Zamalek

Zamalek

The Changing Life of a Cairo Elite, 1850–1945

Chafika Soliman Hamamsy

The American University in Cairo Press
Cairo • New York

Dar el Kutub No. 16553/04
ISBN 977 424 893 7

Designed by Hugh Hughes / AUC Press Design Center
Printed in Egypt

For
A.H.S. and F.S. who started it,
Galal who helped me understand,
Malak, Galal al-Din, Amina, Mona, Fatma, and Ismet,
so that they would know.

Contents

Illustrations

Acknowledgments

I owe this book to my life in Egypt, more specifically, to a life centered in Zamalek, this beautiful island in the heart of Cairo. However, without the invaluable help of sincere and dedicated people, none of it would have been possible. I would like to thank in particular those persons who helped me put the work together.

Djenane Kamel Sirri was the first to know about my project, encouraged me all along, and agreed to read a first draft. I admire her patience and resilience. Dr. Mona Younes, with tremendous generosity, gave me the results of the research she conducted as she studied the role of the Egyptian civil servant in the nineteenth and twentieth centuries. Kamel Hamamsy, my son, with his wealth of information on the history and politics of Egypt during that same period, enabled me to understand situations and evaluate events more accurately than I would have been able to do on my own. Ola Soliman, my sister, whose patience I must have taxed to the limit, endured long and often confused tirades on a past we shared. Kamal Nabih and Ahmad Nabih offered valuable suggestions. In many instances they jogged my memory over incidents of our childhood. Kamal's pertinent and often amusing remarks substantially improved the narrative. Dr. Doris Shukri immediately perceived failings in the text and set me on the right track. Lesley Tweddle's frequent questions provoked answers that helped fill in gaps. Her suggestions brought clarity to an otherwise overly elliptical narrative. Maisa Sid-Ahmed, an excellent proofreader, corrected what I had assumed to be a final draft and cleared it of unnecessary driftwood. Dr. Nelly Boulos Hanna kindly agreed to review the manuscript for possible publication. Her remarks helped me bridge the gap between the 'story' and the historical background in which it is set. My young colleagues of

xi

the American University in Cairo Library—Mohamed Hamed in particular—helped me understand the intricacies of a word processor. Last but not least, I wish to thank my daughters Fatma, who spent many long hours typing a final draft, and Ismet for their unwavering support.

Introduction

This book is an attempt to record some aspects of Egyptian life from the accession to power of Muhammad 'Ali Pasha until the end of World War II. Actually, the period most closely examined covers the years 1850–1945.

During that time, the transformation of the Egyptian sociopolitical scene was spectacular particularly within the confines of the ruling class. Although the narrative, with its occasional flashbacks, mentions various neighborhoods of Cairo, particularly Munira, it is on the island of Zamalek that a greater part of the action takes place.

At the turn of the twentieth century, 'Abbasiya and Hilmiya al-Gadida were no longer the fashionable neighborhoods of gentility; Zamalek had, for a variety of reasons, replaced them and become the preferred choice of a fast-evolving upper middle class. By the 1920s, a number of prominent Egyptian civil servants and rich landowners had built houses there, forming an elite group whose way of life was manifestly more westernized than that of their forebears. That does not mean that this upper crust of society only existed on the island, but simply that instead of being spread out as in other parts of the city, here they were concentrated as a large group. The island became the abode of decision-makers: prime ministers past and present, cabinet ministers, and high-ranking civil servants. These men and their families were, by the fact of their close contact with British officials who lived on the island, exposed to a westernized way of life. Furthermore, many of them had either studied abroad, or were the offspring of men who had traveled to Europe as part of Muhammad 'Ali Pasha's educational missions. Since they belonged to the decision-making apparatus, as well as being avant-garde in their way of life, these families soon became role models.

I was born in one such family at a time when Zamalek was still a beautiful enclave in the heart of Cairo. As I was growing up, it seemed to me that the world in which I lived was the only one that existed. Things then were clearly defined in terms of rich and poor, upper class and lower class, educated and uneducated, westernized or not. It never occurred to me then that the situation might change, as there was, as far as I was concerned, no apparent reason for such an eventuality.

By the end of the twentieth century, however, looking back on the years and events of my life, I became aware not only of the incredible alteration that had taken place, but also of the fact that this little nucleus of society was no longer there. It was not a case of people simply disappearing from the face of the earth, but of a way of life that was gone, and patterns of behavior that had ceased to be meaningful. It seemed important to describe this 'moment' in the social history of Egyptian society. Granted, the characters I deal with do not represent the mass, just an elite, nevertheless they were influential during the period examined.

To tell my story, I relied essentially on oral tradition, what was handed down by word of mouth from one generation to the next. The events that are described I have either lived or was repeatedly told about in the course of frequent family gatherings. As I was growing up, storytelling, particularly family lore, was a favorite mode of entertainment. What happened in the past, what people did or were loath to do, what was socially acceptable or, on the contrary, taboo, became over the years leitmotifs which I absorbed and internalized. Grandparents I hardly knew became familiar figures, and the ways of the past were so often described that they also became firmly entrenched in my consciousness.

Over and above oral tradition, I relied as often as I could on documents, letters, and, in one instance, on the personal diary of Aisha Hanim Sirri (1908–1981), daughter of Isma'il Sirri Pasha.

Most of the characters that appear in the narrative are presented under assumed names. This was done not only for the sake of discretion, but because some of them played a major role in the political arena of the time and hence would have been entitled to closer scrutiny than was warranted considering the nature of the work as a whole. Documents, however, were consulted in the case of some of the characters that appear in their own names such as Dr. Badr, Isma'il Sirri Pasha, 'Abd al-Hamid Soliman Pasha, and Hussein Sirri Pasha.

The urgency to write my story became increasingly felt with the reappearance of the veil on the Egyptian social scene. The *higab*, with its various manifestations, has ushered in an area of religiosity where the demarcation line between the spiritually inspired and the theatrical is often blurred. Women who, throughout the period examined, strove with determination to emancipate themselves, seem now bent on a regression toward values of the past. Whatever the causes of this about-face, the image today is different from the one I describe. It seemed important, therefore, that the world I knew, short-lived as it was, not be totally forgotten.

Characters in the Book

Characters presented under fictitious names

Sadiq family

Isma'il Sadiq
Chafaq Nour   *his wife*

Khadiga
Muhammad
Hussein
Hazim   *their children*
Fatma
'Ali
Muhsin
Anisah

Murad Khidr   *Khadiga's husband*
Malika 'Ilwi   *Muhammad's wife*
Nadra Sa'di   *Hussein's wife*
Dalia Mursi   *Hazim's wife*
'Abd al-Rahman Sallam *Fatma's husband*
Karimah Wasfi   *'Ali's wife*
Inji Khalid   *Muhsin's wife*
Kamal Sabri   *Anisah's husband*

Sallam family

'Abd al-Rahman Sallam
Fatma Sadiq   *his wife*

'Ayn al-Hayah ⎫
'Alia ⎪
'Abir ⎬ *their children*
Chafaq Nour ⎪
Muhammad Hussein ⎭

Non-fictitious characters

Dr. Hasan Badr Bey
Sir Isma'il Sirri Pasha
Sir 'Abd al-Hamid Soliman Pasha

Hussein Sirri Pasha
Nahed Sirri   *his wife*

Nini Sirri ⎫
Doddy Sirri ⎬ *their daughters*

Madame Gollmer   *governess to the Soliman children*
Miss Griffith   *governess to the Sirri children*
Madame Ponsot   *governess to the Foda children*

Zamalek

The Changing Life of a Cairo Elite, 1880–1945

A great part of every day is not lived consciously.
—*Virginia Woolfe*

But if in your thought you must measure time into
seasons, let each season encircle all other seasons, and let
today embrace the past with remembrance and the future
with longing.
—*Kahlil Gibran*

And while Egyptians, like all other people like to
gossip about their friends, they do not relish washing
their dirty linen in public.
—*Afaf Lutfi al-Sayyid Marsot*

Prologue

Usta 'Abdu, the family driver, handed the parcel of *mughat* to Umm Muhammad. "Here you are! Now that the *mughat* and nuts are in the house, I hope we shall not wait much longer. It surely must be a boy this time for three girls in a row is about as much as any man can bear."

"Hold you tongue, old man," answered Umm Muhammad. "Whatever God sends is welcome. May Sitt Hanim be safely delivered."

It was a beautiful October day, warm still but with a gentle breeze. Fatma Hanim, the object of this concern, shifted her heavy body in the large armchair and mentally reviewed all the little odds and ends that needed to be attended to before the baby's birth. The layette was ready, but more important, so was the house—that Zamalek mansion, sometimes referred to by flatterers as Sarayat al-Zamalek. The house stood at the angle of two main streets on the island of Zamalek.[1] According to uncorroborated sources, Zamalek was man-made, the result of accumulated earth thrown into this very large section of the Nile as canals and waterways were dug up by Muhammad 'Ali and his successors in the process of creating modern Egypt. To most people, it seemed to be a lush, green island of peace miraculously born out of the capricious meandering of the river in its race toward the sea. Whatever cause lay behind its existence, the island was beautiful with its lovely shaded streets, where acacias and poinciana lent their glorious hues of pink, purple, and red in summer, and promising branches of scattered green leaves in winter.

In the 1920s and early 1930s, it became the fashionable neighborhood of Cairo gradually replacing Hilmiya al-Gadida and Munira. In fact, the westward movement of the city was sustained all through the nineteenth and early twentieth centuries sliding down as it were from the Citadel and moving from 'Abbasiya (in the east), where the upper classes of the nineteenth century had built their residences, to Hilmiya, Munira, Garden City (also called Qasr al-Dubara), and Zamalek. There were, of course, less elegant neighborhoods that ran along as well, such as Manial, Dokki, and parts of Giza.

But Zamalek in the 1930s was the jewel of the capital despite the fact that the British Residence and other embassies were located in Garden City. The British, who after the defeat of 'Urabi in 1882 became the 'protectors' of Egypt, very soon realized the beauty of the island and managed to obtain a piece of land there, where they created the Gezira Sporting Club.[2] The site was presented by the Khedive Tewfik to the British High Command in the early 1880s, carved out of the Khedivial Botanical Gardens—hence the acacias and jacarandas that adorned it. In the 1940s the club boasted an eighteen-hole golf course—one of the best in the world—two swimming pools, several tennis courts, squash racquet courts, a club house, a pergola, which surrounded the pools usually referred to as 'the Lido,' and a dining room where typical British meals were served. Welsh rarebit, and steak and kidney pie were offered for lunch, hot scones and raisin cake for tea, and trifle for desert. Membership at the club was originally restricted to the British—in other words, the resident general (later to become ambassador), his staff and British military personnel of officer rank only—as it was originally meant to serve the British Army of Occupation. Gradually, however, Egyptian high officials were offered memberships, and these 'happy few' of the early 1920s could, if they chose to, have a taste of the English way of life.

'The club' or the 'Gezira,' as it was often called, was a little piece of Victorian England, where proper decorum *à l'anglaise*, discipline, and high standards of sportsmanship were preserved. In the late 1930s, a new club secretary, Captain Eric Charles Pilley, came on the scene. He was the last of a long line of eminent gentlemen entrusted with the formidable responsibility of protecting and preserving this British entity created in the heart of Cairo. He followed in the footsteps of Captain Humphreys of the mounted infantry and Haywood Walker Setton-Carr (1859–1938) who set the rules and made sure they were respected. Captain Pilley was the epitome of Britishness. Tall, gray-haired, with steel-blue eyes, which glared down at any unfortunate native gardener who encountered his displeasure, he toured the grounds all day long on his bicycle and maintained by his presence the exact orderliness of an already extremely orderly set-up. His aloofness was legendary, and his distrust of natives equally well known, and yet he was perceptive enough to know where to draw the line and whose toes not to tread upon.

Edward Said in his autobiography remembers with a certain measure of bitterness his early encounter with Captain Pilley who, having caught him in an out of bounds section of the club, told him with disdain, "Arabs aren't allowed here and you're an Arab."[3] Such behavior can only be ascribed to Captain Pilley's innate British snobbery for, although he was well aware that Edward Said was a club member, he also knew that he was not a pasha's son but just an 'out of place' little boy. Offspring of Egyptian members were usually not antagonized by Captain Pilley as long as they behaved themselves and followed scrupulously all rules and regulations. For instance, children under the age of sixteen were never allowed into the big swimming pool or on the right hand side of the Lido, the side with awnings that were drawn everyday at noon and pulled back after sunset. Dogs were never allowed on the grounds but were kept in kennels provided for them, and under no circumstances were non-golfers to tread the greens. Children had to leave the club at sunset and were not to bring friends along who were non-members.

To survey his domain and keep the youngsters in check, Captain Pilley had a second in command, a Mr. Williams, otherwise known as 'the Control.' Mr. Williams was a short and stocky man whose diffident manner barely concealed a powerful determination to be obeyed. Under the pith helmet he wore all year round, he had a rubicund face but lips that seldom smiled. He patrolled all day from the playground, where nannies and young children were segregated, to the tennis courts, the swimming pools, and the dining room to ensure that Captain Pilley's instructions were followed to the letter. He knew each member and every member's offspring and was known to have, on occasion, politely requested a non-member who had 'trespassed' to "please leave quietly and make no fuss." Both he and Captain Pilley commanded the youngsters' respect and the club under their aegis was indeed a well-controlled place.

Captain Pilley lived on the grounds in a lovely British-style house, surrounded by perfect lawns with bougainvilleas of many colors creeping up the walls. In fact, the whole club was often perceived as his private garden with acacias, jacarandas, and poincianas planted at strategic points to ensure that pink, blue, and purple would contribute to the harmonious effect of perfect landscaping.

From the very early days of the club's existence, the major social events held there were races and polo matches. One of the first races took place in the mid-1880s. Jockeys were imported from England but in time Egyptian-trained riders joined in, and the heavy European horses were replaced by the swift and agile Arabian ponies. Attendance at the races was always considerable and looked forward to by the British colony and Egyptians as well. As for the polo matches, ten or twelve were held every year, and as early as 1908 a 'challenge' cup was offered by Seif Allah Yusry Pasha, Princess Chivekiar's[4] second husband.

In the early 1920s, very few Egyptians were club members. Those invited to join were usually men who had distinguished themselves in their chosen field of activity, but were not necessarily pro-British. Had that been required, few Egyptians would have wanted to join, as anti-British sentiment, though not always apparent, was very much part of the Egyptian consciousness. It stands to reason, however, that a very vocal anti-British official would not have been sought out as a desirable element in this exclusive—and one might add, elitist—group. On the whole, however, politics was not an issue which concerned Egyptians as much as social standing within the framework of society at the time. To become a club member was assuredly a status symbol perfectly acceptable to an Egyptian candidate as recognition of personal achievement. To be sure, not much use of the membership was made by these families in the early 1920s and 1930s, as most Egyptian men, with notable exceptions such as Seif Allah Yusry Pasha, did not attach much importance to sportsmanship, while wives and children did not even consider it as a social option.

Hoda Sha'rawi, the famous Egyptian feminist, founder in 1923 of the Egyptian Feminist Union, wrote in her memoirs[5] that she never went to the Gezira Sporting Club; neither would she go to a restaurant for a meal or attend mixed parties. These were frivolous occupations that ran counter to the norms of the education she had received and the class to which she belonged. It was one thing to cast off the veil in a grand gesture which had tremendous sociopolitical implications, quite another to reject wholesale the traditions of her social milieu. This is all the more surprising because, according to the account she gives of her life, she was indeed far more emancipated than most ladies of her time and deeply involved in political pursuits. She was encouraged by her husband, 'Ali Sha'rawi Pasha, to become the first president of the Wafdist Women's Central Committee. For a lady who befriended Eugenie Lebrun, wife of writer, feminist, and politician Hussein Rushdi Pasha, and frequently attended her 'salon,' this reluctance to go the Gezira Sporting Club may have seemed anachronistic but only indicated that her adherence to tradition ran very deep. Therein lay her strength, for not all women of the next generation shared this clarity of vision and were able to navigate successfully the rough waters of modernism's tidal wave.

With the advent of World War II, the younger generation of the time, cooped up in Cairo for the summer since Alexandria and most coastal towns were considered dangerous, discovered under the watchful eyes of their governesses the joys of swimming in the pool or playing tennis. Virtually overnight, scones and jam, Welsh rarebit, and steak and kidney pie became household words. A brand new world opened up for these young Egyptians, a world of British discipline paired with a certain measure of emancipation, if not freedom. Soon enough, for these boys and girls aged ten to fifteen, the club became a focal point in their life. It is quite surprising that Egyptian families allowed their offspring so much freedom within the confines of the club, or allowed them to go there in the first place. It must have been a case of global emulation, a pattern followed by the Zamalekites, as well as others, with zest and alacrity. Another reason must have been that there was precious else they could do since the only other outlet for pent-up energies in the heat of the summer months would have been the Grotto Gardens, so named after the grotto that housed an aquarium, surrounded by patches of green lawns and well-traced alleys. There was nothing much one could do there except for an occasional game of hide-and-seek, during which the hiding always took place behind a lone tree with pursuit easily and successfully concluded! Despite its beauty, the garden had an oppressive atmosphere because of the eerie silence of its surroundings, or perhaps because of the gloomy aquarium from the ceiling of which bats hung, like so many stalactites, both ominous and repulsive.

The island of Zamalek was linked to the mainland by three bridges, two on the eastern shore, the Qasr al-Nil Bridge and the Bulaq or Abu al-'Ila Bridge, and one on the western shore, the Badi'a Masabni Bridge (also known at the time as Kubri al-Ingiliz, or Englishmen's Bridge, renamed the Gala' Bridge after the 1952 Revolution).[6] The most beautiful one, the Qasr al-Nil Bridge, was built in 1933 by a British company to replace the narrow causeway originally devised in 1872[7] by Maurice Adolphe Linant de Bellefond, French Saint Simonien engineer who at one time became chief engineer of the Suez Canal. With increasing traffic to and from the island, a more substantial structure became imperative. The new bridge was elegant, its stiff steel structure decorated by lamp posts which "shimmered over the Nile like a bride on her wedding night."[8] However, its most outstanding feature was the four bronze lions—two guard the bridge at either end—the work of Alfred Jacquemart, a French sculptor. The lions were originally meant to stand around Muhammad 'Ali's statue in Alexandria, but Linant de Bellefond thought better of it and appropriated them for his bridge, where they have stood ever since. The Bulaq Bridge was two decades older, inaugurated in 1912 by Isma'il Sirri Pasha, the incumbent minister of public works. It has been variously called the Bulaq Bridge, after the neighborhood which it links to the island, the Fuad al-Awwal Bridge, after the reigning monarch, and later the Abu al-'Ila Bridge after a minor shaykh, Hussein Abu al-'Ila, whose shrine stands nearby. Whatever the name, it dutifully served its purpose well until the end of the century when it was pensioned off and replaced by the Fifteenth of May Bridge. Traffic over the Bulaq Bridge was heavy as it linked Bulaq to the main thoroughfare of the island. This two-way avenue, originally called Fuad al-Awwal Street, renamed after the Revolution the Twenty-sixth of July Street, boasted in the early 1920s and up to the early 1950s a tramway that crossed the island from east to west and back. From the 1920s to the 1940s, this avenue functioned as a frontier, a demarcation line that separated the 'good side' of Zamalek in the south from the 'bad side' in the north. On the 'good side' stood the Gezira Club, the Grotto Gardens, the Gezira

Palace, lovely houses, and tree-lined avenues. Most British officials, connected with either the Agency—later known as the Embassy—or the Egyptian government, lived there. Little by little, perceptive Egyptians realized that this was indeed a lovely neighborhood and started acquiring land there as well. The price of the square meter at the time varied from LE1 for the 'bad' side to LE3 for the 'good' one. The best way of describing the 'good' side of the Zamalek of the time is perhaps to compare it to a small village in the English countryside. It exuded the same peaceful atmosphere with the early morning sound of birds chirping in the trees and their dusk riot when settling for the night. There were no stray dogs then, just family pets or hounds guarding villas and gardens. Every person was identifiable, every *bawwab* recognized each of the children who cycled by, and safety in the street was ensured by an occasional *shawish* (policeman). These were the glorious days of Zamalek.

On the other side of the demarcation line lay the 'bad' side. Actually, there was nothing wrong with it except that it was still untamed, partially covered by marshland or uncultivated plots with a few palatial houses along the Nile facing Bulaq, such as the Tewfik Doss villa or the Aisha Fahmi miniature palace. And yet, maybe because it was where squatters' huts survived longer that an overall gloomy and derelict atmosphere prevailed. Whatever the reason, in the 1920s, and well into the 1940s the distinction was very clear. The third bridge, the Badi'a Masabni Bridge on the western side of the island, links it to Giza, the first outpost of Upper Egypt. It is a small bridge spanning the narrow branch of the Nile. It owes its early name to the famous belly dancer Badi'a Masabni whose cabaret stood at the end of the bridge on the Giza side. The Casino Badi'a played a prominent role in the sociopolitical scene of the first half of the twentieth century. Important political figures would meet there to discuss issues of the day while watching the graceful, if somewhat opulent, gyrations of Madame Badi'a performing her dance. The rumor that she was a British agent, actively engaged against the Axis forces, as was occasionally asserted, may or may not have been true. It could have been spread by Hitler's admirers in Cairo as a piqued reaction to her lack of enthusiasm for the Fuehrer's cause. Whatever the case, beyond doubt she played a role in launching the careers of famous belly dancers such as Samia Gamal, Tahia Cariocca, and Bebba Ezz al-Din.

Though her casino was not a 'salon' or a political club, it was often said that ministerial cabinets were sometimes formed, or dissolved, during these evenings of oriental merry-making.

The idyllic situation in Zamalek eventually deteriorated and its peaceful beauty gradually disappeared. With the advent of the 1952 Revolution and the sudden population explosion of the early 1960s, the 'good' and the 'bad' slowly merged. And, like everything else since then, Zamalek became a microcosm of Egypt, a place where ugliness competes successfully with beauty, where attempts to maintain a modicum of aesthetic standards are an uphill battle fought daily by a few valiant souls who believe that good will ultimately prevail. In the 1930s however it was still a beautiful island, a world all on its own and right in the heart of it stood Fatma Hanim's home.

Part One

An Egyptian Family

1

'Abd al-Rahman Sallam, Fatma Hanim's husband, had a life that might be described as a success story. Born in 1888 in the small village of Fashn near Minya, one of the major towns of Upper Egypt located some 153 miles south of Cairo, he was the son of a venerable *'alim*. The family originally owned substantial land in and around the village and upheld for a long time the tradition of sound Azharite education. Ahmad Sallam, 'Abd al-Rahman's eldest brother, however decided to study engineering at the Cairo School of Engineering, or Madrasat al-Muhandiskhana, as it was called at the time. His example was later followed by 'Abd al-Rahman who was seventeen years younger than his brother. By the time he was born, the family had lost most of its land, the grandfather having signed a promissory note covering the debts of his eldest cousin. Unfortunately, the cousin died before he could repay the debt and the land was lost. 'Abd al-Rahman grew up in straitened circumstances and yet in an atmosphere where piety and Islamic principles of honor and integrity were basic. He was a precocious and intelligent child who sailed smoothly through his elementary and secondary studies. He was easily admitted into the Cairo School of Engineering, which was still at the time a very small college having a graduating class that did not exceed ten students. Instruction was given in English and the curriculum was based on the English system. 'Abd al-Rahman was a fast learner with an amazing ability to absorb foreign languages. He very quickly became fluent in English and graduated top of his class with a degree in irrigation engineering. He immediately obtained a job in the Ministry of Public Works where he was noticed by the minister, Isma'il Sadiq Pasha, who made him his personal secretary. In no time, the young man established himself as an efficient and knowledgable engineer with a quick mind, always ready to absorb more information. And yet he had two major drawbacks as far as Sadiq Pasha was concerned: he lacked experience of the world and he could not speak French.

"You are one of the brightest young men of your generation," Isma'il Sadiq told him a few weeks after he had been on the job, "but you cannot hope to make a name for yourself in tomorrow's Egypt with just a degree in engineering. Your knowledge of English is quite good; so is your accent. However, French is the language of the civilized world. You must learn French. You must know more about European culture, about arts other than the Islamic and pharaonic arts of Egypt, and above all you must travel, see the world, and broaden your horizon. I will send you to France for one year. Come back having learned the language."

'Abd al-Rahman left in the early months of 1912 full of hope and anticipation. He fell in love with Paris, captivated by everything he saw and heard. Here was indeed a world he had never imagined. Following Sadiq Pasha's advice he had, before leaving, spent many hours with M. Quillemer, a Frenchman attached to the royal court, who gave him a beginner's insight into the life of the French capital and the rudiments of the language. They conversed in English and were both amused at the oddity of an Egyptian and a Frenchman communicating in yet a third language. Like most educated Egyptians of his generation, 'Abd al-Rahman knew a great deal about French history and Napoleon. The erstwhile invader of Egypt was a figure he much admired. As he first stood before the Emperor's tomb, he was awed by its grandeur and pierced by a sudden awareness of the sense of history, a history of yesterday measured on the human scale, unlike his country's formidable figures shrouded for all eternity in their mythical past. He felt elated when he walked down the Champs Elysées, admired the Arc de Triomphe and watched with interest the slow movement of traffic on the Seine. The river fascinated him; it was so different from the Nile, so much tamer with a color that shifted from gray to grayish-blue, and always seemed to flow so peacefully between its banks, unhurried, at times almost at a standstill.

Having made the grand tour of the French capital and its surroundings, including a lengthy visit to Versailles, he applied himself to his primary task, which was to learn French. He did not follow the unorthodox approach of some of his countrymen, which was to find a French mistress for the duration and learn French in this pleasant way. Instead he sought a M. Martin Morin, recommended by M. Quillemer, who for a fee taught him French from the basic grammatical rules all the way up to the delights of French poetry. Conversation was an important component of the curriculum. M. Morin encouraged his pupil to express himself clearly, and trained him to listen attentively to the sound of his own voice so as to correct inflections and ultimately master the proper accent. Fortunately both men struck up a solid friendship that lasted until M. Morin's untimely death in the battle of the Somme.

'Abd al-Rahman learned French fast; he devoured the information imparted by M. Morin as well as what he acquired by reading until the early hours of the morning. He had made a promise to Sadiq Pasha and he intended to keep it.

Twelve months to the day after he set out on his voyage of education, he came back to Cairo perfectly fluent in French, which he spoke without a trace of a foreign accent. His experience in France had given him more than the knowledge of a new language. It had introduced him to a different way of life, to a European perception of refinement, which he embraced wholeheartedly. It was not a case of rejecting his own background, traditions, and beliefs, for these were never put in question, but rather of incorporating a wider range of possibilities. The young Egyptian came back polished, on a par with his European counterparts but at ease with himself because his core remained unscathed, only the outer layers of his personality had been brought up to date.

Sadiq Pasha was pleased. 'Abd al-Rahman had passed the test. He had never doubted the young man's capacity to learn French because he had done much the same in his own day, but he had no way of predicting what the impact of this experience on his protégé's personality would be. Fortunately, 'Abd al-Rahman did not come back as an insufferable pseudo *khawaga* like some of his contemporaries, but like men of Sadiq's generation, he took what was best while holding onto what he already owned.

"You have done well, my son," said Sadiq Pasha when he first met 'Abd al-Rahman upon his return to Cairo. "You are now ready to start your career. I believe you will go very far. You have not let me down and, as a token of my appreciation, I shall reward you, as you deserve. I shall give you my daughter Fatma in marriage, but as she is only six-teen you will have to wait another two years before you marry."

'Abd al-Rahman was speechless. He had expected a reward, or some sort of recognition from the Pasha but this surpassed his wildest dreams. To marry into the Pasha's family was a great honor and he was quite prepared to give his heart to the young girl since his affections were not engaged elsewhere. If he had any curiosity about her he quickly set it aside for it was quite immaterial to know, at that point, whether she was beautiful or not. Marriages were usu-ally arranged, not affairs of the heart. Love came afterwards, of that he was convinced, provided there was mutual understanding and harmony of mind. Besides, he had often seen two of the Pasha's sons at the ministry and they were both good-looking young men!

This arrangement suited Sadiq Pasha perfectly. He had no inten-tion of repeating the mistake he made when he married off his eld-est daughter, Khadiga. Having accepted a suitor on the basis of his university degree and 200 *feddans,* he had occasional misgivings about this decision as the young man proved to be strong-willed and at times opinionated. Actually, Sadiq Pasha admired his son-in-law's manliness, but his wife did not or rather would have much preferred that he be more compliant. Furthermore, Fatma was her mother's favorite and as such should be treated with special care.

2

U nlike his future son-in-law, Isma'il Sadiq was not of Egyptian origin. His father, Sadiq Effendi al-Maghrabi, was an Upper Egyptian landowner of some means whose own father had traveled to Egypt by camel from the Maghreb, hence his name, on his way to Mecca to perform the pilgrimage. He liked the country and its people and determined, should he survive the journey, to settle in this pleasant valley. According to family lore, he carried his fortune around his waist in small leather pouches filled with gold coins. The story does not tell whether he landed on his return trip in the port of Suez and traveled thence to Minya or whether he left Saudi Arabia at the port of Yunbu' which is across the sea from Upper Egypt. All that is known is that upon arrival, he acquired land in Minya and thereafter led the typical life of the Egyptian landed gentry.

His eldest son, Sadiq Effendi, married young. Although he was known to have had at least one other wife, a black woman of great beauty, his official wife was a free-born Caucasian lady given him by Sa'id Pasha, the *wali* of Egypt, in appreciation of Sadiq Effendi al-Maghrabi's hospitality following a visit to Upper Egypt. The practice of offering a woman out of the royal harem as a gift to important notables was still current. Up to the end of Khedive Isma'il's reign, polygyny[9] and harems, particularly in royal households, were standard practice. Whereas his successor, Khedive Tawfiq, only had one wife, Princess Amina Ilhami, Khedive Isma'il's harem counted no less that fourteen wives—though no more than four at a time—and numerous slaves.[10] His great-grandson, Nabil[11] Hassan Hassan, explains the situation as follows:

> In Egypt, harems seem to have proliferated happily in all spheres
> of life. Princely harems of the nineteenth century were usually

enormous affairs, highly organized households, with great importance attached to precedence and rank. First came the four official
wives permitted by Islam, the Four Princesses; these ladies were
referred to as the First Princess, the Second Princess, and so on, as
higher form of discretion, since using their names would have
been a minor invasion into their privacy. The head of the family
would maintain precedence and be treated with particular respect
by everybody else, as seniority was the key word to all proceedings and way of life of the period. . . . After the Four Princesses
came the Kadin Effendis, who enjoyed the same material privileges as the princesses, their children inheriting and holding the
same rank as those of the first four ladies. . . . All these ladies
would be treated as respected aunts by junior members of the
family who were not their descendants.[12]

The harem slaves referred to above were Caucasian ladies who, as
little girls, had been sent to Egypt by their parents to live and be
brought up in the khedivial household. This category does not
include girls sold on the slave market. Neshedil Hanim, Sadiq al-
Maghrabi's wife, belonged to the former category of harem ladies.
Though she was the official wife, she had to contend with the
other one. According to family-lore, they seem to have lived
together in peaceful harmony probably because, following the
Khedivial court's accepted practice, she was the mistress of the
household, the First Wife. Isma'il, born in 1861, was their first
child; his fine features and fair skin bespoke his ancestry and Sadiq
Effendi was very proud of him. The boy was handsome, intelligent,
and absorbed knowledge with uncanny rapidity. Sadiq Effendi
himself was not learned, he could read but his intellectual activity
was limited to a daily dose of Qur'an reading. Isma'il's mother, like
most Caucasian ladies of good standing brought up in the
Khedivial palace, was taught to read and write Arabic as well as
Turkish. In fact, her education was quite refined even by today's
standards. She was taught to appreciate poetry, music, and to read
the Qur'an in the right and proper way. That is not to say that she
was erudite in religious matters but simply that she was familiar
with the basic tenets of the faith as set in the sacred book. She had
memorized certain *suras*[13] and could refer to them in support of an
argument or to draw sustenance in times of stress.

She was, therefore, better educated than most ladies of the social milieu to which she now belonged. This, of course must have frustrated her to some extent, yet she must have acknowledged that her fate was not bad since it was better to be married to this handsome, half-educated wealthy man and be safely tucked away in a good home in Minya than to risk being kidnapped by Turkish white slave traders and sold to a life of bondage and misery. She knew that these poor girls, used and abused by their masters, either died young or lost their beauty very quickly with the result that they were discarded like unwanted objects. As stated before, Caucasian parents who felt unable to protect their daughters, particularly the pretty ones, usually took the initiative of sending them to Egypt to be brought up in the Khedivial palace or in one of the royal households. Though often referred to as slaves, they were treated as members of the family, received a fine education and the culture offered by their surroundings. As is usually the case, some were luckier than others; some were happily married to Egyptian notables or, occasionally, to members of the Khedivial family.[14] Some ended up with abusive husbands, while others remained old maids living on with the family and eventually receiving the reverence society bestows elders. Whatever the case, the choice was not theirs but of their 'adoptive'[15] parents, with fate playing a major role.

It is said that, occasionally, the Caucasian girls would grow to womanhood, marry, and through some chance encounter meet up again with members of their original family in Turkey. This was apparently the case with Hoda Sha'rawi's mother who came to Egypt at a very young age and was married around 1878 to Sultan Pasha,[16] an extremely wealthy landowner who played a decisive role in the events leading to the British occupation of Egypt in 1882. He was, like some of his contemporaries, illiterate but was endowed with a powerful intellect, which, as is often the case, amply made up for this deficiency. Unlike other men of his generation, he was not attuned to the Western frame of mind but loved Arabic poetry with a passion and frequently entertained Arab men of letters. His marriage to the beautiful Caucasian girl was a happy one though it did not last very long, as he died in 1884 leaving two young children and an estate of 4,000 *feddans*. His widow, who had fully adjusted to life in Egypt, enjoyed a limited, though pleasant, social life.

In the course of one of the ladies' receptions she attended, she met another Caucasian lady and felt irresistibly drawn to her. Both women conversed amiably, talked about their past and reminisced about their experiences before they came to Egypt. They compared notes, reconstructed events, described as best they could what they remembered of their long lost families when, suddenly, names came up that were similar, houses uncannily alike, brothers who bore the same name and a sister with a black mole on the left shoulder that had caused many jibes on the part of her siblings. Hoda's mother was stunned. She looked up and told her new friend, "I still have the mole and you must be my sister." The story has it that they fell into each other's arms, dissolved in tears, unable to speak or quite believe in the miracle of their reunion.[17]

Isma'il's mother, however, never met a member of her original family again as she rarely left her home in Minya. Like her husband, she took pride in her son's achievement and looked forward to the day when he, like many other boys of his generation, would travel to Europe and become holder of a degree from one of its great universities. In 1878, aged seventeen, Isma'il graduated from his secondary school in Minya well versed in whatever knowledge was given at the time in Egyptian schools. His teachers recommended that he be sent abroad for further studies despite the fact that in Cairo there was a school where he could have studied irrigation engineering, his preferred subject. The Nile River with its yearly floods fascinated him; he loved to sit on its banks and watch its slow movement in winter, its rapid and mud-laden rush in summer, full of treacherous whirlpools and deceptive currents. He wondered at its origins even though by the time he was old enough to contemplate the issue, John Hanning Speke, Samuel Baker and his wife, Charles Chaillé-Long, and many others had done their work of discovery and established finally the sources of the Nile, he still felt there was a mystery attached to this phenomenon that crossed the length of his country and flowed uncontrollably toward the sea.

However, when the time came for decisive steps to be taken in view of sending him abroad, his mother felt a surge of panic. Isma'il was her firstborn, her pride and joy, and just seventeen years old. He was young, far too young to undertake such a perilous journey. She argued very strongly for him to remain at home a little while longer.

If he must travel, let it be to Cairo where she had heard there was a very good School of Engineering. The Madrasat al-Handasa founded in Bulaq in 1821 had developed substantially. By 1834 it had become Madrasat al-Muhandiskhana, flourishing under the impetus of men such as Ya'qub Artin Bey and 'Ali Mubarak.[18] This school had apparently been founded originally to train land surveyors, a job performed at the time solely by Copts. However, they used a system no one else could understand, hence the necessity to create a school that would teach a system based on international standards. The creation of this school, its importance, and development coincided with the arrival in Egypt of the Saint Simoniens such as Lambert Bey,[19] Linant de Bellefond, and others. The school developed consistently through the years and by 1878 was, according to Isma'il's mother, good enough for her son, however brilliant he might be. But she argued to no avail.

Sadiq Effendi al-Maghrabi was adamant: he had made a decision and was not going to change his mind. In Egypt, as probably elsewhere, global emulation is a very strong factor directing movements of social development. Muhammad 'Ali Pasha had set the tone by sending missions of young men abroad, to receive an academic education not yet available in Egypt. The founder of modern Egypt wanted a base of educated men on which to build the foundation of his new country. In 1805, Egypt was indeed a 'new country,' and its links with pharaonic past and Arab grandeur belonged to the realm of collective memory. Muhammad 'Ali was creating, molding as it were, a new entity, and plunged into this endeavor with powerful determination. Education was imposed upon Egypt as the quintessential panacea that would raise her to the level of great nations. The intellectual impact of the French in their three-year sojourn in the country provoked, in a certain way, the epiphanic visions of Muhammad 'Ali. He would shake the country out of its lethargy, he would upgrade his *pis fellah* (dirty peasant), he would create an educated elite that would be the fulcrum with which he would uplift his nation and conquer his empire. Such was the dream, which, in a large measure, he realized.

As years went by, the importance of education took hold in Egypt. Young men were no longer conscripted into educational schemes but actively sought them, and fathers were not only willing but eager for their sons to excel academically. Sadiq Effendi was one of those fathers and decided to send his son out at his own expense, not wait for a government scholarship. Since Isma'il was leaving presumably for many years, the matter of his marriage had to be settled before-hand. Sadiq Effendi feared he might get involved with a *khawagaya*, consequently he decided to immediately announce Isma'il's engage-ment to his cousin Hoda, daughter of his brother, Mahfuz Effendi al-Maghrabi. Both Isma'il and Hoda accepted the arrangement though they hardly knew one another, because such was the custom and nei-ther had any reason to object. Besides, their opinions were not sought; Hoda was just thirteen years old at the time and barely able to understand what was happening, while Isma'il did not care much one way or the other as his mind was totally wrapped up in the big adventure he was about to undertake.

Isma'il was dispatched to France where he was enrolled in the College Saint-Louis in Paris and thereafter joined L'Ecole Centrale des Arts et Manufactures de Paris, from which he graduated top of his class in 1883. This was no small feat, for when he arrived in Paris, he could not utter a word of French. He learned the language in record time, competed successfully with French boys and obtained a degree in irrigation engineering, a discipline that was much in demand at the time.

As could have been expected, the six years he spent in Paris great-ly changed his outlook. Having seen a different world, he acquired over and above his academic credentials a new vision of life. Though he was perfectly willing to go back to Egypt, to his family and tra-ditions, to his beloved Nile, and to a world whose values he never questioned, he was no longer willing to form a matrimonial alliance that held for him no particular attraction. If he was to enter into an arranged marriage, as was the custom of his day, he would choose one that suited if not his heart at least his ideals or best interest. He had read enough of Voltaire by the time he came back to Egypt to be infused with a spirit of rebellion and the desire to assert his human rights, not least of which assuredly was the right to choose his own wife. He knew that he would have to fight a bitter battle against family tradition, a battle that might even create a permanent rift between his father and his uncle, whose daughter he was reject-ing. As soon as he arrived in Minya, where he was to spend a few days before taking up his post at the Ministry of Public Works, he announced his decision to break off his engagement to his cousin.

His father flew into a rage. His mother wept in her room fearing the hidden existence of a French girl to be sprung on them in the near future like an evil genie. His sisters watched him aghast, unable to understand his bizarre behavior. An atmosphere of gloom pervaded the house. Sudden salvation came through his younger brother Mahfuz, who had for some time been secretly in love with his cousin Hoda, whom he had occasionally seen at family reunions. He announced his desire to marry the girl, thereby saving the day, and averting a major family feud. No one knows what transpired between Sadiq Effendi and his brother or how the substitution of one son for another was explained. All that mattered was that harmony reigned again and that Isma'il, vastly relieved by the fortunate outcome of this episode, was able to leave for Cairo and give his full attention to his career.

3

Isma'il arrived in Cairo in the fall of 1883. He was a young man of twenty-three, secure in the awareness of his worth as an educated engineer, and devoured by an overwhelming ambition. This ambition, however, was of a very particular brand: it was civic-oriented rather than self-oriented, as was usually the case with his contemporaries. He wanted to fit into the grand scheme that Muhammad 'Ali Pasha had defined for the advancement of his country, to be an important and effective component of the team that was forging ahead for the benefit of this Egyptian nation that was so very old and yet still new. Self-advancement would be a natural by-product never to be forgotten, or lost sight of, as was proven later when he selected his wife.

Egypt in 1883 was a country with a tremendous history, the keeper of a civilization that had enthralled the world ever since the deciphering of the Rosetta stone. When the *Description de l'Egypte*, was first published, it revealed to an amazed Europe the splendors of a distant past across the sea and fired imaginations with the possibility of what might still be uncovered. Napoleon's expedition to Egypt was a military failure but a tremendous cultural and scientific success. And yet, when the French left in 1801, Egypt was, by modern standards, an infantile country, which had much to learn before it could take its place in world events and be on a par with other nations, particularly European ones. Using modern terminology, Egypt was, at the turn of the eighteenth century, an 'underdeveloped' country with an internal situation bordering on chaos. Gross mismanagement on the part of the Mamluks had driven the country to near anarchy.

One of the main causes of the problem was that the center of power was not clearly defined. There was "a primacy among equals and not a constitutional position with rules of succession. On the contrary, the succession was on occasion decided by pitched battles in the streets or suburbs of Cairo. Deference was still paid to the Ottoman sultan, through his viceroy, but the viceroy's position was becoming nearer to that of an ambassador, with some useful legal powers, capable of exploitation in the power game. The Sublime Porte still received the tribute when the Mamluk households were in some sort of balance, but if one became very powerful, its chieftain tended to retain the bulk of the revenue in Egypt."[20] This chaotic situation was "paralleled by a deep cultural decadence. The great university mosque of al-Azhar continued to function, but its teachers had ceased to produce original work. They repeated old textbooks to their students or at best wrote commentaries on commentaries. Academic posts exhibited a tendency to become hereditary. The medieval primacy of the Muslim world in astronomy and medicine had long been lost to Europe, and the healing art was being invaded by magic and astrology. Religion was being corrupted by mystics and dervishes, who were either mental inadequates or dishonest tricksters. While the ruling class fought for power, the common people were sinking into misery and superstition."[21]

It should be noted, however, that despite their many failings, Mamluks had brought some civilization to the country as attested by the monuments they built. But that was not enough as they had been remiss in their primary duty, which was to attend to the welfare of the population. As a ruling elite, they kept very much to themselves and, by the time Napoleon arrived on the scene, had so indulged in a life of pleasure that they were easily routed. Egyptians realized with dismay that their masters had been unable to protect the country. That was the disastrous situation Muhammad 'Ali found when he was sent by his Ottoman master initially to free the country of the French invaders and thereafter to control the unruly Mamluks.

In 1805, Muhammad 'Ali became *wali* of Egypt and by 1814 had rid himself and the country of their cumbersome presence. Thereafter, he channeled his energies toward one monumental goal, which was to create modern Egypt. A country, he perceived, is rendered great by the quality of its people and the power of its army. He, therefore, embarked on a dual program: create an army and educate Egyptians. On both scores his efforts were relentless and his

energy indomitable. Selections of candidates for educational missions abroad were not made on the basis of religion or social standing; in fact most of the students were from poor families and traveled at government expense. In some of the early lists one comes
across names such as Petru Effendi, Yusuf Istifan, Mahmud Ahmad
al-Falaki, Paul George Jiyani, Yusuf al-Nabarawi, and many others.[22]
When Sa'id Pasha, Muhammad 'Ali's son, acceded to the throne in
1854,[23] there were no less than seventy-two Egyptian students
studying in Europe.

During the reigns of Muhammad 'Ali and his immediate successors the best and the brightest benefited from his enlightened
approach to the problem of education. That does not mean that
Muhammad 'Ali Pasha wanted an 'educated' country, or that he was
overly concerned with his countrymen's illiteracy. His plan was
essentially pragmatic: he wanted a nucleus of very bright young men
who would serve as a basis upon which the ruler could build a viable
government infrastructure. When his son Ibrahim Pasha requested
new schools to educate more native Egyptians, "the Pasha said that
he had no intention of spreading education among the masses in
Egypt. He told his son to look at what happened to European mon-
archs when they attempted to educate the poor. He added that he
should satisfy himself with educating a limited number of people
who could assume key positions in his administration and give up
ideas about generalizing education."[24] Despite this elitist approach,
often enough several birds were killed with one stone: the student
acquired an academic degree hence specialized skills, he brought
back this knowledge for the benefit of others at home, and thereby
opened up Egypt to a current of new ideas and technologies.
Whereas Napoleon and his scientists transported Egypt to the outside world and in so doing offered it a phantasmagoric voyage into
the past, Muhammad 'Ali and his successors opened up Egypt to the
winds of change.

Isma'il Sadiq was well aware that, through his father's foresight and
generosity, he now belonged to the country's elite, albeit at the bottom of the ladder. He was proud to be part of this group of educated men and determined to eventually put his mark on his time. His
role models were numerous, but two of them in particular attracted
his attention. The first one was Dr. Muhammad 'Ali al-Baqli Pasha

and the other one Dr. Muhammad Hasan Badr Bey. Both were natives of Zawiyat al-Baqli, a small village of Munufiya, which like most Egyptian villages was drab, dusty, its houses packed together, and totally devoid of esthetic beauty. Families there were closely knit and people were either relatives, friends, or acquaintances; traditions were observed scrupulously, and life followed unchanged patterns. Nothing of interest ever happened in that village, which should have been dismissed as yet another insignificant conglomeration of inhabitants were it not for the fact that out of it emerged great scholars and eminent men.

Muhammad 'Ali al-Baqli—his name was derived from his native village—was one of the early success stories of emerging modern Egypt. Born in Zawiyat al-Baqli around 1800, he first went, like most boys of his time, to the *kuttab*. There he learned to read and write and studied the Qur'an. Thereafter, he went to the school of Abu Za'bal and then joined the School of Medicine. The School of Medicine in those days bears no resemblance to what it later became. At the time, children were sent there to study the basics of chemistry, natural science, botany, anatomy, ophthalmology, and pathology. Thereafter, they were organized into small groups and sent abroad to France, Italy, Germany, Austria, or Great Britain to complete their studies. Selected students were conscripted into the educational scheme, clothed, fed, and given a small allowance the greater part of which went to their family. Unlike most of his fellow students, al-Baqli did not have an Azharite background and being the youngest pupil at the school in the year the mission to France was organized, his name was not included on the list. But providence played its role. When one of the selected students was suddenly taken ill and died before the mission left, Muhammad found himself included at the very last moment and on his way to Europe. Actually, he had already drawn attention to himself—as many years later Dr. Badr would do as well—by the sheer brilliance of his mind and his innate gift for medical studies.

The French doctor Antoine Clot Bey[25] and his colleagues were always on the lookout for such young Egyptians who could fulfill the role Muhammad 'Ali Pasha wanted them to play in the development of modern Egypt and who would, by their success, prove that their often criticized educational system could work. In al-Baqli they found a gem, a natural, a wonder boy who would, provided he was given appropriate training, be a star in Muhammad 'Ali's firmament. So, by a quirk of fate, Muhammad 'Ali al-Baqli left for Europe in the early years of the nineteenth century and became a brilliant surgeon, by far the most accomplished member of his group. When he came back to Egypt, he was considered an exceptional young man and regardless of his humble origins was given the military grade of *bikbashi*, or lieutenant colonel.

Under 'Abbas I, he was given an important post, but while there, he had a monumental quarrel with his French colleague, which resulted in his transfer to another department. Though bitterly disappointed at the outcome of the incident, he nonetheless was proud to have stood his ground. Many years later he told a young colleague, "Never fear to speak out when you are right and when your opinion is based on scientific evidence; never assume that your mind is of a lesser quality than the mind of the *khawaga* though they would like us to believe it is so and thereby hold us down." Upon Sa'id Pasha's accession to the throne, he was made the army's director of medical services, quite a prestigious position at the time, but more important still, he became Sa'id Pasha's private physician, the ultimate accolade. At the accession of Khedive Isma'il in 1863, he succeeded Arnoux as director of schools and hospitals. What he liked best of all in his professional life, other than treating patients, was teaching in the School of Medicine. One of his young pupils was Muhammad Hasan Badr al-Din, later shortened to Badr, who caught his attention the moment he set eyes on him. Even though he was still an adolescent, he perceived in him the same intellectual curiosity and natural gift for medical studies as his own. In him he saw an alter ego and immediately took a keen interest in his affairs.

After graduating from Qasr al-'Ayni School, which he had entered at the age of seven, young Badr passed successfully through the Khanqa and Mubtadayan Schools and, on October 31, 1850, he left for Edinburgh attached to that year's mission. Under 'Abbas I, whose reign lasted from 1848 to 1854, many of Muhammad 'Ali Pasha's educational projects had come to a standstill. For one thing 'Abbas, unlike his grandfather, disliked everything foreign. Yet, despite the often-reiterated assumption and generally accepted historical fact that he put an end to education in Egypt, he, in fact, did no such thing. He closed down schools that were doing poorly, probably through bad management, but allowed missions abroad to continue. The main difference lay in his moving away from the dominant French influence and putting a greater emphasis on other countries. In 1849, one mission was sent to Bavaria; in 1850, three to England, one to France, and one to Italy; and in 1853, one to Berlin. 'Abbas I diversified, which is all to his credit because, despite his execrable character, extreme chauvinism, and undeniable xenophobia, he did, according to recorded fact, render a great service to his country by sending out these young men wherever knowledge could best be obtained.

Young Badr, with the assistance of Muhammad 'Ali al-Baqli Pasha, was included among the selected few in the Edinburgh mission. Despite the fact that he could not speak English, he looked forward to the challenge that lay ahead. He took to life in Edinburgh like a fish to water and proved to be a brilliant student. While there, he received a medal of excellence and a notice in the newspapers to that effect. The young prodigy was making his mark. The head surgeon of the Edinburgh hospital offered him the position of assistant head and the possibility of settling in Scotland. He declined because he missed his family and his country. Besides, his love of adventure was such that he feared boredom in the staid atmosphere and perfectly organized life of Edinburgh. However, he did spend seven years there, in the course of which he obtained his medical credentials and perfected his knowledge of the English language, which he spoke to the end of his life with a Scottish brogue. When he came back, 'Abbas I had been assassinated, and the amiable, enlightened, gregarious, and pro-French Sa'id had succeeded him. The viceroy demanded to meet this young doctor who had made such an amazing impression in Edinburgh. Thereafter, as was to be expected, Dr. Badr's career became linked to the Egyptian court, the bond being further strengthened by Sa'id's successor, Khedive Isma'il, who named him personal physician to his son, Prince Hasan.

Meanwhile, Muhammad 'Ali al-Baqli Pasha had other plans for his young compatriots. He had worried lest the young man fall in love with a Scottish girl and marry outside his religion and his country. Had not many of his fellow-members of the first mission sent to France come back with French wives? He had nothing against French women or Scottish ones for that matter, but was wise enough to know that mixed marriages are often risky since they entail adjustments that often cannot be made and demands that cannot be met. A difficult marital situation would deter young Badr from pursuing what his mentor hoped would be a brilliant career. With this end in view he had selected the perfect candidate, his niece Halimah, his brother's only daughter. The matter was settled almost immediately upon Badr's return to Egypt. He also preferred an Egyptian wife who would be less demanding than a European one, more attuned to his needs, and better capable of securing his home front. He felt immensely proud to have been selected by a man he admired more than any one else in the world. The wedding took place in the spring of 1858 in Zawiyat al-Baqli.

Sitt Halimah, or Sitt Umm Muhammad, as she was called after the birth of her son Mohammad 'Ali, was a simple woman whose world was circumscribed by her little family and her often absent husband. *Si al-Duktur*, as she usually called him, never ceased to surprise her. He was so unpredictable, so wrapped up in his career, forever moving to a new expedition or another voyage quite unlike other male members of her family who were perfectly content to spend their whole life in the little village of Zawiyat al-Baqli. She was not a pretty girl though her features were regular and her hair silky, very long, and usually twisted in two long braids. Though not dark, she was not fair like Caucasian women. On the whole she presented an amiable physique. When informed of her uncle's choice, she had been very happy because she trusted him implicitly and liked the idea of marrying a doctor and moving to the big city, away from the dull existence of her village.

Sitt Halimah was illiterate but did not lack intelligence and, like all young girls of her social milieu, was certainly well-versed in the lore, folklore, manners, and customs of her rural background. She felt quite ready to meet the challenge of marriage head on, to become a wife and a mother, for such was the preferred destiny of any decent girl. What she was not prepared for, however, and this came as a shock on her wedding night, was her husband's height. Dr. Badr was just over five feet tall! Being so short and slight, he looked far less than his twenty-eight years. Could there have been a mistake? Was she being married to a younger brother? Her misgivings were short-lived for Dr. Badr proved a man of decisive action and commanding disposition. He established his authority immediately and left her in no doubt about who was master in the household. She soon fell in love with her young husband who was generally courteous and even-tempered.

The couple settled in Cairo where by that time, over and above his official functions at the court of Sa'id Pasha and later of Khedive Isma'il, Dr. Badr taught medicine at Qasr al-'Ayni. His was a very busy life; he traveled frequently not only all over Egypt, but to Europe as well. In 1867, he went to France as the official doctor of the Egyptian delegation to the Exposition Universelle. Meanwhile, Sitt Halimah was kept busy in Cairo as she had presented her husband, in rapid succession, with three sons, Muhammad 'Ali, named after his great-uncle, Isma'il, and Hasan, and three daughters, Tawhidah, Chafaq Nour, and 'Ayn al-Hayah. His children, except for the firstborn, were all named after members of the Khedivial family.

It was upon his return from one of his frequent trips abroad that Dr. Badr and his wife had their first, and probably last, big quarrel that almost led to her repudiation. It was not a quarrel actually as there was no heated exchange of invectives or even of arguments. Sitt Halimah did not retaliate in any way but simply withstood, head bent, the violent outburst of anger hurled at her. The reason for this unexpected rage was brought on by her casual remark that during his absence she had been with the children to visit her mother in Zawiyat al-Baqli. While there, she had asked Umm Hamidah, the midwife, to circumcise their eldest daughter Tawhidah. The words were scarcely out of her mouth that he jumped up and shaking her violently shouted, "How dare you? How dare you commit such a crime?"

Shocked beyond words, she looked at her husband whose eyes seemed lit by a demonic fire, his lips were drawn back from his teeth, his fingers like iron clamps were digging into her shoulders mercilessly, and he was shouting over and over again, "This is a crime! How dare you? How dare you?" Halimah was dissolved in tears; she could not understand what was happening. Her mind was about to snap as she found herself propelled into a terrifying situation. Crime? What crime? Was it because she had acted without his permission? The boys had all been circumcised without mishap and surely in the case of a girl it was women's business. What was it then? She could not think as he was shaking her and shouting.

Suddenly, he let go of her and pushing her away stalked out of the room, in fact left the house altogether for several hours. Halimah was stunned, prostrate. She had never seen her husband behave in such a way and the worst of it was that she could not understand the cause. When he came back, his face was grim, the anger was still there but controlled. Halimah was crying, tears streaming down her face, unable to think, almost unable to move. In a measured tone he asked, "What about the others, have they been mutilated as well?" Halimah answered in a barely audible voice "No, because Hayah and Chafaq came down with the measles." "May God be praised," he answered, somewhat relieved.

He had spent the past few hours walking the streets of Cairo, berating himself for his negligence while trying to come to terms with his anger. Yes, the fault was as much his as hers for he should have known better than to entrust the welfare of his children so totally to a woman who had, after all, received no formal education and whose intellectual development was conditioned by and limited to the traditions of Zawiyat al-Baqli. He had been unfair, he should have tried to educate or at least warn her about certain practices. He should have tried to educate her. Sobered, if not repentant, he walked back to the house determined to salvage the situation as best he could. Reassured about his youngest daughters, he sat down with Sitt Halimah to explain the reason for his anger. This operation, he told her, was unnecessary from the religious point of view. Whereas the *sunna* requires it for boys, there is no such injunction for girls. He did not know the source of the tradition, but he had seen the practice applied in Morocco as well as in the Sudan. There, the mutilation was often beyond repair, performed under terrible conditions often with disastrous consequences.

He groped for words trying to explain, as best he could, the problems excision usually created for the unfortunate girl submitted to this awful operation. Here, of course, he had a problem for how could he explain about frigidity and orgasm? These were not topics one discussed with a woman, let alone one's wife! He therefore limited his explanations to the more obvious and immediate aspects of the problem, the possibility of hemorrhage and infection. He had often seen girls die of septicemia because the operation had been performed under unhygienic conditions.

"But *Si al-Duktur*," interrupted Sitt Halimah in self-defense. "Umm Hamidah is a very clean and capable woman, besides she stopped the bleeding by applying coffee grounds on the wound. . . ."

She went no further as she saw on her husband's face signs of mounting anger. She started to cry again, partly out of fear but mostly out of frustration. She had done no wrong. She had performed her duty as a mother. She had followed tradition.

"Anyway," said Dr. Badr. "The deed is done. However, I forbid you ever to do such a terrible thing to Hayah and Chafaq Nour."

Sitt Halimah had recovered herself sufficiently to be able to organize her thoughts. Not do the same? That was an appalling suggestion. Her daughters would be freaks!

"But *Si al-Duktur*, however shall we marry them? Surely no self-respecting man will accept an uncircumcised bride?"

"How will he know beforehand, Umm Muhammad? Do you plan to inform the matchmaker?"

"But such things can't be hidden, word gets round, your daughters will be considered. . . ."

"Considered inferior? Of lesser quality? Not worthy of a good match? So be it, but they shall never be circumcised."

His word was law and the subject was never brought up again. Hayah and Chafaq, who were respectively two and four years old at the time this incident took place, never realized how close they had come to this ghastly experience. When Dr. Badr left for one of his frequent trips to Upper Egypt a few days later, he was perfectly confident that his youngest daughters were quite safe and would not be touched by Umm Hamidah.

4

Five years after Dr. Badr and Sitt Halimah set up house in Cairo, Isma'il, Muhammad 'Ali Pasha's grandson, became viceroy of Egypt on January 18, 1863. The name of this monarch will forever be linked to the Suez Canal and its grandiose opening ceremonies, to the Cairo Opera House, where Verdi's *Rigoletto*[26] was performed, to the Gezira Palace in Zamalek, built for the same occasion, and to the lavish expenditures of this latter day Croesus, who was ultimately defeated by his visions of grandeur, though some historians effectively argue that he was the victim of superpower machinations. Whatever the case, it nonetheless remains true that Isma'il, who later and at an exorbitant price obtained from the Ottoman Sultan the Persian title of Khedive and the hereditary right to the crown of Egypt for his immediate descendants, was an enlightened monarch. And yet, it was a broken and disillusioned man who wrote to his suzerain from exile in Italy a letter listing his many achievements:

> I have just terminated sixteen years of dedicated service. Under my administration, a network of railways has covered the country; the area under cultivation has been increased, the soil enriched by the building of new canals . . . the sources of slavery in Central Africa have been destroyed, and the flag of the Empire has been raised in countries where until then it was unknown. The canal of the two seas has been built and given to the world; and lastly after a long resistance, the reform of the judiciary system has been inaugurated, which will prepare a means of establishing a true justice between the civilizations of the Orient and the Foreign Powers.[27]

Khedive Isma'il's interest in Africa was prompted by a number of reasons. He wanted to extend his empire to the equator. This was his long-term project. Meanwhile, he had to secure his southern borders particularly when, in 1866, the Sultan of Turkey ceded his interest in the Port of Massawa to Egypt. Soon after this, Egyptian forces occupied Keren, the capital of Bogos, which the Negus claimed as being part of his domain, and in 1875, Isma'il acquired the Port of Zela. Having thus expanded his territory, the Khedive felt the necessity to consolidate and protect his possessions. This was bound to lead to an armed conflict with the Negus. Furthermore, Khedive Isma'il was determined to eradicate the flourishing African slave trade. In 1869, three years after his accession, he issued a Firman that gave Sir Samuel Baker complete power and authority in the territories south of Gondokoro. Khedive Isma'il greatly admired this British explorer whose forays into the heart of Africa, accompanied by his wife, enabled him to discover in 1864 Lake Albert Nyanza, one of the sources of the Nile. The mandate he gave Baker was to put an end to the flourishing slave trade in Central Africa, the starting point of which lay 2,000 miles south of Cairo. In so doing, he exhibited a certain measure of courage because Egypt's social structure relied heavily on the use of slaves. His show of moral rectitude, which threatened an established way of life, was definitely not popular among the upper classes of society and, perhaps, not even among the poorer classes whom he was depriving of the dream of being slave owners too some day. Khedive Isma'il's motive was probably not entirely humanitarian. As an enlightened and ambitious monarch, driven by the desire to pursue his grandfather's dream, he had his eye on the vast territories that lay south of his kingdom, and the hounding of slave traders may have been a good excuse to start forays in the Sudan and beyond. Besides, there was always the question of the sources of the Nile that were still to be ascertained in a more definitive way than had so far been achieved.

In order to implement his many projects, and fully aware of his countrymen's limitations, he secured for his African ventures the help of *khawaga*s. As mentioned above, one of them was Samuel Baker who had secured for the Egyptian monarch all the territory that lay between Gondokoro and the Equatorial Lakes. He furthermore had successfully cut off the Nile route to slave traders. When he retired from the Egyptian service, Nubar Pasha, then prime minister of Egypt, persuaded Charles George Gordon to become governor-general of

the Egyptian Equatorial Provinces. This capable English officer established an excellent rapport with his second in command, Colonel
Chaillé-Long, an American officer employed by Khedive Isma'il.
Together they worked in perfect tandem and achieved wonders as the
cool reserve, dedication, and stubborn determination of the
Englishman were reinforced by the daring, courage, and extraordinary
resilience of the American.

The presence of American officers in the Khedive's expeditionary
forces was a novelty, the result of his acute perception of world
events. When, in 1862, Napoleon III decided to invade Mexico, he
obtained from Muhammad Sa'id Pasha, the ever-devoted friend of
France, a contingent of Egyptian soldiers to be sent to South
America. Though they fought valiantly—"They are not soldiers,
they are lions," Marshall Forey said of them[28]—they were unable to
prevent a French debacle. The reason of this defeat and the aban-
donment by France of Mexico, and its erstwhile Emperor
Maximilian to his fate, soon became apparent to Khedive Isma'il.
After Appomattox, the American soldiers, blue and gray, once again
united under the same flag, had rallied to their neighbor in the South
to uphold the principles of the Monroe Doctrine. Isma'il immediately realized "that if the Americans were sufficiently powerful to
expel France from Mexico, they were the men whom he needed to
give driving power to his arms."[29] These Americans for their part,
found themselves at the end of their own Civil War in an unenviable
position: the Southerners were disheartened at the outcome of the
conflict, and the Northerners chafed at their current inactivity. Many
came to Egypt in search of adventure or a new lease on life. It would
not be fair, however, to dismiss them as mere mercenaries. They came
not just for financial gain but to discover new horizons, satisfy their
love of adventure, and do what they knew best: train an army and
fight a war.

There were fifty such officers who came to Egypt at the behest of
Khedive Isma'il. Among them was General Stone who hired Gordon;
Colonel Chaillé-Long who annexed Uganda to the Egyptian crown,
and in July 1874 discovered Lake Kioga, another source of the Nile;
Colonel Colston, who conducted a reconnaissance of Kordofan in
1874–75; Major Prout, who took over when Colonel Colston's
health broke down and completed the assignment; and Colonel

Erasmus Purdy, the only one to have a mausoleum erected in his memory in Cairo's Protestant cemetery. These were but a few. It must be noted, however, that even though employing American officers in Egypt's expeditionary forces was a novelty, a precedent of a sort had already been established by Muhammad 'Ali Pasha. When in 1822 the Sudanese slaves he captured to form the nucleus of his army died like flies, some on the long march to Cairo, others after reaching the Egyptian capital, he wrote to Boghus Bey, his Armenian advisor on foreign affairs, "ordering him to hire a number of American doctors to treat the slaves. They were preferred to European physicians since they had experience of dealing with 'this race.'"[30]

In any event, the American officers hired by Khedive Isma'il came to Egypt with enthusiasm. Of all their achievements, the one that is of particular interest to this narrative is the incursion into the heart of Africa because Dr. Badr found himself at the epicenter of this venture under the command of "the one-armed and battle-scarred Indian fighter and confederate veteran, General William W. Loring of Florida."[31] Like his fellow Americans, Loring arrived in Egypt around 1870, and like his compatriots was immediately involved in Khedive Isma'il's ambitious projects. All of them must have been impressed by the lavishness of the Egyptian court, and if they had to wear a *stambulina* to be introduced to the Khedive, so be it, though it is doubtful any of them mastered the graceful salutation of the *tamanni*. In any event, they were all eager to get down to work and prove their worth.

General Loring became involved in the Abyssinian campaign, which, unfortunately, marks a black episode in the history of American soldiers in Egypt. Problems with the Negus were increasing. King John had not taken kindly to what he considered the Khedive's high-handed annexation of some of his territories, or to the Egyptian presence so close to his boundaries. Matters came to a head when, on November 11, 1875, an Egyptian contingent was attacked and defeated at Gundet and its leader, Colonel Arendrup, a Dane, was killed. When news of the disaster reached Cairo, there was total consternation. Khedive Isma'il and his government took the decision to retaliate immediately so as to secure the Egyptian position and restore confidence in the power of the Egyptian Army. An expeditionary force under the command of Ratib Pasha, a Turk "ever small of stature but shriveled up like a mummy with age"[32] was sent to Massawa whose governor at the time was a certain Ahmad Bey, nephew of Isma'il al-Mufattish.[33]

Ahmad Bey, who owed the position to his uncle's influence with the Khedive, was an inexperienced and pompous young man who had replaced the much more efficient former governor, nephew of Nubar Pasha. Ratib Pasha's second in command was General William W. Loring and his nominal superior was Prince Hasan, the Khedive's third son. The prince, who was studying at the Military Academy in Vienna, was given leave of absence to fight in his father's army and thereby gain first hand experience at warfare. He was an amiable young man of twenty-two, handsome like most of the Khedive's offspring, but totally inexperienced and thrown in at the deep end without warning, albeit under the protection of Ratib Pasha. Dr. Badr, who distinguished himself at the inauguration of the Suez Canal by successfully treating one of the Khedive's royal guests (Prince Henri, brother of the king of Holland) was rewarded by the Khedive who named him the personal physician of young Prince Hasan. When the latter was dispatched to Abyssinia, his physician went along as well.

Dr. Badr was delighted at the prospect of a new adventure and, if Sitt Halimah minded, she certainly never voiced an objection, as it would have been unseemly. Besides, the honor bestowed on *Si al-Duktur* amply compensated her for any misgivings she might have had. Dr. Muhammad 'Ali al-Baqli Pasha, who by that time was quite advanced in age, volunteered to join the expedition and Khedive Isma'il welcomed the suggestion as he wanted to give the whole venture an aura of importance. Thus by the end of December 1875, there was at Massawa an Egyptian expeditionary force headed by an aged Turk, encumbered by a young prince, at the mercy of an inefficient governor and under the virtual command of an able and experienced American general whose hands were more or less tied. The combination could not but lead to disaster. Ratib Pasha was an old man, overly cautious, whose only concern seems to have been the safety of the Prince, while Loring, who knew all about military strategy, could have won the day had he not been at loggerheads with his superior. To add to this unfortunate combination of elements, lines of communication and army supplies, which should have been insured by a herd of at least ten to twelve thousand camels, were left to a mere three hundred, and those were Massawa camels of much weaker stock than the Arab ones. Poor communication, bad feelings between commanding officers, open antagonism between Ratib Pasha and General Loring led to delays and confusion. To these one might add the arrogance of Ratib Pasha who grossly underestimated the enemy. Given these liabilities the expedition was doomed to fail despite the presence of able Egyptian officers such as 'Uthman Nagib Bey, Ahmad Effendi, and Dr. Badr whose courage and valor on the battlefield were later highly praised.

The Egyptians suffered a resounding defeat, all the more humiliating, as they were equipped with Remington rifles and modern weapons against the half-naked warriors of King John's army who fought mainly with sabers and lances. What matters in our context is Dr. Badr's involvement in these events and his amazing prowess.

On March 7, 1876, disaster struck. The Egyptian army was routed and Dr. Badr taken prisoner along with other officers such as Rashid Pasha, Muhammad 'Ali al-Baqli Pasha, Dr. Johnson, Major Dorholtz, and many others. As the battle raged, Ratib Pasha had remained in the fort, according to some sources, in order to protect the Khedive's son, but according to other less generous accounts, through sheer cowardice. Whatever the case, he, as the responsible officer leading the expeditionary force, lost the day. A first hand account of that defeat was recorded by General Loring in his book, *A Confederate Soldier in Egypt*. The following quotation will shed light on the general atmosphere that prevailed on the battlefield, on the attitude of some of the participants, and on the gallant role played by Dr. Badr:

> That night and early next morning a number of our wounded came into camp and reported a great many still in the valley and on the hills, one or two miles distant. The next day, the 8th of March, the commanding general was pressed to send his cavalry to collect his wounded. The valley was open, and it could maneuver without fear, and being an old cavalry officer I proposed to take command with the entire staff, and bring them in. He [Ratib Pasha] would not let a soldier go out of the fort, and if he saw one on the outside he was fired upon. He was told that officers like

Racshid Pacha, Mehemet Ali Pacha [al-Baqli], Dr. Johnson, Major Dolholtz, and a great number of others might still be alive there. These were all friends of mine, and aside from a feeling of humanity and duty that was an additional reason, if there could be one, to induce me to urge action. I said that it was inhuman to leave them out in the burning sun by day, and in the extreme cold at night; that they were naked, having been stripped of all clothing, and were suffering for want of water and food; that many of us would be glad to take our lives in our hands and go out after them. . . . I told Ratib the whole civilized world would hold him responsible. He clung, notwithstanding these forcible appeals, to his fort, and would not let a soldier stir. . . . Ratib, always thinking of his personal safety, had another fort constructed inside his regular fort, out of the great quantity of hard bread called by the Arabs boxomat, which he had piled up in the fort. He stated that one object he had in constructing it was that he might have a safe place for the prince, but everyone knew that he worked for his own safety. . . . The bread fort was, however, a happy thing, as it afforded perfect shelter to our wounded officers, completely covering them, so that they could neither see nor be seen. It was not long before Abyssinians, with sabers and lances, and shields covered in barbaric splendor with brass and silver, were seen glittering in the morning sun. They looked, as they stood in masses, as one might fancy the phalanx of Alexander the Great—the king in his chemma, the princes and priests in their kuaries, and the soldier in his taub, each resembling the Roman toga with red stripes through its center. These folded around them or gracefully fluttering in the morning breeze gave the air of the military civilization of an ancient day. . . . Soon the fight began in earnest. . . . The young artillerymen fell fast and thick at the guns at this angle, it being the point where the attack was fiercest, but others moved up rapidly to take their places. It was near here that my aide-de-camp Ahmad Effendi, a gallant young officer, was killed. On looking around for Ratib, he was found in his bread fort, and being told of the determined attack was advised to come to the post of danger. He took so long a time to light his cigarette that he was left in his place of security. . . . Yelling and brandishing their shining shields and weapons over their heads, the Abyssinians on the sides of the hills were with shout and song urging their assaulting party to leap the parapet, while they stood, to all appearances, ready to rush madly on at any moment. Upon seeing their men approach with their steady fire within thirty or forty feet of us, they sounded applause with a loud shout, and their instruments played notes of victory. At this stage the scene on the hillsides, in the valley, and in the fort was picturesque and exciting—a tableau of interest only to be found in the north–east corner of Africa. After several futile attacks, those of the enemy in our immediate front gave way. When they had fled a considerable distance, running as though they had abandoned the fight, a sortie was made from the fort, the Krupp guns still continuing to pour well-directed shots into the enemy on the slopes of the hills, and these too showed signs of weakening. The scattered throngs in the valley around us, seeing the discomfiture of their assaulting party, fled precipitately; those on the hills catching the excitement, music and shouting ceased, and King John and his army took to their heels. . . . The enemy left a number of killed and wounded on the fields near the fort. As soon as the Abyssinians had disappeared from the hills the Egyptian (Sudanese), officers and men, now that all danger was past, rushed out of the fort at once, and showed their prowess by killing the wounded . . . mutilating the dead, cutting off their hands and feet and scattering them about . . . . As soon as this came to my knowledge I hastened to Ratib Pacha and urged him to stop such devilish work; but I found him unequal to the occasion. . . . I reminded him that King John had nearly one thousand Egyptian prisoners, naked and bound hand and foot, in his camp not two miles off; that as the great outrage had already been committed of killing the wounded, the only thing to be done now was to bury the dead so deep that the Abyssinians could not find them when they came to seek their wounded in the coming night, as they would certainly do . . . that on their coming under cover of darkness and finding their dead so horribly mutilated, just as certain as the sun rose the next day every Egyptian they had in their camp would be murdered, and that Ratib Pacha would be held responsible for it . . . the commander did not take energetic steps . . . The Egyptians did not succeed in burying the dead, and in many instances a ghastly and hideous spectacle was left for the Abyssinians to look upon. The next day the hills resounded with the discharge of firearms and the cry of the unfortunate Egyptians who were prisoners in their power. It was the horrible cry of over six hundred officers and men who were shot down and lanced in cold blood in the camp of the enemy which had caused the ominous noise. Dr. Johnson, an American, and Major Dorholtz, a Swiss, who were naked and bound in this camp, were saved because they were white and Christians. . . . At dawn on the 9th of March I was on the parapet of the fort watching for the Egyptian wounded. . . . It was at this early hour that I was pleased to see Dr. Badri Effendi coming, without any clothing on but his boots, wounded, and dragging himself slowly along. In giving an account of his capture and suffering he said that the enemy had led him, wounded, naked, and bound, into their camp. As he was quite a small man, no particular guard was placed over him. During the night one of the young women cast toward him pitying glances not unmixed with playful fondness, which as he lay bound hand and foot, he observed by the flickering light near which she sat, prevailing upon her to give him water he saw that she was still further attracted. She then loosened the cords, which were most painful, while extracting from him a declaration that he was a Christian, which, as he was a Mahometan, was most humiliating. With the loosing of each cord this was repeated until he got to think he really was a disciple of the Saviour. Courtesies were extended, and she took care that his cords did not bind too closely. After the fires had burned out and all were asleep, ridding himself of his bonds, he rolled over carefully as if he were a log, and watching his opportunity silently stole away and left his fair friend in a happy state of unconsciousness. As soon as he could get into the thick forests of the mountain he circled round the whole night in his wanderings, though only two and a half miles from the fort, before he reached it. . . . These kindnesses of the women of Abyssinia were of frequent occurrence, and their recipients were not always as particular as the doctor in relating how pleasantly he had confessed himself a Christian. . . . The medical department was very unfortunate. Dr. Badri Effendi could barely walk on account of his wounds, Dr. Wilson was *hors de combat*, Dr. Johnson was a captive in the hands of the enemy, and Dr. Mehemet Ali Pacha [al-Baqli], noted as a distinguished surgeon, who had arrived shortly before the battle of the 7th of March, was cruelly murdered while a prisoner in the power of the Abyssinians. . . .[34]

It appears, from other accounts of the day's events, that Dr. Badr despite his many injuries, set himself to work almost immediately upon reaching the fort. The injured and the near-dying all needed his attention and there was no one to help as most other medical personnel of the expedition were either captive or dead. Disregarding his own discomfort, he worked relentlessly to relieve the suffering of his men and thereby won the admiration and respect of his fellow officers, American and Egyptian alike.

Setting aside the personal bias of Loring and the bitterness with which he judged his commanding officer, one cannot but admire the vivid account he makes of that unfortunate day. Whether, as Loring claims, Ratib Pasha was an incompetent coward, or whether Loring, as Ratib Pasha for his part assured the Khedive in his account of the events, was to blame for having been impetuous and careless, it emerges from this whole affair that the valor, courage and ability of the Egyptians as exemplified by the behavior of Dr. Badr, 'Uthman Bey Nagib, Ahmad Effendi, and Dr. Muhammad 'Ali al-Baqli were firmly established.

Dr. Badr came back to Egypt a hero and was rewarded by the Khedive with the title of *Amiralay* (Brigadier), which automatically gave him the right to append the title of Bey to his name. His valor was recognized, his reputation established both as a surgeon and as a soldier, and yet he was deeply sad for he had seen the horror and mutilation suffered by both camps, the wanton destruction of human life, and the agony that it was all for naught. Above all, he had lost his mentor, Muhammad 'Ali al-Baqli Pasha so cruelly massacred by the Abyssinians. He gained tremendous experience on the battlefield, but more important, he developed a keen interest in the activities of the American officers he met during the campaign. He was fascinated by accounts of the various assignments they and their countrymen fulfilled in Africa on the orders of the Khedive. He was told of the Locket and Mitchell expeditions in Abyssinia, whose purpose was to draw topographical surveys of the territories the Egyptian armies traveled through; more exciting still were the expeditions of Charles Chaillé-Long to the sources of the Nile. It is not clear whether he ever met Chaillé-Long though the possibility exists since both men had connections with the Khedivial court. What is known from family lore is that he often spoke with admiration of this American explorer and of his achievements.

Upon his return to Egypt and after an appropriate period of mourning for the loss of his wife's uncle, he quickly recuperated and plunged once again with energy into his various activities. He was, by nature, a gregarious fellow who soon delighted his friends with stories of his captivity and fortunate escape. During these entertaining evenings, he never spoke of the horrors he had witnessed. He felt it would be a betrayal to use the suffering and death of his companions as dinner party conversation. Rather, he turned his tremendous sense of humor upon himself and his diminutive size, often mentioning his Abyssinian savior.

"Pity I could not bring her back with me. I am sure Sitt Halimah would have welcomed her, for after all, she saved my life."

"Tell us again what you told her when she asked if you were Christian."

"I said, 'Yes, yes, Christian, Jesus, Mary.' I nodded all the time I was saying it."

"I am sure you crossed yourself as well," his friend Ya'qub Effendi said mischievously.

"No! That I did not do. How could I, my hands were tied?"

They all laughed uproariously.

"You see," added Dr. Badr, "had I been bigger and stronger she would not have taken pity on me. I looked so helpless, so. . . ."

"'Naked is the word, my friend," interrupted 'Ali Bey and they all laughed again.

The story went on and on but little was added to the original facts as they themselves defied imagination.

5

While Dr. Badr was thus engaged in his busy professional life, Sitt Halimah reigned over her little kingdom. This was no small feat as her six children and large household with many servants required her undivided attention and a good deal of administrative skill. With her husband's advancing fortunes and growing fame, it was incumbent upon her to present a worthy front. That is not to say that she was ever seen in public for she rarely ventured out, and when she did was covered from top to toe; but it was important that it be known through the grapevine—that was usually through the servants—that within the walls of this respectable house in 'Abbasiya, life was lived on a grand scale. And indeed it was. Dr. Badr, like most men who suddenly meet success, wanted his personal life to reflect his new status. As a result, Sitt Hamidah found herself at the head of an imposing household, which comprised many servants, mostly maids from the village, and a gatekeeper. In time, however, Dr. Badr following the modern trend of his day, insisted that a male cook with an under cook be employed. Sitt Halimah communicated with these men through her head maid, Nabawiyah, who was also her daughters' nanny and her confidante. As the official go-between, Nabawiyah gained tremendous prestige in the eyes of the other servants.

Meals were served in the dining room, with all the dishes set on the table, and plates flanked by a lone spoon with which rice or soup were eaten. Actually, Sitt Halimah and her children rarely made use of spoons. Sitt Halimah supervised proceedings and since Dr. Badr was often absent, she was the one in charge of discipline and table manners. However, as is often the case in Egyptian households, she exercised her authority more stringently upon her daughters than her sons. She loved all her children dearly with a marked preference for her eldest, Muhammad 'Ali. Gradually, as her sons became adolescents, she felt awed by them and assumed, as was the custom, that disciplining them was her husband's responsibility for, after all, they were men and as such commanded everyone's respect, even hers. It is amazing that given their father's frequent absences, they never got out of hand.

With her daughters the situation was totally different. They were indeed her responsibility. She had to teach them, prepare them to become good wives and mothers, and her reputation rested on their success. This being the case, she painstakingly taught them all she knew and whatever she had learned from her own mother in the quiet village of Zawiyat al-Baqli. First and foremost, her daughters had to learn about cleanliness—of the body as well as of their surroundings—hence she was a taskmaster at table. The girls did not use cutlery and therefore had to wash their hands carefully before and after meals. Woe befell the unfortunate one who let a morsel drop outside her plate thereby soiling the tablecloth! A rap on the hand was the immediate reaction of her mother. It was quite fortunate for these girls that none of them was left-handed as they were instructed that only the three fingers of the right hand could be brought to the mouth. Though the boys were often loud at table, the girls had to express themselves in measured tones for women should never draw attention to themselves by raising their voice. Never a bully, Sitt Halimah, however, often became exacting in her demands for she felt insecure in the new and elevated position that was her lot now as the wife of the prominent Dr. Badr.

The Badr boys all went to school. By the time Muhammad 'Ali was seven years old, few people of standing would have accepted the notion of having illiterate sons. Muhammad 'Ali became a doctor, like his father and great-uncle, and the other two studied law and in time became eminent jurists. For the girls, however, oddly enough since they were Dr. Badr's daughters, the option was never given. Village custom in their case prevailed. They stayed at home and received a totally different kind of education. Under their mother's tutelage they became recipients of a large body of knowledge with an undefined but varied curriculum. While it may seem surprising that the daughters of a brilliant surgeon educated in Edinburgh should have remained illiterate to the end of their life, it is understandable, if one examines more closely the social scene in Egypt at the end of the nineteenth century, and more particularly the Badr family, which was typical of a very large segment of that society.

Even though Dr. Badr was an educated man who reached prominence early in life, his wife, Sitt Halimah, was the product of her middle class rural background, and as was the custom solely in charge of the home. She set the tone and preserved norms, beliefs, and way of life. This pattern was not challenged by Dr. Badr who, in any, case would not have had the time to do so; besides, it most probably suited his purpose to follow tradition. With all his achievements, Dr. Badr could not be considered a social reformer, or for that matter an educator. The predictable result was that the girls remained illiterate but under their mother's tutelage perfected their Egyptian upbringing, learned the mores of the society to which they belonged, and took pride in being the recipients of a culture rooted in Islam and handed down to them through successive generations. By the time they reached puberty, they had memorized an impressive body of folk tales, legends, and village lore. They knew and could quote with ease and in a most appropriate manner sayings and proverbs whose origins were lost in the very distant past but had come down unchanged through the ages to reflect both the wisdom of the ancients and the perspicacity of their observations. Faced by the vagaries of life, they could sum up each event by one of these little maxims, which encapsulated the whole situation. One in particular surely must have been at the back of Sitt Halimah's mind and guided her attitude toward her daughters:

Ikfi al-idra 'ala fummaha
Titla' al-bint li-ummaha.

Which roughly translates into:

'Imprint on the sand made by the urn
Will be the exact replica of the urn.'

In other words, "Like mother, like daughter" but rendered more forceful by the suggested image and the rhyme. This was a system of oral tradition and education at its best. As these women never used books and could not fall back upon a text, they each developed a formidable memory that became a store of the culture of their country, a store that almost never failed them. Tawhidah, Chafaq Nour, and 'Ayn al-Hayah had no misgivings about their lack of a formal education because they were firmly convinced that the culture they were receiving was a precious gift to be preserved to the best of their ability in its pristine condition.

Over and above concern for table manners and nourishment of the mind, there was a plethora of rules of etiquette the girls had to absorb. They had to know how to behave on the rare social occasions that came their way. For instance, they were told never to sit on the sofa, this being reserved for elderly ladies (or at least married ones). They were instructed never to take part in conversation unless invited to do so and always to stand up when an older person entered the room. Their mother expected them in that respect to become living yo-yos! They also had to kiss the hands of their elders, men and women alike, when greeting them. This was a custom that remained in vigor until the early 1950s, albeit restricted by then to elderly ladies or one's father.

Such was the situation for the Badr family, which was more or less the norm in Egypt at the turn of the twentieth century. However it was not an absolute rule. Many contemporaries of the Badr girls were educated women such as Safeya Zaghloul and Hoda Sha'rawi, who could not only read and write but shared in the political life of the country. These ladies, of course, belonged by birth to the upper echelons of society, the former being the daughter of Mustafa Fahmi Pasha and the latter the daughter of Sultan Pasha. It is interesting to note that among the Coptic community of Upper Egypt, formal education for Egyptian girls was accepted and applied as early as the mid-nineteenth century. Hanna Wissa writes of his grand mother Balsam:

> Balsam, the eldest daughter of Wissa . . . had been sent to Dr. Hogg and Miss Martha J. McKowan when they intimated to Wissa that they wanted to start a girl's school in Assiout in the mid-1860's. Balsam was one of the first three girls who joined the new school. Wissa had stipulated to Dr. Hogg and Miss McKowan that he wanted his daughter to be brought up as a good Christian, able to read and write, but at the same time he wanted her to be able to look after a large house and a family.[35]

Balsam was a contemporary of the Badr girls, perhaps a little older, but her case was not infrequent among the Coptic community of Asyut, due probably to the missionary activity of Dr. Hogg and his colleagues.

What was novel in Sitt Halimah's life was the presence of the many servants who were now part of the household. How she fared with them or treated them, no one knows for sure. One can but assume that she played it by ear and adjusted gradually to their presence. What may have been an oddity for the mother, perhaps even a problem, was perfectly natural for the daughters who grew up knowing the exact place of everyone in the organization of their home. They knew that their mother was the head—the father being an almost mythical figure revered from afar—their brothers belonged to a category of their own, not quite like their father in the respect they were due, but certainly superior to them. Nabawiyah was one rank above the other maids, hence could not be ordered about as they would the others. Above all, they knew that they should never address directly the male gatekeeper or the cook. The girls grew up understanding these relationships and knew instinctively how to behave toward servants and how to dominate them. What was for Sitt Halimah an acquired attitude was for them perfectly natural. All these 'do's and don'ts' were instilled in daily doses by their mother who may have been unaware that she was actually teaching, not simply doing what comes naturally.

One wonders how these women spent their time in an age when outings were limited, books beyond their scope, and television not yet invented. Setting aside the time devoted to the only formal instruction they received, namely the memorization of certain *sura*s of the Qur'an, which their mother taught them, as she was taught herself, through oral repetition followed by recitation, they apparently passed the day pleasantly enough. They chatted among themselves, learned the arts of crochet or embroidery, or listened for endless hours to Nabawiya's stories and folk legends with which she enchanted their evenings. Sitting behind their *mashrabiya*s they would look out to observe what little activity went on in the street below. However, it seems that they also indulged in long sessions of gossip, which came in bouts whenever they heard of a divorce, an engagement, or a quarrel in the family. There again and early on, their mother taught them what topics were allowed and what others were taboo on moral or religious grounds, hence not to be discussed.

If they experienced boredom, they accepted it as a momentary unpleasantness in their day. Since they knew no other way of life,

they never rebelled but, on the contrary, became staunch conserva-
tives, upholders of the flame and the proud recipients of traditions
they were taught to respect. Not for them was Hoda Sha'rawi's
defiant attitude. Casting off the veil was, as far as they were concerned, an incongruous, if not immoral, act. Neither would they ever
participate in a political demonstration, whatever the cause, and
unlike so many women both in Cairo and in the provinces, they did
not rush out into the streets in 1919 chanting slogans in support of
Sa'd Zaghloul and his nationalist endeavors. Their place was at home,
of this they had no doubt. There was a certain incongruity in the
Badr family set-up. What was usually viewed as a patriarchal family
dominated by the powerful personality of the father, was in fact a
matriarchal one governed by a submissive wife thrust into a position
of authority through her husband's frequent absences. This in turn
fostered in her own and her daughters' psyches the belief that the
role of the wife and mother is of prime importance.

Unlike Tawhidah and 'Ayn al-Hayah, Chafaq Nour was not pretty. She had inherited her father's strong features and her complexion,
though not dark, was not as fair as her sisters'. But she had also inherited his powerful intellect and formidable memory. She was strong-
willed, at least as far as it was possible for a girl to be in those days,
and witty with her father's acute sense of humor. Her family could
always count on her for a joke to enliven a conversation but her sisters feared her tongue. Her amazing capacity to use a proverb as a
weapon was like a dart, devastating in its accuracy. Her father was
amused by this clever little girl and often thought she would make a
tough but also reliable and entertaining wife for any man with ambition and character.

Tawhidah was married off at the age of eighteen. She was the eldest and the prettiest of the three. She had many suitors of good standing but, for a while, none seemed adequate enough until her father
finally opted for a young engineer with a substantial income who
seemed to be an appropriate match even though he was, as far as
could be ascertained, a rather ordinary young man. Tawhidah, who
was eager to start her career as a wife and mother was elated by her
father's choice though she had never seen her future husband. She
was sent off with a nice wedding, an impressive trousseau, and her
baggage of culture accumulated through the years. Dr. Badr was

satisfied. He had done well enough for his eldest daughter. Chafaq Nour, he feared, would not be as easy to settle into matrimony. For one thing, she was not as attractive as her sister. Though she was totally segregated, this fact was common knowledge carried through the usual information channels, in other words, aunts, cousins, or family maids. More important still was Dr. Badr's reluctance to let go of his favorite daughter whose intelligence and personality he had come to appreciate with growing interest over the years. This girl, he thought, deserves a man of superior mettle, an educated person, intelligent, sensitive, who will appreciate her worth and get the best out of her.

He turned down suitors who were rich but otherwise mediocre, and others whose credentials were good but whose personality was not promising, at least not meeting his standard. Sitt Halimah was at her wits' end and could not understand what *Si al-Duktur* was up to. Did he want the girl to become an old maid? She was already eighteen years old and not yet spoken for. Occasionally a horrid thought crossed her mind. Could her husband have suddenly remembered that both Chafaq Nour and 'Ayn al-Hayah were flawed because they were uncircumcised? Could it be that he want-ed to avoid a scandalous repudiation of the bride on the *sabahiya*, the morning after the wedding? She kept her thoughts to herself though but spent many sleepless nights worrying over her daugh-ters' future especially Chafaq, who was the plainest of the three and the next in line.

Sitt Halimah's dilemma and profound anguish were relieved sud-denly in a most unexpected way in the spring of 1886. Dr. Badr, who now resided in Cairo almost permanently, came home one evening and announced to his bemused wife that Chafaq Nour had a suitor whom he intended to accept. The surprise was immense and the relief even greater. Sitt Halimah could hardly contain herself. Her prayers had finally been answered and the terror of what might have been was immediately forgotten.

"Who is he?" she asked after a few moments of speechlessness.

"He is the son of Sadiq Effendi al-Maghrabi of Minya. His mother is Caucasian and the family is well to do. More important in my view, the young man has a degree in engineering from France and is currently employed in the Ministry of Public Works, where he is a deputy irrigation controller. He has built a very good reputation for himself. I have met him and am quite impressed with his professional standing."

"May God be praised! Shall I tell Chafaq?"

"No, not a word to anyone until Sadiq Effendi al-Maghrabi and his son come here to officially request an alliance with me. After we have read the *Fatiha*, you can announce the betrothal of your daughter, not before."

It was never clear who, in fact, made the initial approach. Was it Dr. Badr who, in his quest for an appropriate husband for Chafaq Nour, had been on the lookout and upon hearing of Isma'il Sadiq's good reputation at the Ministry of Public Works sent discreet feelers to the young man? Was it Isma'il who, having settled down in what seemed to be a promising career, was eager to secure his situation by making an advantageous marriage?

Whatever the case, it was an arranged affair like all marriages of the time. What was odd, according to prevailing custom, was that Isma'il made his choice and thereafter informed his father. What prompted him to select an Egyptian girl whose family came from a village in Munufiya rather than a Caucasian beauty like his cousin Hoda? Were not Caucasian girls reputed for their refinement, education, and beauty? Did they not on the whole surpass their Egyptian counterparts? To all these questions Isma'il and everyone else in Egypt for that matter would have answered in the affirmative. It is to the credit of this young engineer that he did not attach importance to such considerations but chose instead the daughter of a man who had fired his imagination and provoked his admiration: the famous Dr. Badr, the hero of the Abyssinian campaign, the man who had sailed up the Nile beyond its Egyptian frontier. In fact, the young girl's background was quite suitable. If he, Isma'il Sadiq, was the son of a wealthy landowner, who had at one time held an important government post, she was the daughter of an equally important government employee. Both men, in other words, belonged to the same class. In order to deflect his father's anger at his highhanded behavior and secure not only his approval but his full support, Isma'il pointed out all the advantages of such a marriage, not least of which was the boost it would assuredly give his career. This was the magic argument because he knew the tremendous importance Sadiq

Effendi attached to his son's career, and the pride he felt when the latter was given a position in the Ministry of Public Works.

This ministry was at the time one of the most important in the government. Once they occupied the country, the British very quickly realized that in order to rule Egypt effectively they had to control its irrigation, the country being first and foremost an agricultural one. Bearing this in mind, they selected men such as William Willcocks, William Garstin, and Hanbury Brown, all brilliant hydraulics engineers, to play a vital role in the running of the country. These were the first generation occupants of a government position through which the British imposed their rule. The position itself was that of the honorable irrigation inspector. It was conceived by Sir Colin Scott-Moncrieff, deputy minister of public works, who often quoted Nubar Pasha as saying, "The Egyptian question is the irrigation question." The first contingent of these inspectors were army officers brought over from India. The inspector's position was central and of paramount importance as the following extract from the July 16, 1889 edition of *al-Ahram* will indicate:

> A communiqué from the honorable irrigation inspector of the first sector requests the provincial director to announce to the farmers that they should commence irrigating their fields rapidly, and to the best of their abilities, as the blessed Nile has begun to rise quickly, which may threaten to ruin the levees and force the closure of the Eastern Nile canal. The inspector is prepared to wait until the water arrives to the most needy and thus, the people's praise and gratitude to our honorable provincial director and our honorable irrigation inspector . . . will be twofold.

The job of the inspector was not always an easy one and disputes often erupted with landowners who resented the government's policy as regards the distribution of water. On one occasion, landowners of the Beheira province met in Damanhur and denounced the cruelty of the inspector's orders. One of the main duties of the irrigation inspector was to ensure that landowners not make openings in the sand dikes and irrigate their fields at the expense of their neighbors. The ministry was responsible for dredging canals and reinforcing levees because the yearly floods of the Nile could drown entire villages and the fertile silt could accumulate at the bottom of canals. Under Khedive Isma'il, and before the British occupation, the Ministry of Public Works had been the target of some criticism because part of Egypt's debt was caused by the huge cost of drainage works. This, however, was a necessary expenditure and if the Khedive was blamed—rightly or wrongly—for his financial excesses, prodigality, and unawareness of the value of money, he was certainly justified on that score.

Khedive Isma'il shared his father's vision, intelligence, and ambition both for himself and for the country. When the Khedive was deposed in 1879, Isma'il Sadiq was a very young man who may have admired the monarch but was more concerned at the time with the pursuit of his education. In Khedive Tewfik he found a ruler who lacked his father's genius, zest for life, and political acumen. When threatened by 'Urabi, he had the weakness—some would argue, the wisdom—to seek British protection for his country thereby opening a new phase in its history. The Mamluks had come and gone. The French had come and gone. Egypt for a while fared well enough as a semi-independent satellite of the Ottoman Empire, and now the British had established their presence with its accompaniment of political arrogance, technological expertise, a refined way of life, and, above all, the stubborn determination to do things their own way and to remain. John Bull dug his heels in and went to work.

The moment in time is often crucial in the direction a person's life might take. Opportunity, circumstances, and personal assets all combined to propel Isma'il Sadiq to the forefront of his country's affairs. He came back to Egypt at a time when the seeds planted by the French scientists were flourishing. He soon realized that he could play a major role in the development of his country. His personal ambition was one of achievement; his French teachers at the Centrale gave him the academic expertise he needed, while the years spent in France refined his spirit and clarified his vision. He never for a moment thought to remain there longer than necessary. He would go back to Egypt and live up to Muhammad 'Ali's dream, he would put his expertise at the service of his country, he would build dams to tame the Nile and control its flow, he would learn, he would observe, and he would achieve. His ambition was tremendous for it transcended personal considerations.

Early in 1884, he became one of the first Egyptian deputy irrigation inspectors like his life-long friend, Isma'il Sirri.[36] He perfected the academic training he received in France under the tutelage of the British irrigation inspectors who, at the time, were actively engaged in the ministry. Men such as Brown, Scott-Moncrieff, Garstin, and Willcox taught him as much, if not more, than what he had learned at university. These men he admired profoundly and though not an anglophile politically, he definitely became one on the professional level. "These people," he once told his friends Yusuf Wahbah and Aslan Cattaoui, "have the knowledge we need. It is up to us to learn from them as much as we can and to use this knowledge to our best advantage." This professional attitude of Isma'il Sadiq, which he shared with Isma'il Sirri, Ahmad Lutfi al-Sayed, Hussein Heikal, and many others, was an intellectual stance, an evaluation of worth. He never changed or reassessed his position in that respect.

Unlike many of his contemporaries, he never became a 'nationalist' because he was never a politician but simply a technocrat, a man who distrusted slogans and fiery speeches, but believed first and foremost in the exact science of engineering. And he believed in the reality of a job well done, in the no-nonsense attitude of the British irrigation inspectors whose total dedication to their job he never had cause to doubt. As for the nationalists' demand for immediate evacuation of the country, he viewed it as a potential evil in the short run, but as a right to be fought for, and achieved by, future generations when Egypt through the ability of her own men could stand up and claim her independence. This was definitely an elitist attitude, but understandable in the context of the time. Actually, it was all a matter of nuance and of timing, love of country paired with pragmatic common sense. But for the moment, Isma'il Sadiq was a twenty-five-year-old deputy irrigation inspector on the verge of entering into a matrimonial alliance of his choice.

6

Isma'il Sadiq and Chafaq Nour were married on July 12, 1886. Once Sadiq al-Maghrabi was pacified by his son's arguments, a mechanism of official procedures was set in motion. First of all, he had to pay a courtesy visit to the bride's father and officially ask for her hand in marriage. Dr. Badr would never have consented to a request made by the son. Had he done so, there would have been much loss of face for the bride, for the underlying assumption would be that the groom's parents did not approve of this alliance. As was expected, Sadiq Effendi was quite impressed by Dr. Badr and the evident comfort, if not opulence, which surrounded him. He observed that the *bawwab* was wearing an impeccable jibba and caftan and the traditional white turban. The drawing room, where they were introduced, was impressive, with gilt furniture in every angle of the room reflecting the light of the crystal chandelier. Sadiq al-Maghrabi also observed that juice, and not sherbet, was served first, the latter belonging to the next stage of the proceedings—after the request has been granted and the *Fatiha* recited. The maid attracted his attention not because she was young and pretty (it was Nabawiyah who officiated) but because her *gallabiya* was neat, her feet encased in closed slippers, and her eyes modestly downcast.

"So far, so good," thought the Upper Egyptian gentleman. He glanced at his brothers, Maghrabi and 'Uthman, and noted with satisfaction that they seemed pleased. For this first visit, they had come in full force, rounding up the male relatives of the groom in order to impress his future in-laws with the strength of his *'izwa*. They had to know from the start that Isma'il belonged to a powerful clan. If no maternal uncles could be produced for the occasion, since these were lost somewhere in Anatolia, his father's side would make up the difference.

Dr. Badr was observing as well. Though his mind was already made up, and the visit a conventional formality, still he was curious about this future son-in-law. He noticed that the young man was extremely diffident in the presence of his father and never spoke unless spoken to. It was quite clear that the parent was in charge, as he should be. Furthermore, the suitor was undoubtedly handsome, rather tall—which for Dr. Badr was a definite asset—light-skinned, and his hair, which was abundant and wavy, had an indefinable color. "Is it reddish?" wondered Dr. Badr. "Could he be a red-head or is the light of the chandelier playing tricks on my vision? Whatever the color he surely owes it to his Berber ancestors or perhaps the Turkish ones. No matter, it will improve our lineage." After almost endless exchanges of courtesies, Sadiq Effendi came to the point and Chafaq Nour's fate was sealed by the formal recitation of the *Fatiha*. "May God be praised," they all intoned in unison.

Immediately a chorus of ululations burst forth and, as if by magic, turbaned *sufrajis* hired for the occasion appeared on the scene and moved among the guests passing round trays of sherbet. As of that moment, Chafaq Nour was, to all intents and purposes, married to Isma'il Sadiq. The two basic requirements of an Islamic marriage were fulfilled: recitation of the *Fatiha* to sanctify the proceedings, and *ishhar*, or formal announcement, guaranteed by the presence of witnesses and broadcast by the ululations, which carried the good news beyond the confines of the Badr residence. However, relying on the principle of *usul*, the formal marriage of the betrothed was to take place at a later date to allow both sides to prepare adequately.[37]

Back in Minya, Neshedil Hanim, Isma'il's mother, was seething. This whole affair was to her mind extremely distasteful. She could not understand her son's choice or his father's acceptance of it: an Egyptian girl whose family came from a village in Munufiya! She would almost have preferred the French girl who had for some time lived in her imagination but never materialized.

"But Anna," asked her daughter Zaynab. "Why are you so upset?"

"How should I not be upset? Your brother would have been better off with a French girl."

"But why, Anna? Why?"

"Because a French girl would be just different. This one, I am much afraid, will be inferior."

"Inferior in what way? She is, after all, the daughter of the famous Dr. Badr."

"I know that. But is she fair? Can she read and write? Is she refined in her ways? Your brother has never set eyes on her and yet there he goes, throwing himself blindfold into this silly marriage. No good can come out of such madness."

Poor Neshedil Hanim was laboring under the weight of an impressive mass of misconceptions. This was, of course, the unavoidable consequence of the life she was leading in Minya. As the wife of one of the outstanding notables of the city, she socialized with women who were, for the most part, of an inferior educational or cultural background. As a result, she developed toward them a certain condescension. She was never haughty, nor did she flaunt her refinement but at the same time was aware, as they were too, of her own superiority. That her eldest son should have picked out a person like them instead of like her was galling to an almost unbearable degree.

In any event, what she felt was neither here nor there. Her son had chosen, her husband had accepted the choice, and there was precious little she could do except swallow her discomfiture and proceed with the formalities to the best of her ability. It was now her duty to acquire an appropriate *shabka* for her son's future bride. With a heavy heart she made the round of the jewelers in Minya. She was fully aware that the *shabka* reflects the groom's social standing, hence despite her own feelings, she was determined to buy the best. After much hesitation she selected a gold *kirdan* incrusted with tiny diamonds and a matching pair of earrings. When her husband came back from Cairo, she plied him with questions in an attempt to visualize the situation. Of course, the crucial question had to remain unanswered since neither he nor Isma'il had seen the bride.

With every passing day Neshedil Hanim's curiosity and anxiety increased, until finally, three weeks before the wedding, the family traveled to Cairo. The big house in 'Abbasiya, which Sadiq Effendi al-Maghrabi had acquired in the 1830s and used on rare occasions, was opened by the servants sent down in advance, and prepared to receive them. She was finally going to see her future daughter-in-law in the course of her first official visit to the Badr family. In anticipation of the visit, Neshedil Hanim had prepared a present to offer the bride, which consisted in a little silver mesh handbag in which she had placed a gold bracelet to match the *kirdan* and earrings of the *shabka*. At the appointed hour, accompanied by her three daughters, Zaynab, Fatma, and Aisha, her daughter-in-law Hoda, and 'Uthman's three daughters, she presented herself at the Badr residence. Having feared the worst, she was somewhat relieved.

The girl—as she had referred to the bride so far—was neither ugly nor pretty. She was not dark, if not fair. She was not tall, but not too short. Her hips were not narrow so she would bear many children and yet she was not plump. Her hair was soft but of indifferent color. Her hands were small and her voice gentle. She defied accurate description and yet her countenance exuded a certain dignified reserve that pleased her future mother-in-law. Chafaq Nour knew that she was under scrutiny, therefore she tried to remember all her mother's instructions. She kept her eyes downcast and when addressed answered in a barely audible voice. Neither Neshedil Hanim nor the ladies who met Chafaq Nour for the first time that day realized that they had missed the salient points of her personality: her intelligence and her wit.

Isma'il was on tenterhooks. He had spent the afternoon pacing his bedroom in a frenzy of anxiety because now that the die was cast, he reeled at his audacity. What if the girl were scarred, or worse still, deformed? How would he cope with an ugly duckling or a simpleton? His panic mounted at the thought of his mother's horrified reaction should the girl prove to be a freak or strongly objectionable for whatever reason. Much of the anxiety was brought on by Neshedil Hanim's often voiced reservations, and no matter how independent Isma'il might have felt, yet deep down his mother's opinion mattered a great deal. At long last, he heard the horse-drawn carriage that brought his mother back stop at the gate. With a beating heart, he ran to the garden, opened the carriage door and helped her down.

"Well, Anna, what did you think of her? What is she like? Did you dislike her? Did she receive you well?"

Neshedil Hanim stopped in her tracks and looking at her son severely said, "*Al-Sabr tayib, ya ibni*—Patience is a virtue, my son. Let me catch my breath and reach the house. I shall tell you everything in good time."

"Answer just one question please: is she horrible?"

With a repressed smile and taking pity on her son, she answered shortly, "No, she is not."

Later, after she had performed her evening prayer, she called Isma'il to her room.

"My son, I will tell you now what I have seen and what I feel concerning your future wife. These are certainly well to do, decent people. Sitt Halimah and her daughters received us very well. Their household is akin to ours in Minya, from which we may surmise that they are neither superior nor are they inferior to us. Now for the girl, I truly cannot tell."

"What do you mean, Anna? Surely you have seen her?"

"That is just the point, my son. She is neither pretty nor is she ugly. There are no obvious characteristics that would enable me to form a definite opinion about her."

Vastly relieved, Isma'il asked again, "She is not deformed then? She is not impossibly ugly?"

"Of course not, and neither does she have a third eye on her brow."

"Anna, I really feared the worst."

"Well, that was rather silly for had she been handicapped in any way Dr. Badr would never have allowed matters to reach this stage of the transaction. It would have been for him a horrible scandal had we withdrawn our request on the basis of his daughter's infirmity. No, rest assured, she is, as far as I can judge, perfectly normal. It will be up to you to discover what charm lies hidden behind her bland exterior. I still cannot understand why you chose her instead of one of your uncle 'Uthman's daughters or one of the Musa girls?

"My choice, Anna, was based on her father's reputation. I am essentially seeking an alliance with Dr. Badr whom I admire greatly. Now that you tell me his daughter is all right, I am prepared to meet my fate and live with it."

"*Al-Jawaz, ya ibni, 'isma wa nasib*—Marriage, my son, is a matter of fate and one's allotted share in life. May God protect you. Congratulations!"

Both mother and son were somewhat relieved and spent the next few days preparing the wedding. The date was set for July 12, to take

place in the Sadiq residence. In the Badr house, a joyous atmosphere
and bubbling activity reigned all day. The bride had to be bathed in
scented water, her hair perfumed, her heels, which were already soft
as silk, scrubbed, one more time with a pumice stone. A smoking
incense burner hanging from a chain was dangled over her clothes
and all her belongings to ward off the evil eye. The house reeked of
incense and the noise of running footsteps, sudden exclamations,
peals of laughter, was punctuated at intervals by the shrill notes of a
ululation. Occasionally the first couplet of the traditional wedding
song could be heard:

Itmakhtari ya hilwa, ya zina
Ya warda min juwwa jinina.
('Walk playfully, gracefully, pretty one, beautiful one,
O flower in the heart of a garden.')

Finally, at eight o'clock in the evening, 'Amm 'Abdu, the *bawwab*,
announced that the Sadiq carriage had arrived. The bride, her face
covered by a thick veil and wearing a beautifully embroidered
gown, was driven with her family to the Sadiq residence in a procession of horse-drawn carriages. This was a great moment for
Chafaq. She was formally leaving her past life and starting a new
chapter in a world of unknowables. Was she frightened? Most probably, and yet her fear was tempered by the knowledge that this was
the fate of all girls. If others had done it before her, there was no
reason why she should not do so as well. There was also on her part
a tremendous curiosity to be assuaged, for the only unknown element she cared about at that moment was her husband, the man to
whom she must devote her life and whose children she would bear.
Rocked by the movement of the carriage and exhausted by the
activities of the day, she slowly drifted into a trance-like somnolence
from which she was suddenly jerked out when it came to a stop.
Helped by her sisters and cousins, she slowly mounted the stairs and
walked into the foyer of the big house. Neshedil Hanim and all the
ladies of her family received them and directed the veiled ladies to
the main drawing room where the wedding party was to take place.
The men all gathered in a tent erected in the garden where a sumptuous buffet was served.

In the drawing room, Chafaq Nour watched the belly dancers in
a daze and listened absentmindedly to the songs, the music, and the

clatter of conversation. When dinner was served in the main dining room, she could hardly eat for anxiety. After dinner, Neshedil Hanim indicated it was time for the bride to retire to her room. Helped by her mother and her mother-in-law, she was taken up to the bedroom where she was to spend her wedding night. Left alone, her face covered once more, she sat on a divan and waited with trepidation for an outcome of some sort, which she could not, for the moment, anticipate.

Later that evening, after the male guests had left, Isma'il came into his wife's room. He walked up to her, lifted the veil and smiled. Slowly, she forced herself to look up and the face that met her gaze appeared to her as the most beautiful she had ever seen. Her joy was such that it reflected itself in her eyes, which suddenly came alive as if lit internally. She smiled back and from that moment fell irrevocably in love with her husband.

Two days after the wedding, Isma'il and Chafaq Nour left for Sohag where he had been appointed deputy irrigation inspector. During these two days in the Sadiq residence, as custom demanded, they hardly left their room, taking their meals together, slowly learning to get acquainted with one another. It was Neshedil's turn now to be devoured by curiosity about this daughter-in-law she hardly knew. She wondered whether Isma'il had found her to his liking or whether her worst predictions would be realized. She spent her day sitting alone in her room fretting and waiting for news. On the afternoon of the second day, an hour before they were to leave, Isma'il went to his mother's room. She looked at him anxiously but seeing the smile on his face felt immensely relieved.

"Come my son and sit with me for a while."

"I have come to say goodbye, Anna. Chafaq seeks permission to present her respects and take her leave."

"I too would like to see her. I hope she has been satisfied by our reception and that you will visit us in Minya. Sohag is not far and both your father and I would like to spend some time with you and get to know your wife a little better."

"Well, Anna, I don't think you will be disappointed though she differs in some ways. . . ."

Isma'il did not finish the sentence. Instead he quickly got up to fetch his wife. A few moments later they were back.

"Well, Chafaq," said Neshedil Hanim, "I hope you have found everything to your satisfaction."

"Yes, Tayza. . . ."

"Tayza?" interrupted Neshedil Hanim. "No, no, you must call me Anna, just like Isma'il."

"Yes, Anna," answered Chafaq Nour obediently.

"Take good care of my son, Chafaq. He is a good man; and always remember that on a woman's shoulders rests the responsibility of a successful marriage."

Chafaq Nour needed no reminder because this was a fact she had always known.

7

Traveling to Sohag was, for Chafaq Nour, a great adventure. She had rarely left her home in 'Abbasiya except for occasional trips to Alexandria where she and her sisters spent their day in the *mashrabiya* verandah overlooking the garden. But now she was traveling to Upper Egypt, this exotic place, as the wife of the deputy irrigation inspector. Her husband's position impressed her but not nearly as much as the man himself. He was so handsome, this husband fate had given her, so kind, and apparently so clever! This was a voyage of discovery: the young *centralien* (Centrale University graduate) and the girl from Munufiya were exploring the unknown territory of each other's personality. The first time they had a meal together, she was surprised by the dexterity with which he used the utensils that were set by the plates. She observed that smaller ones had been provided for dessert. It mattered little to her because she used none at all. As was her wont, she washed her hands meticulously before the meal and picked the food delicately with the right hand using the left one only to help separate smaller pieces. Isma'il was bemused. Did she not know how to use cutlery? Probably not. He chuckled inwardly imagining his mother's indignation when apprised of the fact. Should he offer to teach her? Would she be offended? Could he just ignore the issue and pretend he had not noticed? Ever a straightforward and practical person, he decided to face the issue immediately, come what may.

"Chafaq, why don't you use a knife and a fork?"

"Oh no, I cannot."

"Why? Don't you know how?"

"Neither do I know, nor do I wish to know."

"Why ever not?"

"Because I cannot bear the thought of putting into my mouth a fork that other people have used, no matter how often it has been washed."

"But eating with your fingers. . . ."

"What is wrong with that? My hands are clean and my fingers have never been used by anyone but myself."

Isma'il found this logic disarming and burst out laughing.

"You are right. However, I am used to eating with a knife and a fork, and shall continue to do so."

In fact, he found himself laughing quite often in her company. She amused him with her repartees and unexpected reactions. Despite the fact that she was so innocent, so unused to the ways of the world, he detected behind this unassuming façade a quick mind and a strong will. One thing about her he noticed immediately was her obsession with cleanliness. Over and above the ritual ablutions before prayer, she would bathe whenever she felt hot or had perspired. August is a hot month, so the wife of the deputy irrigation inspector seemed to consume an inordinate amount of water for her frequent baths. This, of course, drew comments on the part of the small Sohag community who were torn between the desire to imitate this fine lady from Cairo who had quickly become a role model, and their own entrenched habits. As she grew older her fastidiousness increased noticeably. No one was allowed to use her teacup, coffee cup, silver goblet, or water pitcher. This last item in particular drew a comment from her husband who chided her very gently the first time he saw her drinking from it.

"Use a glass, Chafaq. The *'ulla* is for everyone to use."

"Not this one. I had it brought from Qina and it is much smaller than the other ones. You see, I love the taste of water mixed with the scent of clay. It feels more natural, as if straight from a spring. I can't explain it any further."

"Have it your own way, Chafaq. Have it your own way." "She has done it again," thought Isma'il, convinced by this very simple argument. Though he never drank out of an *'ulla* himself, yet he respected her decision to do so and understood that Chafaq was determined to hold onto her identity. At the end of August, Chafaq Nour suffered a miscarriage brought on, according to the midwife who was rushed in to help, because she had probably drunk cinnamon tea. Chafaq loathed the stuff but was too prostrate to argue. By the end of the summer of 1889, however, Chafaq realized that she was pregnant again. Both she and Isma'il were elated and looked forward to the arrival of their first child. The good news was sent to Cairo and to Minya where it was received with joy. Despite occasional early morning sickness, Chafaq never felt better. She loved the life of Sohag and the close community of the small society there. She was never bored. There was always someone coming to visit, such as the wives of the *'umda*, the commissioner, the secretary, or any women of the community. She enjoyed running a household of her own and soon enough her strong personality became obvious. Maids—of these she had four—feared and respected her. She imposed her will not so much out of authoritarianism but through an innate sense of propriety, discipline, and justice. Gradually, Isma'il began to trust her judgment in matters concerning family affairs and, occasionally, he even discussed with her issues relating to his work. Her good common sense and acute perception of human nature amply compensated for her lack of formal education.

Chafaq derived much pleasure listening to her husband's discussions pertaining to events outside the home. He was, in a sense, her window to the world and, unaware of it, satisfied her natural curiosity, triggered by an intellect that demanded more than domestic life could offer. Isma'il, for his part, was delighted to have such an avid listener. She loved to hear him talk about the Nile, its flow, its power, its mysterious annual ferocity, when its dark, mud-laden waters would overflow its banks and inundate the fields that bordered them.

"Surely the peasants must dread the moment," she observed the first time they discussed the subject.

"Not at all. They await impatiently for the time in the fall when the river's rage is spent. You see, Chafaq, this is one of the great phenomena of nature, that this water when it withdraws in late autumn, leaves as a gift to the peasants, the most enriching mud in the world."

"So the good comes from the bad?"

"You might put it that way. Anyway, we always try to control this flow by building dams across the river. In that way we are still—up to a point—the masters."

"Amazing! Surely building a dam must be a very difficult undertaking?"

"Well, this is one reason we study engineering."

He smiled at her and her admiration for him increased. She was not the only one to be impressed by Isma'il. William Garstin, the British irrigation inspector, had also noticed him and thought very highly of this young engineer. Actually, the respect and admiration were mutual. It was just a matter of time before Isma'il would be transferred to Cairo to occupy an important post in the Ministry of Public Works. Chafaq was not aware at first that her husband was a rising political star. All she knew and cared about was that he was clever, educated, and had a good and interesting job in Sohag.

With every passing week, her pregnancy became more obvious. It was decided that she would not travel to Cairo or to Minya for the birth but would remain in her husband's home in Sohag. Actually, this had been her unilateral decision, which she persuaded Isma'il to present as his own in order to deflate potential objections from either set of parents. Umm Hanifah, the best midwife in Sohag, was hired which of course substantially increased her importance in the eyes of the community: she was going to deliver the deputy irrigation inspector's baby.

Khadiga was born on May 25, 1890. Disappointment at the sex of the child was short-lived because she was beautiful. Besides, two weeks after her birth, Isma'il came home one afternoon and announced that he had been promoted and transferred to Cairo. Chafaq received the news with mixed feelings. She was, of course, very happy about the promotion and yet she loved her life here in Sohag, among the simple people of this provincial town. With her unerring instinct, she perceived that in Cairo she would have to share her husband with a much more demanding job. On the other hand, she looked forward to life in the big city, close to her mother and sisters.

"Where shall we live in Cairo?" was the first question she asked.

"At first in my father's house in 'Abbasiya until our own home is ready."

"Do we have a house in Cairo?"

"Not yet, but I plan to build a large residence in Munira."

"Where is that?"

"Well, not too far from 'Abbasiya. It is the new, up-and-coming neighborhood where I have acquired, through a friend in Cairo, a large plot of land."

"That must have cost a fortune?"

"Well, actually it was my parent's wedding present."

The house was in fact almost built. Isma'il had seen and approved the plans before leaving for Sohag and entrusted the supervision of construction to his best friend, Isma'il Sirri. Sirri lived in Munira (hence Sadiq's choice of the neighborhood) and had at his disposal a number of young engineers and contractors who, for a reasonable fee and a promise of everlasting friendship, worked at high speed and to the best of their ability.

Like many houses built in Egypt in the course of the nineteenth century, Isma'il Sadiq's boasted a *salamlik*, or men's quarter, and a *haramlik*, or women's quarter. This architectural concept was apparently the outcome of the social development that took place in Egypt during the seventeenth and eighteenth centuries.[38] During the Mamluk period, much of the activity that normally had taken place outside was gradually incorporated within the precincts of the house particularly where important personages were concerned. For instance, the *shaykh al-balad* (village chief) would have appended to his house a prison and a place of execution. Women had to be segregated in special quarters in order to protect them from violence and unseemly sights. By the nineteenth century, the concept became a status symbol, a way of life mirroring that of the ruler. In the last decade of the century, the practice was still quite common and Isma'il Sadiq adopted it not only to conform to the current fashion but as the practical solution for his growing social life. He might be considered as the prototype of the foreign-educated Egyptian of the turn of the century, poised mid-way between adherence to tradition and belief in modernism. He knew that some traditions had to be upheld at all costs while others should be abandoned if society were to develop in the right direction.

Bayt al-Munira, as the house was called, reflected this dichotomy hence the necessity of a *salamlik* where he could receive his male visitors, of which he expected a growing number, without inconveniencing his wife who considered segregation the proper way to live. Chafaq Nour remained throughout her life a staunch conservative who never stepped out of her nineteenth century mold. She never went outdoors with her face uncovered but always wore a *habara* and a *petsha* that covered her nose, mouth, and chin. Her sense of propriety was such that she would have been horrified had anyone suggested she show her face to the carriage driver, the gatekeeper, or passersby in the street. It was not at all on her part a question of religious belief or an interpretation of Islamic precepts concerning women's dress. It was in essence a social attitude shared by most women of quality of her time: she owed it to herself to preserve the mystery of her identity. There must have been at the core of this collective thinking a little dash of snobbery as well, for the upper-middle class had its own role model to emulate, the Khedivial court whose women were totally segregated and veiled. A segregated household presupposed the presence of eunuchs or at least servants, whereas poorer classes had to manage by themselves and could ill afford such luxury. In any event Chafaq Hanim held unto her *petsha* with determination.

Once the house was completed, the division of power was firmly established: the *salamlik* was Isma'il's domain, while she reigned supreme in the *haramlik*. The *salamlik* consisted of a large dining room that could seat twenty-four guests and a large drawing room, where gilt sofas upholstered in burgundy velvet alternated with armchairs and straight backed chairs for lesser guests. It also had two bedrooms, a bathroom, and a pantry, where coffee and tea were prepared. The *haramlik*, which was linked to the *salamlik* by a vaulted corridor with a ceiling of stained glass, comprised the bulk of the house. This women's quarter consisted of three floors. On the ground floor were the family dining room, the main drawing room, a study where Isma'il Sadiq received informally male members of the family, and a pantry. On the first floor were the bedrooms, sitting rooms—one for summer facing north and one for winter facing south—two bathrooms and the maids' room. In the basement was installed a cavernous kitchen. The top floor remained undefined until more bedrooms were needed for a growing family.

The family was indeed growing at a regular pace; after Khadiga came Muhammad in October 1891, followed in quick succession by Hussein, Hazim, Fatma, 'Ali, Muhsin, and Anisah, interspersed with several miscarriages.

Chafaq, repeating the pattern of her father's home, took over the responsibility of the household because her husband's career made great demands on his time. What is of particular interest in the Sadiq household is that to Isma'il's occasional avant-garde views, Chafaq Hanim opposed a firm conservative front. There was no tug of war, no fundamental difference, simply because Isma'il's ideas were addressed to his public life, to whatever was happening outside his home, to the overall grand scheme that was meant to shape the future of the country, but rarely to his home front. In fact, he remained to the end of his life a conservative Upper Egyptian gentleman of the old school. It may well be that the possibility of allowing modernism to penetrate his home never crossed his mind except on the issue of his daughters' education. At any rate even if it did, Chafaq Nour was standing guard determined to perpetuate the traditions she knew and understood.

Chafaq Hanim liked her role and fulfilled it well, while Isma'il felt secure in the knowledge that she had the necessary skill and personality to deal effectively with any situation. As the children grew up they knew that Nayna, as they called their mother, ruled over their life, while perceiving that Baba, their father, was the ultimate authority particularly when it concerned the boys.

At the age of nine, Khadiga was a very pretty child who looked like her father and shared his light complexion and regular features. Isma'il doted on her but her mother had perceived that she was not as bright as her brothers, or even perhaps as Fatma, who was just a baby at the time but showed every sign of having an alert mind. She would follow her mother with her eyes, smile with glee when picked up, grasp fingers or toys that were handed to her, and seemed to be watching whatever went on around her with keen interest. Chafaq Hanim felt drawn to this baby in a way she had never felt before, and though it was clear that she would never be as pretty as her sister, this never made a difference.

Whether Khadiga had brains or not was totally immaterial as far as Isma'il Sadiq was concerned. His daughter might not be as clever as her mother would have wished her to be, nonetheless it remained imperative that she receive an education and learn a foreign language. Khadiga was a sweet child, quiet and submissive. She certainly was not stupid but lacked the sparkle of a quick wit. Chafaq, who had always taken her own intelligence for granted, could not understand, or perhaps accept, a lesser mind. How was it possible that she and Isma'il had produced a child who was not the brightest? The boys were all right, in fact, Hussein seemed to be a chip off the old block. This, in a way, irked Chafaq Hanim who, with her strong sense of hierarchy, would have preferred that Muhammad, the eldest, be the one who was best and looked most like his father. Fate had decreed otherwise and it turned out eventually that Hussein and Fatma were the brightest of the lot. As years went by, Chafaq Hanim's preference for Fatma became very obvious and oddly enough, was accepted without acrimony by the others. Actually, Fatma was everybody's favorite because of her warm and generous nature, her wit, and engaging personality. When Anisah, the youngest child came along, almost as an afterthought, she lived her life in Fatma's shadow, enthralled by her sister's charismatic figure.

The problem of Khadiga's education weighed heavily on her father's mind. He could not conceive having an illiterate daughter, yet he did not know how to discuss the issue with his wife without hurting her feelings. He need not have worried because Chafaq Hanim, with her usual perspicacity, had understood that her own illiteracy, which she had accepted without question, was a thing of the past not to be suffered by her daughter. A few days after Khadiga's birthday, she broached the subject with her husband.

"Should we not bring in a shaykh to teach Khadiga?"

"Teach her what, Chafaq?"

"Well, I thought perhaps a little bit of reading, writing, the Qur'an."

Greatly relieved at his wife's attitude, Isma'il promptly answered, "No, a shaykh will not be able to give her all she needs. We shall bring one in to teach her the basic principles of Islam and a proper reading of the Qur'an. However, she needs more than a shaykh."

"What do you mean?"

"She should go to school."

Totally taken aback by her husband's unexpected declaration, Chafaq Hanim gaped unable for a few moments to react. In her mind's eye, a rapid succession of images unfurled: Khadiga at school among foreigners, Khadiga in the street on a daily basis, Khadiga not at home where she belonged. She recovered very quickly however, and asked, "What is this school you wish to send her to?"

"The Bon Pasteur Convent for girls. It is a good place. There she will learn French which, I believe, is essential for girls nowadays."

Chafaq Hanim was slightly peeved.

"I can't speak French, neither can my mother or my sisters."

"This is not an argument, Chafaq. Times change and we need to adjust to the change."

"Do you mean to give Khadiga the same education as her brothers?"

"No, I would not go that far. She will not go to university, just to school for a few years. The nuns will teach her a foreign language, how to read and write. But more important she will learn the ways of the world. . . ."

"Of the world?" interrupted Chafaq Hanim. "What world is that?"

"Not ours obviously, since she will get the best of it from you," answered Isma'il immediately to mollify her. "I mean the world of the foreigners. You never know what life has in store or what the future may hold for her. In any event, I strongly believe it is essential that she be prepared."

Chafaq Hanim sighed deeply because she knew she had lost the argument and had the wisdom to accept it graciously.

The Bon Pasteur Convent was, at the time, what might be considered a finishing, or rather a 'polishing' school. Pupils were not submitted to strenuous intellectual exercises or high standard academic requirements; they were taught to read, write, count, and to pronounce French properly. The curriculum had a broad spectrum. The girls were given a little geography, history, elementary science, and general knowledge on a variety of subjects. They were taught the art of embroidery, some of them took up drawing, and all of them shared a mid-day meal in the course of which they were taught the etiquette of table manners.

Khadiga loved school, where every moment was filled with an interesting activity. So much better than staying at home where her only options were to follow Nayna as she went about her daily chores or sit on nanny Fikriya's lap to listen to her limited, therefore repetitive, stories of Shatir Hasan, the epic folk hero. She would come home every afternoon bustling with energy and contained excitement. Chafaq Hanim was pleased. The school was doing wonders for her placid daughter. One day, a problem arose which Isma'il Sadiq had anticipated for some time. Meals at Munira were always taken in the *haramlik* presided over by Isma'il and organized by Chafaq Hanim. Each child upon reaching the age of seven was included around the table, the younger ones taking their meals in the children's playroom. In that respect, Isma'il Sadiq was behaving like a modern man. Eschewing meals taken separately, either in the *salamlik* or with his sons in the *haramlik,* he chose to eat *en famille* with his wife and his children regardless of their sex. As on their first day together, Isma'il Sadiq and Chafaq Hanim followed their own rules of table manners and Isma'il had, so far, been loath to impose on the children an etiquette their mother chose to ignore. While he used cutlery, his wife still ate with her fingers and this difference was bound to provoke questions. So far this had not happened either because the children were too young to notice, or perhaps because they assumed that Baba and Nayna were different. Isma'il worried about the issue, and in a rare show of indecision for such a determined man, simply ignored it in hope that somehow the problem would resolve itself.

This is precisely what happened a few weeks after Khadiga attended school. Sitting down to lunch with the family on a Sunday, she suddenly asked in her clear and childish voice, "Nayna, why do you eat with your fingers? The nun told us never to put our hand in the plate or touch food except with a fork or a spoon."

"Because this is the way I enjoy my food," answered Chafaq Hanim somewhat put out.

"But it is not right, Nayna," persisted the child. "Sister Marie-Helene told us that it was a very bad habit and that we should never do it."

Chafaq Hanim's face flushed a deep crimson and Isma'il Sadiq, anticipating a thunderous outburst spoke up immediately.

"It depends how it is done, Khadiga. Look at the way your mother is eating, how delicately she handles her food, and how clean her hands are. You must never generalize, child, and probably if Sister Marie-Helene had no fork or knife she would never be able to eat in your mother's refined way."

Khadiga shook her head stubbornly.

"No, Sister Marie-Helene said we must always eat with a fork, a knife, and a spoon as well, just like you do, Baba."

"Very well then," said her father, "as of now you shall all learn to use cutlery but, beware, whoever drops food on the table cloth will leave the table immediately."

Chafaq Hanim sat in stony silence while Muhammad and Hussein looked on with interest at the unfolding drama. With the percep-tiveness of children, they had sensed that all was not right around the table. Nayna seemed angry, though not Baba, and Khadiga was say-ing very strange things. Chafaq Hanim was fuming and after lunch expressed her anger in no uncertain terms.

"Is that what we have sent our daughter to learn at school? To be disrespectful to her mother?"

Her anger was exacerbated because it was not focused. It was dif-fused between her daughter who had dared criticize her table man-ners, the nun who was teaching the child to be disrespectful to her parents, and her husband for humoring Khadiga instead of scolding her for impudence.

"The child meant no harm, Chafaq. Surely you must understand that the ways of Europeans sometimes differ from ours."

"Even so, she is my daughter, an Egyptian girl who should follow me and not this *khawagaya*. What was right for me, for my mother, for her mother before her should be good enough for that silly girl."

"Look, Chafaq, I am all for upholding traditions but sometimes we must discard some along the way. It is up to us to select what is important. This issue is not an important one as it only concerns appearances not the core. . . ."

"Precisely," interrupted Chafaq Hanim. "The nuns are teaching her to look down on our ways. Remember, Baba, the proverb, *al-'ayn la ti'la 'an al-hajib*—The eye cannot raise itself over the eyebrow."

"Absolutely," agreed Isma'il, "but remember also the saying, *kull shaykh wa lahu tariqa*—Every shaykh has his way. Sending her to school will give her the chance to learn more ways of doing things; thereafter the choice will be hers."

Chafaq Hanim was mollified if not convinced. At any rate she let the matter drop and life resumed its course in the Sadiq household. The boys were sent to government schools to receive a formal aca-demic education and English-language instruction, while concern over etiquette at home was minimal; consequently, they developed according to their own inclinations. Muhammad and Hussein, par-ticularly the latter who always tried to emulate his father, behaved at the table with decorum, but Hazim, the third boy, was forever trying to attract attention. What better audience would he have than the family gathering at meal times? He was a gregarious little fellow with a gargantuan appetite; he gobbled up his food, asked for more, and never seemed to have enough. "The boy is a glutton," observed his father, "and if he does not learn to curb his appetite he will soon be as big as an elephant." Chafaq Hanim indulged her son because he made her laugh and was not as pompous as Hussein. Hazim's table manners were appalling and he doggedly refused to use cutlery like his siblings; his voice was loud—a trait he retained to the end of his life—and he poked fun at everyone, himself included. On more than one occasion, his father in a fit of anger sent him out of the dining room.

In 1905, Fatma reached the age of seven, which meant that she would take her meals in the dining room. On the first day that she joined the family for lunch, shrill screams were heard outside the door, shuffling of feet, and bizarre noises. Isma'il Sadiq quickly got up to find out the cause of the disturbance while the others sat in stunned silence waiting for the outcome.

"What is this riot?" thundered Isma'il Sadiq.

He was addressing his six-year-old son, 'Ali, who was howling at the top of his voice.

"*Sidi*, he wants to go in with Sitt Fatma," said the maid.

"Quiet 'Ali or I shall have to thrash you."

The menace took effect immediately. Meanwhile, Fatma quietly slipped off her chair, ran out into the hall and taking her brother by the hand told her mother: "Nayna, we always eat together, 'Ali and I. Let him have lunch with us."

Her request was granted and 'Ali, still sniffling, found himself seated next to his sister at table.

The year 1905 was an important date in Fatma's life for another reason as well. Her father decided she was old enough to go school and need not wait until she was nine years old, like her sister, to be allowed out of the house on a daily basis. There was another major change in her case, for instead of sending her to the Bon Pasteur Convent with Khadiga, he opted for a new school that had opened in Bulaq, the Pensionnat de la Mère de Dieu. According to some of his friends at the Ministry of Public Works, this school's academic standards were higher and the nuns were all recruited from the best families in France. Chafaq Hanim was easily convinced because, by that time, not sending her daughters to school was an option she no longer envisioned. Therefore if the Mère de Dieu was a better school, that was where Fatma would go, for nothing short of the best would do for her favorite daughter. She bristled at first at the name of the school.

"Mother of God! This is a sacrilege. How can anyone utter such nonsense? Don't these nuns know that God was not begotten and did not beget?"

"They do not mean it in quite that way," answered her husband. "You see, I doubt very much that any of them has ever read the *Sammadiya*.[39] They do not realize that this name is a little bit ridiculous. I think it is their round about way of expressing themselves, so instead of naming it School of the Virgin Mary they tried to be a little bit more sophisticated and as a result they sound pedantic. Anyway, none of the ladies at the school chose the name so you can rest assured that your daughter will be safe there and will receive a good education."

Fatma loved her school from the very first day. She felt quite at home there and perfectly at ease with these ladies who spoke so very softly in a language she could not understand. To make things easier, an Arabic-speaking nun of Syro-Lebanese origin attended every class and translated what was said in French. Soon enough, the little girls picked up a limited vocabulary, words such as *crayon, craie, merci, cahier, tableau noir*. They were taught to address the nun in charge of the class as *Ma* Mère and curtsy before speaking to her. In a matter of weeks, the little pupils had picked up enough vocabulary for the Arabic-speaking sister to be dispensed with. Actually, this nun belonged to a lesser category and was mainly employed in the kitchen, or the *réfectoire*, where she served the girls their mid-day meal. The student body was very small as few Egyptian parents, in those days, would have opted for a formal education for their daughters and when they did usually preferred an Arabic school such as Madrasat al-Saniya.

Curriculum at the Mère de Dieu was basically the one used in French schools but adapted, or adjusted, to the requirements of Egyptian students. In other words, French was a subject taught at all levels, while others were added as the children grew older. Mère Saint Ignace, a venerable lady said to belong to a noble French family, taught history and geography. Until they were old enough to attend her classes, the pupils' day would be spent in half hours of calligraphy, drawing, arithmetic, and spelling, given in little doses with numerous breaks. Fatma learned very quickly and at the end of the first year spoke French well enough to gain a prize and a good report. Later on, when she was allowed into Mère Saint Ignace's classes, she enjoyed them tremendously and for many years kept among her treasured possessions a photograph of that nun facing her class, holding a long stick, which she pointed at a large *mappemonde.*

The nuns did as much as they could for their students in the short time they had them. Most girls did not stay at the school beyond the age of sixteen, and almost none were interested in obtaining an academic degree. For them, school was a place where they could enjoy a social life of some sort while pleasantly learning a foreign language. Fatma made the most of it and later on in life remembered her school days as being perhaps, if not the happiest, at least the most enjoyable and carefree she ever knew.

8

While Fatma was thus being 'polished' at the Pensionnat de la Mère de Dieu, many events had already taken place, or were taking place, on the international scene and in the Sadiq family. In 1898, the Fashoda incident had led to the creation of the Anglo-Egyptian Sudan. Considering Dr. Badr's interest in that country, which had developed in the course of the Abyssinian campaign of 1876, it is not surprising that the events taking place in that remote outpost of the Sudan should have captivated his interest. Fashoda was no more than an abandoned fort on the banks of the White Nile south of Khartoum. It became the focal point of the Anglo-French struggle for supremacy in Africa. These were the years of colonial expansionism. Laying claim to Fashoda, where the French had already planted their flag, became vitally important for Great Britain whose colonial policy was based on the principle "that the valley of the Nile should continue to be entirely and exclusively in the British sphere of influence."[40] A confrontation ensued between the two colonialist powers. Ultimately after much escalation and decrease in tension between Lord Kitchener, Great Britain's representative, and his counterpart Marchand, the British won the day. On December 13, 1898, the French abandoned the fort and the Egyptian flag replaced the French one.

Dr. Badr was elated. However he did not survive these momentous events. In 1902 he died of a heart attack in his house in 'Abbasiya. Sitt Halimah was distraught as might be expected. Her much admired *Si al-Duktur* would no longer be there to guide her through life's vicissitudes. All she hoped for now was to join him in everlasting companionship. Chafaq Hanim mourned her father and during the *mahzana* plunged headlong into morbid speculations on the hereafter and in an irrational death wish. She was pulled back to life with a jerk when informed that Fatma was very ill in Munira. The child had contracted scarlet fever. All thoughts of her own death were set aside and worry over her daughter's mortality took over. She rushed back to Munira where she found the child delirious and a doctor in the room with her husband.

Decorum required that she not enter the sick room as long as a foreign man was in it, but the moment he stepped out she took over and never left her daughter's bedside until the fever broke and she was declared out of danger. Poor Fatma, who had burned with fever, hardly able to swallow, semi-delirious most of the time, was now starving. The good doctor's treatment for her ailment was a diet of milk and nothing else. Her hunger pangs were such that she dreamed of food all day long and waited impatiently for the hourly drink she was given. Chafaq Hanim thought of a nice way to break the monotony of the diet, the beverage was served in a variety of containers: a porcelain cup, a silver goblet, a terra cotta bowl, a stemmed glass, a tiny *'ulla*, or whatever else could hold the milk. After about two weeks, Fatma was declared cured but was totally depleted, almost unable able to walk.

The year 1902 was decidedly not a good one for Chafaq Hanim because little Fatma had barely recovered when Isma'il Sadiq announced he had to leave for Aswan where a dam across the Nile was to be constructed. This was for him an extremely exciting prospect but not good news for Chafaq Hanim who hated her husband's absences. Not that she felt unable to cope with a large household, but she missed the companionship and their daily conversations, which had become her mind's sustenance. She had resented his trip to Italy in 1899, where he had been sent to study the system of irrigation in that country. At the time, his friend Isma'il Sirri had been the head of the delegation. On their return, Sirri published a document[41] which impressed the nationalist leader Mustafa Kamel so much that he later recommended him for a ministerial position. Sadiq was very proud of his friend's achievement and a little while later published a report of his own, which was also very well received. Proud as she was of her husband's success, Chafaq Hanim nevertheless much preferred that he remain in Cairo. The boys were, on occasion, getting out of hand, particularly the ever-boisterous Hazim and little 'Ali who promised to be as difficult as his brother.

If 1903 passed uneventfully, except perhaps for the birth of Muhsin, their fifth and last son, 1904 was marked by an event that had immense repercussions in the Middle East and Egypt in particular. In that year, an Entente Cordiale was signed between France and Great Britain which parceled out the Middle East into spheres of influence. Great Britain's prerogative over Egypt was reaffirmed and in return France received Morocco, thereby curbing Germany's presence in North Africa. At the same time, Italy was ensconced in Ethiopia and eyed Libya as well. The seeds of World War I were being sown and in its aftermath the whole of North Africa fell into France's sphere of influence, while England was content with Egypt, the jewel of Africa, which secured her passage to India through the Suez Canal.

On the personal level, 1904 was a very sad year for Isma'il Sadiq as he lost both parents within a few months. Sadiq Effendi al-Maghrabi died of a stroke while riding his horse on a hot July day and Neshedil Hanim followed soon after, the victim of a heart attack.

On May 25, 1905, Khadiga celebrated her fifteenth birthday. Her mother decreed that she would not be sent back to school in the fall but would stay home and learn the art of good housekeeping. It is not clear whether Khadiga minded or not, as she never expressed an opinion, being fully aware that Nayna's decrees were usually not to be discussed. Besides, she may have been convinced of the judiciousness of her mother's decision. As with the previous generation of Egyptian women, a girl's ultimate goal was still to get married, the younger the better. Khadiga knew that the time was drawing near when the selection would be made and her fate sealed. Two young men had already presented themselves but were rejected immediately. The first one was socially acceptable but had the reputation of being a libertine; the other was illiterate and had relied on 200 *feddans* and a hefty bank account to give weight to his request.

A few weeks after Khadiga's fifteenth birthday, what seemed to be the right person came along. He was a rich landowner with a law degree and an impeccable background, and he was quite handsome as well. That he was fifteen years her senior did not weigh negatively on the scale. In fact, it was considered an advantage as an older man would surely be more responsible, better able to take care of a young and inexperienced wife. Khadiga was not consulted. She was just informed that she had a suitor and that her father was giving the matter serious thought. She knew, nevertheless, that the big day was drawing near. She was elated, excited, and looked forward to the moment when she would enter 'real life.' Isma'il Sadiq was not absolutely confident that this man was the best choice for his daughter. There had been something about the young man, an indefinable negative aura that Isma'il perceived as so many pinpricks of warning. And yet he could not focus on a definite reason for turning him down. Chafaq Hanim sensed her husband's unrest and in her usual forthright manner put the question to him.

"What is bothering you? What is the problem with this young man?"

"I frankly don't know. Nothing seems wrong. In fact, he is eminently acceptable. It is just a feeling."

"Well, feelings can be deceptive, particularly when one is about to give away one's daughter. I hope nothing is wrong with this young man, but of course, we shall never know before the wedding. Anyway, can we guarantee that the next one will be better?"

"No, certainly not. Well, we must also consider that Khadiga will soon be sixteen years old and it is time she settles down. However, I need to give the matter more thought."

Isma'il Sadiq's dilemma was compounded by the fact that a few weeks previously, he had been granted the title of pasha in recognition of the tremendous work he had performed at Aswan. As a pasha, he had to uphold his rank and ensure that his children's matrimonial alliances, or *nasab*, present impeccable credentials. Murad Khidr had them; there was no question about it. But, as the bride's father, he wanted more than that. He wanted assurance that the man was all right, that he would behave in the proper way toward his daughter for he did not wish to be confronted with an unhappy marriage, or worse still, with a divorce whether quick or protracted. This latter eventuality would result in much loss of face for him as well as for his daughter. And yet, he could not hold back an answer much longer for fear of offending the suitor, which would hardly be a good beginning for any relationship let alone a matrimonial one. As usual, he sought his wife's opinion.

"Well, Chafaq Hanim, what shall we do?" he finally asked his wife and best advisor.

"Frankly, Basha," she said, for this is how she addressed her husband from the day he received the title to the end of his life, "I am just as perplexed as you are. I have not seen Murad Khidr and my opinion is based on what you have told me about him. His credentials are perfect and unless you truly feel something is wrong with the man I do not see how you can refuse. If you do, this might earn our daughter the reputation of being difficult to obtain, and frighten away other suitors."

"You are right, Chafaq Hanim," he replied, returning the compliment by appending to his wife's name this official form of address. "I shall give him a positive answer tomorrow, *insha'Allah.*"

Khadiga's wedding was not a grand affair. Soon after the engagement, 'Uthman al-Maghrabi died which, of course, dictated a period of mourning of one year. The groom, however, was reluctant to wait out the period but suggested that the marriage ceremony be restricted to the immediate family with no *zaffa*, no ululation, and no music. Chafaq Hanim considered this a preposterous idea because Khadiga was the eldest daughter of the family, the first one to marry. She should be sent off with all the pomp and fanfare that befit a pasha's daughter! Isma'il Sadiq, however, being of a more practical nature, acceded to the groom's demand despite his wife's claim that this was not a good omen. Khadiga, as usual, did not express an opinion, and if she was disappointed, hid it well. Later on, when Murad Khidr proved to be a domineering husband, understandably so since he was older than his bride and more educated, Chafaq Hanim developed the typical mother-in-law syndrome.

"You should have realized, Basha, that this young man was strong-willed and determined to run his house with an iron will. Anyway, that is Khadiga's fate and she will have to accept it."

"Her fate is not all that bad," answered Isma'il Sadiq with a smile, "Murad Bey is a husband many women would envy because he is a man of quality, intelligent, educated, and quite handsome. Your daughter wants for nothing in her home and, despite his intransigent attitude, he treats her very well. Many men in our country behave in exactly the same way. Anyway, she seems quite happy and does not complain about him."

"You know quite well that Khadiga rarely complains or demands. Let us hope that her first born is a boy for it might improve the situation."

As it happened, the first child was a girl born in the early hours of a bleak December day in 1906. The baby's father indicated his discontent by not casting a single glance at his newborn daughter. His disappointment was profound. As far as he was concerned, until his wife had given him a son he would not have considered that he had procreated because girls never carry on the family name, but are men's possession to be made use of and no more. He justified his attitude by declaring that his severity toward his wife, her virtual incarceration at home, his reluctance to allow her to visit her parents' house in Munira, were all indicative of his profound love for her. "Jealousy is a form of love," he would often declare. "It is because I love my wife and mean to protect her that I do not let her out of the house." Khadiga did not seem to mind and had, for some obscure reason, fallen in love with Murad Khidr, or perhaps convinced herself that she had. Fatma, as she grew older, often wondered at her sister's fate. How could Abla Khadiga be happy? She disapproved of her brother-in-law's attitude toward her parents, particularly her mother whom she adored. Was it not a mark of profound severity on Murad Bey's part to often refuse his in-law's invitations to lunch? Poor Khadiga, how on earth was she able to adjust to her new situation? The main question she often asked herself was, "How can I avoid a similar fate?"

Chafaq Hanim was also worried and occasionally discussed the problem with her sisters Tawhidah and 'Ayn al-Hayah. However, details were never given out in the course of these discussions, as it would have been considered bad form. If their sister chose not to elaborate on her daughter's private affairs they, in turn, would respect her discretion and speak only in generalities. Between themselves they gossiped to their hearts' content, filling in gaps as they went along, but always careful to keep their conversations secret as they had no wish to hurt their sister's feelings. Khadiga for her part kept quiet and never divulged details about her marital difficulties. She knew that it was important for her standing within the family that Murad be made to appear as an admirable, lovable, and desirable husband, which in a certain sense he was. Murad in his own way enjoyed his wife. Her refinement, her beauty, and family connections gratified his ego, and being essentially a man of his time, he decided to make the most of his marriage, in other words, bend his wife to his will and ultimately secure for himself the ideal companion.

The year 1906, in which Isma'il Sadiq and Chafaq Hanim became grandparents for the first time, witnessed the unfortunate events of Dinshway. On June 13, a group of British officers in uniform went shooting pigeons near the village of Dinshway. Unfortunately, they shot a woman. Peasants in a frenzy of anger turned on them to seek revenge. The officers took to their heels; one of them dropped dead, either from shock or from sunstroke. These tragic events led to the creation of a special tribunal to judge the Egyptian peasants who had taken part in the incident and were being accused of having killed the British officer. The tragedy and its sequels upset Isma'il Sadiq profoundly. His particular brand of 'anglophilia' was not put in question since it bore no relation to political events, and yet his sense of justice and his pride were deeply hurt. Because of his position in the government, he was fully informed of the details of that unfortunate incident, which as is often the case, triggered off a chain reaction of blunders and mistakes. "This business is a mess," he told Chafaq Hanim. "My heart goes out to the poor *fellahin* who have been flogged and to the families of the ones that were executed. I deplore this whole affair."

"The British are ruffians," answered Chafaq Hanim who was irate. "I cannot accept what they have done to these poor *fellahin*; as for Boutros Ghali and Ahmad Zaghloul, I wish they could hang as well. Can you imagine Egyptians participating in a special tribunal that was set up as a farce to condemn Egyptians?"

"Come now, Chafaq Hanim, don't be so harsh in your judgments. Would you have preferred that such a tribunal in our country have no Egyptian representative? I think not."

Anyway, this was a moot point and the events of Dinshway became a pivot around which popular nationalist sentiment gathered. Despite his attempts to justify the existence and comportment of the special tribunal, Isma'il Sadiq was deeply shaken. His attitude toward the British had always been positive; he admired them, learned from them, accepted them as enlightened teachers. Suddenly he felt betrayed and it became difficult to separate their dual role as occupiers of his country and as mentors. Yet, he realized that was precisely what he had to do because, while he rejected absolutely the behavior of the former, he still retained for the latter the same respect and the belief that their continued presence, at least for the time being, was in the best interest of the country. Isma'il Sirri, his friend and colleague, shared his views and they spent many hours examining the problem as dispassionately as was humanly possible.

The dilemma that so profoundly disturbed both men, as well as others technocrats of their generation, was the unavoidable consequence of the historic development of the Egyptian civil servant class through the nineteenth and early decades of the twentieth centuries. Under Muhammad 'Ali Pasha, office holders were essentially Turks. Because the *raison d'etre* of Egyptian bureaucracy was service to the viceroy and his family, these civil servants had to enjoy the absolute trust of the ruler. Consequently, they were drawn from members of the latter's family including in-laws, all of them Turks. Under 'Abbas I, the situation changed ostensibly. A new class of civil servants appeared on the scene, albeit on the lower rungs of the ladder, as the result of Muhammad 'Ali Pasha's educational reforms. The concept of *ahl al-thiqa* (those one can trust) was gradually supplanted by the concept of *ahl al-khibra* (those who have knowledge and expertise).[42] The latter class, mostly drawn from the Egyptian population, did not view with much sympathy their less educated but more powerful Turkish superiors. It became of paramount importance for them to establish and consolidate their position. Their numbers grew steadily and by "the middle of the nineteenth century, perhaps for the first time since the Pharos, native Egyptians in significant numbers could be found in high posts in the provinces and in Cairo . . . the new cadre of Egyptian officials were not *'fallahin'* by the standards of native society. Quite the contrary, the new Egyptian officials represented some of Egypt's most prominent elite."[43] In 1858, Arabic replaced Turkish as the official language of the country, and by 1868 many Egyptians became holders of responsible jobs. A case in point is 'Ali Mubarak, who at that time became minister of education. These men took pride in their achievement for it was based on their intrinsic worth. The following often-quoted saying of the time confirms this attitude:

Laysa al-fata man yaqul hadha abi
Bal al-fata man yaqul ha ana dha.
Which roughly translates into:
'A hero is not he who proclaims, 'this is my father'
But he who proclaims, 'this is who I am."
This was the forceful affirmation of the self over lineage.

The British invasion of the country in 1882 added a new element to this complicated equation of relationships. These newcomers to the Egyptian scene became the 'protectors-rulers' of the country. Advancement could hardly be obtained without their recommendation and support. This was particularly true in the Ministry of Public Works. Willcocks, Garstin, Brown, to name but a few, entertained an excellent rapport with the young foreign-educated Egyptian engineers. To be sure, there was an element of interest involved in this relationship, for if the British realized the worth of these Egyptians in the realization of their plans, the latter for their part knew perfectly well what they owed the British. This being the case, it seemed unwise to stand up against the occupier when there was still so much that needed to be accomplished. These were pragmatic apolitical technocrats. In Egypt in the early decades of the twentieth century, the currents that governed the sociopolitical scene ranged "from one extreme, a pro-western approach, to the other, an anti-western, purely Islamic one, with gradations of mixture in-between . . . pro-western supporters, who by the thirties were indigenous Egyptians, opted in favor of westernization with an areligious bend."[44] One of the most vocal politicians of the period, Lutfi al-Sayed, "advocated moderation in nationalist demands, and would have cooperated behind the scenes with the British authorities in return for a promise of eventual evacuation."[45] The rationale behind this policy was that Egyptians should bide their time until the country was ready for its independence. Besides, there was always the underlying belief that the British would eventually depart.

This attitude was shared by some English politicians as well. Lord Milner for one, as early as the 1890s, wrote: "I am not one of those who hold that everything that has been done in Egypt since 1882 is due to Englishmen. I am the first to recognize the very important part that has been played in the revival of the country by natives and other Europeans. I do not believe that the indefinite continuance of British control in its present form is essential to the ultimate welfare of Egypt."[46] This statement cannot be construed as an open demand for immediate evacuation of the country by the British, but can be seen as a hint in that direction. In any event, the Dinshway affair was an extremely upsetting element in the precarious balance of Anglo-Egyptian relations.

Having examined the problem from every possible angle, Isma'il Sirri finally said, "My friend, let us examine the issue as engineers, that is to say without emotion as we would a mathematical problem that needs a solution. The situation can be resolved in the following way: if the British have a dual role, so do we; we are first and foremost Egyptians and secondly seekers of knowledge and technical expertise. As Egyptians we should never compromise when our integrity and Egypt's best interests are at stake, but as students we must learn as much as possible and as fast as we can."

Both men agreed this was the only solution. A few years later, Isma'il Sirri had the chance to prove his point when he resigned from the ministry over the issue of Nile water storage in the Sudan. The plan devised by the British, if adopted, would have run counter to the best interests of Egypt. The controversy had raged for well over a year. What angered Isma'il Sirri and provoked his resignation was that the discussions were conducted in secrecy and the Committee of Inquiry studying the problem did not include a single Egyptian expert. Isma'il Sirri's resignation was a blow to the Agency, the name of the British Embassy at the time, but it earned him the respect of his British superior, Sir William Willcocks, and of his Egyptian colleagues. When Isma'il Sadiq reported the fact of this resignation to Chafaq Hanim, her response was typical.

"Good for Isma'il Sirri! If we had more of the likes of him the British would know how to behave in Egypt." She also served him immediately one of her often quoted proverbs:

Ya Fara'un far'ant lay?
Ma la'itsh illi-yashkumni.

('O Pharaoh, why are you such a despot?

Because I found no one to stop me.')

Isma'il Sadiq smiled sadly and said, "There are many, Chafaq Hanim, many who try."

The years 1908–1922 might be considered the golden years of Isma'il Sadiq's career. During that period, he became minister several times, was elected as member of the Institut d'Egypte and of the Senate, received the Legion d'Honneur, and published, while minister of war, an important paper on the use of the Nile water in the Sudan. It might seem odd, in retrospect, that an engineer trained essentially in the field of irrigation should have, at some point in his career, become minister of war. However when one examines events of the time, as well as the career of some of Isma'il Sadiq's contemporaries, that fact is no longer surprising. Egypt in the first half of the twentieth century was a country at peace, with a well-organized system of government and a handful of extremely capable men. As early as the mid-nineteenth century, Great Britain and the Porte had viewed with concern Muhammad 'Ali's growing power, particularly in Syria. At Great Britain's instigation, the Convention for the Pacification of the Levant had convened in London in July 1840 to examine the 'Eastern Question' and find a way to coerce Muhammad 'Ali and force him out of Syria, Adana, Crete, and Arabia. He, however, presented an intransigent front and refused to comply with the demand that he order Ibrahim Pasha to withdraw from these positions. Ultimately, a British force landed in Beirut forcing Ibrahim Pasha to withdraw his troops from Syria and return to Egypt. However by 1841, a compromise was reached between all the parties concerned: on June 1 of that year, the Sultan issued a Firman that recognized Muhammad 'Ali as governor of Egypt for life (he now posed no threat to Great Britain), the position and title to be inherited by his male descendants in order of primogeniture. In return, Muhammad 'Ali agreed to reduce his army to 18,000 men.[47]

Forty years later, after the failure of the 'Urabi Revolt and the occupation in 1882 of the country by Great Britain, the Egyptian army found itself not only reduced but with nothing much to do. Consequently the Ministry of War became a relatively unimportant one. Soldiers were employed as cheap labor to dig wells in outposts near the Sudan border, build barracks, or perform repair work on dams across the Nile. These chores fell within the sphere of public works, consequently the incumbent minister of public works was often entrusted with the Ministries of War and Navy as well. Isma'il Sirri Pasha, Sadiq's best friend and colleague, is a striking example of the civil servant of that period. He cumulated the Ministries of Public Works, War, and Navy for an uninterrupted period of twelve years, from 1908 until 1920. Isma'il Sadiq's career in many ways resembled that of his friend. In any event, during the very active years that covered the period of 1908–1922, he gained tremendous prestige both as an engineer and as a statesman.

9

While her husband was thus putting his imprint on the affairs of the country, Chafaq Hanim was also growing in her role of materfamilias and gaining prestige of her own in Cairene society. Choosing her had been a terrific gamble for Isma'il Sadiq, but now he definitely felt he had made the right decision. Chafaq Hanim had met the challenge head on and proven her worth. And now that he was a prominent figure in the Egyptian establishment, with close ties to Khedive 'Abbas II and later to Sultan Hussein, he was sure she would be able to cope with her husband's growing success. And she did, because as her personality developed, its strength became apparent. It never disintegrated into obnoxious authoritarianism because she was endowed with a tremendous sense of humor and the ability to observe herself as well as others with clear, almost clinical, objectivity. Very soon, she became an outstanding figure on the Egyptian social scene, not as a socialite but as the respected representative of the conservative segment of that society. After the birth of Su'ad, her first grandchild, her status grew. She was now the *Sitt al-kibira*, a venerable matriarch although she was herself the mother of a six-month-old baby.

Bayt al-Munira, or simply Munira as the family called it, was to a large extent a typical Egyptian household of the early twentieth century. Isma'il Sadiq was, of course, the dominant figure, but the real power was Chafaq Hanim. The norms of this family were the result of an incredible combination of Turkish etiquette with Egyptian patterns of behavior, upon which were sprinkled dashes of Europeanisms brought in by Isma'il Sadiq and later on by his sons who had studied abroad. Even with the children, this admixture of cultures was apparent. While the girls went to a French convent, the boys were sent to government schools, and while the girls were never expected to achieve academically or travel abroad, four of the Sadiq sons completed their studies in Europe.

In Munira meals were always an event, especially lunch and dinner. Chafaq Hanim, though not an Upper Egyptian, prided herself in observing in her home typical Minyawi hospitality. Minyawis are often compared and contrasted with Asyutis; the former are usually depicted as more generous, even lavish in their way of life, whereas the latter, no matter how rich, are noted for their avarice. In Munira great store was placed on the table, on the quantity and the quality of the food served. The staff consisted of a Nubian cook who had learned his trade in one of the Khedivial palaces, two undercooks, two *sufrajis*, and maids headed by Sakan, the widowed daughter of the faithful Nabawiyah. Chafaq Hanim had, therefore, no problem producing meals at regular intervals for any number of people. It was assumed that over and above the immediate family, guests could be expected any time. This was a very Egyptian attitude. People thought nothing of arriving unannounced at meal times. In fact, they considered it an act of courtesy on their part to accept the invitation to share the family meal in an impromptu fashion, while the mistress of the house drew immense satisfaction in knowing that she could cope and that her table would be impressively laden with food.

Meals in the *haramlik* never included outsiders: people who dropped in had to be related to the family in some way. If relatives from Minya came to Cairo, it was understood that they would be houseguests in Munira. The visit could, in some cases, extend to several weeks or even months. Breakfast always included homemade jams, honey, black olives, plates of *ful midammis*, white cheese, eggs, molasses, and occasionally *fitir mishaltit*, over which was spread fresh cream. At around 2:00 PM lunch was served. It was always an extremely informal affair with food laid on the table and everyone helping themselves with gusto. A typical meal would always consist of a meat course, chicken, either fried or roasted, stuffed vegetables, rice, and at least one vegetable, which in summer would be okra or *mulukhiya*.

Cairenes and Upper Egyptians, unlike most people who live in coastal towns of Egypt, rarely ate fish. This was usually reserved for parties, where it would be served in an elaborate mayonnaise concoction. Occasionally, however, a member of the family would ask for fried fish to supplement the menu, while Chafaq Hanim always served *bakala* fish for breakfast on the first day of the feast marking the end of the month of Ramadan. Dinner, served at 9:00 PM or thereabouts, was a simplified version of lunch unless an unannounced guest appeared, in which case another course was added and perhaps another dessert. If guests were formally invited for either meal, a roast turkey would surely be presented, and possibly stuffed pigeons as well. Whenever Sadiq Pasha entertained in the *salamlik*, an *uzi* was often part of the menu. Desserts offered at the Sadiq meals were varied and comprised essentially homemade puddings and pastries such as *umm 'ali*, rice pudding, *mihallabiya*, *kunafa*, baklava, and *sadd al-hanaq*. However, other desserts were also bought from famous pastry shops in town, such as Groppi.[48]

This was the house of plenty, as both Isma'il Sadiq and Chafaq Hanim were extremely hospitable and enjoyed extended family gatherings. Oddly enough that was precisely the reason for which Murad Khidr boycotted his parents-in-law's invitations. He told his mother-in-law quite bluntly: "You do not expect me, *Yafandim*, to allow my wife's cousins and male relatives to set eyes on her face now that she is married to me? And surely, you do not expect her to eat wearing her *petsha*?" Chafaq Hanim was stunned by the rudeness of the remark and her irritation at her son-in-law increased perceptibly.

If Khadiga lived outside the family circle, making rare appearances at Munira, the other children remained very close. Fatma and Anisah went to the Mère de Dieu convent every morning but were always eager to be back in the afternoon. Life at home was very pleasant because so much was happening there all the time. There was always an aunt or a cousin visiting, as well as Nayna's weekly reception attended by a variety of ladies mostly drawn from the establishment. On these occasions, Chafaq Hanim would receive these ladies formally in the *haramlik* ground floor drawing room, wearing a very simple floor-length, dark-colored, long-sleeved dress and a veil that would hang loosely over the head. It is quite amazing that despite her illiteracy she could hold her own so well on these social occasions. In fact her gatherings were usually very well attended and looked forward to by her friends and acquaintances alike.

It was often remarked in the family that Safeya Hanim Zaghloul would often seek her advice on personal matters and Hoda Hanim

Sha'rawi would usually make an appearance despite her busy political life, and the fact that Chafaq Hanim did not approve of her views
concerning women's emancipation. Chafaq Hanim was a few years
older than Hoda Hanim and possibly thought that, given time, her
young friend would mend her ways. Her tolerance was such that she
accepted her regardless of their differences.

There was also at Munira the continuous bustling activity of a
household where seven boys and girls were growing up. Isma'il Sadiq
took his sons' education very seriously; he expected them to do well
academically and to obtain a university degree if not from Europe,
at least from Cairo University. All of them studied abroad, except for
Hazim who chose to study agriculture in Egypt. Muhammad, the
eldest, was rather good-looking, not as handsome as Hussein but
definitely less boisterous than Hazim. As the eldest son of Sadiq
Pasha, he was considered one of the most eligible young men of his
generation. After a stint at Oxford where he perfected his English
language proficiency and obtained a degree, he came back to a government job that was not overly demanding. Muhammad was a bon
vivant with little ambition other than to lead a pleasant life as Sadiq
Pasha's eldest son. If the father was pleased with Muhammad's performance at Oxford, he was delighted with Hussein's academic
achievement, which matched his own. Hussein had followed in his
father's footsteps, joined the L'Ecole Centrale des Arts et
Manufactures de Paris, from which he graduated, like him, top of his
class and came back to Egypt on the eve of World War I determined
to distinguish himself as an irrigation engineer.

The devastating conflict in Europe which began in 1914
inevitably had its repercussions in the Middle East. It was also a
momentous year for Egypt as it witnessed the removal of the two
most outstanding personalities on the Egyptian political scene: Lord
Kitchener, who never returned from his annual home leave, having
been called to arms, and Khedive 'Abbas II, who was in Istanbul
when war broke out and was told by the British not to come back
to Egypt; in other words, he was deposed. His constant tug of war
with Cromer, later with Kitchener, and his suspected pro-German
sympathy made it imperative that he be removed from Cairo at a
time when Great Britain needed to secure her position in the
Middle East. The Khedive's deposition was received with mixed

feelings. By and large, Egyptians resented Britain's intrusion in Egyptian affairs, which they perceived as yet another attack on their national pride and constitutional rights. And yet, 'Abbas II had been unable, during the years his reign lasted, to secure his subjects' unanimous support and unfailing loyalty. Perhaps he was himself disillusioned by his countrymen and, despite his unquestioned· devotion to them, was unable to establish the bond of mutual understanding, which is an essential basis for unflinching support. In his memoirs, published many years after his death, his ambivalence of feelings is clearly expressed:

> I knew that Egyptian patriotism existed and was widespread, but in that troubled age, there were many degrees of patriotism. Many demonstrated their love of their country only in words; rare were those who dared to express it through action.[49]

or again:

> The common man was still ignorant of the idea of nationhood, perhaps because those who espoused it did little to propagate it, and there was still no apostle in sight to preach the nation's creed. The Sheikhs, for their part, served me as intermediaries with the soldiers. Perhaps they were not completely disinterested. Faith is not always enough to nourish the men of God, and whatever their admiration for the joys of Paradise, they are not averse to following the righteous path in as comfortable a fashion as possible.[50]

A few pages later comes the following devastating observation:

> It is true that during my rule I encountered no suitable Egyptian who could help me and show me the right path to take.[51]

Furthermore, he had a falling out with Shaykh Muhammad 'Abdu, the nationalist leader and Egypt's outstanding religious reformer, who had a tremendous following.

'Abbas II's removal was received with sadness but equanimity in the Sadiq household. Isma'il Sadiq was perfectly aware of the Khedive's problems, hence while not condoning Britain's action, he understood it and approved without reservation the choice of his successor. Unlike 'Abbas II, Sultan Hussein, the man chosen to succeed him, commanded the unanimous support of Egyptians.

Selecting him was a clever move as it deflated opposition and, though Sultan Hussein had initially been reluctant to accept, he ultimately realized it was in everybody's best interest that he did. He was Khedive Isma'il's favorite son, a man of integrity and courage, a family man who treated his kindly wife, Sultana Malak, with respect and devotion.

While these various dramas were unfolding on the national and international scenes, Chafaq Hanim was involved in matrimonial pursuits of her own. In fact, these became her main activity for the next decade. The first in line was Muhammad, who despite his reluctance to give up his carefree existence, knew that he would eventually have to submit to his mother's wish and marry the girl of his parents' choice. Isma'il Sadiq, following the proper channels, let it be known that he was looking for a bride for his eldest son. Considering his status in the Egyptian society, the use of a match-maker would have been inappropriate and the quest was limited to a certain segment of society, the upper class with Turkish connections. At that time, social stratification was clearly defined with a Turkish-Caucasian-Georgian upper class, a Coptic, Arabic, Syro-Lebanese middle class—with occasional connections to the upper class—and the artisans, workers, and peasants as the lower class. The arrogance of the Turkish ruling class often antagonized Egyptians who in many cases were far more educated and capable than the Turks whom they considered obstinate and narrow-minded. If the Turks called Egyptians *pis fellah*, they, in their turn retaliated by labeling Turks *mukh turki*, or obstinate Turk. However, after the post-war cotton boom, illiterate peasants made enormous fortunes and this sudden enrichment brought strange results, one of which was a blurring of the old class distinction. Men such as Muhammad Badrawi 'Ashur found themselves all of a sudden propelled to the forefront of the country's social map.

But Isma'il Sadiq, because of his lineage—Caucasian mother, Moroccan grandfather—as well as his close connection to the court, had never felt the brunt of Turkish disdain, therefore he limited his search to the upper class. Very soon, a perfect candidate was identified. She was the daughter of 'Ilwi Pasha, a Turk who owned extensive land in Egypt and yet retained very close links with his native country. This, of course, was an added asset for it meant that the family had preserved the aura of refinement usually associated with the Ottoman Empire, albeit at the tail end of its glorious past. Furthermore it was said that Malika 'Ilwi was a great beauty with fair hair and blue eyes. All transactions between Isma'il Sadiq and 'Ilwi Pasha were conducted through intermediaries; 'Ilwi Pasha considered the match favorably because of Isma'il Sadiq's outstanding position in the country, his wealth—which was often assumed to be far greater than it actually was—and his excellent reputation. It was an alliance that would do justice to his own sense of superiority as a Turk. As far as he could judge, Isma'il Sadiq had, through his achievements, transcended his 'Egyptianness.' At any rate, Malika could not hope for a better match in Istanbul. In Cairo 'Ilwi was a big fish in a small pond. Within his Cairene existence the match with the Sadiqs was the best he could hope for since in Istanbul, competition among the elite strata was far greater. Eventually, the marriage deal was concluded and the *Fatiha* recited.

Muhammad, even though he affected an air of indifference, was actually very curious about this Turkish beauty everyone was talking about. Had it been up to him, he would have remained celibate for quite a while longer as he was living a very pleasant existence. His job, which was just a sinecure obtained through his father's influence, did not make too many demands on his time. Isma'il Sadiq knew that Muhammad needed a front but would never be as achieving as his brother, Hussein. Muhammad was not at all stupid; in fact, he could have equaled his brother had he made the effort. He just did not see any reason for such diligence, lacked ambition, and was often irritated by Hussein's earnest dedication to his work and desire to excel. In any event, he now had to go ahead, pursue the next phase of his life, and face, whether he liked it or not, the serious business of marriage.

Chafaq Hanim came back from her visit to the 'Ilwis delighted because the young girl was indeed beautiful, worthy of her son Muhammad. Fatma and Anisah were just as impressed because she was so well dressed; her hair, which she wore very long, was fair and held back in a thick braid, and her hands were small, the fingers thin, and the nails perfectly rounded. Anisah looked at her own hands and immediately closed her fist to hide her nails, cut squarely like a boy's. What impressed them more than anything else was that she spoke

French fluently whenever she addressed her governess who, at Malika's insistence, had been present during the visit. Their own knowledge of French was quite good because the time spent at the Mère de Dieu convent was doing wonders for both girls. The nuns were giving them culture more than education, and their Egyptian upbringing was covered by a thin layer of Europeanism. This layer they wore like their mother's *habara*, which could be shed or picked up again at will. They had the amazing ability to step in and out of these very different cultures depending on the demands of their daily life and never felt at odds with their surroundings because the core was untouched: they were Egyptian and had no ambivalence about their identity.

Preparations for Muhammad's wedding were soon in full swing. Chafaq Hanim was feverishly busy preparing the groom's part of the event. Guest lists were drawn with care and since the *kitab* was taking place in the bride's parents' house, they discreetly informed them of the number of guests the Sadiqs were bringing along. Proceedings had somewhat evolved since the days of Isma'il's own wedding, as now the *kitab* was given great importance in the sense that it was a ceremony in the course of which the bride officially gave her consent in the presence of witnesses. The festivities marking the event, or *farah*, were to follow later and would be a grand affair. The problem in Muhammad's case lay in the fact that some of his uncles and male relatives lived in Upper Egypt and were totally ignorant of the ways of the modern world, yet protocol demanded that they be invited. Isma'il Sadiq knew that despite his importance in Cairo and the respect accorded him by his family in Minya, he could not afford to snub anyone as it would make him 'lose face' in his home town; and if he did Muhammad's *'izwa* would be lessened and his own as well, for that matter. He knew that the *'umda*, his cousin, had to be on the list despite the fact that he would surely appear in his jibba and caftan, and that his old uncle, the venerable Mahfuz al-Maghrabi, who headed the list, often belched in public.

"'Ilwi Pasha will surely look down upon my family for their lack of social sophistication," he thought. But out of two evils, he chose the lesser one: better shock his new in-laws than antagonize his blood relations. Upper Egyptians were, and still are, a very proud people, proud of their ways and ancestry and, unlike Cairenes, not overly impressed by the refinement of the Turkish way of life. They have their own codes of conduct, their own brand of refinement onto which they hold with determination. Isma'il Sadiq was well aware of the situation and made his choice accordingly. He, as usual, had sought the advice of Chafaq Hanim who, despite her delight with the new *nasab*, had immediately realized how different they were. The presence of the French governess in the drawing room the day of their first visit had shocked her, and the fact that Malika had once or twice spoken French, a language her future mother-in-law could not understand, had annoyed her. She had not mentioned these incidents to her husband because he would think them trivial, but they had not passed unnoticed. Though she worried that the Sadiqs might be looked down upon by their future in-laws, yet she had the wisdom to recognize that pretending they were alike would be impossible simply because it was not true. Her logic dictated her conduct and the advice she gave her husband: "Look, Basha, we are different but not worse. They have agreed to give their daughter to an Egyptian family hence should accept us as we are. Remember the proverb, *man fatu qadimu tah*—He who forgets his past is lost. If we antagonize the family in Minya by not inviting them, we would surely lose face there and we would be starting a relationship with the 'Ilwis in the wrong way. They would assume that they were superior and act accordingly and I, for one, could not bear it! It might induce me to behave toward them in an inappropriate manner and, as you well know, *al-nasab zay al-laban, in it'akkar ma yisfash*—Family relationships through marriage are like milk; when they curdle, they cannot be made good again."

Isma'il Sadiq felt reassured. Consequently, he drew up a list that was systematic and comprehensive. No one who should be invited was left out and he did not commit the error of requesting that they dress in a certain way. He knew that they would come attired in what was absolutely proper according to their own code of social behavior, in other words, all caftans would be silk, all 'abayas would be of fine hand-woven wool, and all turbans would be immaculately white. During the short ceremony in the course of which only sherbet and *milabbis* would be offered, the chance of anyone belching was reduced to a minimum!

Since both fathers were important men in Egyptian society, the shaykh al-Azhar had been invited to bless the ceremony and deliver a small speech. All proceedings were based on Islamic tradition, therefore, the bride's consent had to be given in front of witnesses. She was in her room with her mother, future mother-in-law, sisters-in-law, and a few ladies of her family. She was dressed in almost full regalia. The complete splendor of her wedding attire was reserved for the *farah*, which was to take place in the evening. Then she would wear a gown of fine lace embroidered with sequins and pearls, and her hair would be covered by the wedding veil her mother had worn. Attached to her hair and falling in cascades on each side of her face, would be the silver threads of her *talli*. Now, however, her dress was not white but pink, and in her long braids were interwoven strings of pearls while above her ears two little strands of orange blossom were securely held by invisible hairpins. Malika's feet rested in a silver basin in which floated green mint leaves while at the bottom lay a pair of scissors, and in her mouth was a lump of sugar. Green mint leaves symbolize abundance and fertility, scissors are to cut the path of the evil eye, and the lump of sugar represents sweetness of the tongue, or refined speech.

Her aunts were busy with the incense burners full of incense from Mecca. Chafaq Hanim observed her daughter-in-law with satisfaction but a twinge of worry. Was anything wrong with Malika? She certainly did not look joyful despite the occasion. Was she not happy? Did she not approve of Muhammad? That was not possible because she had not yet laid eyes on him. Chafaq Hanim experienced a moment of dreadful foreboding, a sense that things were not as they should be, and the atmosphere was suddenly strained, charged with anxiety almost as if danger were lurking in the corners of the room. She immediately recited sotto voce the *Ma'udhatayn* and her inner tension was somewhat relieved. She forced herself to discard the uneasiness she was feeling and, looking at her daughter-in-law, convinced herself that there was nothing wrong except perhaps excessive shyness on the part of a young girl who hardly knew them. Fatma and Anisah were sitting quietly in a corner of the room and observed all these proceedings with interest. This was their first big wedding since Abla Khadiga's, which had been a small affair, and they felt very important as sisters of the groom.

There was a gentle knock on the door and 'Ilwi Pasha walked into the room flanked by his sons in order to receive Malika's consent.

'Ilwi Pasha adored his only daughter but never indulged in open expressions of affection because to do so would have been considered unmanly for a Turk of the old school. He was proud of her beauty and since she was the youngest of his three children and only daughter, she was his favorite. Actually, Malika was everybody's darling at home and, consequently, a little spoiled. Tarandil Hanim, her mother, had given her what she assumed to be a fine education. When the child was two years old, she hired a French governess, Mademoiselle Tabouret, to teach her French and give her the refinement of a European education. By the time she was five years old, Malika was fluent in French, which she spoke with Mademoiselle Tabouret, and in Turkish, which she spoke with her parents and family in Istanbul. Unlike her parents though, she could hardly speak Arabic and had no desire to do so. She thought of Arabic as the language of the servants and therefore to be looked down upon. Since she was receiving her instruction at home and not at school, she had virtually no contact with Egyptian girls her age and was perfectly content in the company of her governess.

The curriculum taught by this French lady was not comprehensive, yet in some sense it was adequate. It was based on one principle, which was that only through reading could one learn. Malika was taught to read and to love books. Mademoiselle Tabouret discarded mathematics as unnecessary for a young girl of quality who would never become an engineer or an accountant, but concentrated instead on the masters of French literature. After La Fontaine, they read together Ronsard's sonnets, pages of Montaigne, delighted in the stories of Rabelais and his gargantuan hero, spent many hours with Racine's tragic heroines and Corneilles' gallant heroes. Molière offered a pleasant interim of comic relief after an arduous hour of tragic recitation. By the time they reached the Romantics, Malika was totally addicted to poetry. She adored Musset, was moved to tears by Vigny and, if she could not quite accept Rousseau's 'noble savage,' much preferring the civilized modern concept of life, she understood his nostalgia, his pining for a long lost world.

Malika enjoyed the hours she spent with Mademoiselle Tabouret in the course of which they read poetry or discussed fine points of literature. She was convinced that in doing so she was establishing herself in the category of the 'educated' and even tried her hand at poetry. Her education, of course, was lop-sided and incomplete because her teacher knew nothing of science, very little of geography, and totally ignored philosophy or even history except for the French modern period. But she had the veneer of run-of-the-mill culture, which she imparted to her pupil. Tarandil Hanim, though she could speak French, Turkish, and Arabic, had little culture. She was not interested in literature or poetry, rarely picked up a book, and had since her marriage been wholly wrapped up in domestic affairs. She was quite impressed with the education her daughter was receiving and given her own limitations, she failed to perceive that Malika was acquiring a superficial Frenchified version of education while losing her own culture, whether Turkish or Arabic, and the incredible wealth of knowledge and ideas that they encompassed.

Moreover, it had not seemed important to Tarandil Hanim that Malika learn about Islam or Islamic religious practices. Though she, Tarandil Hanim, performed her ritual prayers five times daily, fasted the month of Ramadan and always gave alms to the poor, she performed these acts mechanically as part of a routine to which all Muslims must subscribe without giving them much thought. At any rate, she had overlooked that aspect of her daughter's education and took it for granted that the girl would, somehow, be a good Muslim. As a result, Malika grew up in an artificial atmosphere, a mixture of the conventional and the traditional with Mademoiselle Tabouret's version of culture. That she was lost somewhere in between is undeniable and while she thrived on the Occidental part of her daily life, she dismissed her oriental roots. The result was that Malika in a certain sense was an outsider. She lived in Egypt and for all practical purposes was destined to go on living in Egypt, yet she felt totally alien to the Egyptian society, a society to which, as far as she could see, only people like her mother's maids belonged.

What little Arabic she knew, she could not use since her governess forbade her to speak with the maids, saying their language was uncouth and that Malika might pick up 'bad things' from them, although the nature of the badness and its extent were never clearly defined. 'Ilwi Pasha interfered very little in his daughter's education, convinced that Tarandil Hanim and Mademoiselle Tabouret were doing their best. Malika's main problem, though, was that she was endowed with limited intelligence and unlimited obstinacy.

This being the case, she lacked the intellectual curiosity that would have demanded more knowledge about her own background or the ability to encompass both worlds and be enriched by their compounded value.

When 'Ilwi Pasha entered his daughter's room, he stood for a moment awed by her beauty and overcome with emotion. Here was his beautiful Malika ready to be handed over to another family. Much as he loved his daughter and dreaded the separation, he had stood firm and exercised his full parental authority in the face of Malika's vehement rejection of this marriage. "Never," she had cried. "Never will I become the wife of an Egyptian *fellah*. This Muhammad Sadiq, I am sure, cannot speak French. I do not care if they have all the money in the world, they are just a bunch of une-ducated *Sa'idis*."[52] 'Iilwi Pasha's Turkish blood boiled over in the face of such effrontery and a violent slap put an end to the conversation. Malika threw herself on her bed and sobbed uncontrollably more out of anger and shame than of pain. This was the very first time her father had struck her. She felt betrayed and in a state of utter despair because she had no doubt that her father would never change his mind and that she would have to marry this *pis fellah*.

She cried for hours despite Mademoiselle Tabouret's half-hearted efforts to console her; the poor woman was distraught at the sight of her pupil's despair and was just as shocked and angry at what she termed *une mésalliance*. No doubt she was also reflecting on the fact that once Malika was out of the house, she would be out of a job! By that time, Tarandil Hanim had been crying as well because even though she approved of the proposed match, her daughter's reaction pained her tremendously. She would so much have wanted matters to be different, to see everybody happy, and feel that her daughter was looking forward to her coming marriage. Malika, unwilling, or per-haps unable, to accept her fate and make the necessary adjustments, vowed to hate Muhammad Sadiq and his family to her dying day.

For the time being, however, none of this was apparent. Malika's upbringing was such that she was able to control her emotions in the presence of her new family, and if she could not bring herself to smile, at least she did not cry. She looked at her father as he came into the room and wondered at his sudden appearance. Chafaq Hanim, Khadiga, and Fatma pulled their *petsha*s over their noses but not Anisah who was still too young to wear one. "Malika," said 'Ilwi Pasha, "I have come to receive your official consent in front of witnesses. Do you accept to marry Muhammad Sadiq?" As he spoke the words, he experienced a sudden rush of panic: would Malika commit the unthinkable and refuse her consent? He glared at his daughter willing her to give the right answer but for a few seconds she remained silent while everyone watched. She had lowered her eyes to conceal the tears that were threatening to flow and, for a mad moment, felt the urge to cry out, "No! Never, never!" Instead, in a barely audible voice she answered, "Yes." Moments later the whole house resounded with the shrill peals of Sakan's ululations. Sakan had come at the insistence of Chafaq Hanim who suspected that her future in-laws would be too Europeanized to have in their household a woman capable of ululating. Fatma and Anisah had pleaded with their mother not to bring her, fearing that they might appear *baladi*. Chafaq Hanim, however, had been adamant. "This is our tradition and I will uphold it. It would be a bad omen not to have ululations on an occasion such as this one. This is a wedding, not a funeral!" As it turned out, 'Ilwi Pasha was enchanted and kept repeating, " '*Azim! 'Azim!*—Wonderful! Wonderful!" Malika, however, was horrified and Mademoiselle Tabouret pressed her hands to her ears to shut out the dreadful noise.

In the evening, the *farah* took place in Munira. It was a grand affair attended by all the cabinet ministers and most outstanding families in Cairo. Because of Isma'il Sadiq's position and his close relationship with the palace, a representative of the Khedive was sent to offer the monarch's congratulations and a wedding present. Elaborate buffet diners were served simultaneously in the *salamlik* and in the *haramlik*. At the end of the evening, Muhammad came over to the women's quarter to fetch his wife and take her home.

After the wedding, Muhammad and Malika settled into a life that was quite mysterious as far as the family was concerned. Malika was 'too tired' to attend the Friday lunches. At first, she had made the effort to come, not daring to be blatantly rude, but soon enough realized that she could not cope with the rowdiness of the gathering. Though she would not admit it, even to herself, what she experienced was not discomfort but fear. She had been plucked out of a very sheltered existence and thrown suddenly unprepared and defenseless into the midst of a very large, boisterous, Arabic-speaking family. Her initial disdain of Chafaq Hanim had turned into awesome respect when she realized that her mother-in-law controlled everyone in Munira, perhaps even the Pasha. The others she looked down upon except for Fatma with whom she was able to communicate and rather liked, and Hussein who was so handsome and polished. The others she simply detested. Hazim, of course, never stood a chance as far as she was concerned.

As he grew up, Hazim's childhood desire to be noticed increased and he deliberately adopted outrageous attitudes from which he derived much pleasure. Forever playing the buffoon he established himself within the family as a sharp-tongued, quick-witted, and funny character. He loved to shock his 'refined' sisters, but usually failed to do so because Fatma saw through his antics and was amused by them, and Anisah always followed Fatma. But for Malika, he was a nightmare, a constant reminder of the low state to which she had fallen. Her main problem, however was not Hazim or the family but Muhammad, the husband her father had imposed upon her. Theirs was definitely not a marriage made in heaven. In response to his wife's aloofness, Muhammad went back to his bachelor's way of life and in order to humiliate her, made a point of publicizing his many affairs. Malika sought comfort and solace in her books, her poems, and her daydreams.

Shortly after her marriage, her father died in a car accident while vacationing in Istanbul. With her share of the inheritance, she acquired a small property in Giza, near the pyramids, where she built a small house with many little corners where she would retreat with her books. Tiny windows that let in very little light gave the interior a gloomy, almost mysterious atmosphere. This was her retreat and there she lived alone the rest of her life, while Muhammad remained in the town house. Hazim wryly observed that Muhammad and his wife were truly 'poles apart.'

"Poor Abla Malika," sighed Anisah one Friday morning. "It is so sad that she never comes to lunch with the family."

"It is sad for Nayna as well," answered Fatma. "First Murad Khidr who is keeping Abla Khadiga away most of the time, and now poor Muhammad who has to put up with such nonsense. And, of course, it is Nayna who suffers the most. Anyway, it is Malika's loss and if she prefers the company of her books to ours, that is her problem. She is depriving herself of much fun."

Fun was exactly what everybody seemed to have at Munira. In an age when radio broadcasts were not yet introduced and television non-existent, entertainment was provided by the family themselves. There was always someone coming in with a new story to tell or a juicy bit of gossip to be dissected ad infinitum. Gossip was certainly one of the main activities the ladies indulged in during the long hours they spent together, particularly when relatives came to visit from Minya. Chafaq Hanim, however, drew the line at some point. She would never allow an improper accusation to be made in her presence. She shocked the assembled family one day when, rather abruptly, she reproached her husband for doing it. He had come one afternoon from lunching with friends and casually informed the family that I.S. Pasha was having an affair with the daughter of one of their colleagues Y.I. Pasha. Chafaq Hanim's response was immediate.

"Have you seen them in the act, Basha?"

"Upon your life, Chafaq Hanim. How could that be possible?"

"Then, it would be better if you did not repeat this story because one cannot be sure about such things unless present to witness them." A stunned silence followed her remark. Isma'il Sadiq frowned at first, but seeing the consternation on his daughters' faces and the look of gleeful anticipation on Hazim's, smiled gently and said:

"You are quite right, Chafaq Hanim. One should never wantonly destroy people's reputation."

Fatma had been surprised at her mother's unusual sharpness toward her father and was at a loss to understand the cause. She mulled over the issue for some time and finally decided to question her.

"My dear," answered Chafaq Hanim, "there are certain limits that should never be transcended. If you reflect on the kind of gossip we indulge in as a pleasant pass time—even though between you and me that also is not good—it is not really sinful, just a little harmful."

"But what is the difference, Nayna? Yesterday we were all discussing cousin Su'ad's awful treatment of her maids, her avarice, and the poor upbringing of her children. We were gossiping, were we not?"

"Ah, but there is a tremendous difference. All we said about Su'ad are verifiable truths. None of us approves of the way her household is run, or the way she treats her servants. We are irritated by her behavior, though I must admit it is none of our business. Discussing her among ourselves relieves the pressure of our disapproval and is not harmful. But what your father said is an open accusation of adultery without proof. In our religion, it is a sin punishable by eighty lashes. Never indulge in gossip that is so sinful."

Fatma understood the wisdom of her mother's response and the depth of her religious commitment. She always remembered this incident, and to her dying day never indulged in 'sinful gossip.'

10

Chafaq Hanim was not happy these days because all her careful planning seemed to have gone awry. Her children's matrimonial alliances did not develop as she had anticipated, or even hoped. She perceived the failure of her son's marriage as a personal offense, and the unhappy situation of Khadiga was an added grievance. Muhammad's 'debacle,' as she termed his marriage, was like a sickness for which there is no cure. No one could have foreseen that 'Ilwi Pasha's daughter would not be quite right in the head and that her eldest son would be so publicly rejected by this silly girl who, apparently, now lived as a recluse. As for the other couple, they were a constant source of frustration and often extreme irritation. Murad Khidr's severity did not decrease with the years, if anything it was getting worse as if he wanted to prove that he and he alone had jurisdiction over his wife and his children. This arrogance pained Chafaq Hanim almost as much as his rigid attitude toward her daughter because, in her opinion, it was so laden with disrespect. Her husband was amused by such anger because he suspected that deep down it was basically a question of mother-in-law syndrome. He never voiced this opinion, of course, as it would have been very badly received by Chafaq Hanim who was further aggravated by the fact that she could not retaliate in any way without damaging Khadiga's situation. She consoled herself instead with yet another often quoted proverbs:

Al-dunya 'allaba
Yawm laka wa yawm 'alayk.
('Life's fortunes change
Up one day, down the next.')

It now became for her a matter of family honor that the next marriage in the family be successful. In 1916–17, three of her children

were lined up to jump the hurdle: Hussein, who with his degree from
the Centrale was an extremely eligible bachelor of twenty-three;
Hazim who had recently graduated from the School of Agriculture
and needed to settle down before he committed some irreparable
outrage that would disbar him from the more exclusive Egyptian
families; and Fatma who would turn eighteen at the end of the year
and should be launched into a life of her own. Chafaq Hanim sighed
deeply, there was so much to be done, so many decisions to be taken
and so many risks involved! Fatma was the only one about whom she
felt somewhat reassured. Her future husband had already been selected and Sadiq Pasha who had never ceased to observe the young man
had recently declared himself satisfied. He was a fine man, even-tempered with a gentleness of manner that was deceptive, for when put
to the test, his Upper Egyptian sense of pride would immediately take
over leaving no doubt as to his ability to command respect.

"What I like best about him," Sadiq Pasha told his wife, "is that he
has refinement of the spirit, politeness of the heart. I believe jealousy
and pettiness are totally alien to him. He has ambition and wants to
rise and prove himself."

"Praise be to God!" sighed Chafaq Hanim. "When do you plan to
announce Fatma's engagement?"

"In a month or two, just as soon as the next list of deputy irrigation inspectors has become official. 'Abd al-Rahman will be posted
to Sohag."

"Sohag? Why should they be sent so far?"

"But Chafaq Hanim, that is where we started our life together,
and as I recall you enjoyed it very much."

"Yes, that is true. But I hate the thought of her going so far.
Anyway, it can't be helped, may God provide what is good. Let us
concentrate on the other issues. What are we going to do about
Hussein and Hazim?"

"I think I have found a good candidate for Hazim; at least I hope
it is a good choice, though God only knows how such matters eventually develop."

"Who is she, Basha?"

"She is the daughter of Muhammad Basha Mursi from Minya. My
cousin 'Uthman is a friend of his and though he has never seen the
girl, he speaks very highly of the family."

"Muhammad Basha Mursi? Isn't he the one who owns the beautiful mansion on the banks of the Nile in Minya?"

"That is the one. It is an excellent family and, as I understand it, they are not only wealthy but they enjoy a very good reputation as well. I have learned, from some discreet inquiries I made, that they would welcome an alliance with us. 'Uthman, as I told you, has not seen the girl, but has heard that she is pretty, though rather stout."

"But, Basha, if she is such a good choice why not give her to Hussein who is the eldest and should marry before his younger brother?"

"No, she won't do for Hussein. You see, she has lived all her life in Minya, and is probably quite provincial. Hazim will know how to deal with her and will, I hope, derive much pleasure from her company, but Hussein needs someone totally different."

"You mean someone 'modern'?" asked Chafaq Hanim with a twinge of irony.

"Perhaps! Well, anyway, Dalia Mursi is a good choice for Hazim."

Muhammad Pasha Mursi was a very wealthy landowner whose property extended many miles along the banks of the Nile in Minya. His palace, for it could not be described as anything else, was built by his father and enlarged extensively over the years. It overlooked a huge garden on the western side, while the eastern side abutted a little wall in which a door—locked most of the time—led to an embankment from which one could step onto a felucca moored there. The house was furnished with gilded wood furniture very much the fashion since Empress Eugenie's visit to Egypt in 1879, and the huge crystal chandeliers, which hung from high ceilings in the ground floor reception rooms, threw light on marqueterie floors covered with exquisite Persian rugs. This is where Dalia, the Pasha's daughter, had grown. She was raised in the manner typical of girls living in Upper Egypt at the time, that is to say, she never went to school but was taught at home to read and write and not much else.

She spent most of her day lounging on sofas or chatting with the maids and relieved the boredom of her existence by indulging in overeating. The result was that she grew very fat, but because her eyes were green and her skin fair—probably due to an indiscretion of one of her ancestors at the time of the French occupation—she had the reputation of being beautiful, at least from an Upper Egyptian point of view. When a description of his bride to be was given to Hazim, he declared himself satisfied, because, as he said, he had no wish to spend his life with an ethereal creature who shunned good food and thrived on poetry. He wanted a woman who would share his appetite for life and, as he told his mother, "If she is fat, all the better, I will have more to embrace!"

In April 1916, Hazim and Dalia were married after grandiose festivities in Minya and settled in a house in Giza. Just as soon as this young couple was organized in happy matrimony, the Sadiqs turned their attention to the next in line. The ideal bride for Hussein had not yet been found and since the official list of irrigation inspectors had been announced, a date was set for the marriage of Fatma and 'Abd al-Rahman Sallam.

The wedding took place in June 1916. Again, it was a grand affair, and Sultan Hussein, who held Isma'il Sadiq in high esteem, sent one of the palace carriages with a guard of honor to escort the bride to her husband's house. Sultan Hussein's gesture was not uncommon in those days. Hanna Wissa recounts that when his father, Fahmy Bey Wissa, married his cousin, Esther Fanous, "Khedive 'Abbas Helmi sent a Khedivial band and carriage to Asyut for his wedding."[53] In a typical gesture of courtesy current at the time, Isma'il Sadiq had given strict instructions that the khedivial band that accompanied the procession march silently as they passed before the Abu Usbu' house. The Abu Usbu' family were close friends of the Sadiqs and a year had not yet elapsed since the death of the head of the family.

A few days after the wedding, the young couple left for Sohag where, upon arrival, they were received with all the honors due to the irrigation inspector and his wife. They set up house in a very large and comfortable villa that had bathrooms and plenty of running water but which, unfortunately, was not free of insects and reptiles. 'Abd al-Rahman explained to his wife that certain precautions had to be taken very seriously at all times. For instance, all four legs of their brass bed had to be immersed in deep bowls filled with water as a deterrent to scorpions. Shoes and other closed footwear when not used had to be placed on a shelf for the same reason, and feet were never to be inserted in slippers at the foot of the bed until the slippers had been shaken to chase out roaches and the like. Heavy nets enveloped beds to protect sleepers not only from flies and mosquitoes but from other winged insects that abounded in the area. If Fatma was put off by this very ominous and alarming situation, she apparently adjusted to it very well, perhaps assuming that since Nayna had lived through the same experience so could she. Her husband never had to explain about the proper attitude to observe toward the women of the community with whom she would inevitably be in contact. As soon as they arrived, he noticed that she had instinctively done the right thing. Her attitude was neither haughty nor condescending—which would have been even more offensive—but cordial, while at the same time retaining a certain distance dictated by her husband's position.

The job of irrigation inspector had lost none of its importance. In fact, it had increased because the British engineers of the time of Isma'il Sadiq had relinquished their hold over it, leaving their Egyptian counterparts masters of the field. Like her mother before her, Fatma enjoyed life in Sohag. It was different from Munira, but every day had its share of excitement and discovery. She learned to speak the dialect of the Sohagi women and to share in their concerns, and all the while she was getting to know better this gentle man who was so affectionate and soft-spoken, with sudden bursts of wit that made her laugh to tears.

Fatma loved to laugh and had a very positive outlook on life; problems, whenever they crossed her path, were either solved or ignored. Though Muhammad, her eldest brother, was her favorite, especially now that his personal life was so disappointing, she was in many ways more like Hussein and Hazim. She shared Hussein's brilliant intellect inherited from their parents and Hazim's boisterous *joie de vivre* and delightful sense of humor. However, having been drilled by Chafaq Hanim and polished by the nuns at the Mère de Dieu convent, she never shared his grossness, which she found at times very trying. By the end of summer, she happily announced to the family in Cairo that she was pregnant. The baby was due in late spring and since the weather in Sohag is abominably hot in summer, and probably in order to please her mother as well, it was decided that she would travel back home and have her baby in the comfort of her father's house. However, a few days after her arrival in Cairo, she suffered a miscarriage, which left her prostrate for quite a while. She had been carrying twins.

"*Al-'ayn, ya sitti, 'ayn wa sabit*—It is the evil eye, Madam, the evil eye that has struck," Sakan kept repeating. "*Si* 'Abd al-Rahman Bey is such a kind man and Sitt Fatma Hanim seemed so happy."

"'*Ayn walla ghayruh*—The evil eye or whatever else," answered Chafaq Hanim. "Fatma lost her babies because she was too small to carry both." A scientific explanation was more reassuring for Chafaq Hanim than the evil doings of mysterious powers beyond one's control. She feared the evil eye more than she feared sickness or death because these were part of life, part of the human condition, but the evil eye was something altogether different. Its very elusiveness and unpredictability terrified her and as years went by, she devised all sorts of little stratagems to counteract its power such as reciting the *Ma'udhatayn*, burning incense, touching wood, or spreading her open palms before her face. In any event, Fatma had lost her babies and no amount of prayer, wood rubbing, or incense burning would bring those back. "Better luck next time," she thought, because she never doubted there would be a next time. She would have dearly liked to keep her daughter in Cairo but knew that was not possible. A wife's duty is to follow her husband wherever the demands of his career take him. She also knew that she could not ask her husband to use his influence in order to obtain 'Abd al-Rahman's transfer to Cairo because Isma'il Sadiq had always declared his aversion to favoritism. Besides, Fatma did not seem eager to be transferred to Cairo for though she adored her mother and often missed her, she thoroughly enjoyed her newfound independence.

With the resilience of youth, she slowly emerged from the bout of depression that followed her miscarriage and allowing her natural zest for life to take over, she quickly recovered her health and looked forward to her next pregnancy. The only concession Sadiq Pasha made was to allow Fatma to spend the summer with the family in Alexandria. He always rented a large house by the sea where they spent the summer months from June to September. This year, however, they decided to leave later as Dalia's first baby was due in early June—"almost at the same time as Fatma had she not miscarried," thought Chafaq Hanim. Dalia gave birth on June 10, 1917, to a son who was named Isma'il, after his grandfather. This was the first grandchild who would perpetuate the family name. Consequently, festivities surrounding his birth were spectacular, both in Minya, where Muhammad Pasha Mursi ordered six head of cattle to be slaughtered and the meat distributed to the poor, and in Munira, where the baby was born. Isma'il Sadiq was profoundly happy at the birth of this grandson who bore his name.

In Munira, the *salamlik* was filled with visitors who came to congratulate the Pasha, some sincerely while others to ingratiate themselves with a man in power. The real festivities, however, took place in the *haramlik*, where all the family were gathered to celebrate the *subu'*, which on the seventh day of his birth marked Isma'il's official entry into the world. Dalia sat in her bed propped up by cushions, wearing a pink satin nightgown. Her blond frizzy hair was braided, she wore gold pendant earrings and around her neck, almost like a choker because she had grown so fat, was her gold *kirdan* that matched the many gold bracelets that encircled her forearms. The baby, a tiny bundle wrapped up in shawls despite the heat of summer, looked incongruously small in the arms of his mother, almost lost between her ample breasts, and the mound that raised the satin sheets might lead one to believe she was still pregnant. The room was filled with as many members of the family as it could contain. On the floor sat Sakan holding a large sieve; next to her were a copper pound and pestle. On the table was an earthenware *abriq*, decorated with as many of Dalia's jewels as possible so that the evil eye would be attracted by them rather than by the newborn and his mother. The jug was filled with jasmine-scented water in which grains of wheat had been added to symbolize fertility and abundance. When everyone was seated around the bed, Durriyah Hanim, Dalia's mother, lifted the baby and placed him in the sieve, which she rocked gently from side to side, while Sakan pounded vigorously the copper pestle and chanted, "Be obedient to your father, Isma'il. Be obedient to your mother."

"And to his grandmother," someone shouted.

"Be obedient to your grandmother," repeated Sakan and immediately added, "Be obedient to your grandfather. Be obedient to your aunt Sitt Khadiga Hanim. Be obedient to your uncle Si Muhammad Bey."

The litany went on and on until all members of the baby's family on both sides had been named, and all the while the hammering also went on. To the din of the metallic pounding was added the

shrill crescendo of ululations outside the room. Dalia was compla-
cently enjoying the proceedings. She sat there, queen of the day,
mother of a son, which, as far as she could perceive, was the greatest
feat a woman could accomplish. Chafaq Hanim observed her daughter-in-law with a critical eye. "She truly is a very plain woman," she
thought, "and her corpulence is getting out of hand. However, if she
pleases Hazim, that is all that matters. Let us hope that he will continue to find pleasure in her company." Chafaq Hanim hid her feelings well and pretended to be enjoying the celebration while her
heart was grieving. How she would have wished this be the celebration for Fatma's *subu'*. But in her wisdom she perceived that there
was nothing she could do for her daughter at that point except submit to God's will and hope she would soon become pregnant again.
Fatma had experienced serious twinges of jealousy that day and,
fearing her own evil eye might hurt the baby, had recited the
Ma'udhatayn several times as her mother had taught her. At the end
of summer, she went back to Sohag, at peace with herself and looking forward to the future.

11

October 1917 was a sad and troubled month for Sadiq Pasha. On the ninth day of the month, Sultan Hussein, his monarch and friend, died after a short illness leaving him disconsolate and worried about the immediate future of the monarchy. When King Fuad, his brother, replaced him on the throne, he had misgivings because this prince knew little about Egyptian affairs, having spent most of his life in Italy. He could hardly speak Arabic and did not seem to have the same rapport with his countrymen Sultan Hussein had enjoyed. Still, there was the strong possibility that he would rise to the situation and prove to be an effective ruler. "Time will tell," he thought. More problems, however assailed his mind. In Russia the Bolsheviks had toppled the monarchy, upsetting the ordered pattern of that country and the revolution was spreading like wildfire. Isma'il Sadiq was by principle an anti-revolutionary. During his years in France, he had read about the 1789 French Revolution, the seeds of which were sown by philosophers of the previous century, picked up by the intellectuals, nurtured by the masses, its fire kindled by opportunists and anarchists, its victims sacrificed in the name of liberty, equality, fraternity. The concept of the 'guillotine' had repulsed him and he wondered at the barbaric inventiveness of a man who would devise such a ghastly instrument in a country, which was, at the time, the epitome of civilization and refinement. As he read more accounts of the dramatic events that took place in France during the revolution, he noticed that the ingenuity of the torturers was diabolical. Surpassing the horror of the dreaded guillotine were the *Mariages de Nantes*, where victims marked for execution were tied together, a man and a woman, placed in a leaking barge as many as it could hold, and launched on the river where it would sink slowly drowning all aboard. Ultimately, all had come to naught, a moment of intense suffering borne by a nation who, in 1917 after relapses into royalty and short periods of empire, was once again in the throes of a new form of horror, as the First World War was in full swing. His observations about the French Revolution convinced him that despite its lofty aims, it had been in fact evil and destructive. He feared this Russian uprising might trigger similar movements elsewhere, and most of all he feared for Egypt.

"What is wrong, Basha?" asked Chafaq Hanim. "You are so pensive."

"News is not good, Chafaq Hanim, not good at all. These Bolsheviks are causing havoc in Russia."

"Upon your life, Basha. Why should that worry you? Russia is so far away. It has nothing to do with us."

"I would not say that. Revolutions are often contagious and there is a lot of unrest in Egypt—for different reasons, of course. Who knows if these events 'so far away,' as you say, won't have repercussions here?"

When the war in Europe finally ended with the armistice of 1918, Egypt's internal situation was tense. Relations with Britain took on a new dimension. Before the war nationalists demanded some sort of self-government. After the war nothing less than full sovereignty would be acceptable. In fact, right after Armistice Day on November 11, 1918, Sa'd Zagloul, the nationalist leader, 'Ali Sha'rawi Pasha, and 'Abd al-'Aziz Fahmi Bey, asked for an interview with Sir Reginald Wingate, the British High Commissioner, who received them on November 13. At that meeting, the Egyptian delegation "asserted that the ultimate aim of all Egyptians was complete independence. They considered themselves just as capable of independence as Bulgaria and Serbia, and more capable than the Arab States likely to be set up at the Peace Conference. . . . When [Wingate] inquired about this, the British government's answer was categoric. Britain had no intention of abandoning her responsibilities."[54]

There ensued an escalation in the tension that already existed between the nationalists and Great Britain. Sa'd Zaghloul, humiliated by Britain's refusal to let him represent Egypt at the Paris Peace Conference, rallied all nationalists to his cause. In March 1919, he and four other leaders were exiled to Malta. These were somber days for Egypt and Isma'il Sadiq's worst predictions were realized when, as a result of this treatment of Zaghloul by the British, the country was plunged in a revolution albeit much tamer than either the French or the Russian ones. But it was nevertheless a revolution. "In its violent stage, the rebellion was short but bloody. Because of the peasant resentment against the British, which had built up during the war, there were some serious atrocities. . . . About 1,000 Egyptians were believed to have been killed, while thirty-six British and civilians also lost their lives."[55] The crisis was fortunately short-lived and on April 7, 1919, Zaghloul was released and allowed to attend the conference. There, the setbacks for the Egyptians were tremendous. Over and above being snubbed by British authorities, they suffered a severe blow when on April 19, they and the rest of the world were informed that "The United States recognized the British Protectorate over Egypt. The champion of the doctrine of self-determination thus decisively destroyed the recently revived Egyptian hopes for an international settlement at the Peace Conference."[56]

Isma'il Sadiq was indignant and shared his countrymen's anger and frustration. Despite his respect and admiration for the British and his belief that "Progress for Egypt" was a better, more educated slogan than "Egypt for Egyptians," he rebelled against the duplicity of politicians, British and American alike. If his wife and daughters did not join other women who rushed out into the streets of Cairo in protest, it was not because they did not share in the popular sentiment but because propriety forbade it. It is interesting to note that in the provinces such scruples were less pronounced. Zaynab Hanim al-'Alayli, daughter of 'Abd al-Salam Bey al-'Alayli, one of the most prominent notables of Damietta, told the author that she as well as other ladies of the family, wearing *habara* and *petsha*, had run out in the streets to shout their support for Sa'd Zaghloul and his cause. When asked if her father, the venerable patriarch of the family, or her husband, had not attempted to prevent them, she immediately answered, "Of course not, in fact they encouraged us."

Meanwhile, Chafaq Hanim had agonized over another problem. Right after the end of the war, Fatma had sent word that she was pregnant again. Chafaq Hanim was overjoyed because more than eighteen months had elapsed since her daughter's miscarriage. But now, frightening events were taking place in the towns of Egypt and her husband held pessimistic views about the political situation. She feared that Fatma might well have to deliver her baby in Upper Egypt in mid-August with the temperature soaring to over forty-five degrees centigrade. In early 1918, 'Abd al-Rahman had been transferred to Girga and in recognition of his outstanding performance in Sohag was granted the title of bey, albeit of the second class. Despite her son-in-law's promotion that pleased her very much, Chafaq Hanim was alarmed by the transfer to Girga, which is further south on the Nile and even warmer than Sohag.

There was a definite release of tension when Zaghloul left for Paris, which helped alleviate Chafaq Hanim's worries. However, all was not well, as despite his presence in Paris, Zaghloul could not prevent the reaffirmation of Britain's presence in Egypt as stated in the Treaty of Versailles. Great Britain, in an attempt to deflate the mounting tension in Egypt, decided to send a mission there headed by Lord Milner. The mission was announced in March and arrived in Egypt on December 7. Prime Minister Muhammad Sa'id, as was his wont, preferred to resign than to face the inevitable clash that would occur between the nationalists and the British occupiers of the country. This is precisely what he did on November 15. Yusuf Pasha Wahbah, a Copt, both capable and honest, replaced him. The nationalists in Egypt had hoped that no one would accept the position so that the Milner Mission upon arrival would find itself stranded, as if it were in a country without a government. In any event, a boycott was declared and controlled by members of the Nationalist Party. It was in effect, as a historian later put it, "a refusal of all assistance to, or acceptance of, the objectionable authority."[57] No ministers, no politicians, no journalists, nobody in fact had any contact with Lord Milner's Mission or other British representatives.[58] Egyptians presented a wall of passive resistance to the much-discredited Mission. But calm was restored, for the time being at least, and in July Fatma and her husband were able to travel from Girga to Alexandria where on August 16, 1919 the baby was born. 'Ayn al-Hayah instantly became the center of 'Abd al-Rahman's life, the love of his heart, his most adored little girl. There was no disappointment at the sex of the child because all that mattered was that she had arrived safely.

Chafaq Hanim was totally engrossed in this new situation and consequently paid little attention to what was going on outside her home. It mattered little to her when Muhammad Sa'id became prime minister or when he resigned, though she was delighted when Isma'il Sirri, her husband's friend, became minister of war in the newly formed cabinet headed by Yusuf Pasha Wahbah. However, what pleased her more than anything, in fact made her intensely happy, was that 'Abd al-Rahman had finally been transferred to the Ministry in Cairo. She need no longer feel guilty at having kept her daughter in Munira after the summer holiday was over, using the pretext that the baby was too small to undertake such a long train voyage back to Girga.

"Surely you realize, 'Abd al-Rahman Bey, it could jeopardize her health," she had said, "Even perhaps endanger her life."

She knew that this would be an unbeatable argument and of course she secured his approval. Now everything was fine because Fatma had the right to be in Cairo. In the early months of 1920, 'Abd al-Rahman settled his family in a little villa on the Island of Zamalek. At about the same time, Isma'il Sadiq told his wife in confidence that he had finally found the blue bird, Hussein's future wife. Chafaq Hanim's heart skipped a beat; she knew how very important it was for the choice to be the right one. Hussein was not only more handsome than Muhammad but more intense and sensitive: an unhappy marriage could well destroy him. There was also the question of honor to be redeemed, the necessity to restore their public image somewhat tarnished by the rejection—no longer a secret in Egyptian society—of Muhammad by his Turkish wife. She had not considered Hazim's marriage, or even Fatma's for that matter, as sufficient reparation for the damage done. To her query about the girl's identity Sadiq Pasha answered, "She is the daughter of Muhammad Sa'd al-Din Pasha. . . ."

"Sa'd al-Din Pasha?" interrupted Chafaq Hanim. "But I thought you did not like him."

"Actually I don't but for reasons that should have no bearing on the choice of his daughter for Hussein. I know that his political attitudes differ from mine and that his ambition sometimes leads him astray, nevertheless he is an *ibn dhawat*.[59] I might not wish to give my daughter to his son because in that case my grandchildren would carry his name, but I would readily accept his daughter in our family. As you well know, Chafaq Hanim, it is the mother that counts in such cases and everyone knows that 'Adliyah Hanim is eminently respectable and, from what I have been told, has done an excellent job with her daughters."

"'How did you find that out, Basha?"

"From Yusuf Zaki Pasha, whose son is married to her sister."

"Yes, but isn't 'Adliyah Hanim a Turkish lady and haven't we decided not to enter again in a matrimonial alliance with Turks?"

"Well, I don't think we are because Sa'd al-Din Pasha is not Turkish. He is an Alexandrian Egyptian. Of course I cannot guarantee his origins up to the seventh generation, all I know is that he is not today a Turk like the 'Ilwis. What is more important in my view is that he belongs to our class, and as you said yourself often enough, in marriage one should not aim above or below one's state. Also, I believe that this girl will be good for Hussein, as she has been given a fine education."

"It seems to me, Basha, that you have made up your mind. May God bless your decision."

The Sa'd al-Din household was far more Europeanized than the Sadiq's. Though in straightened circumstances, they still lived in a very large villa in the residential neighborhood of Zizinia in Alexandria. Nadra was their second daughter. Zubaydah, her older sister, was married to Sherif Zaki, a young lawyer. Nadra was the prettier of the two in an exotic sort of way: very large dark eyes, a sensuous mouth, and very soft, jet-black hair that she wore cut short, as was the fashion in Europe in the 1920s. She was a very trendy sort of person, at least tried to be, and with her sister had attended the prestigious Dames de Sion convent in Alexandria. She was more emancipated than either Fatma or Anisah, and though she still wore a *habara* and a *petsha* she became one of the first women in the family to discard them. She spoke French and English fluently, Arabic not as well, and Turkish not at all—this language having been banned from their home by Sa'd al-Din Pasha in his moments of nationalist fervor. Nadra took pride in the fact that she could pass for one of the European girls she had known at school and whose parents were pillars of the Alexandrian society of the time. She was firmly convinced that to be European meant to be superior.

The Sa'd al-Dins, though more westernized than the Sadiqs, still upheld certain basic social customs, one of them being that under no circumstances could their daughters choose their own husbands. The girls led segregated lives, never met men outside the immediate family circle, where there were no eligible cousins of the right age, much to Nadra's regret, for she would have dearly wished to choose her own husband and make, to use a standard cliché of the time, *un mariage d'amour*. She was so Europeanized in her attitudes that she bristled at her parents' adherence to what she considered outmoded norms. However, there was nothing she could do about it because Sa'd al-Din Pasha was the standard authoritarian father who meant to be obeyed and always was. At any rate, however European the Sa'd al-Din family may have assumed themselves to be as a result of their frequent contact with the foreign communities of Alexandria, it was only an appearance, a surface coating, or, as a foreign diplomat once observed, a cosmetic uplifting to suit the time. When it came to the institution of marriage, traditional customs prevailed.

Nadra, who was two years younger than Zubaydah, had mulled at length over the issue; she thoroughly disliked her brother-in-law, perhaps because she had overheard that he was not too discreet about his extramarital activities and wished to live a different life from her sister's. She wanted to go out, entertain, and be entertained. She wanted to meet people, even those who did not necessarily belong to her milieu, and most of all she wanted to shine, proud as she was of her looks, her education, and her refined background. Suddenly, Hussein's proposal burst in her life like a meteor, frightening and yet illuminating. Through her parents, she had heard about Isma'il Sadiq's achievements and, unlike Malika, was flattered at having been selected by such a prominent family. She had heard her parents discuss the young man when they thought she was out of earshot. He was, she had learned, the bright one of the family, the one who had studied in France, and was the Pasha's favorite son, destined to a brilliant future. She was vastly relieved and her ego was gratified that her future husband-to-be could speak French and had learned the ways of the western world.

The marriage took place in Alexandria after which Hussein and Nadra settled down in a little house in Zamalek within walking distance from the Sallam's. Nadra was accepted in the family unreservedly because she was charming and different from Malika in almost every way: where Malika was aloof, she was warm; while Malika was shy and reserved, she was forthcoming; and where Malika clearly resisted entanglement with her Egyptian in-laws, Nadra welcomed it because they were a happy change from the austere and stiff-backed family to which she belonged. More important, she perceived immediately that she could 'shine' among them through her superior European education and her more sophisticated social behavior. These had actually been the reasons that had determined Isma'il Sadiq's choice for his son. He had been on the lookout for a young girl who would lend an active support to his son by being perfectly at ease with the more open society that was emerging in Egypt after the war; a girl like Dalia, though perfectly suited to Hazim, would have been a hindrance to Hussein because he needed a different setup, a more 'modern' one.

Nadra, at first dazzled by her new status and her own sense of superiority, committed the occasional faux pas for which she was rebuked, gently but firmly. The first was by far the most outrageous, according to the family, because it involved the Pasha and his deep-rooted self-respect. The incident took place a few weeks after Hussein and Nadra had returned from their honeymoon in Paris. In the course of a Friday lunch at Munira, Nadra, who had been feted by the family, had taken on a little air of superiority, which had immediately been noticed by Chafaq Hanim. She had said nothing at first but knew that sooner or later she would have to address the problem before it got out of hand. She needed to set her daughter-in-law on the right track and have her understand the delicate and intricate texture of family relationships. As it happened, it was the Pasha who took matters in hand on that fateful Friday. The whole family was gathered in the private sitting room in Munira and Nadra, who was seated in front of her father-in-law, suddenly crossed one leg over the other and assumed a casual deportment. The Pasha noticed Nadra's attitude but made no comment. His annoyance, however, was shared by Chafaq Hanim who was just as irritated as her husband and on the point of making a remark such as, "Nadra, please uncross your legs when sitting before your father-in-law." But she refrained from doing so because she was reluctant to upset her son and make an enemy of this girl who obviously meant no harm.

She also did not wish to compound the problem the family was experiencing with Malika and her impossible behavior. Fatma and Anisah who had never dared sit in this way in front of their parents were also shocked. Just as Chafaq Hanim was mulling over this problem, voices were heard in the hall and a moment later the Pasha's half-sister walked into the room. 'Ammiti Murganah, as the Sadiq children called her, was a tall, almost statuesque black woman. Her skin was the color of ebony and her hair, loosely covered with a veil, was absolutely frizzy and closely cropped. Her nose was slightly squat and her eyes small but widely set. She was a handsome woman with a dignified gait, an almost regal air.

"Morning of blessing, my brother. Morning of blessing, my brother's wife," she said.

The Pasha got up immediately went over to his sister and taking her by the hand led her to the armchair next to his. Chafaq Hanim got up as well, kissed her sister-in-law on both cheeks, and greeted her warmly.

"Chafaq *Yakhti*, before I sit down, let me greet the family." They had all stood up the moment she had entered the room, her nephews to kiss her hand and then her cheek, while 'Abd al-Rahman Bey bowed deeply as he took her hand. Fatma and Anisah were hugged warmly. She then looked around and addressing herself to Hussein asked, "And where is our bride?" Nadra had not moved, mesmerized by the fact that this black woman, whom she had at first assumed to be a maid, was related to the family. She was absolutely stupefied and when 'Ammiti Murganah walked over to her, she remained seated, one leg crossed over the other, and stuck her hand out to the older woman. The Pasha glared at his daughter-in-law, his usually light complexion took on a dark hue, and his piercing gray eyes like twin daggers bore on the young woman. Chafaq Hanim perceived her husband's mounting anger and, fearing an explosion, intervened immediately. "Nadra," she said, "come sit by your aunt Murganah. She would like to get to know you better." Nadra rose and walked over like a robot not quite believing what was happening to her. Who on earth was this woman? How could she be the Pasha's sister? And what had she done to provoke his anger? Being very intelligent, she had perceived that she had somehow angered him. Totally mystified and deeply shaken, she sat down next to the older woman who patted her hand and smiling gently said, "How beautiful your are, my dear. Hussein has indeed made a good choice. May God bless you both."

Hussein for his part was quite upset. He knew that Nadra had offended his father, albeit unwittingly, and feared the consequences. "My God, what a mess," he thought. "How will I ever make Baba forgive Nadra?" He was miserable because he had, in the few weeks of his marriage, fallen deeply in love with his beautiful, warm, fun-loving, and sophisticated wife, and was enchanted by his parents' choice. But now catastrophe had struck! And yet, this was one of the unavoidable clashes that often occur during the initial period of a new relationship. While the Sadiqs and the Sa'd al-Dins belonged essentially to the same milieu, there were differences, or nuances, in their respective rules of protocol. Nadra may have assumed that being now a married woman it was acceptable that she sit with one leg crossed over the other in front of an older person, while according to the more conservative Sadiqs it most certainly was not. Where she erred almost beyond repair was in having greeted 'Ammiti Murganah without standing up deferentially. The atmosphere in the room was charged. Fatma and Anisah, who were very fond of Nadra, regretted an incident that could have been avoided had the latter been forewarned. Had this been the case, Nadra would have undoubtedly behaved with her usual graceful cordiality. The very tense silence was broken by Sitt Murganah's gentle voice.

"Chafaq *Yakhti*, we are all very hungry. Is lunch not ready yet?"

During the meal, conversation resumed its normal tempo and the mood of genuine conviviality was gradually restored. While making her best to put up a brave front, Nadra was still shaken and confused. She kept going mentally over the whole unpleasant episode trying to understand its cause and evaluate the consequences. This had been for her an extremely brutal awakening. She had been so sure of her superiority, of her complete control of her situation within the framework of her new family, so convinced that she dominated them all by her charm, her sophistication, and her modern ways. Nadra was an intelligent person but she often misjudged situations or misunderstood people. This was due to the fact that though basically kind, she was also self-centered and viewed life through the spectrum of her own self-interest. She was deeply offended at finding out that she was now related through marriage to a colored person who furthermore dressed like her mother's head maid. How would she ever be able to explain her existence to her family and to her friends? Her condescending attitude had been a spontaneous response, an implicit rejection of a relationship for which she had been totally unprepared. Though distressed at having angered her father-in-law for whatever reason, she was also irritated. "I wonder what other surprises lie in store for me," she mulled, while listening absentmindedly to the animated conversation that took place around the table. Hazim was at his best, teased every one (except Nadra, of course, whom he felt instinctively was, for the moment, out of bounds) and ate as usual more than was good for him. Chafaq Hanim observed her daughter-in-law and whenever their eyes crossed, she would smile and press more food on her.

Back in the safety of her Zamalek home, Nadra immediately demanded an explanation.

"Hussein, why was your father so angry with me? What did I do wrong?"

"Two things, my dear, which might seem unimportant to you but are of paramount importance to my father, and if I may add, to my mother as well. First of all, you sat before him with one leg crossed over the other, and worse still, you did not get up to greet my aunt who is an older person. . . ."

"But Hussein," interrupted Nadra " surely she is not one of us?"

"Nadra," Hussein's tone was sharp, "never forget she is my father's sister and my blood relative from the strong line."[60]

"But how can that be? He is so fair and she is so black."

Hussein smiled touched by her confusion.

"Because my dear, our grandfather had an Ethiopian wife and 'Ammiti Murganah is her daughter, whereas my grandmother was Caucasian hence the difference in color. Have no fear, our children will not be black," he added jokingly.

"I never thought of that Hussein. It is just that I was surprised."

"You mean shocked, and I understand. It is my fault, I should have warned you. You see, Upper Egyptians, particularly Minyawis, are very strict in their rules of social behavior, so always remember never to offend a blood relative, never lack respect to an older person, and," he added with a smile, "never sit one leg crossed over the other in front of my parents."

Nadra nodded slowly as she realized the enormity of her mistake and the extent of the offense that she had unwittingly committed. However, her nature was such that the practical side of her character took over immediately so she asked: "Hussein, are there many more that I still don't know about?"

"Yes, all that branch of the family who are the offspring of my grandfather's Ethiopian wife. Though I dare say you will rarely meet them, if you do, remember to treat them nicely."

"Hazim is such a tease. Do you think he will bring this subject up next time we are at Munira?"

"You have nothing to fear. You are Hussein's wife and as such command everyone's respect."

Nadra never forgot this incident. She was sobered by it but her spirit was not broken because she was tough and, unlike Malika, eminently adjustable and on the whole rather fond of her new family.

Part Two

Cultural Encounters

12

"What happened, Basha? What happened? Is it true the prime minister has been killed?"

"No, Chafaq Hanim. He is safe and so is Isma'il Sirri."

"But what happened?" She asked again.

"A bomb was thrown at his carriage by an anarchist, or a revolutionary, or perhaps a madman. No one knows yet and the situation in town is troubled."

"How will it end, Basha?"

"God only knows."

"I wonder why Wahbah Pasha was targeted for such an attack? He is a mild reasonable man and has not sullied his hands by condemning his countrymen as Boutros Ghali has done. That one, God forgive me, truly deserved what he got, for it is said in the Qur'an: 'He who kills will also be killed, no matter how long it takes.'"

"Come, come, Chafaq Hanim. The verse in the Qur'an refers to murderers and Boutros Ghali did not murder anyone but acted in all good faith as his conscience dictated. But to answer your question, any number of reasons could be behind this attack: frustration at a weak government headed by a Copt, anti-Coptic sentiment in general, anger over the long protracted negotiations that seem to be at a standstill, anti-British sentiment, and who knows what else. Hotheads have accused Yusuf Basha of being a traitor to our cause because he accepted the position of prime minister after Muhammad Sa'id Basha's resignation. But the sad news is that Isma'il Sirri has resigned as minister of public works. I regret his decision because he is an extremely capable and honest man and now people will assume that his decision was prompted by fear, which is not the case at all. You see, he was in the carriage with Yusuf Basha when the bomb exploded. 'Abd al-Rahman saw him after the attack and says he was totally unmoved. No, what apparently troubles him deeply is this whole business of the Nile water distribution; he insists an Egyptian should be member of the Nile Water Commission and I share his views absolutely."

"The British are truly impossible, Basha. First they come here under the pretext of protecting the foreign community and bring order to the place, then they declare a protectorate—whether we want to be protected or not—and now they want to interfere with our water. Amazing!"

"Don't be too harsh in your judgments, Chafaq Hanim. Not all British are as arrogant as Cromer or Kitchener. There are good men among them such as Willcocks—who incidentally is in disagreement with his own government over their handling of our affairs— Charles Kenneth Scott-Moncrieff, William Garstin, Wilfrid Scawen Blunt, and many others. These men gave us a great deal Chafaq Hanim. Never forget it."

"Well, perhaps you are right. Do you have news of 'Ali, Basha?"

"Yes, I received a letter this morning and meant to tell you about it. He is well and enjoys—so he says—life in Edinburgh. I hope he follows in your father's footsteps, though I know it won't be easy."

'Ali, Isma'il Sadiq's fourth son, had left for Scotland right after his brother's wedding to study medicine at Edinburgh University. He had his future all planned: first his degree, then his marriage to Karimah Wasfi, whom he had known all his life, and then a medical career in Egypt in which he hoped to emulate his grandfather. It seems strange. that in the early 1920s a young man could marry his childhood sweetheart or even have one in the first place. Actually, this was not exactly the case. Hamid Pasha Wasfi, Karimah's father, was a close friend of Isma'il Sadiq, and his wife, Zaynab Hanim, was a friend of Chafaq Hanim. Both ladies visited one another very often and Zaynab Hanim had always deplored the fact that, though she had been married for over fifteen years, she had never been able to have a child. One day when it was least expected, she announced with tremendous pride that she was pregnant. This happiness, however did not last long. She died giving birth and Hamid Pasha, who was well over fifty and disconsolate, vowed never to marry again but to devote all his attention to his only child. He hired maids to take care of the baby but, because he was not experienced in that area, he often employed women who were gross and whose vocabulary left much to be desired. When the child was about five years old, Chafaq Hanim would often fetch her to spend the day at Munira with Anisah who was of the same age. The first time she came, Chafaq Hanim noticed immediately that she was not well taken care of. She had stains on her dress, her shoes were not polished, and worst of all, she used a vocabulary that was totally unacceptable for a little girl of her milieu.

Appalled by this state of affairs, she decided that something ought to be done to safeguard her friend's daughter. There was little she could do actually short of taking the child to live at Munira, which of course would have been unacceptable to Hamid Pasha. She opted for the next best solution, which was to have her over as often as possible and, at the same time, persuaded her father to enroll her at the Mère de Dieu Convent in hope that the good nuns would, somehow, instill in her the rudiments of refinement and proper behavior. This solution worked well enough for some years as long as the children were small. Karimah was a very clever little thing, bright as can be, full of mischief, and perfectly at ease in Munira. The older boys, Hazim in particular, liked to tease her and the younger ones, 'Ali and Muhsin, were amused by her antics and enjoyed having her around. Over the years, a problem inevitably arose; the older Sadiq boys were getting married but the younger ones, both handsome and eligible, were still living at home. It was socially unacceptable for a young girl to be frequently seen in a house where bachelors lived; her reputation would be damaged, as her presence there was unexplainable. As far as Chafaq Hanim was concerned, the solution to the problem was self-evident: Karimah would have to be 'spoken for' by one of the boys.

"The time has come, Basha, for us to do something about Karimah."

"What do you mean, Chafaq Hanim?"

"We must ask Hamid Basha for her hand in marriage."

"In marriage, Chafaq Hanim? But she is still a child."

"Of course, I do not mean for her to marry now but simply to come to an agreement with her father, an informal *Fatiha* perhaps. Unless we do that people will talk."

"Talk about what, Chafaq Hanim?" asked her husband bemused.

"What is happening to you, Basha? Don't you see the problem?

Unless she has an official status she can no longer come freely to our house. It would damage her reputation because we have boys in the house."

"Fine, fine, you are right. We shall give her to Muhsin. He is the youngest and by the time he is ready to marry she will be ready as well."

"Muhsin? Of course not. It is 'Ali I have in mind."

"But 'Ali is leaving for Edinburgh; he will never agree to be tied down before going off for a number of years to study. I have been through this experience and know how frustrating it can be."

"Times have changed, Basha. Besides, of the two, 'Ali will be, I believe, more compliant. I have often noticed that he is amused by her funny remarks and he seems to enjoy her company. Muhsin is much more aloof. Karimah does not interest him in the least. But the more important reason for my choice is that she is dark and plain, 'Ali is dark as well, whereas Muhsin is fair and the most handsome of all our sons. It is never good for a plain girl to marry a handsome boy: he will look down upon her and the marriage will be a failure."

"Have it your own way, Chafaq Hanim; I see you have made up your mind and I must admit you do have valid reasons. I fully agree that she is a very good match. Her mother, may her soul rest in peace, was well-born and her father is one of the outstanding men of our generation. We could not have wished for a better or more honorable *nasab*."

'Ali, when approached by his mother voiced no objection. In fact, he rather liked the idea of marrying this funny little thing who was always at Munira with his sisters. He wisely assumed that since he had known her for so long the risk of a nasty surprise was greatly diminished. Soon after, an informal agreement was reached between Isma'il Sadiq and his friend Hamid Pasha, though nothing official could be done for the moment because Karimah was still too young, and 'Ali was off for a few years. However, Chafaq Hanim made it her business to spread the news 'discreetly' and ensure that anyone who mattered was apprised of this happy development in the Sadiq household.

Karimah was delighted! As she grew up, her looks improved noticeably. Her figure was lovely and whatever she still lacked was amply compensated for by her wit and sparkling gaiety. While she made an effort to refine her language, particularly when at Munira, she could not hide the fact that she also had a little streak of malice that occasionally would show itself in her relationship with people. Anyway, these were minor defects in the overall picture and, as Chafaq Hanim pointed out, "No one is perfect and what we know is better than what we don't know."

'Ali left for Edinburgh in the fall of 1919 and a year later Muhsin left for France to study law at the Sorbonne. Chafaq Hanim felt that, for the moment, her home front was well organized. She had accepted Khadiga's situation since there was nothing she could do to either change or improve it. As for Muhammad, he had reverted to his bachelor life but did not mention divorce, which was just as well. A very harmonious relationship was developing between the Sallam and the Hussein Sadiq families. Fatma and Nadra got along very well and 'Abd al-Rahman, though about ten years older than Hussein, was on friendly terms with him. Both men were engineers and both were pursuing the same career as irrigation inspectors, the main difference between them was that while 'Abd al-Rahman, like his father-in-law before him, had no political ambitions and was primarily a technocrat, Hussein definitely had political inclinations. He may have perceived that only through politics could he surpass his brother-in-law, perhaps even his father.

By 1920, 'Abd al-Rahman had established his reputation as a remarkably capable engineer. At Isma'il Sirri's insistence, he became a member of the Nile Water Commission and in 1921 was part of the official delegation headed by Adly Yeghen Pasha that went to London to discuss the question of Egypt's independence. In 1923 he was awarded the Order of the Nile, received the title of Pasha and was offered membership at the Gezira Sporting Club. These successes of course spurred on Hussein who was determined to emulate his brother-in-law and, if not surpass him, at the very least catch up with him. Meanwhile, both young couples had a trait in common: neither of them had been able as yet to produce a son. In 1923, Hussein and Nadra had their first daughter, Nadia, followed in 1925 by another, Yasmine, while Fatma's second daughter, 'Alia, was also born in 1925, and a third, 'Abir, eighteen months later.

This succession of girls was perceived by Chafaq Hanim as just punishment for the Tutankhamen episode. When Howard Carter and the Earl of Carnarvon discovered the tomb, Chafaq Hanim did not attach a great importance to the event because as she pointed out, Egypt seems to be one vast cemetery with tombs everywhere, none of which so far had surpassed the Giza Pyramids. However, when on November 26, 1922, Isma'il Sadiq announced that he would attend the opening of the tomb as part of the Egyptian delegation, which consisted of Prince Omar Toussoun, Adly Yeghen Pasha, Isma'il Sirri Pasha, Tewfik Nesim Pasha, Hussein Rushdy Pasha, 'Abd al-Khaliq Saroit Pasha, Isma'il Sidki Pasha, and 'Abd al-Hamid Soliman Pasha, she went up in arms.

"Upon my life, Basha," she begged her husband. "Don't go to this opening. It will bring a curse upon us."

"What are you talking about, Chafaq Hanim? This is an archaeological exploration. This tomb will reveal a big chunk of history."

"Nevertheless, Basha. Tutankhamen was a human being and he must be allowed to rest in peace until Judgment Day. If you attend this opening, you will bring a curse upon us."

"Nonsense, Chafaq Hanim. This is idle talk. Of course Tutankhamen was a human being. Who would deny it? But," he added with a twinkle, "he was not a Muslim. He did not believe in the one God, so perhaps taking a peek at his tomb won't be so terrible!"

"I give you my life, Basha, if you would desist. Nothing good will come out of this affair and we shall all be punished."

"Knowledge of the future is God's alone," answered her husband sternly and with this pronouncement the subject was closed. However, Chafaq Hanim's discomfort endured. She refused to listen to the description of the event that Isma'il Sadiq later gave to the family. Instead, she went to her room to pray and ask God's forgiveness for what she still considered a sacrilege. With the birth of four granddaughters in the family in quick succession, she became absolutely convinced that was the price they had to pay.

In any event, Fatma did not concern herself with the issue as she had a more pressing problem on her hands: she was unable to nurse her third baby. She had no milk at all and the newborn was crying pitifully. A professional wet-nurse had to be found immediately. This was not as difficult as it might appear for in those days women of the upper echelons of society often chose not to breast feed and since baby formulas were not yet available, wet-nurses from the poorer classes were eager to supply the service. They were for the most part unfortunate

women whose babies had died at birth or shortly after, and whose supply of milk could, for a fee, be put to good use. The ideal wet-nurse
was quickly found. Farhah was the family driver's sister-in-law, whose
baby had just succumbed after a short unexplained illness, and whose
breasts were so full of milk that it was flowing all over the front of her
gallabiya. She was a very simple-minded and kindly girl whose heart
was full of grief for her lost infant, but also full of love, as the death of
her child had not killed in her the natural instinct of motherhood. It
is said that the first time she ever crossed Boulaq Bridge was the day
the Pasha's driver came to fetch her for her interview with the family. On that day, she wore her only good *gallabiya* made of shiny pink
satin with a cut across the front and falling very loosely around her
ample body. Her head was tightly covered by a kerchief and she was
wrapped in her *milaya,* holding one side under her elbow and the tip
of the other side drawn over her face. On her feet were her good soft
leather slippers, the ones she kept for special occasions.

Farhah was grieving at the loss of her baby but she had reasoned
with herself and decided that since it was God's will that the child
die so quickly after its birth, it was written and such was her fate.
Besides, the baby was just a girl, and she would surely have been
more distraught had it been a boy. She could not understand her
mother and her grandmother who always said that girls bring
abundance and prosperity to a home, and yet were only happy
when the newborn was a boy. Anyway her little girl, though dead,
did send her a good armload of prosperity, for she was now in the
Pasha's car, being driven across the river to live in a beautiful house
where her only duty would be to eat her fill and produce good
milk for the Pasha's baby. She smiled at the prospect, already visu-
alizing the lovely roast chicken, the *ful midammis* covered with a
thick layer of *tihina,* the rice puddings, and the many other delica-
cies that would be her daily fare. Milk, she would drink gallons of.
She loved milk with a large spoonful of honey and surely the
Pasha's wife knew that the best milk-producing beverage was
almond syrup. She had never tasted almond syrup but had been
told by the midwife that refined ladies who nurse their baby always
had some before breast-feeding.

Most of the food she fantasized about she rarely ate, for how
could she have afforded it? Had her baby lived, her meals would

have consisted of a plate of *ful* with one large onion, one loaf of bread dipped in milk and a glass of *hilba* brew, which was known to be, like almond syrup, an excellent beverage for nursing mothers. Anyway, she had no problem with her milk production, in fact, right now she was soaked. Usta Hasan, her brother-in-law, had explained that this was just an interview and that she would get the job only if the Pasha and Sitt Hanim liked her, and more important still, if she passed all her medical tests. She had no idea what they would be looking for since she felt perfectly well, had a healthy appetite, and had enough milk for two babies let alone one. Suddenly a horrifying thought crossed her mind: maybe they were looking into the cause of her baby's death? Surely it was not her fault, it was written. What is written on the brow, the eye must see, and there was no way that either she, the Pasha, his wife, or the doctor could have altered what had been decreed by fate. She was suddenly deeply disturbed.

"*Ya* Abu 'Ali, what is the medical examination for? What are they trying to discover? What will they do to me?"

"You are going to have blood tests to determine if you are carrier of a disease that could be transferred to the child through your milk. Also the Pasha will want to know if you are suffering from tuberculosis."

"What is tuberculosis, *ya* Abu 'Ali?"

"It is the sickness of the lungs."

"Oh that! Of course I don't have tuberculosis. I have never coughed in my life."

"Well then you have nothing to fear. Anyway, we have reached our destination."

The moment she walked into the house, she was overwhelmed by the size of the place. She had never imagined that rooms that size existed, that ceilings could soar so high, that floors, though made of wood, could shine like marble and reflect the rays of the sun that came through the open window. Usta Hasan should have taken her up through the back stairs reserved for the servants but he had wanted to impress her and show off the opulence of his employer. However, he knew that he was not allowed on the first floor where the family had their private quarters, therefore, he crossed the main hall followed by a stupefied Farhah, and went to the pantry where

Idris, the head *sufraji*, was busy sorting out china and cutlery in preparation for the family lunch.

"*Salam*, Idris. Where is Umm Muhammad?"

"*Wa 'alaykum*, Usta Hasan. Is this the wet-nurse?"

"Yes, take her up. They are waiting for her."

"Right away. I am told the baby has cried all night long." Turning to Farhah, he said, "Come with me. I'll take you to Sitt Hanim."

Farhah followed Idris who took her up through the back stairs to the first floor. He crossed a small hall and knocked at a door, which opened immediately and there stood Umm Muhammad, Fatma Hanim's head maid.

"What is it, Idris?"

"The wet-nurse is here."

Having said that, he retreated behind Farhah and gently pushed her toward Umm Muhammad, his mission accomplished.

"Come in, woman. Don't just stand there!"

Farhah obeyed and walked into the most beautiful room she had ever seen. Her attention however was immediately distracted by the pitiful wailing of a tiny infant lying in a crib that looked like a wedding dress, all frills and lace. She walked over without so much as a glance to the baby's mother, removed the muslin netting, picked up the infant, and opening the front of her *gallabiya* pushed an overflowing nipple into its tiny mouth. Umm Muhammad gasped in horror. She would have snatched the baby away had not Fatma Hanim interfered immediately.

"Let her be, Umm Muhammad. The baby is starving."

"But, Sitt Hanim, she is not clean. We have to give her a bath, check her hair for lice. Should the Pasha come to hear what has just happened, he will be very angry."

Umm Muhammad was furious. Farhah had overstepped the set boundaries of servant hierarchy and taken matters into her hands in a cavalier fashion, disregarding the fact that she, Umm Muhammad, was the head maid hence in a position of authority, and that all the maids including the wet-nurse were under her jurisdiction and had to refer to her in all matters. She glared at the woman squatting on the floor but held her tongue knowing that she would have ample time later to straighten up matters in her own way and teach this newcomer her place.

Utter silence reigned in the room for about ten minutes. During that time, Farhah never lifted her eyes from the baby's face imagining all the while that she was holding her own little girl in her arms. Her milk flowed freely and with it all the pent up emotions and maternal instincts that had lain dormant since her baby's death. Finally, little 'Abir fell asleep and Farhah gently put her back in her cot. She then turned round to face her employer and Umm Muhammad.

"What is your name?" asked Fatma Hanim gently.

"Farhah, Sitt Hanim."

"That is a nice name. We will not change it. Umm Muhammad, take her with you and attend to her needs. You know what must be done."

"Certainly, *sitti*, but how about the tests and the medical examination?"

"It will be taken care of. Don't worry. But now give her a meal, a bath, and clean clothes."

Umm Muhammad left the room followed by Farhah. A while later she came back to report that the woman had eaten an enormous breakfast, had been scrubbed from top to toe by Umm Muhammad herself, and that she had no lice for the simple reason that she did not have a single hair on her body. Umm Muhammad had never seen anything like it. The woman's head was as sleek as an ostrich's egg. Upon hearing this, the Pasha burst out laughing and said: "Well that is one less problem to worry about!"

Eventually, Farhah passed all the tests with flying colors. She was indeed a very healthy person endowed with an enormous appetite and a pleasant disposition. Feeding herself, producing milk, and in turn feeding the baby became her daily occupation, punctuated by long stretches of dreamless sleep. She loved her life in Zamalek and got along very well with the staff. Umm Muhammad's initial resentment soon disappeared because Farhah was an obedient and simple woman who never questioned the head maid's authority. So, in the fall of 1926, she became part of the Sallam household. This household had grown substantially over the years with three children and probably more to come as both 'Abd al-Rahman and Fatma made no secret of their desire to have a son.

Over and above the servants, in a category all her own, was the family governess. By the time Farhah appeared on the scene, Madame Duprée had been with the family a little over three years.

She was a tall, heavy boned French woman with steel-gray eyes and brown hair tied back in a chignon. After an unhappy marriage to a young French officer who, at any rate, was killed in the war leaving her penniless, she left her native France in 1919 following the trail of so many English, French, German, and Italian women who after World War I fled the poverty and destruction of their homeland and sought refuge with rich families in Egypt. In 1923, when ʿAyn al-Hayah was four years old, Madame Duprée was hired by ʿAbd al-Rahman Sallam to teach his eldest daughter the French language and generally take care of her. Madame Duprée was a strict disciplinarian with well-defined sets of ideas and a powerful will to enforce them. Her jurisdiction over the child would have been restrictive had not the Pasha set firm rules from the start and explained that she was not meant to replace the parents but simply help them educate the child and that they, not she, would always be the final authority in all matters concerning discipline. As he was very perceptive, he had immediately sensed that Madame Duprée could, if given a free hand, be dogmatic and overly strict. He had hired her, nevertheless, because he had seen in her the perfect governess who would teach his daughter what he considered essential for the offspring of an ambitious and successful cabinet minister: namely good manners and good French.

13

'Abd al-Rahman Sallam's initiative to hire a foreign governess for his daughters was not unique in Egypt at the time. From the turn of the century to the early 1950s, there was in Cairo a group of foreign women who were very much part of the Egyptian social scene. These were the foreign governesses, the *khawaga*s, as the Egyptian servants called them. In Zamalek, these ladies—for this is how they thought of themselves and more often than not quite rightly so—fell roughly into two distinct national classifications: the French *gouvernante* and the English lady companion with the occasional German Frau. The phenomenon was triggered off on the one hand by the desire of a rising upper class in Egypt to Europeanize themselves, and on the other hand by the penury that struck the French, English, or German middle classes as an aftermath of World War I. Egypt in the early years of the century was flourishing. The British had established a successful system of government and the educated Egyptian elite was quite ready to receive this 'foreign aid' that added an element of glamour and refinement to their households.

The reasons for which the ladies opted for Egypt could be explained in a variety of ways. For one thing the climate was good, certainly preferable to India's. The families they worked for were, if not totally westernized, certainly refined, therefore adaptation was not difficult. The pay was usually adequate, and the lure of the Orient had become almost irresistible after Khedive Isma'il's spectacular extravaganzas of the Suez Canal inauguration. It seemed to these ladies that this Egyptian monarch was a modern Croesus who had invited all the crowned heads of Europe to attend the ceremonies and displayed for them the dazzling opulence of an oriental prince whose lavish generosity seemed unlimited. For the British contingent, there was the added attraction that Egypt was occupied by Britain. They felt at home there, secure in the knowledge that a Cromer, a Kitchener, or later a Sir Miles Lampson reigned supreme and guaranteed their safety and the continuance of a certain British way of life in this outpost of the Empire. Even though they were just governesses working for Egyptian families, they were first and foremost British citizens and therefore assumed to be superior. They identified with the Agency and basked in the reflected glory it offered them.

Whether French or English, the governesses were hired to perform essentially the same duties. They were employed to teach their charges the governess's native language as well as give basic instruction until the children were old enough to go to school. Thereafter they would stay on to teach them good manners and instill in their young minds the love and admiration one ought to have for one's own country but which often enough turned out to be that of the governess! The children, for the most part, accepted their presence and never questioned what might have been considered an oddity, for in many cases the governesses became surrogate mothers. The system worked, but through it the children often developed dual identities: they were little French children or little English children, as the case might be, but they were also Egyptian children speaking, when the need arose, their own native language and absorbing their own culture, albeit to a more limited degree.

In some cases, the dichotomy was profound because the partitioning of influence was not even, with the result that the children identified with and became more attuned to the foreign element they admired in the person of the sophisticated governess, and turned away from the native background which by their nationality they actually shared with the maids and other domestic servants in the house. If, in addition, they were sent to a foreign language school, the problem of identity would often become serious: were they Egyptian children with a European mentality or European children with an Egyptian passport? For the generations of the 1930s, 40s, and 50s, the sense of not quite belonging became acute and tore at their psyches. Some learned to live with it. Others rejected their own background to adopt the foreign one, or, following the exigencies of the day, on the contrary, plunged headlong into a wholehearted embrace of whatever was native, firmly turning their back on what they considered an error of education.

The impact of governesses on girls was far greater than on boys. When a boy reached the age of twelve to fourteen, families usually decided that he should no longer be under the tutelage of a woman. For a girl, however, the governess was an essential appendage, a presence she would have to accept willingly, or contend with, until she married. The reason, of course, is that it would have been unthinkable in those days to allow a girl out of the house unaccompanied. Families who employed governesses believed very strongly in the necessity to respect decorum and it was the accepted convention that daughters of well-to-do families be chaperoned wherever they went as an indication of their social rank. In the late nineteenth and early twentieth centuries, girls hardly ever went out, but as society developed under the impact of modernization and emancipation gained ground, women ventured out more often. At first, muffled to the eyes, they would be accompanied by a eunuch; gradually the eunuch was replaced by an elderly maid of the house who, in turn, was replaced by the governess.

Until the 1950s, girls usually accepted this state of affairs, in fact they derived a certain smug pleasure at being seen in the company of these refined ladies unlike some of their acquaintances whose families either could not afford to employ a foreign governess or were not sufficiently westernized to feel the need to do so. In these cases it was the native maid who was the companion. Hence the governess, French, British, or German, was an educator, a lady companion, and a status symbol. If few appear on the scene in the early years of the twentieth century, by the 1930s and 40s, with war raging in Europe once again, their numbers grew. On the island of Zamalek in the first half of the century there were many such ladies employed in Egyptian households. Mooro Pasha, the eminent surgeon, had Mademoiselle Philippe for his boys; Kamel Pasha Nabih, who lived two streets away, had Madame Gantes; Hussein Sirri Pasha, several times prime minister during the reign of King Farouk, had Miss Griffith (who had replaced Mademoiselle Carère, the later having gone to work for the Attal family). The Assems had Mademoiselle Mariette; 'Abd al-Hamid al-Shawarby Pasha had Miss

Blygh; 'Abd al-Hamid Soliman Pasha had Madame Gollmer, who replaced Mademoiselle Marguerite, and was followed in rapid succession by Miss Grey, Miss Wheelen, Mrs. Donovan, and finally Miss Florence Maddock. Though not in Zamalek, there was also at the time a delightful French woman, Madame Ponsot, who worked for the Hussein Bey Foda family. Madame Ponsot became an institution among Egyptian families, as did the Soliman's Madame Gollmer.

These women had one thing in common: they were expatriates. Otherwise they differed not only in character and nationality but in the social milieu to which they originally belonged. Some came from an impoverished middle class, some from impoverished nobility, some were staunch Victorians in their attitudes, others dedicated republicans or fervent royalists. Armed with their individual personalities and backgrounds, they came to Egypt determined to earn a good living, enjoy a comfortable existence, establish their authority as dispensers of a superior culture, and generally redeem their egos from the frustrations of a life of genteel poverty in Europe. All of them made one basic adjustment: even though they functioned as teachers and felt superior because they were European, they accepted the status of hired help in an oriental family, thereby falling into a lesser category. The system, on the whole, worked rather well. They taught manners and a language and in return received security and recognition.

Friendships among governesses developed, as did enmities. Their relationships depended very much on the families for whom they worked and their social life was extremely limited since they were granted one afternoon off a week (and Sunday morning, if they wished to go to church). Their social activity was conditioned by and dependent upon that of the family for whom they worked, which meant that these French, English, or German ladies were often in each other's company regardless of their personal preferences. Their life was totally taken up by the family. In a certain sense they identified with it, lived its life, shared its joys and sorrows, and felt that they belonged. In most cases their devotion was beyond question. However, there would occasionally be the odd one out, the cruel, overbearing, arrogant, or supercilious foreigner who would antagonize the family to such an extent that she would be summarily dismissed.

That is precisely what happened to Miss Ashby, the first British governess employed by 'Abd al-Rahman Sallam. This was the summer of 1936 and Madame Duprée having decided to take a one-month vacation in France, the Pasha felt that a 'British interlude' would benefit his children. He interviewed Miss Ashby, was quite pleased by her appearance, her refined manners, her poise. Very soon, however, he realized that while she had the necessary qualifications for the job, she lacked refinement of the mind. He gradually became irritated by her affectation, her haughtiness, and her constant stressing of British superiority. Though he admired British refinement, way of life, sense of duty, and discipline, he did not for one moment lose sight of his own worth as an Egyptian gentleman. He did not want his children to develop a subservient attitude toward what Miss Ashby considered a superior brand of humanity. They were the Pasha's children, brought up in the tradition of their country, among their people, and Miss Ashby was merely an added element in the décor that surrounded their daily existence. Furthermore, as he pointed out to his wife, Fatma Hanim, politics in whatever shape or form ought not to be part of their education—not yet, at any rate. With every passing day his irritation increased.

"The woman is a fool," he told his wife, "and a bore. She has no sense of humor and spends all her waking hours trying to perfect her role of memsahib. I think we should get rid of her."

"Well, we are soon leaving for Europe and Madame Duprée is meeting us in Marseilles. It won't be much longer now so we may as well put up with her until we leave."

"Very well, I just hope she will not push me beyond endurance."

Matters came to a head one morning through an incident mischievously provoked by the Pasha himself. Miss Ashby and the children were having breakfast, a meal that she considered of prime importance in the course of which porridge, eggs, toast, and marmalade were consumed, accompanied by tea for herself and hot chocolate for the children. She was about to take her first sip when the Pasha, still in his bathrobe, poked his head through the dining room door and said, "Good morning, Miss . . ."

The sentence was cut short by a gasp, almost a wail from the governess who stretched her back as far as it would go and uttered, "Pasha, in your bathrobe!"

At that point, the Pasha pushed the door wide open, entered the room, took his place at the head of the table and calmly poured himself a cup of tea. Miss Ashby sprung up as if bitten by a scorpion and throwing her napkin on the table, marched out of the dining room, her head held high, her back ramrod straight, followed by the mesmerized gaze of the children. Having finished his cup of tea, the Pasha went to his study and prepared an envelope, which was delivered by Idris on a silver tray. It contained Miss Ashby's salary and a curt note of dismissal. That was the inglorious end of Miss Ashby in the Sallam household.

Cases such as this were not frequent and usually occurred when the relationship between employer and employee was not based on mutual respect. The cotton-boom class of nouveaux riches that sprung up after World War I, desiring to better themselves, occasionally resorted to the employment of governesses; the latter, however were usually not impressed and looked down upon families who lived as peasants in imposing houses. Besides, it was mostly unqualified women who accepted such posts, their basic claim to refinement being the knowledge of a foreign language. Because of the new craze for English-speaking governesses, employment was available and the lack of discrimination on the part of the ignorant employer was often matched by the lack of discretion of the employee. Anna Cacchia, in her memoirs published by her son in 1999, tells of her experience as governess in an Upper Egyptian family of Asyut in the early 1930s.

When she first entered the house, she was awed by the elegance of the reception rooms, which glittered with gilded wood furniture, the high ceilings, and the numerous vases filled with fresh flowers. However, as soon as she walked up to the first floor and entered the living quarters, she was struck by the surrounding squalor and when she was taken down to visit the kitchen, shock turned to horror when she saw the multitude of cockroaches that swarmed everywhere in broad daylight, and the indifference of the servants who did not seem to mind either the filth or the crawling insects. If, sixty years later, she still remembered the culture shock of this first encounter with an Egyptian family, one can well imagine what she must have told her friends at the time. Of course, one cannot generalize, and loyalty, or the lack of it, must have varied from one person to the other, but one can fairly assume that whenever the selection was made in the right and proper way, chances of a harmonious relationship between employer and employee were very good. This was usually the case with almost all the families who lived in Zamalek in the 1930s and 40s.

Snobbery was often evident among governesses. They gloated if their employer was a pasha, still more if a cabinet minister or someone related to the royal family. This attitude, unfortunately, often had its impact on the children who would find themselves caught up in a confusing situation: on the one hand they were constantly reminded of the virtue of humility, while on the other they were instructed always to keep in mind their parents' elevated position. Miss Griffith, for instance, would often tell her charge "never forget my dear that you are a pasha's daughter and cousin to the Queen, therefore, not all girls you meet at school can be invited in your home. They are of a 'different' milieu." By 'different,' she meant 'inferior.' Madame Gollmer, who worked for the Soliman Pasha family, often exhibited the same intransigent attitude, consequently the Soliman children found themselves living in a rarefied atmosphere. The governesses' argument was that it was their duty to protect the children from contamination, social or otherwise, which could be brought on by contact with the wrong people.

To be fair, in the Soliman family, Madame Gollmer's snobbery was often curtailed by the Pasha himself or his wife. One such incident took place when their youngest daughter was about seven years old. They were all at the farm in Mahalla al-Kubra to spend the Easter holiday. The house at Mahalla was a two-story building of modest proportions with running water but no electricity. Madame Gollmer did not enjoy the place but the children loved it, as it was such a wonderful change from their Zamalek way of life. There, they lived much closer to their parents and discipline was more lax. As was usually the case, the supervisor came to pay his respects and receive his orders. He was told to gather all the children whose parents were employed at the farm and have them line up in the garden. The Pasha then asked Madame Gollmer to come down with her charges for them to distribute candies and sugared almonds to the little peasants. Madame Gollmer was appalled. How could she allow the children to get close to these unwashed, evil-smelling little urchins! Yet, she knew that these instructions were not to be discussed let alone disobeyed. Therefore, with a heavy heart, she stoically marched down to the garden holding each child firmly by the hand, and there was met by a chorus of piping voices.

The little girl, sensing her governess's disapproval, was not happy. When told by her father to take a handful of candies and give it to one of the children who was waiting, hand extended, dirty palm up, she recoiled in horror and said, "*Oh non, il est trop sale*—Oh no, he's too dirty." Her father frowned ever so slightly and said quietly, "*Donne-lui une poignée de bonbons, il est un être humain comme toi*—Give him a handful of sweets. He's a human being like you." His stern tone was rendered more compelling by the fact that he never scolded and rarely showed disapproval. He did not raise his voice but conveyed through his quiet determination the necessity to be obeyed. The girl did as she was told, not out of fear but through the sudden awareness that her initial reaction had been the wrong one and that she needed to redeem herself in front of her father. She never forgot this lesson in humility and probably neither did Madame Gollmer.

Friction frequently erupted between governesses, particularly between those of different nationalities. The English ones upheld the British way of life, the 5:00 PM tea ritual often derided by the French, the dressing up for dinner and the stiff upper lip attitude they were determined to teach their charges. The French ones, on the other hand, stressed the importance of calligraphy and the use of florid language. Euphemisms were encouraged since well-bred young ladies should never utter certain words. Fortunately for the Soliman and the Sallam girls, Madame Gollmer's and Madame Duprée's good common sense ruled out exaggerated daintiness. Both categories of ladies, the British and the French, were sticklers where table manners were concerned. Madame Gollmer, for instance, always insisted that children ask permission to drink at meals and the question had to be worded in the following way: "Madame, I have wiped my mouth. May I drink?"

To which the answer would invariably be, "Yes, you may, but wipe your mouth afterwards as well."

Madame Gollmer, who had befriended Madame Duprée and was often considered the doyenne of this little corporation probably because of her powerful personality, was quite a character. French by birth and German through marriage, she had been widowed young, yet retained throughout her life a profound admiration for her husband's country and anything Teutonic. She was an extremely able and intelligent woman, totally devoted to the family, a strict disciplinarian with definite opinions about almost anything under the sun, a determined educator who gave the children a cultural polish they would not have obtained at school. Her impact on them was tremendous and, oddly enough, on some of their friends as well. Antagonism between her and other governesses was unavoidable because she was strong-willed, domineering, and often dogmatic. She would dismiss without qualms whatever opinion differed from her own as being inconsequential or wrong.

"Madame Gollmer knows everything," was a statement often heard, uttered by some ironically but most often with awe if not reverence. The Soliman children believed in her implicitly: she was a tower of strength, a fount of knowledge, a dispenser of love, warmth, and strict discipline. Miss Griffith who worked for the Sirri family was an altogether different proposition. She was the typical British old maid of good background who came to seek her fortune in Egypt, because, despite excellent qualifications, her chances of success in England were very poor. To begin with, she had very little money therefore could not establish herself on her own. Secondly, she was an albino and could hardly see, so finding a job as a governess in England would have been far more difficult than in Egypt. Besides, the climate of Egypt suited her much better than that of her original Wales. Hussein Sirri Pasha, having interviewed her was impressed by her education and genteel demeanor, consequently hired her and never regretted his decision.

The Sirri family and the Soliman family were very close and perfect harmony reigned between both sets of parents and their offspring. Alas, not the same could be said about the governesses who were poles apart in every possible way. Ultimately, the innate antipathy between the French pro-German governess and the British imperialist one came to a head. Miss Griffith objected to Madame Gollmer's dictatorial behavior while Madame Gollmer disapproved of the stiff-necked attitude of *cette anglaise* as she called her. The situation was further complicated by the fact that the families lived very close together and the children were first cousins. A modus vivendi was reached, however. In order to avoid an open clash between the two ladies which might have resulted in the dismissal of one or both, the two mothers agreed that whenever the Soliman girls went to their uncle's house Madame Gollmer would stay home and Miss Griffith would be in charge, and the reverse would happen when the Sirri girls went to their aunt's around the corner.

This arrangement worked well enough for some time. The children in both families had the benefit of an Anglo-French education and their young minds were exposed to a broad spectrum of concepts, ideas, and principles as well as a variety of idiosyncrasies, which were their daily fare at the hands of these two determined women. However, what neither family had foreseen was the impact of international politics and world events on this seemingly perfect arrangement. With the advent of World War II, the mood in Egypt became tense. Everyone knew that King Farouk favored the Axis powers and, had he been free to do so, would readily have joined ranks with Germany to spite the British in general and Sir Miles Lampson, whom he abominated, in particular. The latter disliked Farouk, spoke deprecatingly about him and never missed a chance to remind him that he was a young king, a 'boy' at the head of a country occupied by Great Britain. Politicians such as 'Ali Maher and 'Aziz al-Masri shared Farouk's views, perhaps even inspired them, while others fervently wished that the Allies be the victors.

At the time of the Battle of al-Alamein in 1942, 'Abd al-Hamid Soliman Pasha was in failing health and living in semi-retirement while Hussein Sirri Pasha was vigorously engaged in the political activities of the country. Both of them, albeit for different reasons, were definitely anti-German. 'Abd al-Hamid Soliman Pasha, like Isma'il Sirri Pasha, his father-in-law, had devoted most of his career to the Ministry of Public Works. Even though he had never worked under Willcocks or Scott-Moncrieff, he had met and worked with many other British engineers and appreciated the technological expertise Great Britain offered his country. He was never interested in politics per se but loved his profession as an engineer with passion and, like his father-in-law before him, became an anglophile of a sort. Though he wished, like all nationalists of the time, that an early end be brought to the protectorate, he believed, at the same time, that Egyptians should make the most out of Britain's undesired presence in the country. This was definitely a very pragmatic approach to the problem, one possibly suggested by his father-in-law or brought on by the rational thinking of an engineer.

A more forceful reason, however, made him opt for Great Britain in her conflict with Germany: he distrusted Hitler and his motives profoundly. As far as he was concerned, fascism, dictatorship, and fanaticism were abominations, the Brown Shirts were terrorists, Hitler a malevolent buffoon with tremendous power and therefore tremendously dangerous. He condemned unequivocally Hitler's racism and politics of segregation, convinced that any man who would consider blacks little better than apes and Jews a cancer that should be excised from the body of the human race was a madman bent on a course of destruction. Hussein Sirri's motives were of a more political and less philosophical nature. Though related to King Farouk, he did not share his views as far as the war was concerned and never doubted even in 1942 when Rommel was at al-Alamein, a few miles from Alexandria, that the Allies would eventually emerge victorious.

Both families, therefore, were in the same political camp—not so, however, the governesses. As the war raged on in North Africa and the Germans' entry into Cairo seemed imminent, Madame Gollmer could hardly contain her excitement, which bordered on exultation. She boasted openly about the might of the magnificent German war machine, about the cleverness of 'the desert fox,' about the supremacy of the Teutonic culture that would soon dominate the world. Her remarks were duly reported to Miss Griffith by one of the Gaullist governesses she had befriended. In a frenzy of anger she demanded an audience with the Pasha on a matter of the utmost importance. Intrigued by this unusual request, since governesses were his wife's domain not his, he nonetheless received her immediately suspecting a major problem he would have to deal with in person. "Treason," she clamored, "It must be reported immediately! Madame Gollmer must be dismissed, thrown into a concentration camp, or better still, hanged in Abdin Square to serve as an example."

Her frustration and anger were such that she actually cried. Hussein Sirri Pasha who had listened attentively to this tirade, calmed her as best he could and finally pieced together a coherent picture from the almost incoherent story the distraught woman was telling. He promised to discuss the matter with his brother-in-law. "Not enough, not enough," she stubbornly repeated, "The woman is a Boche and must be dealt with accordingly." She only calmed down when Hussein Sirri Pasha promised that the culprit would be punished. The matter was indeed serious because the country was in real danger of being invaded. Most landowning families in Cairo had taken refuge from impending disaster in their farms away from the capital. Official papers were being burned at different embassies and this was certainly not the time for such statements to be made by a pro-German governess working for an Egyptian family. Consequently, Hussein Sirri Pasha went to see his brother-in-law 'Abd al-Hamid Soliman Pasha, whom he found in a somber mood.

The news of the war was bad, and despite his staunch belief in the ultimate victory of the Allies, he dreaded the intervening period and the dire consequences of a German invasion, even if short-lived. Moreover, he was angry, very angry indeed. That very morning, as he was listening to the news over the radio, Madame Gollmer had knocked at the door of the study and asked if she could talk to him for a few minutes. Though surprised, he acquiesced, remembering that his wife was attending a Red Crescent committee meeting and that a crisis of some sort had taken place. As he reported to his wife later on, what she said amounted to the following: the Germans would be in town any moment now. Since the Soliman villa was one of the grandest on the island, it would undoubtedly be requisitioned, an unavoidable hazard of war. Madame Gollmer therefore wanted to reassure the Pasha that she would use her influence—for after all, her loyalty to Hitler and the National Socialist party were well known—to persuade the German military high command that only officers should be allowed in the house, not soldiers. The Pasha was flabbergasted.

Madame Gollmer, mistaking his silence for profound emotional gratitude, had added, "You see, Pasha. We have girls in the house and we cannot allow them to be in close contact with soldiers even though I can assure you these German boys would know how to behave."

This was the supreme impertinence that 'Abd al-Hamid Soliman Pasha could not accept. He dismissed her curtly and told her he would discuss the matter with his wife. Somewhat taken aback at her employer's coolness, which she put down to the seriousness of the situation, Madame Gollmer left the room all puffed up with her

newly acquired self-importance, convinced that she had just rendered a tremendous service to the family.

His brother-in-law's visit and what he came to say increased his
anger and indignation.

"The woman," he told Hussein Sirri, "is out of her mind. Does
she truly believe that I would allow my daughters to have anything
to do with German officers? Tomorrow, if the news does not
improve, I shall take the family to the farm at Mahalla, and German
officers as well as soldiers can have the house."

Later on, having discussed the issue with Fatma Hanim, he decided that Madame Gollmer would eventually have to be dismissed
because her pro-German attitude would sooner or later have an
impact on the children. Another reason was that the same tug of war
between governesses was occurring daily in their home. When two
of the older Soliman girls became engaged in early 1941, 'Abd al-
Hamid Pasha decided that Madame Gollmer, who had been an
unsuitable chaperone for his eldest daughter and her fiancé, should
not be called upon to play the role again. She had been meddlesome
and had often tried to monopolize the conversation and dominate
the situation. Someone else would have to be hired. In the early
1940s, 'Abd al-Hamid Soliman Pasha was still sailing a middle course
between Egyptian conservatism and European emancipation. While
he fully concurred with the idea that his daughters and future sons-
in-law should be given the chance to get better acquainted before
marriage, he did not consider it proper that they should be left alone
together. Hence a chaperone would be employed. The lady's sole
duty was to sit in the drawing room with the young couple, albeit in
a corner so as to give them a certain measure of privacy.

The first one he interviewed turned down the job because she felt
it beneath her dignity to sit there like patience on a monument, or
as she said, "like another piece of furniture." The second one, however, accepted with alacrity because she was told that part of her
duties would be to accompany the young couples on their outings.
The prospect pleased her; besides, she had no money and no better
offer. If her ego was bruised, she nursed it in the privacy of her room.
So Miss Grey entered in the life of the Soliman family. It soon transpired that while Miss Grey was totally mute in the drawing room,
she was quite vocal otherwise. Furthermore, she thoroughly despised

Egyptians and expressed her views frequently, which made her unpopular with the children, and while not as patriotic as Miss Griffith, she was constantly needling Madame Gollmer about her political bias with the result that the children's floor often rang with the noise of their heated discussions.

Hussein Sirri Pasha and his wife Nahed Hanim often criticized the Solimans for employing two governesses at the same time particularly as one of them was pro-German and the other one English. However, this is how matters stood for some months. Miss Grey followed the engaged couples wherever they went and Madame Gollmer took care of the little ones in the family and fought her private war with Miss Griffith while railing against *ce cataplasme hypocrite*, as she had dubbed Miss Grey.

"I will tell Madame," she warned her once.

"What will you tell her I wonder?"

"I shall tell her that you speak very badly about Egyptians. *C'est honteux! Vous gagnez votre pain en Egypte*—Shame on you! You are earning your bread in Egypt."

"I have said nothing against the family, nothing to offend her. After all the little Egyptians in the street are dirty. Would you allow the children near them?"

"Of course not."

"Well then, what are you complaining about? That is all I have said. Besides, your charges are very nice." The last sentence was uttered in an ironic tone, which implied she meant the contrary.

Miss Grey's haughty and imperialistic attitude had not escaped the Pasha. He knew that sooner or later he would have to get rid of her but, because the situation in the country was very tense and he had more urgent business to attend to, he postponed the dismissal of Miss Grey for the time being. Miss Grey's days in the Soliman family, however, came to an abrupt end in the most unexpected way. Madame Gollmer woke up one morning feeling extremely unwell and was unable to get out of bed. In the afternoon the two youngest children in the family, a girl of ten and a boy of eight, grew restless so their mother asked Miss Grey to take them to the Grotto Garden to look at the fish in the aquarium. She accepted reluctantly because as she told her employer, "I am a lady companion, Madam, not a nanny." Anyway, she did take the children to the Grotto as the garden was called. All the while she was unpleasant to them, scolded them for walking slowly, snapped at them for no apparent reason, made them stand longer than they wished in front of the turtle tank, laughed at them because they feared the bats that were glued to the ceiling of the cave making ominous noises.

Both children were tired, angry, and fed up. On the way back they came across a group of little children clad in torn *gallabiya*s, who were playing with a soft ball made up of rags tied together. Miss Grey lifted one eyebrow and said haughtily, "Get out of the way, dirty little Arabs." The boy's reaction was as swift as lightening. He went round behind Miss Grey and with the full force of his eight years kicked her on the backside. She let out an unladylike yelp, which was more of anger than of pain. She would have hit the boy had his sister not grabbed him by the hand and both of them ran all the way home where they locked themselves up in his room expecting the worst. Panting and sweating, Miss Grey arrived back at the house and went immediately to Mrs. Soliman to complain about the children's behavior and demand that they be severely punished. Her employer listened in utter dismay. What on earth had possessed her son to behave in such an incredible way? The child was usually well mannered and not particularly aggressive. She decided to investigate the matter and get to the bottom of this story. The children were questioned by their parents and gave their version of the event. The little boy added in a defiant tone, "We are not dirty Arabs. We are clean Egyptians."

"But she was not talking about you," said his father. "She was referring to the children in the street."

"No, she meant us," answered the boy stubbornly. "All Egyptians. Would she be happy if we said 'dirty English'?"

"Of course not and neither should you say it."

In the morning, a beaming Umm Muhammad announced that Miss Grey was leaving. She had been fired. Madame Gollmer was delighted when she heard the news. She was gratified by the dismissal of a woman she had come to consider as 'the enemy,' and gloated over the fact that she was, once again, the only governess in the house. Unfortunately, two weeks later she made her own fatal mistake and was dismissed as well. Madame Gollmer's dismissal was the first acutely traumatic experience suffered by the two youngest

Soliman children. They loved her dearly as she had guided them every step of the way from the moment they were born, and had dominated their young lives to a point where they could not imagine being without her. It was, in a certain sense, their first encounter with death, the death of a permanent relationship. It was for both of them their very first heartbreak.

Madame Gollmer was not given a 'character' for none was needed; her reputation as governess was well established. Had she wanted another job, she would have found one readily, not only because she was good but because she had been employed by the Soliman family. Actually, she was not told the reason for her dismissal because both 'Abd al-Hamid Pasha and his wife felt that they owed her too much to hurt her feelings by referring to her German connection and to the terrible faux pas she had committed. They knew that she had acted in good faith but her political allegiances were not acceptable to them. She was told that the children now needed someone who could teach them English. As it is, she never worked again. Soliman Pasha with his accustomed generosity pensioned her off and helped her secure a small flat downtown in Falaki Street and his wife extended an open invitation to come for lunch every Sunday with the children, which she did to the end of her life in 1957.

14

In the Sallam household the relationship between the family and their governess was very harmonious. At the time of 'Abir's birth in October 1926, Madame Duprée had already been with the family three years. She enjoyed her life there and looked forward to many more years of security, taking care of children of whom she had grown very fond. She was still mainly responsible for 'Ayn al-Hayah who was a bright and pretty little girl of seven; 'Aliya was handled by Umm Muhammad and 'Abir totally taken over by Farhah. Madame Duprée was grateful to God for having sent her this good job, where there always seemed to be something new or exciting taking place.

In January 1927, she was given her first taste of Egyptian festivities on a grand scale when Chafaq Hanim invited her to attend the wedding of 'Ali and Karimah that took place in Munira. 'Ali was now a doctor recently returned from Edinburgh, and Karimah finally an official member of the Sadiq family. Madame Duprée enjoyed the wedding tremendously and was very touched when Chafaq Hanim gave her a gold coin to keep as souvenir. She could not get over the fact that the young couple had been showered with gold coins which, as she told her friend Madame Ponsot, Egyptians call *badra*; that was truly amazing, but no more amazing than the three dresses the bride changed into in the course of the evening, or the display of jewelry worn by the ladies from Minya. However, she disliked the music and the singer's nasal voice, and as for the belly-dancer, she found her obscene! Still, it was quite an experience and she was delighted to have been invited to share it.

In early June, Fatma Hanim announced that the family would accompany her mother and her still unmarried sister, Anisah, to Europe.

"All of us?" exclaimed an incredulous Madame Duprée.

"Yes, all of us," answered Fatma Hanim, "including Farhah and the baby."

The projected trip had been Chafaq Hanim's idea. She had for some time considered the possibility of traveling to Europe now that her children, with the exception of Anisah and Muhsin, were all settled in lives of their own. Anisah was unofficially engaged and Muhsin was still studying at the Sorbonne. She often wondered at Muhsin's protracted absence. Why on earth was it taking him so long to get a degree? In any event, as she told her husband, she wanted to see *bilad barra*—countries overseas. It was time now for her to loosen the bond that tied her to her traditional past and to venture into the modern world of the *khawaga*s. She had no preconceived idea about what she would find there, or even what she expected. She had an open mind ready to receive this new experience and make the most of it. Isma'il Sadiq was immensely surprised by his wife's request and at first, wary of this adventure, tried to dissuade her.

"Chafaq Hanim, what is the necessity of such a trip?"

"'No necessity, Basha, simply my desire to see the world before I die."

"May evil always be far from you, Chafaq Hanim. What will you do in Europe? You can't speak a foreign language."

"This is not a problem since I will be traveling with 'Abd al-Rahman Basha, Fatma, Anisah, and Madame Duprée."

"And where do you plan to go?"

"Baris, Basha, Baris. I want to see the city of light and I also want to see Muhsin. Frankly I cannot understand what is happening to that boy. He used to be so bright, just like Hussein."

"Don't count on seeing Muhsin, Chafaq Hanim, because by the time you arrive in Paris he will be on his way back to Cairo."

"Oh, has he finally obtained his degree?"

"We'll see, we'll see," was her husband's noncommittal answer.

Muhsin's problem had, for the past four years, weighed heavily on the Pasha's mind. His youngest son was just as bright as the others and yet he had seemed, so far, unable to finish his studies and obtain a degree in law. The first three years he had passed his exams brilliantly, but in the summer of 1923, at the end of his fourth and supposedly final year, he sent home a letter to announce that he had failed his final examinations. There was total consternation in the

Sadiq family for this had never happened before. He explained in the letter that influenza had been the cause of the problem. Muhsin was a very independent character with a mind of his own. The moment he had set foot in Paris, he had fallen in love with the city and with the women who flocked around him and with whom he was having a wonderful time. Back in Cairo, the Sadiq family relationships were being formed, adjusted, organized, consolidated, or otherwise sorted out, but in Paris, Muhsin was having a ball. Going home was definitely not a prospect he looked forward to, therefore, when he reached his final year though he succeeded brilliantly at his exams, he decided to send word that he had failed and thus bought himself a year's reprieve.

He repeated the stratagem in the summers of 1924, 1925, and again in 1926. He deluded himself into believing that his father, busy with a heavy schedule and the demands of a growing family in Cairo, would accept his excuses and dismiss his regular failures as an unfortunate turn of events in an otherwise very successful academic career. Perhaps in time, his father would get used to the idea of a son in Paris who demanded nothing more than a regular—and preferably generous—allowance. He was, however, gravely mistaken. Isma'il Sadiq's respect for education was rooted in the very core of his being. He was deeply upset not only at his son's repeated failures, the cause of which he had suspected for quite some time, but at his irresponsible attitude toward learning, oblivious of the fact that Muhsin had indeed brilliantly completed his studies. Working on the assumption of his son's repeated failures, he decided that the latter deserved neither his trust nor his pity, therefore he treated him with the ruthlessness of an Upper Egyptian landlord.

In the summer of 1927, Isma'il Sadiq traveled to France with Chafaq Hanim, Anisah, Fatma, her husband, and children cum governess and wet-nurse. He settled the family in a large house in Passy after which 'Abd al-Rahman Sallam, Fatma's husband, left for London and he proceeded to his favorite hotel in Paris, the Claridge on the Champs Elysées. The reason he did not stay with his family in the house at Passy is that he wished to see the many friends he had in Paris and do it at his own pace unencumbered by family routine. Chafaq Hanim did not question her husband's decision on that score as she had the wisdom to understand that men need, from time to time, their own space. The next morning at 9:00, he arrived at Muhsin's lodgings at the Rue Royale, and after bidding the concierge good morning walked up to the second floor and rang the bell. Receiving no answer, he rang again but this time he kept his finger on the bell. After about five minutes, Muhsin opened the door, his hair disheveled, his eyes puffed out from sleep. On seeing his father, he thought for one moment that he was hallucinating. He stood there speechless, gaping and unable to move.

"Good Morning, Muhsin. Am I to stand at the door for the rest of the day?" asked the Pasha in a quiet voice. Muhsin moved aside to allow his father in and closed the door. By that time he had somewhat recovered so he rushed to his room to retrieve his dressing gown and warn his current paramour not to make a sound. Isma'il Sadiq sat on a chair deliberately ignoring the sofa thereby indicating that his visit would be short. Muhsin was relieved but not for long. Crossing his legs and resting both hands on the pummel of his cane, the Pasha told his son, "Muhsin, pack your things now because you are taking the 11:00 AM train to Marseilles. There, you will board the boat that leaves tomorrow for Alexandria. 'Uthman Effendi will travel with you. He is downstairs and will be up in a moment to help you pack. When you reach Alexandria, you will proceed immediately to Cairo and remain at Munira until I come back."

"But Baba, university starts in September. . . ."

"Forget about it," interrupted his father. "From now on, no more university for you, my boy. You are evidently quite incapable of obtaining a degree. Furthermore, you will have no allowance and whatever money you need you must earn. Your expenses during the trip will be taken care of by 'Uthman Effendi who will present me with a very detailed account upon my return."

Muhsin was crestfallen! Sentence was passed and he knew that no amount of pleading would alter his father's decision. Even Nayna, had she been present, would not have been able to interfere for this was men's business. Anyway, she probably agreed with the Pasha.

Muhsin was set up as an example in the family. The story was told and retold with glee by some, with sorrow by others, but the consensus of opinion was that Muhsin had played with fire and been burned as a result. The rest of the story is less grim. Muhsin ultimately married a beautiful, young girl, quiet, affectionate, and a superb housewife. Everyone in the family liked and admired her, and Muhsin, though he never publicly expressed it, was enchanted with his parents' choice. She vastly compensated him for the boredom of the clerical job his father had secured for him in the province and, in due time, gave him two daughters he doted upon. Because he had become such a taciturn person as an aftermath of his enforced exile, the family thought he was unhappy. Chafaq Hanim, however, knew better. She understood that Muhsin had made the necessary adjustments and refocused his life. Since he could no longer have Paris and its glorious days, he settled for the best Egypt could offer him: a leisurely existence in an undemanding job that gave him all the time he needed to enjoy domesticity with a beautiful wife and two lovely daughters. It was often remarked in the family that out of courtesy for Inji, his wife, who spoke no foreign languages, he never uttered a word of French after their marriage. It was almost as if he had forgotten it or wanted to close that chapter of his life.

At the time of Isma'il Sadiq's fateful visit to Muhsin, Chafaq Hanim and her daughters were enjoying their trip abroad. Madame Duprée had overcome her initial surprise but Farhah was quite disoriented. When told that she would accompany the family to Paris, she had been delighted though she did not understand what it meant. She had heard of Alexandria where there is a very big sea of salty water, and of Tanta where her mother went to visit the shrine of Sayid al-Badawi and from whence she brought back a box of *halawa tahiniya*, but Paris she had never heard of before. As far as she was concerned, that was another source of wonder in a life that now seemed so full of surprises. The major problem was her husband. Reluctant at first to let her live across the river in Zamalek, he was now refusing to allow her to cross a sea and live among *khawaga*s in a foreign land. He said he feared she would change or perhaps be contaminated by new ideas. This was of course not the reason at all. He knew well enough that Farhah was impervious to new ideas. Though her mind was not a tabula rasa, yet it had closed forever around a small body of knowledge, to which she held with dogged determination and which she had no inclination to enlarge. No, he had cunningly realized that she had become indispensable to the Sallam household and that his reluctance would be overcome by a financial compensation. This is precisely what happened. He was induced to change his mind in the usual way: he was given an envelope containing the equivalent of two months of his wife's wages. 'Abd al-Rahman Sallam was a fair and generous man who would have been loath to take advantage of someone's poverty, but he knew nonetheless that it was not love, or concern over his wife's mental and spiritual welfare that had prompted the husband's attitude. It was greed, pure and simple. Consequently he chose the course that satisfied all parties concerned: the husband would get some money, Farhah would go to Paris, and the baby's daily supply of milk would be guaranteed.

The problem was thus solved in an expedient way and Farhah found herself one morning on the deck of a big ship, clutching the baby to her bosom and silently reciting all the verses of the Qur'an that she knew. She had been looking forward to this great adventure but now she was terrified and a little sick. The crossing lasted six days during which she flatly refused to leave the cabin because the sight of the vast expanse of water filled her with dread. Finally, they docked at Marseilles and, once she set foot on firm soil, she regained her composure, and with it, her appetite. At Passy she lived just as in Cairo. She ate, slept, and fed the baby, but after about ten days, she gradually developed all the symptoms of homesickness. She missed the sights and sounds of her homeland. She missed the sun, the heat, even the dust and flies. She missed the smell of fried *ta'miya* and above all she missed her mother, her sister Badriyah, and even her husband, unpleasant as he was. With every passing day her mood became more somber. She would sit for hours on end at the window of her room watching Pascal, the gardener, tend the garden and the graceful movement of sparrows on the lawn. She rarely spoke for there was no one she could share a thought with and, being of a gregarious nature, she suffered from this enforced silence.

Gradually, she started to lose her appetite though, oddly enough, her milk production was not impaired. Chafaq Hanim and her daughters had noticed the change and feared that in the long run her health might be affected. Finally, Madame Duprée suggested that she be taken out for a drive in the family's rented car. They all thought it was a good idea so, on the first sunny day, Chafaq Hanim and her daughters got in the back of the car and Farhah with the baby sat up front. They had tried to persuade her to leave 'Abir with Madame Duprée but she would have none of it. She trusted no one with her baby. So off they went from Passy to the Champs Elysées with Fatma and Anisah pointing out sights as they drove along. When they reached L'Etoile they asked the driver to slow down so that she could get a good glimpse of the Arc de Triomphe. Finally, they reached the Concorde and Fatma pointing at the Obelisk said, "Look, Farhah. This comes from Egypt."

"What is it doing here?"

"It is a gift from Egypt to France. You see, we wanted French people to know that we also can make beautiful things."

"Amazing!"

"And look at this square," added Anisah. "Isn't it beautiful?"

Farhah craned her neck, looked around and after a moment pronounced in a determined voice. "*Wallahi, ya Sitt Anisah*—By God, Sitt Anisah, Ataba Square in Cairo is far more beautiful."

Both Fatma and Anisah were shocked into silence, but an amused Chafaq Hanim asked, "What do you mean, woman?"

"Sitt Hanim, with your permission, I speak the truth. In Ataba Square, there is life. Here it is like a big cemetery with cars going round and round in silence. Where are the peddlers selling their wares? Where are the vendors with their baskets of *'asaliya*? And the *saqa* and the *'irq sus* merchant? I long for a glass of *tamr hindi* or mango juice. Don't you miss *libb* (sunflower seeds) and *hummusiya*, *sitti*? There are no donkey carts here. Don't they have donkeys in this country? This is truly a sad square. It has no soul."

This was a final judgment and the ladies, though amused, remained silent. They drove back home disappointed at having failed to impress Farhah or relieve her depression. They wondered what would happen next and Fatma vowed never again to travel with an ignorant servant. But the strange thing is that after this outing, Farhah's mood improved perceptively.

This miraculous recovery was brought on by Chafaq Hanim who took matters into her hands. She called Farhah to her room and, not beating about the bush, told her in a stern voice, "Pull yourself together, Farhah. No one in my house is allowed to mope or pull a long face. I abominate long faces. Besides, it is not good for the baby who will surely grow into a sour and unpleasant girl if she is fed sour milk, which is probably the kind you are currently producing."

She then threatened to put her on the next ship sailing for Alexandria and send her back to her husband unless she stop her nonsense and behave in the right and proper way. At that point, Farhah started to cry. "Upon your life, no tears," scolded Chafaq Hanim "I detest tears even more than long faces." Poor Farah was at her wit's end. The prospect of a long voyage alone across the big sea terrified her but the thought of being separated from 'Abir was even worse. She swallowed hard and tried to control herself not wanting to anger Sitt Hanim any further. Chafaq Hanim remained silent a few moments to let the effect of the threat sink in. When she spoke again, her tone was gentle.

"Look, Farhah. I understand that you should miss your family and life at home. This is perfectly normal. I also believe your suffering must be compensated. Therefore, if you promise to control your feelings, to smile again as you do in Cairo, and forget about being sad, I will give you the same amount of money my daughter is paying you. In other words, I will double your salary." Farhah's spirits lifted immediately. She grabbed Chafaq Hanim's hand to kiss it, for her relief at knowing she was not to be sent back was immense. The money helped, of course, but what had worked the miracle was the threat followed by a reprieve. Chafaq Hanim had gambled, albeit with minimal risks. She had judged Farhah accurately and understood from the start that this simple woman would have died rather than undertake the trip back alone or be separated from the baby.

Once the problem of Farhah was sorted out, the trip was thoroughly enjoyed by everyone. The house in Passy had enough rooms to accommodate the whole family in comfort and was surrounded by a large garden where the little girls played under the watchful eye of Madame Duprée. It came with two maids, Marguerite and Honorine, mother and daughter, and a gardener, Pascal, Marguerite's husband. Having settled down in the villa, Chafaq Hanim fully expected to live there as she did in Cairo. Very soon the clash of cultures became obvious. Chafaq Hanim insisted that meals be served at the same hours as in Cairo, which meant breakfast any time between 8:00 and 10:00 AM, lunch at 2:00 in the afternoon, and trays for herself and her daughters at 9:00 in the evening. Marguerite accepted the hours because she understood that foreigners live differently and that her 11:00 AM snack followed by a frugal diner at 6:00 PM could not satisfy her Egyptian employer. What was totally beyond her comprehension, however, was the vast amount of food she was required to cook every day.

These were between-war years in France and people of Marguerite's generation had known deprivation, poverty, and hunger. Thrifty by nature, as most French people are, she was shocked at what she considered wanton waste. It seemed to her sacrilegious that lunch should consist of an entrée, two meat courses, vegetables, salad, and a dessert, while most people she knew would have been content with a roast, salad, and a piece of cheese. The first time Fatma gave her the menu following her mother's instructions, Marguerite innocently asked how many guests were expected. When told that this was the normal family meal, her indignation knew no bounds. She decided that these Orientals were definitely gluttons and would have resigned on the spot had Madame Duprée not interfered.

"Come now, Marguerite, don't be silly. Do as you are told. You will be compensated for your efforts."

"But this is positively sinful—so much food for one family while so many people go hungry in the streets of Paris."

She may have been thinking of her own son and daughter-in-law whose daily meal in their home consisted of a tureen of soup with an occasional piece of bacon thrown in.

"Never mind these thoughts, Marguerite. I can assure you that the Pasha's wife is an extremely generous person and that in all probability you will be given all the leftovers to take home at the end of the day."

Marguerite, though pacified, did not quite believe her because in her experience people did not 'give' food away, but, as Pascal pointed out, it was not their business what these Arabs wanted to eat as long as they paid the wages on time. Madame Duprée, of course, reported Marguerite's reluctance to Chafaq Hanim who was shocked at her cook's impudence. However, she did give instructions that Marguerite and Pascal be given all the leftovers every day. The first time it happened, Marguerite could not believe her good fortune, and Honorine danced with joy as she very quickly packed remnants of a roast of beef, one whole chicken, a full pan of rice, and another of string beans. Thereafter, Marguerite and her family were totally won over and their dedication to Chafaq Hanim's service assured. No questions were ever asked or objections raised, for over and above the daily gift of food, Chafaq Hanim was very liberal with her tips.

"All services have a price," she would tell her daughters. "What is important is to evaluate properly." As a result, Marguerite accepted without question the taboo over pork and the necessity to bring live fowl into the house to be slaughtered over the kitchen sink so that no blood would remain in the flesh as with the French system of strangulation. The first time she did it, Pascal watched stupefied and then walked out of the kitchen muttering under his breath, "*Sales arabes.*" Nonetheless, a harmonious relationship was established between the 'Arab' masters and the French servants and soon enough Marguerite realized that these people were of the class of *seigneurs*, accustomed to be served and have the best. She was definitely impressed by Chafaq Hanim's imposing presence, by her daughters' westernized ways, and by Madame Duprée who belonged to the group. She agreed to apply the high levels of cleanliness demanded by Chafaq Hanim who insisted that all vegetables be washed thoroughly and chicken rubbed with flour and salt and then dipped in vinegar so as to remove all smell of grease, and above all, that Marguerite and Honorine bathe regularly if they wanted to keep their jobs. She would have asked for more had not Fatma quoted one of her mother's favorite proverbs:

> *In aradt an tuta'*
> *Itlub al-mustata'*

In other words, "If you wish to be obeyed, demand what is possible." The issue of personal hygiene was the most difficult to tackle. Both Fatma and Madame Duprée were at a loss how to do it, not wanting to offend the women but knowing that Chafak Hanim could not abide body odors around her. Fatma came up with the idea of offering them perfumed soap bars with Madame Duprée gently explaining what was expected of them. If Marguerite and Honorine were offended, they never showed it, for by that time they had convinced themselves that the frequent bizarre requests of their employer were amply compensated by her generosity.

It amused Fatma and Anisah to hear the comments uttered on both sides of the fence. Chafaq Hanim was shocked at the lack of hygiene of the maids, while they could not understand why their current mistress was forever washing her hands and feet, particularly before praying. Chafaq Hanim was angry whenever Pascal allowed his dog in the kitchen because the animal was not only impure but was full of ticks and fleas, and both Marguerite and Honorine were amazed when they saw their employer eat with her fingers. On the whole, however, there developed between them a relationship based on respect on the part of the French group and benevolent sympathy on the part of Chafaq Hanim, and funnily enough, both sides assumed that the other one knew no better.

Setting aside these domestic concerns, Chafaq Hanim and her daughters performed the standard sightseeing tours of the city. Fatma and Anisah led the way because they had heard so much about all these wonderful places either from Madame Duprée or the nuns at school. They walked around the Champ de Mars and the Champs Elysées, went up to the first platform of the Eiffel tower, spent several hours at the Louvre, enjoyed long afternoons in the Tuileries Gardens and visited the Madeleine Church. Chafaq Hanim always went along and, like her daughters, was fascinated by the beauty of the city. She had no compunction about entering churches which she considered not so much as places of worship but as another sight to be seen. Fatma teased her about it one day.

"Nayna, don't you think you are committing a sin by entering these Christian places where the unbelievers gather to pray?"

"We'll pray a little longer tomorrow so that God may forgive us today's sins," answered her mother with a little twinkle in the eye. Chafaq Hanim's good common sense precluded the acceptance of bigotry. Her curiosity about the city and its sights knew no bounds and she satisfied it without reservation. However, what they enjoyed above all were the long afternoons they spent in the shops of Paris. On the days they went shopping, Chafaq Hanim decreed that lunch should be served at 1:30 PM to allow more time for their outing. Anisah had at first suggested that they spend the whole day shopping, stopping at one of the restaurants on the Champs Elysées for a meal and a rest. The suggestion was turned down flat by her mother. Under no circumstances would she eat in a public place. Neither would she sit in a café. She thought it would be highly improper as cafés, according to her, were for men or *khawagas*, certainly not for an Egyptian pasha's wife and daughters. As a result, their shopping sprees were exhausting, more so for Fatma and Anisah than for their mother, as Chafaq Hanim always managed to rest her feet when a shop attendant, eager to please these good customers, offered the elderly lady a chair. To shop in Paris was, by all accounts, the highlight of the trip for, no matter how sophisticated they might have been, they could not but be dazzled by the displays of the *grands magasins* or those of the small boutiques.

"Why can't we have the same in Cairo?" wondered Anisah.

"But we do, in a sense," answered her sister. "We have Sednaoui, Cicurel, Orosdi Back, and Chemla."

"Yes, but they do not have all this merchandise and the shops themselves are ugly and dusty."

"They are not ugly. Actually, the Sednaoui shop in Midan Khazindar is a very handsome building. As for the dust, it is unavoidable because Cairo is a dusty city. 'Abd al-Rahman told me that when the east wind blows it carries dust from the Muqattam Hills. Remember also that shops in Cairo have to import a good amount of stuff from abroad and clearly they can't get everything."

"Isn't it odd that the biggest and nicest shops in Cairo are owned by Jews, Syrians, or Lebanese?" observed Anisah.

"They are clever," answered Chafaq Hanim, "as well as enterprising, whereas we are indolent. Besides, Egyptians are basically people of the soil. They cultivate and grow things but are not clever in commerce."

Many years later, Fatma Hanim reminiscing on the past and remembering this conversation told one of her daughters, "Your grandmother remembered the donkey cart from which Selim and Sam'an Sednaoui used to peddle their wares. They were very clever, kept their prices down, served everyone with a smile, and little by little their clientele grew and grew and so did their savings until one day they bought a little shop, which also grew and grew and now they have this fine place in Khazindar Square."

"So Youssef Pasha Sednaoui is the son of one of them?"

"Absolutely."

"He is such a nice man and so elegant. Is he a Jew?"

"He is not. He is a Christian from *bilad al-sham* (Syria and Lebanon) and very clever. Have you noticed how he is always around in the shop, always willing to lend a helping hand to the shop assistants, always courteous to the customers?"

"Yes, and I have noticed as well that he always sees you to the car whenever you visit his shop."

However, in 1927 in Paris, Chafaq Hanim and her daughters did not receive such treatment despite their liberal spending. They did not fail to observe that they stood out as different because they spoke Arabic among themselves and dressed differently. They all wore a *habara* though the *petsha* was more often left hanging than pulled up over their faces. In later years, however, when Fatma Hanim accompanied her husband on his frequent trips abroad, he insisted that she adopt a totally western form of dress. Pictures of her as a young woman show her walking down the Champs Elysées wearing an elegant coat over a print dress and a little hat, which looked extremely fashionable. The last few days of the trip were totally devoted to shopping for presents to take back home. No one was forgotten. The list of recipients included not only brothers, sisters, sisters-in-law, cousins, nephews, nieces, and friends but servants as well.

Marguerite and Honorine were goggle-eyed at the sight of the multitude of packages that accumulated daily in the various bedrooms. Finally, on the last day and shortly before leaving the house, Chafaq Hanim called Marguerite, Honorine, and Pascal into the drawing room. Fatma was with her mother to serve as interpreter. Chafaq Hanim thanked them for their good service and handed each one of them a present and an envelope containing their wages. They shook her hand and thanked her profusely. They were sad to see her go for they had grown rather fond of this elderly lady with the bizarre requests and amazing generosity. Marguerite, who was more articulate than Pascal, made a little speech at the end of which she said, "*J'éspère, Madame, que vous reviendrez l'année prochaine*—I hope, Madame, that you will come back next year."

Fatma having translated, her mother smiled and said *insha'Allah*, God willing. But this was not to be.

Part Three

A New Way of Life: Zamalek

15

Chafaq Hanim never traveled again. In the spring of 1928, Fatma Hanim suffered a miscarriage and her gynecologist, Dr. Naguib Mahfuz, recommended that she spend the summer in Alexandria, as a trip abroad would have been exhausting. She soon recuperated, her morale raised by the new heights her husband's career was reaching. Already in 1927 while they were in Paris, he had been named by the French government Grand Officier de la Legion d'Honneur and now, as she was convalescing, he had become minister of communications in the Muhammad Mahmud cabinet. But, above all, she was totally engrossed in the house 'Abd al-Rahman was having built.

Upon their return from Europe in the fall of 1927, 'Abd al-Rahman decided to build a house befitting his social standing. He opted for one of the choicest pieces of land on the 'good' side of Zamalek. Though it did not overlook the river or the Gezira Sporting Club, it was nevertheless very well situated at an angle of two main streets on the south and east sides, while the northern side of the house overlooked a large garden. 'Abd al-Rahman liked the idea of having three sides unencumbered by immediate neighbors. The house looked unimpressive from the outside despite its three floors and ornate wrought iron gate, and this was deliberate. He never meant to finish it completely. It is said that although he was a profoundly religious man yet he was also extremely superstitious and feared the evil eye. If the house looked unpretentious, perhaps even ugly from the outside, so be it, for in that case fewer passersby would envy its owners and cast on them, even unwittingly, the evil eye.

The garden *à la française* boasted a stone fishpond and was enclosed by a beautiful wrought iron fence. At each of the four corners of the garden was a room: one for the *bawwab*, one for the two *sufrajis*, one for the *makwagi*, and the last one was a large garage. The impression of incompleteness or simplicity vanished the moment one walked beyond the main entrance door into the vestibule where four steps led to a landing beyond which, through an arcade, was the great hall with its magnificent oak staircase and marqueterie floor.

'Abd al-Rahman was his own architect. He knew exactly what he wanted his house to be and he knew also that in order to achieve the best results he would have to employ the best artisans wherever they could be found. Hence, he imported carpenters from Aswan for his oak staircase that was held together without bonding material of any kind, and artisans and workmen from Italy for the stuccowork and gilt of the reception rooms. He housed these people in makeshift accommodations in the garden until the completion of their work, and if it is a wonder that no clashes occurred between these men of different cultures, this was probably because the fees they were paid smoothed out potential wrinkles. The vestibule itself was a little masterpiece of elegant simplicity. The steps were flanked by two lions carved in white Carrara marble. On either side of the landing was a room: one was 'Abd al-Rahman's study, and the other his private drawing room, where lesser guests were received. From the central hall opened three very large doors: one led into the main drawing room, the second into the dining room, and the third to the back stairs leading to the other floors of the house, or down to the basement, used by the servants in their daily activities. The south wall of the house on the first landing of the main staircase was dominated by a large glass, colored panel depicting Ceres, goddess of harvests, and the light which filtered through it enveloped the hall in the soft shades of its many colors.

The oak staircase led to the first floor where the Pasha and his wife had their apartments. This first floor also included 'Ayn al-Hayah's room, a guest bedroom, and the summer and winter sitting rooms. The top floor was reserved for the children with their governess. The house, by any standards, could be considered a fine example of architecture and decoration. Every detail had been carefully worked out: the wrought iron balcony and window railings, the stucco work of the drawing room walls, the wood paneling of the dining room with its huge marble fireplace, the pressed velvet floral pattern of the winter sitting room wall paper, the cool colors of the summer sitting room, the marble bathrooms, and the cavernous kitchen with its enormous built-in oven. 'Abd al-Rahman's pride, however, lay in the small but exquisite collection of Persian rugs he had acquired with the help and expertise of his friend 'Ali Pasha Ibrahim.[61]

Collecting objects d'art was still in Egypt of the late 1920s a relatively novel pursuit, but it was developing rapidly and emphasized a marked difference between houses of the nineteenth century and those of the twentieth. This difference was exemplified perfectly by the Sadiq house in Munira and the Sallam's in Zamalek. Everything inside the Sadiq house was functional. There were chairs, tables, brass beds, couches of different shapes including the type usually called *karawita*,[62] there was also an elevator which was installed in the early 1930s when the Pasha could no longer negotiate the stairs with ease. But nowhere, neither in the *salamlik* nor in the *haramlik*, was there a single collector's item. By the 1920s however, the social scene in Egypt had vastly changed. In fact, as early as 1891, art exhibits had become fashionable, a fact that undoubtedly contributed to the development of an aesthetic sense in the rising wealthy middle class. The Egyptian Society of Fine Arts, founded in 1923, was presided over for more than twenty-five years by the internationally known art collector Muhammad Mahmud Khalil who, with the help of his French wife, built an outstanding collection of paintings which included works by Camille Pissarro, Claude Monet, Edgar Degas, Paul Gauguin, Vincent van Gogh, and Pablo Picasso, as well as famous artists of earlier periods.

By the late 1920s when 'Abd al-Rahman Sallam built his Zamalek house, the architectural dichotomy of *salamlik* and *haramlik* was no longer viable and the concept of art collecting was well entrenched. As a man of taste, discrimination, and lover of beautiful things, 'Abd al-Rahman opted for an art form that would reflect his oriental background. In that respect he had followed the advice of his friend Dr. 'Ali Ibrahim and collected antique Persian rugs. His collection, though small, was of the highest quality, and he took enormous pleasure in very gradually adding to it. It was not so much an acquisitive spirit that spurred him on but rather the love of beauty per se. He derived as much pleasure from visiting his friend Dr. 'Ali Ibrahim to admire a new item in his collection as he did from buying one himself.

Some of the furniture of the Zamalek house was imported from France or from Italy, but most of it was acquired in Cairo at al-Mawardi's, the purveyor of custom-made furniture very much in vogue at the time. The house and its furnishings took shape slowly but at a steady pace. By the summer of 1929 'Abd al-Rahman was already discussing the possibility of moving in soon. Fatma Hanim was there every day watching the progress of the work and was loath to leave whenever more urgent business required her attention. Anisah, whose engagement to Kamal Bey Sabri was now official, was planning to marry in the fall and, at her request, her future husband rented a villa in Zamalek close to her brother Hussein and her sister Fatma. The distribution of the Sadiq offspring in the neighborhoods of Cairo was by now as follows: Khadiga and Muhsin lived close to their parents in Munira, although Muhsin worked in the province, he had a flat in Cairo; Hazim and Ali lived in Giza; Hussein, Fatma, and Anisah settled in Zamalek; and Muhammad shuttled between his house in Heliopolis and Bayt al-Munira.

A few weeks after Anisah's wedding, 'Abd al-Rahman announced that he and his family would move into the new house on December 31, 1929, so as to start the New Year in their new home. Fatma Hanim readily agreed but was taken aback when she realized they could only occupy the top floor for a while as the rest of the house was not yet ready and that workmen were still milling around the place like ants in a frenzy of activity spurred on by 'Abd al-Rahman's foreman and possibly by the promise of a handsome bonus should they finish their work before the agreed deadline. In any event, on the morning of January 1, 1930, the Sallam family woke up to a new year in their new home, and a few weeks later they took possession of the whole house in its pristine beauty.

Since the house was vast, a gong was used to call the family for meals. Everyday at precisely 1:30, Idris in his immaculate caftan held at the waist by a large red sash, would stand in the main hall and strike two blows on the gong. There was no elevator in the house so as the sound reverberated across the floors, the Pasha, his wife, daughters, and, more often than not, relatives or guests would walk down the grand staircase and converge upon the dining room. Meals at Zamalek were less elaborate than at Munira but more formal. Dishes were never placed on the table but presented by the *sufraji* to each person in a set order. First an entrée, followed by a meat course, a vegetable dish, dessert, and fruit. Next to each plate were two smaller ones, one for the salad and one on which were a kaiser roll and two pieces of dark *baladi* bread. On the table was an assortment of small salad dishes such as *tahina* or *babaghannug*, white cheese salad, pickled green olives, and pickled cucumber.

Like her mother, Fatma Hanim prided herself in the quality of her cuisine. Her cook was a chef who could equally well produce a roast turkey stuffed with chestnuts, a vol-au-vent, or a soufflé, dishes he termed 'European,' or *mulukhiya*, okra, moussaka, which are typically Egyptian. The range of desserts was varied but often enough *pofiterolles au chocolat, forêts-noires,* or *monts-blancs* would be ordered from Groppi's. These were standard meals for Egyptian upper class households and children born into these families took for granted, as is usually the case, the refinement and luxury that surrounded them. By the same token, less fortunate children inevitably envied them or were marked in one way or another if they came into contact with the life of the upper echelons of society. The envy of the have-nots, though understandable, often expressed itself in the strangest way. When 'Abd al-Hamid Soliman Pasha, a close friend of 'Abd al-Rahman Sallam, was director of the Egyptian State Railways, he was approached by Morcos Ya'qub, the stationmaster of the tiny Saft al-Turab station, who asked for a promotion, linking his request to the imminent birth of the Pasha's fifth child.

"May God grant you a son, Basha," he had said. "I will pray for it to happen, and if it does, I would be most grateful if you would transfer me to Tanta."

The Pasha had been furious at the man's effrontery. How dare he assume that promotions were handed out as favors depending on the director's mood or personal circumstances! He had stopped the man in his tracks and told him he would receive his promotion when it was due. This incident had very strange repercussions. Many years later, two of Soliman Pasha's daughters sold a little villa they owned in Alexandria to a person they thought was a wealthy Saudi Arabian. Once the transaction was concluded, and as they stood in the garden overlooking the sea, the purchaser inhaled deeply filling his lungs with sea breeze. He closed his eyes for a moment as if savoring not only the physical well-being of unpolluted air, but an inner triumph or deep satisfaction.

He then looked at the two ladies and said, "I don't think you really know who I am."

They both looked at him quite surprised.

"What do you mean?" said one of them. "Aren't you Ramzi Ya'qub?"

"Yes, of course. What I mean is that I saw you many years ago," and looking at the younger one of the two added, "You were about two years old at the time."

"Well, in that case, how could I possibly remember?"

"I will tell you how I came to know you and your family. At the time, your father 'Abd al-Hamid Soliman Pasha was director of the Egyptian State Railways and my father was the humble stationmaster of a small station near Mahalla. The pay was poor and my father was due for a promotion. The problem was that, as a Copt, he feared he would be bypassed, as he was told the director was rabidly anti-Copt. At about that time, the Pasha arrived one day at the station of Saft al-Turab and my father saw this was his chance, so plucking up all the courage he could muster, he presented him with a petition stating his case. The Pasha read it, looked at him coldly and said, "When your turn comes you will get your promotion." His tone had been curt and he walked away without a smile or a word of encouragement. My father was dejected and almost lost hope. A while later, he came home from work and proudly announced that he had indeed been promoted and that we were all moving to Tanta. This was in late September. In early October, he read in the newspaper that 'Abd al-Hamid Soliman Pasha finally had a son so he told my mother to prepare a 'visit basket'[63] because he intended to go to Cairo to thank the Pasha for the promotion and congratulate him on the birth of his son. He took me along because he was proud of me and wanted to show me off and also convey the message that since he too had a son he could not be accused of giving the newborn the evil eye.

"We arrived in Cairo and took the tramway that crosses the Boulaq Bridge into Zamalek. We walked part of the way and it seemed to me, as a ten-year-old, that we walked for miles and miles. Finally, we stood before the Pasha's house and rang the bell. A tall

Nubian opened the garden gate, my father introduced himself and after handing over the 'visit basket' asked to see the Pasha. The *bawwab* let us in but instead of walking up the steps to the front door of the house, he took us round the back and down a few steps to an enormous room where men dressed in white were busy cooking. Through the window one could look out into the garden and there I saw a woman walk up and down the paths holding a tiny girl by the hand. I looked around me and was amazed at the quantity of objects that were hanging on the walls or lying on the big central table.

"'Wait here,' said the tall Nubian. 'The Pasha has guests for lunch, he will see you later.'

"We sat on a bench in a corner of the kitchen and presently one of the men handed my father a glass of strong tea and a glass of milk for me. I would have much preferred the tea but drank the milk as I was thirsty and the day was hot. I was also very hungry and the feeling was exacerbated by the delicious smell of food that emanated from the various casseroles and serving dishes. Right next to me, one of the under cooks was decorating a creamy substance in a glass bowl. Its color was grayish and it had a marvelous smell of garlic. It was tantalizing.

"'What is it?' I asked my father pointing at the bowl.

"'This my son,' answered the cook, 'is *tahina* salad and I am decorating it with *sinibar* because this is the way the Pasha likes it.'

"I had no idea what *sinibar* was and as for *tihina* the only kind I knew was liquid and poured over molasses. A minute later, the salad was ready. The cook placed it on a shelf in a square hole like a window in the wall. Suddenly the shelf moved up and the salad as well as the other dishes placed there disappeared into a mysterious void. I was totally mystified. I don't know whether it was hunger or the heat, but I was suddenly overwhelmed by an acute perception of my worthlessness. Here was a world different from the one to which I belonged, a world of luxury and beauty, inhabited by people as remote from me as the legendary figures of our popular ballads. I thought of the Pasha, of his remoteness, of his elevated status, and the more I thought, the more my feverish and fertile imagination endowed him with almost supernatural qualities. The salad that was sent up also took on some of the magic. It was a fare for a king. It was the symbol of his greatness. In the middle of my reverie, I looked at my father in his old suit and dusty shoes and felt pity for his weakness and anger at his mediocrity. I vowed that one day I too would be rich and that I would have a cook to prepare meals for me, and that in my house *tihina* would always be served with *sinibar.*"

Both ladies remained silent for a while. The eldest turned away and, as she confessed later, had been quite put out by the story. "Had I known such envy was possible, I would not have sold him the house." The other one, however, looked at the buyer and boldly said, "I assume, since you have just bought our house, that your dream has come true."

"Indeed it has. I am now a very wealthy man."

"At the risk of being awfully rude, I would like to inquire how you worked the miracle, because if you are able now to move in circles that are light years away from Saft al-Turab, you must have achieved a success of momentous proportions."

At that point he burst out laughing and said, "Of course, if by success you mean a great deal of money. In Saudi Arabia where I have lived for many years it is not difficult to amass a fortune if you follow certain channels."

"One last question, after which I promise not to pry any more: you said at the beginning of your story that your father was a Copt and that my father hated Copts—which incidentally is not true at all—how on earth did you end up making a fortune in a Muslim country such as Saudi Arabia?"

"But I am Muslim," he replied. "You see, this business of religion is, as far as I am concerned, of no importance. I happen to have been born into a Coptic family. Very early on I understood that this fact of my birth could well become an obstacle to success. At about the same time I realized that the only place to make money was Saudi Arabia, as Egypt under Nasser was a country of austerity, deprivation for the rich, and illusions for the poor. I had lived all my youth with deprivation and knew that illusions could never translate into a hefty bank account. I became a Muslim, went to Riyadh, and there was lucky enough to find the right channels. So here we are."

"And now do you always have *tihina* salad with *sinibar?*"

He smiled wistfully and said, "I often do, yet I sometimes wonder whether it tastes as good as the Pasha's."

It probably never did.

The success story of Ramzy Ya'qub struck both ladies as being symptomatic of the new age. The 1952 Revolution gave birth to a different society from the one they had grown up in, a society for whom to achieve no longer meant to contribute but merely to acquire. European civilization ceased to be a source of inspiration while not having been replaced in a meaningful way by an authentic Arab culture. When the petrodollar made its entrance in the world of international finance, it became the ultimate goal for would-be men of worth with its accompaniment of gaudiness and extravagant display of ownership. The difference between the post-1952 Revolution nouveaux riches and those of the cotton-boom generation of the early 20s was profound. The latter were men of the soil, attached to a land which they and their forebears had tilled for generations, eager to better themselves and join the ranks of the established, educated upper and middle classes, whereas the former, dazzled by the glitter that lay elsewhere, usually in the rich oil-producing countries, turned their back on their own and, in a large measure, lost their identity, becoming not quite Arab and not truly Egyptian. A new amorphous class, whose success was defined by the size of its individual bank account, came into being and, in the process, colored or rather discolored, the world around them. The age of culture and refinement was gradually superseded by an era of feverish, money-grabbing activity.

All of this, however, was still many years away. Meanwhile, 'Abd al-Rahman Sallam and his family were enjoying a blissful existence in the very civilized world of Zamalek in the 1930s. 'Abd al-Rahman never allowed alcoholic beverages in the house. At meal times only water was served and occasionally orange juice when fresh oranges were received from the farm. In summer, water had to be ice cold and since fear of typhoid fever was forever present, no ice cubes were ever added, as they were considered unhygienic. In those days refrigerators were not common household appliances; all one had were iceboxes that functioned with the serpentine system. The block of ice was placed on top of the pipes and the water cooled as it flowed through. It was Idris' responsibility to see to it that the icebox was never without its block of ice.

Finger bowls made their appearance at the Zamalek table though they had never been used in Munira. Ever since 'Ayn al-Hayah contracted typhoid fever at the age of five, 'Abd al-Rahman became extremely concerned over matters of hygiene in his home and considered finger bowls a necessity since black dates, though eaten peeled, had to be dipped in them as well as figs. The practice was severely criticized by Miss Ashby, the first British governess, who had joined the Sallam family very briefly during the only home leave Madame Duprée ever took. Miss Ashby pointed out, "These are finger-bowls to dip fingertips in, not wash basins." When the remark was later reported to the Pasha, he answered that his fingertips were free of dust but that if Miss Ashby enjoyed the taste of dust she could certainly eat the fruit with it and dip her finger tips in the bowl afterwards. She, of course, had not realized that figs and dates ought never to be washed before serving as it alters the taste.

The family almost never had a meal alone, as there was often a cousin or a relative who would drop in or be formally invited. 'Ayn al-Hayah had her meals with her parents, while 'Aliya and 'Abir with Madame Duprée were only included on special occasions. Madame Duprée enjoyed that meal, not only because the food was good but because she liked the formality of the procedure and her sense of decorum, perhaps of snobbery, was gratified. She, however, was not included at table when Ahmad Bey, 'Abd al-Rahman's eldest brother, came to visit. Ahmad Bey was seventeen years older than his brother and, although he never reached the latter's prominence, was always treated by the family with deference and respect. Though his word was not law, it was usually given due consideration because he was the head of the family, a wise man not given to hasty judgments or dictatorial attitudes. Since he was a descendant of *'alims*, he was a devout Muslim who practiced his religion with zeal and took his position as head of the family and defender of Islam very seriously. He was not xenophobic, yet he considered unacceptable any encroachment of non-believers into the private life of the family. 'Abd al-Rahman was well aware of that fact and found himself caught in a dilemma: on the one hand was his avowed desire to westernize his daughters and broaden their horizon through the inclusion in his household of a French governess, on the other was the tremendous respect he had for his elder brother. Had Ahmad Bey requested it, 'Abd al-Rahman would have dismissed Madame Duprée. The only solution was to play a little game of deception.

Whenever he came to visit, Madame Duprée would remain closeted in her room and her existence never alluded to. It was not clear whether Ahmad Bey was duped by this little stratagem, but in any event, he played along with it and held his counsel.

Yes, life at Zamalek was in many ways more formal, more governed by westernized rules of conduct than life at Munira and both were the two poles of Fatma Hanim's life. Bayt al-Munira, where she grew up, was a mansion bustling with activity often overly boisterous despite Isma'il Sadiq's imposing presence, while life at Zamalek had moved perceptibly away from the atmosphere of a nineteenth century Egyptian upper-class home. Fatma Hanim loved both houses and, great as it was, never questioned the difference.

16

Fatma Hanim took immense pleasure in her new house. She moved about the rooms inspecting every nook and cranny, determined to control its vast expanse and run it as efficiently as her mother did Munira. Though the staff was increased, she relied mostly on the ever efficient and loyal Umm Muhammad as well as on Madame Duprée whose attachment to the family grew with every passing year. In the early days of February, she realized she was pregnant again and in early March announced the good news to the family. Speculations about the baby's sex started immediately.

"After three girls," said Karimah, "you will surely have a boy. Have you worn one of Shaykh Hamza's talismans?"

"Of course not," answered Fatma Hanim, who was often irritated at her sister-in-law's remarks.

"Perhaps you should have," persisted Karimah, "for can you imagine the catastrophe if you have a fourth daughter?"

Before Fatma had time to answer, 'Abd al-Rahman said in his usual quiet voice, "Catastrophe, Karimah Hanim? How odd to consider a child a catastrophe! Whatever God sends is welcome. In fact, if it is a girl we shall name her Hibat Allah."

Unabashed, Karimah asked again, "And if it is a boy, Basha?"

"In that case, the names are many and we shall choose one in good time."

Fatma Hanim had often wondered at her husband's kindness and understanding. Theirs was truly a marriage made in heaven and Isma'il Sadiq was gratified to see that his initial judgement of his son-in-law's character had been correct.

'Abd al-Rahman's first daughter, 'Ayn al-Hayah, was the love of his life, and considering the beauty of the child and her amazing intelligence, he felt his pride in her justified. She remained an only child for six years and since that period corresponded with the meteoric rise of her father's career, she was in many ways everybody's little darling. The second daughter, 'Alia, came at a time when they had almost given up hope of having another child, hence its sex did not matter as long as it was healthy. A year and a half later, a third daughter, 'Abir, was born and though disappointment in the family must have been great, yet it was never expressed because 'Abd al-Rahman would have none of it, and besides, she also was a very pretty child, the only one of the three to be fair. Fatma Hanim was a loving mother who took pride in her daughters. They were impeccably groomed from top to toe, particularly when each one in turn came under Madame Duprée's jurisdiction who, in that respect, behaved like a sergeant major demanding and receiving immediate obedience. She loved the children though she had a marked preference for 'Alia, and Fatma Hanim wondered whether this was caused by the fact that the child was less pretty than her sisters. She questioned the governess about it one day and was surprised by her answer.

"*Mais non Madame*, I love them all the same and 'Alia when she turns sixteen will be prettier than the other two."

Oddly enough, her prediction was realized and 'Alia grew into an exquisite young girl with perfect features matching an endearing personality. But for the time being, she was an ugly duckling overshadowed by her sisters.

October is a lovely month in Egypt, neither too warm nor yet cold, with no danger of *khamasin* winds that plague the months of March and April, covering the furniture with an ugly veil of dust. "It is a nice month to have a baby," mused Fatma Hanim, "for one can drink *mughat* and enjoy it." Fatma Hanim was very fond of the thick, syrupy beverage, sprinkled with chopped grilled nuts. It had to be drunk hot which was very pleasant in winter, unfortunately much less so in summer. As summer dragged on toward fall, preparations were in full swing and by the end of September the house was in a state of absolute readiness for the baby's birth. The cook prepared daily a chicken soup, as Chafaq Hanim, like most ladies of her generation, believed firmly in the saying, "Replace the baby with a chicken to give the mother strength." "Praise be to God," thought Fatma Hanim, "that I do not live in Minya like cousin Tafidah, who is made to drink a glass of hot melted butter laced with molasses right after giving birth!"

The very thought of such a beverage turned her stomach. Actually she had not been feeling well since morning with occasional waves of nausea sweeping over her and her back ached more than usual. Could this be the day? She knew that the whole family was on the alert waiting for a call to come over and be in attendance. Su'ad, Khadiga's daughter, had been staying at Zamalek for the past week, keeping her company and entertaining her with family gossip to while away the time.

On October 10, 1930, in the early afternoon after a quiet lunch with 'Abd al-Rahman and Su'ad, Fatma Hanim felt that the moment had come. Mahfuz Pasha, the gynecologist, was called in immediately and the family alerted. By the time they had all arrived and settled for what they presumed would be a long wait, the baby surprised them all by making a very hasty appearance. It was a girl! While Mahfuz Pasha attended to the mother, a thump was heard in the room. He looked round and there was Su'ad slumped on the floor in a dead faint, overcome by the immensity of the calamity that had just hit the family. Mahfuz Pasha, always the professional, carried on with his duties unruffled by the condition of the woman lying unconscious at the foot of the bed and more concerned by his patient who asked: "What is it doctor?"

"Believe me, Fatma Hanim, another girl."

If Fatma Hanim was disappointed, as she must have been, she said nothing and stoically accepted her fate. Meanwhile, 'Abd al-Rahman was in his study waiting for news. As the minutes dragged on, he felt his tension mounting. Even though his wife had been safely delivered three times, one could never be sure, mishaps were known to occur, and unforeseen problems could complicate matters. He was worried and wished the whole business to be over quickly and wondered at the wisdom of having tried their luck a fourth time. "It is all in God's hands," he thought. "All one can do is hope and pray." A while later unable to sit still, he walked over to his wife's bedroom but before he reached the door he heard the baby cry. He waited for a few seconds but since no one came out to announce the birth and no ululation was heard from within, he immediately understood that his wish for a boy had not yet been granted. He walked back to his study, lit a cigarette and quietly tried to compose himself and come to terms with his bitter disappointment. Finally, Mahfuz Pasha, his friend, knocked at the door but before he could utter a word 'Abd al-Rahman said, "Thank you, Basha, for helping my fourth daughter into the world."

Relieved at not having to announce this unfortunate occurrence himself, Mahfuz Pasha smiled and answered, "Congratulations, my friend. May she grow up to enjoy your prosperity."

Footsteps were then heard outside the door of the study and Idris, having knocked, opened the door and announce the arrival of Chafaq Hanim. 'Abd al-Rahman stepped out and running down the steps met his mother-in-law in the hall. He saluted her respectfully and said, "Congratulations, *Yafandim*. God has sent us another girl."

The elderly lady had guessed as much, for had it been a boy the house would have by now been resounding with the joyful sound of ululation.

"May God's benedictions be upon you my son," she answered and slowly mounted the stairs. As she walked into her daughter's room, she saw Su'ad, who had recovered, sitting in a corner, tears streaming down her face, and next to her stood Madame Alexandra, Dr. Mahfuz's assistant, holding the baby.

"Go wash your face Su'ad and stop your nonsense," she ordered her granddaughter. "I will not have tears and long faces on this happy occasion. Congratulations, Fatma. Girls always bring prosperity to a house and this one, *insha'Allah*, will be no exception. Have you chosen a name yet?"

"'Abd al-Rahman wants to name her Hibat Allah."

"Hibat Allah? Gift of God. It is a good name. However all children are gifts of God and it would please me if you would name this one after me."

Fatma gasped in astonishment. Her mother had, so far, never allowed her name to be given to any of her granddaughters, not to Samia—Hazim's daughter; not to Su'ad, Sa'diyah, Zaynab, or Ruqayah—Khadiga's daughters; not to Nadia, Yasmine, or 'Adliyah—Hussein's daughters; and not to 'Ayn al-Hayah, 'Alia, or 'Abir. "There will only be one Chafaq Nour in this family," she had said repeatedly. "I will not have my name used and abused whenever you scold your daughters or reprimand them. Never!"

They had all pleaded in vain but not even Fatma, her favorite child, had been able to make her change her mind. The honor was of such magnitude that Fatma, for a while, forgot her disappointment and unable to hide her surprise, asked her mother, "You have never allowed it before. Why this time?"

"Because this child needs protection. If she carries my name no one in the family will dare taunt her with the fact that she is an undesired fourth daughter, at least not openly. She will be Chafaq Nour. She may be the fourth girl in this family but she will be the first and only one to carry my name."

And so, with this very clever move, Chafaq Hanim saved the day for the newborn of the wrong sex. Fatma Hanim and 'Abd al-Rahman never indicated that they had been disappointed by the birth of their fourth daughter. It is amazing that in an Upper Egyptian family so much fortitude was shown in the face of that particular kind of adversity. Fatma had an extremely loving and generous nature, which precluded the possibility of negative feelings toward her own child. She simply loved her as she did the others and accepted her unconditionally. Her disappointment had been of the moment and was immediately quenched by her mother's gesture. As for her husband, he was profoundly convinced that God's ways are not to be questioned, and if his wish for a son had not been granted this time it might well be the next. Meanwhile, his 'Gift of God' must be accepted gratefully. Consequently, the little 'catastrophe' was somehow elevated to the ranks of a much-desired child and never made to feel insignificant or unwanted.

Even though 'Abd al-Rahman was no longer a cabinet minister at the time of Chafaq Nour's birth, still he was a very prominent figure in the Egyptian establishment. His lifestyle was grand, his wife was the daughter of one of the most important figures of the day, and both of them reflected a new and glamorous aspect of the emerging social scene in Cairo. Whereas Chafaq Hanim had always remained in the background, leading a family life, and rarely appearing in public, Fatma Hanim was slowly but steadily moving forward toward her social emancipation. Consequently, the festivities surrounding the birth of little Chafaq were as impressive as if she had been a first-born. There was a constant flow of visitors to the ground floor reception rooms of Zamalek bringing gifts and receiving in return little porcelain boxes containing sugared almonds. Trays of *mughat* were passed around alternating with trays of sherbet and silver platters of chocolate or marrons glacés. 'Abd al-Rahman ordered that two head of cattle be slaughtered and distributed to the poor of Sayida Zaynab and two more at the farm in Mahalla. All the servants in the house received a generous gift of money and Madame Duprée was offered a gold bracelet.

Fatma Hanim lay in her room receiving all the ladies who came to congratulate her. Whether the newborn was a boy or a girl was of no consequence as far as concerned bringing a gift, and all who did had to be received with courtesy. Actually, despite feeling a little tired, Fatma Hanim enjoyed the attention that was lavished on her. Nadra, Hussein's wife, was a little peeved at Chafaq Hanim's gesture though probably quite pleased that Fatma was still producing girls. When 'Adliya, her third daughter was born, she had flatly declared that she had no intention of ever trying again. Her ego was somewhat bruised at having been outdone by Dalia, Hazim's wife, who had three handsome sons, the eldest named after his grandfather. "Something is wrong there," she often thought, because Hussein was, after all, the Pasha's favorite son, the successful one, the one through whom a dynastic entity should be perpetuated. Yet, oddly enough, it was fat Dalia and rowdy Hazim whose offspring carried on the family name. As for Karimah, whose son was two years old, it satisfied her to know that in one area at least she had outdone her sister-in-law. Whatever these ladies' feelings, they hid them well for it would have been bad form to gloat. Besides, Nayna was there to keep everyone in check.

Nayna was indeed the moderator in this ever-growing family with its tangled relationships. She had, over the years, realized how different they all were. It was not just a question of character, but also of social background and education, despite the fact that all her daughters-in-law belonged to the upper crust, the *wilad dhawat*. Malika, Muhammad's Turkish wife, did not count since she had opted out of the family from the start, but how about Karimah who grew up in Munira with Anisah? Chafaq Hanim was often irritated by Karimah's superstitiousness, which far exceeded her own. Karimah also had a tendency to suspect everyone of being envious of her, so when on occasion her latent suspicion was aroused her superstitious nature would take over and her behavior become definitely bizarre. As long as she acted in the privacy of her own home there was no problem, but sometimes she would forget herself and do the wrong thing in front of Chafaq Hanim. When Hasan, her first-born, a beautiful little boy, visited his grandparents at Munira, he was never well groomed and his nanny looked like an old hag from the backwaters of Sayida Zaynab. Chafaq Hanim was upset because her sense of decorum was offended. Karimah seemed to ignore that Hasan was the Pasha's grandson, a Sadiq, and always managed to make him look like his messy nanny's child in need of a bath. This was not the case at all, for after bathing him and dressing him, she would deliberately mess him up again. On the first *'Id al-Fitr* he attended at Munira, his appearance caused quite a commotion. When he came into the room, there was a clearly audible gasp of shock. It must have been Nadra who had gasped, or perhaps Anisah, while Chafaq Hanim remained perfectly still. Everybody was staring at Marika, the Greek maid, who carried little Hasan. His face was covered with smudges of black grease!

"My God, what happened to the child?" cried Anisah. Nadra's face was the image of anger. She often disapproved of Karimah's way of life. As for Dalia, her usually placid face had taken on a quizzical look, while Fatma, always kind and considerate, gently ushered Marika out of the room. Chafaq Hanim, who had understood before anyone else what Karimah was up to, was very angry.

"Karimah, explain to the family the reason for this charade."

"But Nayna, surely you understand. It's for the evil eye."

Everyone in the room looked at Karimah and poor 'Ali tried to cover his embarrassment behind a façade of jollity.

"Come on, Nayna. Let Karimah do as she pleases. Look at me. Aren't I well turned out?"

Chafaq Hanim glared at her son but despite her anger kept her cool. When she spoke her voice was firm and her tone commanding: "Karimah, go wash your son's face with plenty of soap, which seems to be lacking in your house. Bring the boy back when he is fit to be seen and worthy of the family to which he belongs. No one here will give him the evil eye."

"But Nayna," persisted Karimah, "there always is an evil eye. It is written in the Qur'an."

"Indeed it is. It is also said in the Qur'an that evil doers will be punished. It is evil to smear a child's face as you have done. Have you thought of that?"

"But Nayna, I was just trying to protect him."

"Protect him in the proper way. Right now you are just exposing him to ignorant practices."

Karimah walked out of the room defeated but unrepentant. This incident upset Chafaq Hanim deeply for it revealed the strength of Karimah's commitment to superstition and childish beliefs. Though she herself believed in the evil eye as well and always tried to ward it off, yet she did it in a decent, 'educated' way and definitely not by resorting to primitive traditions. To recite a few verses of the Qur'an in order to neutralize evil powers is one thing, but to resort to such stratagems was quite another. Chafaq Hanim was further angered because she had detected in Karimah a little streak of naughtiness, possibly brought on by the circumstances of her childhood, which threatened to get out of hand. Today's scene was not only caused by fear of the evil eye, but by her desire to tease Nadra and Fatma who had, so far, been unable to have a son. "Whatever happens," thought Chafaq Hanim, "and no matter how different they all may be, they will have to manage somehow and keep the family together."

And they did manage. The closeness and affinity of the Zamalek group was evident from the start, cemented by the fact that their off-spring were of the same ages and were educated in the same way. They represented the Europeanized segment of the Sadiq clan. The bonds of friendship and understanding were also reinforced by the fact that the three husbands—'Abd al-Rahman Sallam, Hussein Sadiq, and Kamal Sabry—were following the same careers. They were all three engineers involved in one way or the other with the Ministry of Public Works. Fatma and 'Abd al-Rahman dominated the group because 'Abd al-Rahman was about ten years older than the other two. This group was distinctly different from the other two groups because they strongly believed in the supremacy of a foreign education, all of them employing French or English governesses and sending their daughters to French schools.

Relations between the Zamalek and Giza groups were cordial but formal, based on the predicate of family bonds which, as is usually the case, were defined and controlled by the women. Nadra's background, education, and character precluded any understanding of either Dalia or Karimah though she put up with them for her husband's sake or, as she put it, *pour la forme*. Fatma and Anisah, having been brought up by Chafaq Hanim, were very much aware of the necessity to keep family bonds intact hence were never remiss in performing their duty whether they approved of Dalia or not. Karimah they looked upon as a sister who had grown up in their midst and of whom they were very fond, but Dalia they could never get close to because actually she was too different. Fatma was so bright, vivacious, and witty and had developed intellectually to such a remarkable degree under her husband's tutelage and guidance that she was often put off by Dalia's complacency and indolent way of life. While never voicing her criticism, she nonetheless kept her distance so as not to encroach upon a life that was so different from hers. Yet, whenever Hazim and Dalia invited the whole family— which occurred approximately once a year—both she and Anisah enjoyed the day.

What was true of Bayt al-Munira was also true of Hazim's house in the sense that it exhibited the same opulence and the same importance was given to proper hospitality in an Upper Egyptian way. There were differences, of course, but they lay elsewhere. Dalia lacked Chafaq Hanim's intelligence and not knowing how to conduct a conversation or entertain guests, usually retreated within the confines of her own thoughts. However, spending the day at her house meant having a royally served meal. Entertainment was provided by the guests themselves, all the brothers and sisters with their respective spouses and offspring, dominated by the matriarchal figure of Nayna. Ismaʻil Sadiq rarely attended these reunions, as with advancing years, he could no longer cope with the noise and commotion. Hazim was a superb host: witty, warm, affectionate and, owing in a large measure to his own brand of charm, these gatherings were enjoyed by almost everyone. Nadra had her reservations. She was usually a little wary of her brother-in-law who delighted in teasing her mercilessly. Though he did not actually dislike her, he was often irritated by her superior airs particularly in her dealings with Dalia. He never offended her in his own home because that would have been bad form, but he rarely missed a chance elsewhere and, to the end of his life, derived infinite pleasure from deflating his overbearing sister-in-law.

Left: The author (right) with her father and siblings, 1940.

Below left: Aisha Hanim Sirri on her wedding day, 1929.

Below right: Effat Soliman, daughter of 'Abd al-Hamid Soliman Pasha, on her wedding day, December 31, 1942. The bride is wearing her *talli.*

Egyptian ladies wearing *habara* and *petsha* enjoying an outing in Aswan, c. 1925.

One of the same ladies four years later in France.

Nasiriya School class photograph, c. 1940.

Front row, from left to right: Hussein
Heikal Pasha, Hussein Sirri Pasha,
'Abd al-Hamid Soliman Pasha, Prime
Minister Hasan Sabri Pasha, and other
members of the Egyptian cabinet, 1940.

Galal al-Hamamsy, journalist and
co-author of *The Black Book*, c. 1941.

Miss Florence A. Maddock,
governess in the Soliman Pasha
household, 1945.

Madame Gollmer, governess to 'Abd al-Hamid
Soliman Pasha's children, with her charges in
France, 1936.

Madame Ponsot,
governess to the Foda
children, c. 1942.

Young Zamalekites at play, c. 1936.

Zamalekite daredevils jumping off the Great Pyramid, 1944.

Doddy Sirri and Mahmoud Younes seated in their *kusha* surrounded by bridesmaids and pages, May 1941.

Nahed Hanim Sirri, president of the Ladies' Committee of the Egyptian Red Crescent Society, c. 1941.

Sewing for the poor. From left to right: Princess Chivekiar, Miss Mary Kahil, Mrs. Soliman Pasha, c. 1942.

Ahmad Pasha Hussein, minister of social work, flanked by Princess Nesl Chah on his left and Mrs. Soliman Pasha on his right. Both ladies are wearing the Mubarrat Mohammad 'Ali uniform.

AU BON MARCHÉ — PARIS

RÉSUMÉ DE L'ANNÉE 1926

Last entry in Aisha Hanim Sirri's diary of 1926, recording her fond impressions of that year.

Letter sent by Isma'il Sirri Pasha from Paris to his granddaughter Loula in Zamalek, 1933.

One of the episodes that entertained the whole family, in fact the Alexandria society as well, took place long after Hussein had become a cabinet minister and had received the title of Pasha. Nadra, by that time, had established herself as a pillar of the social scene in Cairo through her husband's connections and her own accomplishments as a perfect hostess. And, of course, as her importance grew through her husband's elevation in the world of politics, so did—in the eyes of the Giza group—her natural tendency to be supercilious. Fatma was never jealous of Nadra, being sure of herself and well established in society though in a somewhat different way, and Anisah, as always, followed Fatma. But Dalia, with her Upper Egyptian pride resented Nadra deeply. Consequently Hazim always tried to put Nadra in her place. One day, Hussein and Nadra were having breakfast on the verandah of their lovely villa in Alexandria. Nadra was planning a dinner party to be held in the pergola and was engrossed in establishing the menu while Hussein Pasha was reading the morning papers. Suddenly they heard someone from the street down on the corniche calling, "Hussein, Hussein. Good morning."

Hussein and Nadra looked down, but could not figure out who it was as there was no one there except for a fat man wearing a *gallabiya* and holding a paper bag filled with *libb*.

"Who is this Hussein?" asked Nadra.

Hussein was puzzled for a moment until the fat man crossed the street and walked over to the *bawwab*.

"Morning of blessings be upon you my son. Please tell my brother Hussein Pasha that I am down here."

Hussein having heard him understood what was happening. He hid his face behind his newspaper and almost choked with repressed laughter. Nadra was livid, appalled by the vulgarity of the scene.

"Hussein, make him stop! Get him into the house before anyone sees him."

Hussein, leaning over the railing called his brother.

"Hazim, come on up have coffee with us and stop your antics."

"Good morning, my brother. Good morning Nadra Hanim and how are you both on this fine day? Why don't you come down for an early morning stroll on the corniche and share my humble breakfast?"

Nadra got up in a rage, but as ill luck would have it, at exactly the same moment Mahmud Sa'di, her brother, and his wife Samia drove

past. Seeing Hussein Pasha leaning over the railing apparently argu-
ing with a man wearing a *gallabiya*, stopped to inquire into this
unlikely scene. Hazim, having had his fun, hailed a taxi and drove off.
Within a few hours the story was all over Alexandria.

Nadra vented her anger on Hussein who tried to calm her down
as best he could. He was just as irritated as his wife at his brother's
silly behavior but knew there was nothing he could do about it.
Hazim was impossible to control and retaliation was out of the question. Nadra knew that too; all she could do was pour out her
mortification, frustration, and deep humiliation to Fatma in a long
telephone conversation.

"Hazim has gone too far," she complained. "Can you imagine my
embarrassment in front of Mahmud and Samia, let alone the *bawwab*?
Hazim looked so awfully vulgar in his *gallabiya* and *bulagh*. What will
the servant think of the family if the Pasha's brother looks like a fat,
uncouth *fellah*?"

Fatma agreed absolutely because she strongly believed that decorum and proper behavior should be observed at all times. She, therefore, fully sympathized with Nadra but, like Hussein, knew that
nothing could be done; it was a clear case of 'grin and bear it.'
Because of her marvelous sense of humor, she at the same time saw
the funny side of the episode but dared not laugh outright. She did
not want to offend Nadra any further, though she gave her the following advice: "If you really want to deprive Hazim of his fun, do
not show your anger or the extent of your humiliation."

The real problem however was not Hazim but his wife Dalia, who
as a typical Upper Egyptian was extremely vindictive. She had so
much time on her hands and so little to occupy her mind that one
of her intellectual outlets was to nurse offenses, real or imaginary,
and create cases out of them. She never forgot and rarely forgave a
slight, and in recent years most of her resentment had centered
around Nadra, whose patronizing attitude angered her tremendously. Although, unlike Hazim, she never initiated an aggression, she by
the same token never accepted what appeared to be attacks on her
dignity. She did not view the episode that so angered Nadra as
funny, amusing, or offensive. It was in her opinion the just retribu-
tion for encroachments on her dignity. Hazim had avenged her, and
that was that!

Indeed, the Sadiq family had many facets and encompassed different segments of society, though all belonged to the upper echelons. With each addition of a new member, adjustments had to be made involving long periods of adaptation fraught with danger. Petty quarrels occurred again and again as did jealousies, resentments, and misunderstandings. Yet despite it all, there was an underlying power that held the structure together, Chafaq Hanim, who instilled in them her belief in the value of the family and its position in society.

17

Isma'il Sadiq sat alone in his study, the door closed, an indication to the family that he had no wish to be disturbed. He was deep in thought and, unusually for him, his thinking was random, disorganized, images and perceptions jostled with one another, driven by the pulse that was rushing the flow of blood to the brain. This went on for a while until, with a tremendous effort, he channeled his thoughts into a more coherent pattern. "So, I am dying," he thought. "But aren't we all from the moment we are born? What matters is how one has lived, what legacy one hands over to the next generation, and ultimately that the final passage be smooth and dignified." He considered himself fortunate. He had enjoyed a long and fruitful life and had achieved professionally the goals he had set for himself. He had settled his children into comfortable patterns of their own, had witnessed the birth of many grandchildren, but now it was time to go.

He was surprised though that it should happen in this way. He had always enjoyed good health, preserved by the organized life he led. He ate sparingly, took his meals at regular hours, rarely stayed up late and, being a devout Muslim, never touched alcohol. His illness had started with what appeared to be a simple cold, which he seemed unable to shake off. Then it was thought that he was finally showing signs of stress and fatigue after a lifetime of intense activity. He actually did have influenza and a very bad sore throat. The best doctors in Cairo were called in and came up with various diagnoses. One of them, however, suspected from his preliminary examination that the Pasha was suffering from cancer of the vocal cords. The dread word was usually not pronounced in front of patients. In fact, the doctor was reluctant to tell the family what he suspected, not wishing to be a bringer of bad news. He knew that in the event his diagnosis was correct there was nothing at all he could do to save the Pasha's life, and if it were wrong then the patient would eventually get better with the treatment he was receiving. And yet, his professional integrity made it incumbent upon him to tell someone from the family what he suspected the truth to be. He obviously could not talk to Chafaq Hanim, as propriety forbade it. He mulled for a while over which son to approach: Muhammad, the eldest; Hussein, the favorite; 'Ali, the doctor. His dilemma was short-lived, for on his next visit Isma'il Sadiq asked to be left alone with his doctor. His sons, who usually attended the consultations, reluctantly filed out of the room. Once they were alone, the Pasha looked straight at the doctor with his piercing gray eyes and asked point blank: "Tell me the truth now. What is wrong with me?"

The doctor hesitated for a few seconds before answering, but quickly perceived that facing him was a man whose intelligence could not and should not be insulted.

"Pasha, I think you are suffering from cancer of the vocal cords."

"I suspected something of the kind. How long do I have?"

"This is a matter for God to decide. The only answer I can give you is that, at your age, cells reproduce more slowly than in a younger person. You may be with us for a long time yet."

Isma'il Sadiq knew better than to insist for a more precise answer. He did ask, however, "Are you certain of this diagnosis?"

"Actually Pasha, I should like to run some tests. . . ."

"If what you suspect is confirmed," interrupted the Pasha, "do you have a cure?"

"I am afraid not," answered the doctor dejectedly.

"In that case what is the point in trying to find out? At my age time is running out anyway and the end is close. God has granted me a long life that I have employed to the best of my ability. All I can hope for now is that the dying may not be too difficult. I will ask you doctor to tell no one what we know. Let us both keep up the pretense. When the time comes I shall tell the family in my own way."

And so the doctor kept the secret and life went on in Munira according to the established routine of many years. The family remained in ignorance of the truth but all could see that the Pasha had curtailed his activities and was spending far more time at home than ever before. There was at first a continuous procession of visitors, but after a while, and at his request, word was spread that the Pasha was better and, though it was not true, had resumed his normal active life. Only his two closest and lifelong friends came to visit daily. One of them was Aslan Cattaoui Pasha and the other one Yusuf Wahbah Pasha. Chafaq Hanim had often wondered how her husband, though a devout Muslim, had come to develop such a close relationship with a Jew and a Copt. She once asked him about it.

"Because, Nayna," answered her husband, "they are sincere and honest men."

"But surely, Basha, there are many honest and sincere men among your Muslim friends."

"Indeed there are many—such as Muhammad Mahmud, Isma'il Sirri, or Lutfi al-Sayed—and countless others, but all of them feel secure in their position as Egyptian Muslims and do not belong to a minority with the drawbacks it entails. I admire Yusuf Basha and Aslan Basha because their personal integrity, loyalty, and friendship have, over the years, eradicated the boundaries that normally enclose minority groups and influence their behavior. They are men of value in their own right irrespective of religious affiliation and I have tried, through my friendship with them, to show everyone that tolerance is of the essence in a mixed society such as ours."

There was no condescension in his understanding of tolerance. It mattered little to him that Yusuf Wahbah went to church and Aslan Cattaoui to the synagogue. What he cared about was the affinity that existed between them, born out of the same understanding of what is important in life and what is right or wrong, good, or bad for their country. Their friendship was in fact closer because of their religious difference, rendered stronger perhaps by having to rise to higher levels of understanding in order to survive. There was no naïvete in his attitude either. He was well aware that prejudice is a fact of life, particularly in a country such as Egypt, where so many different religious groups and nationalities coexist. He had not been shocked to hear that at the Dame de Sion Convent School in Alexandria, girls had to wear little silver chains around the neck with a cross for the Christians and a medallion for the Muslims and the Jews. However, he would not have tolerated such behavior at the Mère de Dieu

Convent where he sent his daughters because this was a blatant expression of prejudice.

He had debated the issue once with 'Abd al-Hamid Soliman Pasha, 'Abd al-Rahman Sallam's closest friend and incumbent director of the Egyptian State Railway, who had at the time created a mini-scandal within the Coptic community. Upon becoming director of the Egyptian State Railway, he had asked for a list of the employees on the payroll. It had occurred to him that the total paid in salaries was exorbitant considering the number of people who should normally constitute a work force, or for that matter the number of persons he saw daily. When the list was finally produced, after repeated demands and ultimately a threat to dismiss the employee responsible, it appeared that only about 60 percent of the names belonged to the actual workforce of the department, the rest were names of deceased employees or their children. The common denominator of all these people was that they were Copts. 'Abd al-Hamid Soliman Pasha put an immediate end to this abuse, with the result that he became overnight the bête noire of the Coptic community.

"I had no choice," he told Isma'il Sadiq who had wanted to know the truth of this affair. Versions of the story ran around like wildfire, most of them wrong, and all detrimental to the reputation of 'Abd al-Hamid Pasha. He was depicted as an anti-Copt, an accusation which angered him, as it was untrue. It was a malevolent reaction brought on by anger, fear, and the insecurity of a minority group.

"Yes, I can see the point," answered Isma'il Sadiq, "however, you seem to forget my friend that Copts have a proprietary vision of their position in Egypt. They were here long before Muslims and the hurt at being supplanted by a strong Islamic majority runs very deep, as does their sense of insecurity. One ought not to exacerbate these feelings by unmasking the various ploys they use to protect their own. Besides, this incident is not symptomatic of what I would term a 'Coptic behavior' versus a 'Muslim' one. It does not go beyond a certain level of society, and I think it would have been wiser to handle the issue in a more subtle way."

"How could I have done that? I could not go on paying a salary to a five-year-old child simply because his deceased father was once on our payroll."

"You are right, of course. I understand there have been threats against your daughter's life?"

"Yes, empty threats. You know how it is. Hotheads usually fear but are not shamed,[64] but I have made threats as well, so they will never dare try anything of the sort."

"I do not believe it either. Still, try to mend your fences Basha, because the vicious circle must be stopped somehow. You see we should not complicate our internal situation. The Copts have over the years suffered less, far less, at the hands of Muslims than from their fellow Christians, the British. Our peasants, Copts and Muslim alike, follow the Coptic calendar, tell the same stories, sing the same songs. They all share the same view of life, believe in the same virtues and reject the same vices. We are in effect one nation."

"I agree totally with you, Basha, particularly as in recent years it is the British who have reduced the Coptic community to a subordinate state."

"Precisely, and now, especially after the Coptic Congress of 1911, their nationalism is firmly expressed and most of their grievances are directed against British Christians rather than toward Egyptian Muslims. We must make the most of it to cement our national unity."

This was the voice of reason, to which 'Abd al-Hamid Pasha and many others subscribed readily.

Isma'il Sadiq's health problems—the gravity of which still remained a secret—were relegated to the background by a sudden crisis in the 'Abd al-Rahman Sallam family. Approximately six months after the birth of Chafaq Nour, Fatma Hanim woke up at 2:00 AM in agonizing pain. Every remedy in the house was tried but to no avail. Umm Muhammad had brewed mint tea to which she added a sprig of parsley and tried to make Fatma Hanim swallow a few spoonfuls. A hot water bottle was held against her lower back, a few drops of laudanum in a spoonful of rose water were given and yet by 4:00 AM the pain seemed to increase in intensity. Finally, at 5.00 AM, 'Abd al-Rahman called Dr. 'Ali Ibrahim. "Thank God winter is over," he thought, somewhat embarrassed at calling his friend so early in the morning. This was early April and the weather in Cairo had much improved. March had been trying this year because the city had been hit by three successive waves of *khamasin* winds with their usual sequel of dust all over the place and flies clinging to windowpanes as if dazed by the noise or hoping to escape the fly swat.

Dr. 'Ali Ibrahim examined the patient thoroughly, gave her an injection of morphine to ease the pain and declared that she probably had kidney stones that ought to be removed. The diagnosis was later confirmed by an x-ray.

So far, 'Abd al-Rahman had told no one of the problem and, after instructing Madame Duprée to keep the children very quiet in their quarter on the third floor, had decided not to inform the family until after all major decisions had been taken. He knew, of course, that a definite protocol had to be observed. In other words, he would have to tell his mother-in-law first and word the information so as to appear to be seeking her advice rather than informing her of a decision already taken. Thereafter, the family would have to be told in order of precedence, starting with the eldest. By noon that day the Zamalek house was filled with family members who had converged from every quarter in the city. They all sat around, as there was nothing much they could do except speculate in muted tones on the possible outcome of the operation. Always the perfect host, 'Abd al-Rahman had ordered a lunch to be served at 2:00 PM. At 4:00 PM, he drove his wife to hospital, accompanied by Chafaq Hanim in his car and followed by all the others in theirs. The hospital administration knew they would have to accommodate not only the patient but members of her family as well. Nayna and Khadiga were given a room next to Fatma's, as it was understood that they would be staying there for the duration. Surprisingly, Murad Bey had not objected to his wife's absence from home. The situation was grave, therefore unusual measures had to be accepted. Two other rooms were converted into comfortable reception areas to accommodate the visitors who would undoubtedly flock in every day.

Medical preparation for surgery was, at the time, rather more casual than it is today. As long as the patient had no major problem (other than the one to be dealt with) such as a heart condition, hypertension, or diabetes, the surgeon simply went ahead and did whatever had to be done. That was Fatma Hanim's case and the operation went without a hitch. The doctor's casual attitude, however, was not matched by that of the family or the friends who regarded surgery as a dangerous, mysterious, frightening undertaking performed by wizards behind closed doors. There was also the ghastly business of chloroform, which induced a death-like sleep that blocked the pain but from which the patient might never emerge. Everyone shared this fear based on collective ignorance. After what seemed to the family like hours, Dr. 'Ali Ibrahim still in his surgical gown came out of the operating theater to reassure the family: two large stones and several smaller ones had been removed and the patient was doing as well as might be expected.

Thereafter a very pleasant arrangement was established at the hospital. Chafaq Hanim never considered the possibility of eating hospital food, which she assumed would be tasteless and probably unclean. So Hajj Mansur, the family driver, brought meals from home for herself, Khadiga, and any other members of the family who happened to be there at meal times. Umm Muhammad was brought in with her coffee-making paraphernalia which consisted of bags of freshly roasted coffee beans, a hand mill to grind them, a small spirit lamp, an incense-burner to fumigate the cups before pouring in them the thick brown beverage, two phials, one containing essence of rose water and the other one essence of orange blossoms, and, of course, a good provision of sugar. She established her quarters in one of the bathrooms and produced innumerable cups of coffee *sada, 'ala al-riha, mazbut* and *ziyada*[65] accompanied by glasses filled with cool scented water.

After the first forty-eight hours of concern over the patient were over, a very pleasant routine was established. Chafaq Hanim and Khadiga slept soundly and at about 11:00 AM they were ready to receive their first visits in one of the reception rooms. Baskets of flowers that had been there overnight were moved into the corridor to make room for the fresh ones that would undoubtedly be received in the course of the day. Khadiga chatted with her mother and tremendously enjoyed this interlude in the dreary routine of her life. Since men were not allowed to enter Chafaq Hanim's reception room unannounced, she felt secure. Murad Bey never allowed her to be in the company of men, even veiled. He maintained that masculine conversation was not meant for ladies' ears. Although Chafaq Hanim was quite conservative, her good sense was often taxed beyond endurance by her son-in-law's dogmatic and intolerant attitude. She occasionally chided him in the hope of bringing a certain measure of flexibility to his rigorous behavior. One afternoon at the hospital she told him, "I am an old woman, Murad Bey"—she always addressed her sons-in-law formally—"and do not approve of modern ways. Had I been able to I would most certainly have put an end to all this nonsense one hears nowadays about women's emancipation. But, on the other hand, the other extreme is also wrong, for Islam teaches us to tread the middle path."

"What is that other extreme you are referring to, *Yafandim?*"

"Well, I have for years asked that you allow Khadiga to come freely to Bayt al-Munira, have lunch with the family, and spend the day, particularly when you are away at the farm. But you have consistently refused."

"But this is quite impossible! Bayt al-Munira is a veritable caravanserai, particularly on Fridays."

"I am not familiar with the word you have just used to describe my house, therefore I will not take offense. No one comes to Munira unless perfectly respectable. The Pasha, as you well know, is very strict in that respect."

"Yes, of course, but how can one trust what goes on in the heart of men? One of them might look at my wife with desire, and the sin would in that case be hers as much his. I am merely trying to protect her soul. The truth of the matter is that I love my wife, and whoever loves his wife must be jealous and guard her from sin and temptation."

"Utter nonsense," answered Chafaq Hanim with growing impatience. "You are a despot, Murad Bey."

With these words she put an end to the conversation for fear of losing her temper altogether. She had, in fact already gone too far by calling him a despot. And yet, Chafaq Hanim was not an emancipated woman nor did she want to be. She just wanted to uphold *usul* and its intricate ramifications. *Usul* was not just politeness, or culture, or tradition but an amalgam of them all, with the roots entrenched in the distant past. She would often tell her daughters: "*Man fatu qadimu tah*—He who forgets his past is lost." The more of *usul* one learned the more refined and educated one became. When she heard of Qasim Amin's famous book on the emancipation of women, she was disturbed. It was always dangerous, she felt, to revolutionize an established situation. In the family, everyone except Murad Bey approved of Qasim Amin and his emancipated ideas. His book, *Tahrir al-mar'a* ("The Liberation of Women"), was discussed at length during long Friday afternoons when the family gathered at Munira. What pleased Chafaq Hanim though, was that he did not argue against the veil but against the excessive use of it. The veil, as he explained in his book, is not an exclusively Islamic garb, it was also standard practice in Europe from the ninth to the thirteenth century. Backwardness is caused by bigotry and ignorance, which manacle society. "Why should a Muslim," he wrote, "believe that his traditions cannot be changed or replaced by new ones and that it is his duty to preserve them for ever?"[66] It seemed to Chafaq Hanim when she heard these lines that this was a subversive question because traditions are the cornerstones of a strong society.

Isma'il Sadiq discussed the issue with her in order to clarify those points that seemed to bother her most and which, he suspected, she had misunderstood.

"You see, Chafaq Hanim," he said, "there are certain practices that are based on falsehoods or misunderstanding of the spirit of Islam. Amin is right to argue against blind adherence to them."

"Good, as long as he does not meddle with our ancestral beliefs. I do not mean the religious ones for these I know he would never attack, but the ones that deal with everyday life."

"They can hardly be separated," answered her husband, "but rest assured, Amin's purpose is not to destroy but to clarify and enlarge. He wants to keep the good traditions based on a true understanding of our religion and build on them, bring us closer to today's world."

"Besides," he added with a smile, "isn't that precisely what we did when we sent our daughter to the Mère de Dieu Convent, and is it not what you often try to explain to our son-in-law?"

"Please don't remind me of this man's stubbornness. May God in His mercy grant him peace of the heart."

After two weeks in hospital, Fatma Hanim was declared well enough to be sent home. Before leaving the hospital, Chafaq Hanim took care of a very important task: the distribution of gifts to all those concerned. Since 'Ali Pasha Ibrahim as a friend had refused remuneration, he had to be offered a handsome present, probably a silver tea set.

"English silver, Basha," suggested Chafaq Hanim, "not one of 'Agati's[67] creations. Egyptian silver is good but 'Ali Pasha is a refined man and he would appreciate genuine English silver." Having settled the question of the main gift, she turned her attention to the nurses, the elevator boy, the cook whose food she had not touched, the gate-keeper, and the nurses at the reception desk; she even remembered the hospital garbage collectors. To all these people she made generous gifts of money, handed to them by her granddaughter, Su'ad.

The day Fatma Hanim left the hospital went down in the family annals as a day of joy and celebration. 'Abd al-Rahman drove home first to make sure that all was in a state of absolute readiness to receive the mistress of the house. Little Chafaq Nour, unaware of the bustle and commotion that was taking place around her, slept peace-fully in her cot while her sisters, in a state of excitement, jumped about the place and went from one window to the other, each hop-ing to be the first to glimpse the car that would bring their mother home. Finally, the shiny black, four-door Buick, curtains drawn over the windows, pulled to a stop in front of the gate. Hajj Mansur held the rear door open and Fatma Hanim stepped out smiling wanly. She felt fine, and was delighted to be home, but following her mother's instructions, she strove to look weak and unwell. She walked very slowly supported by her husband on one side and by her brother 'Ali on the other.

"Remember, my daughter," Chafaq Hanim had said, "the neigh-bors will be looking out of their windows, watching every move you make. You must give the impression that you are still far from well. Make them pity you not envy you. Do not attract the evil eye upon yourself." Fatma Hanim knew better than to argue with her moth-er. She played the role of the invalid, who had to be carried to her bed where she was confined for the next two weeks.

All the festivities that had taken place when little Chafaq was born were repeated and everyone looked forward to a few more days of social gathering with sumptuous meals, laughter, and gaiety. Chafaq Hanim came in everyday to ensure that her daughter followed the prescribed behavior and did not expose herself unduly to the dan-gers of the evil eye. However, no matter how hard she tried, she could not protect her absolutely. This bitter realization came to her about a week after Fatma Hanim had returned home. One of Queen

Nazli's ladies-in-waiting, a close friend of Fatma Hanim, came to visit and innocently reported that her majesty had remarked that Fatma Hanim was indeed a very lucky person since her problem had been solved through surgery, whereas she was suffering from an obscure kidney ailment for which there was no cure and, as a result, was deprived of all the good food she liked and often felt unwell.

A stunned silence of a few seconds followed this casual remark. Fatma Hanim recovered her wits almost immediately and, not daring to look in her mother's direction, quickly changed the subject. The visit lasted thirty minutes during which Chafaq Hanim remained silent but clicked her worry beads with a vengeance. After the guest left, she disappeared for a few moments into the maids' quarters, after which she went back to her daughter's room quite composed and chatted with the family apparently undisturbed by the unfortunate comment of the lady-in-waiting. Suddenly, a very strong scent of incense pervaded the atmosphere. Umm Muhammad and the two maids Fathiya and Sikina, rushed into every room and, swinging their incense burners, shooed away with audible incantations the evil spirit that might have been let loose in the house.

The next day Fatma Hanim woke up with a fever. The Pasha, deeply worried, called in Dr. 'Ali Ibrahim again and Umm Muhammad, anticipating Chafaq Hanim's reaction and equally concerned, descended once again upon every nook and cranny of the house, fumigating, purifying, exorcising evil spirits, almost suffocating in the process, such were her diligence and concern. She believed absolutely in the nefarious power of the evil eye and did not doubt for a minute that the Queen's remark, reported by Su'ad, was the direct cause of her mistress' fever. Oddly enough, the doctor found nothing wrong with the patient, whose temperature in the early afternoon was back to normal. He declared that too much excitement the previous day could have caused the problem, but that there was nothing to worry about. Nonetheless, to her dying day Chafaq Hanim kept a grudge against Queen Nazli and whenever she was mentioned in conversation, just pressed her lips, a clear indication of her silent disapproval. Fatma Hanim, who suspected the reason of her mother's attitude, nevertheless decided to question her. "My daughter," answered Chafaq Hanim, "it is better to remain silent than to express an opinion about the Queen that may be considered disrespectful."

"But why should you want to express such an opinion? What has she done to deserve your disapproval?"

"My dear, *al-lafz sa'd*—Fortunate is the one who can express himself correctly, and no-one should know the truth of this saying more than a queen. The remark she made about your luck in having undergone an operation was inappropriate to say the least. One does not envy another person's good fortune, one controls one's feelings. A queen, above all, must remember *usul* at all times."

"I am sure she does. You know, she is a very unhappy woman who is virtually incarcerated in that gloomy palace. The king, they say, is very jealous and won't let her go anywhere. Anyway, he apparently loves her very much and she is a beautiful woman."

"It must be her French ancestry, though I, for one, do not think she is beautiful."

Chafaq Hanim's mind was made up and she was not about to change it.

18

Life in Egypt in the 1920s and 1930s, despite its many tensions, exhibited (at least on the surface) a benevolent acceptance of the status quo; therefore, an atmosphere of sweet repose and pleasant cordiality dominated the social scene. Yet spasms of political anguish occurred sporadically. There were political assassination attempts, which were at times successful, as in the case of the Sirdar Sir Lee Stack (1924), or unsuccessful, as in the case of Yusuf Wahbah Pasha (1919) and Isma'il Sirri Pasha (1920). At the same time, ripples of the destructive wave that swept over the European and American economic worlds inevitably hit the Egyptian financial establishment. Consequently, the early 1930s were also a period of difficult economic and agricultural conditions marked by endemic agitation and the constant tug of war between the Palace, the Agency, and the nationalists. In 1928, Hasan al-Banna founded the Muslim Brotherhood, a movement that marked the overt resurgence of an Islamic group in the political life of the country.

This organization was covertly encouraged by the British Embassy who saw in it a powerful tool with which to combat the growing power and popularity of the troublesome Wafd Party headed by Mustafa al-Nahhas. Whereas the British had respected Sa'd Zaghloul, they had no such feelings for Mustafa al-Nahhas who succeeded him in 1927 as head of the party. They, for the most part, considered him to be a politician of doubtful credentials and of even more dubious motives, in other words, a man they could eventually use, which they did, while not giving too much credit to his worth. This opinion was shared by a number of Egyptian politicians, including fellow Wafdists, which led to a crisis in 1932, in the course of which al-Nahhas expelled from the party some of its founders such as Fathallah Barakat, Hamid al-Basil, Fakhri 'Abd al-Nour, Ata 'Afifi, Murad al-Shiri'i, and 'Ilwi al-Gazzar. Between 1930 and 1932, the government of the country changed hands at short intervals. In 1930, the Wafd was in power for a few months but al-Nahhas had to resign in May 1930 owing to bad economic conditions. He was replaced by Isma'il Sidki who ruled the country with an iron fist and prepared it for elections, which eventually took place in June 1931. That year was marked by a resurgence of violence and general unrest in the country and political parties boycotted the elections, which in any case were rigged.

In the midst of all this commotion tempered by gentleness, which is fundamental to the Egyptian temperament, life in the Sadiq family was dominated by the Pasha's illness. The dread word had not been pronounced, yet the immediate family, uninformed as it was, realized that the situation was far more serious than was officially disclosed. Chafaq Hanim was nobody's fool and understood that her husband was gravely ill, yet never once did she question Dr. 'Ali, her son, because she instinctively shunned the truth and preferred to ignore a reality over which she had no control. Her children played the same game and the pretense went on for many months. In the early days of 1932, Fatma Hanim knew she was pregnant again; though she was somewhat embarrassed by this belated pregnancy, yet she was also happy, not only because she still hoped to have a son, but because it would be something to look forward to at a time when so many unpleasant events were taking place in the country and the family was so depressed by the Pasha's illness. With Fatma's announcement, spirits lifted immediately and a certain measure of optimism was restored.

'Abd al-Rahman received the news with his usual calm acceptance of events, but Chafaq Hanim was not overly happy because she had worked out that the baby was due in the early days of October. She had come to consider the month of October as an unlucky one for Fatma: both her youngest daughters were born in October and Chafaq Hanim feared the next one would again be a daughter. Was this an omen, she wondered? Though her belief in God and in the tenets of the Holy Qur'an were beyond question, yet like many Egyptians, her life was dominated by an inherent reliance on omens and signs. For instance, she hated owls, and could not even look at

a picture of one because she was unable to forget that on the day
her father died she had seen an owl perched on the lowest branch
of a tree in the garden, and at that moment a maid had told her owls
were messengers of death. She dreaded broken mirrors, as she
believed that breaking one would bring disaster. She feared bad
dreams, particularly those that occur before dawn, for they are rev-
elations that often announce a dreadful happening. By the same
token, she believed that a white dove on the windowsill was a good
omen, and that to be woken at dawn by the muezzin's call to prayer
was an indication that the day would be blessed. Setting aside these
intimate feelings, she never voiced her anxiety and hoped against
hope that just this once fate would play a good hand and the spell
that seemed to have been cast on her daughter would finally be dis-
pelled. As usual, she resorted to daily prayers and arming herself
with patience presented a calm and even front to the world. Most
members of the family were quite pleased with this fifth pregnancy
as it brought the usual promise of festivities and entertainment. As
days went by, winter glided into spring, and with the summer heat
tensions mounted as all thoughts converged again upon Fatma
Hanim's increasing size and eventual delivery.

"I predict it will be another girl," announced Nadra. "Fatma
should have known better than to try her luck a fifth time."

"I think not," answered Anisah, always ready to defend her sister.
"This time it will be a boy."

"No, it will be a girl for it is due in early October, like the last
time and the time before that, and Fatma has again refused to wear
a talisman claiming that she does not believe in such nonsense. I
don't either, yet she had nothing to lose."

"It was Nayna who advised her not to," said Anisah, "because
whatever God sends is His will and the talisman won't alter it.
Besides, who ever said that October is a girl's month? If it were true
then all babies born in October would be girls! Which then would
be the boys' month?"

Nadra shrugged, unable to answer.

Summer that year dragged on with hot and humid days succeed-
ing hot and humid nights in a relentless cycle of unrelieved discomfort. 'Abd al-Rahman had decided that this time again the baby
should be born in Zamalek, so the family did not spend the summer

in Alexandria but had to endure, as best it could, the merciless climate. The children were listless and often bored. Madame Duprée tried to keep them busy all day with a variety of activities; she taught the older girls to knit, skip, or play dominoes. The heat was so intense that she established her quarters in the basement of the house where the temperature was at least five degrees lower than on the upper floors. This basement was separated from the kitchen by a thick wall and had an independent entrance. It consisted of a large hall where the girls had a ping-pong table. Out of this hall opened two rooms: one became a dining room where the children's midday meal was served, and the other a bedroom where three cots were installed for an after-lunch nap.

'Ayn al-Hayah did not always follow her sisters' routine. She often escaped to the second floor of the house, where there always seemed to be a hushed activity. Fatma Hanim could not sleep well at night because her swollen body made it difficult for her to find a comfortable position, therefore, during the hottest hours of the day, she tried to rest and sometimes slept for a few hours. During that time, Umm Muhammad stood guard at her door. Whenever she saw 'Ayn al-Hayah walking up the backstairs, she would stand up, smile, and whisper, "She is resting, make no noise."

"Has the baby arrived?" was 'Ayn al-Hayah's usual question.

"Not yet, Sitt Hayah," would answer Umm Muhammad. "The time has not yet come."

"When is that time coming? How long do we have to wait?"

"God only knows, Sitt Hayah. He alone can decide."

"Will it be a boy, *ummi*?"

"A boy, a girl, all is good. All is in God's hands."

No one dared speculate on the sex of the child in Chafaq Hanim's presence as she had forbidden it, not wishing to add to the mounting tension with unnecessary banter. She was not worried about the actual confinement of her daughter, having gone through it so many times herself, but she hated the thought of the bitter disappointment that would inevitably accompany the birth of yet another girl. She spent many sleepless nights trying to figure out ways of protecting the infant since her one and only name had already been disposed of when her namesake, little Chafaq Nour, was born. Occasionally, when she allowed her thoughts to drift toward a happy outcome such as the miraculous advent of a boy in this family of girls, she would speculate on boys' names. She had never permitted herself to question 'Abd al-Rahman Pasha but was quite intrigued. Her curiosity was relieved a few days before the baby was born. She had just arrived at Zamalek and was slowly mounting the stairs leading to the first floor when she came across 'Abd al-Rahman and Dr. 'Ali Pasha Ibrahim walking down. They stopped to greet the elderly lady.

"Morning of blessing, Basha," she said, the address encompassing both men.

"May it grace your morning," they answered in unison.

"You will soon have another grandchild, *Yafandim*," said 'Ali Pasha Ibrahim, and turning to his friend asked. "Have you chosen a name yet?"

"This time, the girl will be Hibat Allah, what else? As for the boy, I have made a vow to name him Hussein after the Prophet's grandson so as to place him under his protection."

"May names live on," answered 'Ali Pasha with the standard response to the announcement of names for a newborn. "It is indeed a good choice."

Chafaq Hanim did not react but slowly resumed her walk up the stairs. Her mind was in turmoil for although her curiosity was satisfied, she immediately realized the problems that the choice of that name would inevitably generate. By the time she reached her daughter's room she was quite distraught, but years of training as the organizer of family affairs, plus her innate wisdom, dictated that she put up a front and hide her feelings. It would not do at this juncture to voice her fears or even admit she had officially been told of the Pasha's choice. As long as nothing had been formally announced, decisions could be altered and a major problem averted. Yet, what reason could she give to make her son-in-law change his mind? What could she do to avert a serious family crisis? How could she explain to Muhammad, her first born, that he had been by-passed in favor of Hussein his younger brother? Her sons always enjoyed an affectionate and cordial relationship but she knew that Muhammad, though he hid it well, suffered from his brother's favored position with their father. Now he would surely assume that the choice of the baby's name had been dictated by Hussein's growing professional success. By the time she returned to Munira, she was suffering from

a splitting headache and had not solved the problem. To make matters worse, she had to hide her feelings so as not to worry her husband unduly. However, years of close relationship made dissimulation
or secrecy impossible and Isma'il Sadiq immediately sensed that
something was amiss.

"Why are you so pensive, Chafaq Hanim? Is Fatma not well?"

"Not at all, Basha, she is very well. By the way, have you heard that
the baby, if it is a boy, *insha'Allah*, is to be named Hussein?"

"Come now, Chafaq Hanim, don't change the subject. Tell me
what is troubling you."

"That is precisely what is troubling me."

"What do you mean? Would you prefer that she have a girl?"

"Of course not, Basha. We are all praying for a boy."

"What is it then?"

"It's the name, Basha, the name."

"What is wrong with this name? After all it was good enough for
your second son so why should it not be good enough for your
grandson?"

"But don't you see, Basha. This will definitely anger Muhammad.
We both know that even though he and Hussein get along very well,
Muhammad is a little jealous of his brother's success. Should Fatma
name her son Hussein, it will hurt his pride. He would feel he had
been bypassed."

"Well, he has only himself to blame for such feelings. He is a bon
vivant who cares more about good food than about hard work. If
he visited the cafés less often he would have more time to advance
professionally."

"You know quite well, Basha, that he goes to cafés in order to
escape the frustrations of his marriage to Malika."

"But he does not even live with the woman! This is an unhealthy
situation. I suspect he is seeking pleasure elsewhere and God only
knows where this will lead. Anyway, a bit of hard work could alleviate his frustration just as well."

They had often had this discussion though it never ended acri-
moniously. Muhammed was his mother's favorite son because he was
kind, funny, and never afraid to show his feelings. She knew that
Malika was just an excuse; Muhammad always had a predilection for
the good life, which did not include too much work but plenty of

fun. He was the eldest son and for some reason had assumed that life owed him success, which did not seem to be forthcoming. Hussein, who was perhaps more intelligent but certainly more hardworking, grew up to be very much like their father. As the years went by, Muhammad became jealous of his younger brother, though he kept it very well concealed. In this very Egyptian family, it did not matter that the younger brother was more successful. Precedence and rank were always to be respected and Muhammad never let Hussein forget it, or for that matter, anyone else in the family. As long as this convention was respected, he had no cause to express his latent jealousy. Isma'il Sadiq for his part never hid his preference for Hussein. He was proud of his second son, his alter ego, who he knew without a shred of doubt would ultimately follow in his own footsteps and distinguish himself professionally.

After their conversation, Isma'il Sadiq and Chafaq Hanim sat for a while in silence absorbed in their own thoughts. "Yes," thought the Pasha, "Hussein will achieve because he has respect for knowledge and is ambitious. Yet what will the quality of this ambition be, I wonder?" Hussein, mused the Pasha, might get caught up in the general political frenzy of the time, for gone were the days of the great pioneers and builders—men fashioned by Muhammad 'Ali the Great and his immediate successors. Egypt was now a country still much in need, but it was caught up in the throes of political currents and ambitions that could turn some men into self-seeking devious politicians who would not hesitate to sacrifice public interest for personal gain or glory. Had not al-Nahhas and his clique turned down the Anglo-Egyptian treaty negotiated by 'Abd al-Khaliq Saroit simply because they had not been involved in the negotiations hence could not reap the credit?

This thought infuriated Isma'il Sadiq. He dismissed al-Nahhas as a devious politician, a discredited character, inept as a parliamentarian and nothing short of catastrophic as a leader. Thank God for men like Muhammad Mahmud who openly expressed their disapproval of such people and their practices, and for men like Mustafa Riad Pasha, 'Abd al-Khaliq Saroit, or Sa'd Zaghloul. But these were an older generation and times had changed, goals had altered, ambitions followed different paths. How would Hussein fare in the midst of the currents flowing across the political and social scenes of Egypt?

Would he retain the clarity of vision, which is a prerequisite for a man of worth? Would he be able to use his knowledge and academic achievements for the benefit of his country while keeping in mind that self-aggrandizement should only be a fringe benefit, not a primary goal? Would he, like his brother-in-law 'Abd al-Rahman, remain a technician at heart and develop his potentials so as to establish his worth as an engineer? 'Abd al-Rahman had recently been knighted by King George V in recognition of the magnificent work he accomplished on the Nag Hammadi Dam. Isma'il was proud of his protégé who seemed to be following his example despite the fact that he had also felt the need to establish himself socially. With this end in view, he had acquired agricultural land and built his house in Zamalek, and in so doing had consolidated his position and his social standing. This last concern, which Isma'il Sadiq had never felt, had run parallel to 'Abd al-Rahman's devotion to his work but never overshadowed it.

But how about Hussein? The Pasha was worried, for he detected in his son a flaw, a weakness that might, in the long run, be his Achilles' heel. Hussein loved his wife deeply, which was good, but he was also often influenced by her and this was wrong. A man should always be the master of his household because a woman, in his opinion, no matter how glamorous or clever—and he had no doubt that Nadra was both—lacked experience in world affairs. Chafaq Hanim ruled over his household but had always known her limits and would never have allowed herself to overstep them. Men have their place and women theirs and the demarcation line should always be clearly defined and totally accepted. Nadra, he feared, did not know these limits or perhaps chose to ignore them. He resented the fact that she was attempting to control his son's life through the love he had for her and feared that she would ultimately blur his vision and lead him into undesirable paths. "Hussein," he thought, "will have to fight his own battles and be firm if he means to stay the course. Otherwise . . . ," he shrugged the thought away and reverted to a consideration of the baby's name: Hussein ibn 'Abd al-Rahman. He liked the sound of it despite Chafaq Hanim's foreboding.

Next morning, Chafaq Hanim, who had spent a sleepless night mulling over the problem, got up in a cheerful, almost jubilant mood. She announced that she would spend the morning at

Zamalek because this was September 30 and that the baby's arrival was imminent. Isma'il Sadiq was amused because had it been the first day in September she would have gone just the same. What intrigued him, however, was the smile on her face. If he wondered at this sudden shift in mood, he knew better than to ask. Besides, he had an important meeting scheduled with his lawyer because, as the time drew near, he was determined to settle all his affairs while he was still well enough to dispatch this final project with his accustomed efficiency.

Having reached Zamalek, Chafaq Hanim asked Idris, "Is the Pasha home?"

"Yes, Sitt Hanim, he is in his study but will go out very soon."

"Good! Please announce my visit and tell the Pasha I wish to see him. I shall wait in the drawing room."

Idris was surprised for this was quite unusual. 'Abd al-Rahman came out immediately and after greeting his mother-in-law offered to walk her up to his wife's room.

"No, my son," she answered, "not yet. I have come this morning to tell you about my dream."

"Your dream, *Yafandim*? A good one I hope?"

"Yes, Basha, a very good one indeed; though it is said that one ought never tell one's good dreams, for in that case they might not come true. Nevertheless, I shall tell you mine for it is so wonderful I truly feel the need to share it with you. But please, do not breathe a word of it to anyone."

If the Pasha was amused or intrigued, he did not show it out of courtesy for the elderly lady, who seemed to have had a vision of some sort.

"Your secret is in a well," he answered, using a common Egyptian expression.

"Well, Basha, as I was fast asleep just before dawn, I heard a voice telling me, 'Fatma, your daughter, carries a son. He will be born in the first days of October and he is to be named Muhammad.'"

A stunned silence followed this statement. 'Abd al-Rahman was totally taken aback, he did not know whether to laugh—which would have been extremely discourteous—or to allow himself to believe in this omen. He was at a loss.

"Well, Basha, aren't you happy?"

"Yes, of course, *Yafandim*. Of course, but it is all in God's hands."

"Undoubtedly, but the voice I heard was clear. It is a boy and he is to be named Muhammad."

"How can I do that, *Yafandim*? I have already made a vow that he shall be named after the Prophet's grandson and placed under his protection."

"So be it, my son. Why not give him both names and in that way he will be doubly protected?"

'Abd al-Rahman was not fooled. He understood that the dream—if ever there had been one—came at a very opportune moment to force upon him a name different from the one he had selected. What prompted his mother-in-law to behave in that way he wondered? She had always been a model of discretion, a person who matched the respect she demanded from others with the respect she gave them. Her behavior was quite out of character. It suddenly occurred to him that when he had first told her of his choice, her reaction had been indifferent. She had remained silent whereas the normal response should have been, 'May names live on.' What was all this about? She must surely have a reason over and above the dream. And yet, the tremendous respect he had for her prevented questions of an unseemly nature. All he said at that point was, "Very well, *Yafandim*. We shall name him Hussein Muhammad. . . ."

"Upon your life, Basha," interrupted Chafaq Hanim. "How could you possibly have a name precede that of the Prophet's, God's prayers and salutations be upon him? Anyway the voice said very clearly Muhammad. Would you defy such an order? Would you start your son's life with such an act?"

'Abd al-Rahman was wise enough to realize he had lost the argument.

"You are right as always. It will be as you wish. If we have a son, we shall name him Muhammad Hussein and call him . . . ."

"Muhammad," interrupted Chafaq Hanim again. "All is well, my son, now we must wait and pray."

'Abd al-Rahman went back to his study to ponder this bizarre conversation. Why not Hussein? Suddenly, the truth hit him with full force. "Of course! It is because of Muhammad, the eldest! How clumsy of me not have realized that I was about to commit a dreadful faux pas. Muhammad would never have forgiven the slight."

Chafaq Hanim with her clever ploy—for 'Abd al-Rahman no longer doubted it was one—had saved the day. "Bless her heart," he thought. "She could have been a fine diplomat, a resourceful negotiator, and is certainly a woman of substance."

Chafaq Hanim, having successfully accomplished her mission, slowly mounted the stairs, exulting in her success, relieved beyond words at having been able to avert a family crisis. There still lurked at the back of her mind like an evil genie the notion that the child could very well be another girl. In which case she stood to lose some face or, at the very least, be discredited as a dreamer of credible dreams. Pushing that unpleasant thought away, she allowed her practical common sense to take over: better be discredited as a dreamer than have a family feud on her hands.

The very next morning, as she was getting dressed, Sakan, her maid, knocked at the door and excitedly told her, "*Sitti*, 'Abd al-Rahman Pasha requests your presence in Zamalek."

Chafaq Hanim understood immediately the reason behind the summons. She finished dressing and although her mind was filled with apprehension and anxiety, calmly sat down and very slowly, attending to every word, recited *Surat* Yasin. This she always did when an important event was about to take place in the family. She prayed that God in His mercy would safely deliver her daughter but she prayed mostly for a boy, a son for Fatma, her favorite child. By the time she reached Zamalek, the house was in turmoil. The family had, once again, descended upon the place from every quarter of the city. There were the well-wishers who, from the bottom of their heart, prayed for a boy, the ill-wishers who hoped it would be another girl, and the ones who did not care one way or the other but simply hoped for a safe delivery—otherwise they would be deprived of all the festivities that lay in store. And there were also the ones like Chafaq Hanim and Anisah whose main concern was the safe arrival of the baby, preferably a boy. The ladies were in the second floor summer sitting room, the men in the main drawing room. 'Abd al-Rahman would have preferred more privacy because he was convinced that the child would be another girl and hated the thought of the commiserating looks, whether sincere or faked, he would have to contend with. He tried to occupy his mind in a variety of ways and claiming urgent business locked himself up in his study.

In the ladies' sitting room conversation was carried in muted tones out of respect for Chafaq Hanim who sat rigidly in her armchair clicking as always her worry beads. She had a set look on her face and although she was not frowning they all knew she was extremely worried. Umm Muhammad passed round trays of Turkish coffee and rose water. Nadra declared that she needed a cup of strong tea to sustain her—she had heard that Dorothea Russell, wife of the British chief of police, Sir Thomas Russell Pasha, always resorted to tea in times of stress. Su'ad sat in a corner sulking, as she had been banned from Fatma's room by order of Chafaq Hanim, who feared her histrionics whatever the outcome of the birth. Dalia had plunked herself on a sofa because no armchair could contain her ample body and Karimah darted her sparkling black eyes right and left in an attempt to figure out what the others were thinking. Tension mounted with every passing moment. Chafaq Hanim could contain herself no longer. She sent for her son, the doctor who was in the drawing room holding forth, as was his habit, on yet another story of his adventures, or misadventures, in Edinburgh. She asked him to check on the latest news. He came back in an instant and declared that the birth was imminent. A few minutes later, sounds of running footsteps were heard in the hall outside the room. Suddenly Madame Alexandra, Dr. Mahfuz's assistant, burst into the sitting room and, kneeling in front of Chafaq Hanim, kissed her hand and said, "Congratulations, Sitt Hanim. It is a boy."

The words were scarcely out of her mouth than total pandemonium broke loose: Anisah screamed with joy, Nadra spilled her tea, Dalia laughed hysterically, and Umm Muhammad led a deafening chorus of ululation. Chafaq Hanim was transfixed. Her dream had come true! Fatma had a boy and she saved face.

A few hours later, when the commotion had somewhat died down, 'Abd al-Rahman crept into his wife's room. She was sleeping peacefully, exhausted by the day's events. In a corner of the room stood the cradle from which no sound emerged. 'Abd al-Rahman looked at the little bundle, so small, so pathetic and yet of such momentous significance in the balance of his life. After enduring for a while the bustle and noise that had followed the announcement of Muhammad Hussein's safe arrival, he had wished to look at his son at his leisure, unobserved, and to take full measure of his profound happiness. A son at last! Proud as he was of his daughters and fully aware that he would never love this child more than the others, yet he suddenly felt reassured. The boy was a vital addition to the family, a true extension of his self, who would carry on his name and possibly follow him in his career. Yes, he would become an engineer and, like his father, build dams across the Nile.

It seemed now such a long time since he had traveled to France in order to learn French and been rewarded upon his return by marrying his mentor's daughter, Fatma, this very excellent woman whose wit and intelligence he never ceased to admire. So many years had gone by, such efforts, such agitation. He often thought of life as a sequence of agitations, strivings, efforts to achieve set goals. Was this ambition? In a large measure it was, prompted by the need to prove himself worthy of his father-in-law's trust, but more essentially the desire to become a man of substance while serving his country. It suddenly dawned on him that there was a difference between his ambition and Isma'il Sadiq's, a difference not in intensity perhaps but in quality.

His father-in-law's ambition had been geared toward the advancement of his country, toward making Egypt a viable, independent, and successful entity. This had been Muhammad 'Ali's dream, which Isma'il Sadiq had pursued unencumbered by the necessity to establish his credentials on the social level, since he had those from the outset. 'Abd al-Rahman's case had been different because it had been important for him to secure a social position on par with his professional ability, while holding onto his dream and never losing sight of his own reality. The effort, therefore, had been greater and the merit noteworthy. It had not been easy but he had welcomed the challenge and plunged with alacrity in the tremendous task before him. There had been events, whether political or social, that created circumstances where possibilities were offered and choices made. To choose properly had always been his personal aim and what was proper as far as he was concerned had never been limited to what was expedient or pragmatic, but essentially to what was morally right.

He was a profoundly religious man who never rebelled when life became difficult and choices seemed unbearable, for he believed in God's justice and knew that His ways are unfathomable. Had his fifth child been a girl, he would have accepted her as he did the others, but probably with a measure of bitterness. With the tremendous happiness he was experiencing came a vague uneasiness, a primeval fear perhaps of the unknown, of what lay in store for that little life that had just begun and was part of his own and for which he felt totally responsible. Suddenly, from the darkest recesses of his soul, the claws of fear came forth tearing at the joy, almost destroying the perfection of the day. Would his son live to adulthood or would he be snatched away to be survived by his own father? Never as much as in that moment had the frailty of human existence tormented him. 'Abd al-Rahman shook himself out of this reverie that was suddenly leading toward paths unknown and certainly undesirable. The sound of ululation came through the closed door and he smiled, his spirits restored. Whatever the future might be, the present was wonderful and should be enjoyed. He silently walked out of the room and braced himself to meet the exciting demands of the day.

19

Madame Duprée was sitting in the garden under the mango tree watching little Chafaq and Muhammad at play. She had her knitting in her workbasket with today's issue of *Le Progrès Egyptien* neatly folded. It was a late autumn day. The sun was shining in the early afternoon and the air was pure with no trace of humidity. She loved those quiet hours sitting in the lovely garden enclosed in its surrounding wall and the hushed atmosphere of the island. Idris came over with a carafe of lemonade and three glasses, which he put down on a wrought iron table beside her.

"Ah, you came in good time, Idris. The children are thirsty."

"Always at your command," answered the old Nubian deferentially.

To treat Madame Duprée with respect was one of the set rules of the house, even though she was, like them, hired help. Yet she stood several pegs above because she was educated and in charge of the Pasha's children. By the same token, Madame Duprée never exceeded her authority or humiliated them because she knew that the enmity of an Egyptian servant would make her life unendurable.

"Has Sitt Hanim returned from Munira?"

"Not yet," answered Idris laconically.

Once the children had drunk the lemonade—Cha in one gulp and Muhammad sipping his slowly so as to make the pleasure last— they ran off to play with the bright red little car Muhammad had received from his uncle Ahmad Bey. Madame Duprée watched them for a while but then let her mind wander again. Life was good in the cushioned environment of Zamalek. What an amazing country Egypt had proved to be. When she had left her native France to seek her fortune in Africa, little did she suspect that she would stay that long or enjoy it so much. Living with the Sallam family in this beautiful house was certainly a very pleasurable existence despite the fact that political events often seemed to threaten its peace. However, in time, she had learned to take it all in her stride and not make too much of it. The Pasha was now a member of the Senate having served as minister in one cabinet or another. She knew that he was quite important and, though his status had grown very much over the years, he remained modest and unassuming.

She definitely liked 'Abd al-Rahman Sallam who was always courteous and considerate. He was also a man of taste and discrimination whose house reflected his predilection for classical beauty and sober elegance. Someone told her recently that he had been the one to embellish the lovely avenue along the Nile in Zamalek known as Gezira al-Wusta with the superb poinciana trees, which now ten years old, shone gloriously in the sun engulfing the street in the splendor of their orange hue. Did he dislike Sir Miles Lampson as much as the other Egyptians did? She wondered. He probably did because the man behaved as if he owned the place. Well, perhaps he had a right to, she thought, because he was the 'protector' of the country, wasn't he? The king, she was told by a friend, was a problem also. Everyone said he was hard and authoritarian quite unlike his brother, the late Sultan. Besides, the constant change of government was also rather disturbing as one never knew who was friend and who was foe, at least she didn't. Consequently one could never assess what impact the changes might have on the fortunes of the family. Anyway, Sallam Pasha always seemed unperturbed, almost unconcerned, unless chosen to be a minister himself.

She had heard, about the time of Muhammad's birth, that al-Nahhas Pasha had resigned and been replaced by that other fellow Sidki, who was said to be a ladies' man. Though very intelligent and capable, he was having affairs all over the place and had so much charm that women succumbed to it despite the fact that he was not handsome at all. Apparently the king had grown displeased with him and replaced him too. Now Sir Miles was ambassador. He was pompous before; God only knew how he would behave now. "He may burst, like La Fontaine's frog, through an excess of pomposity," she thought, and smiled because the very idea amused her. It was said that the king was gravely ill. Would he die, she wondered. Hopefully not yet for poor Prince Farouk is so young. Madame Duprée sighed deeply. She looked around the garden with its green patches of lawn neatly bordered by alleys and at the multi-colored bougainvillea that covered the garage wall. It truly was a lovely sight to behold and yet despite the enjoyment of the moment she felt uneasy.

Madame—for this is how she addressed Fatma Hanim—was not back from Munira and this was not a good sign. Munira had, for sometime, been the center of the family's attention because of Sadiq Paha's illness. Madame Duprée never dared ask a direct question, but she was kept informed of the latest developments by Umm Muhammad: *al-Basha al-kabir*[68] was gravely ill and Chafaq Hanim was beside herself with worry. She had also been told that the Pasha and his doctor had known for quite some time that his condition was incurable. He had seemed at times to be better and had even occasionally attended the Friday family lunch. As always, he dressed immaculately when going out and his white beard was always carefully trimmed. However, as time wore on, he had felt his strength ebbing and could no longer stand too much noise or activity around him. Lately, he never left his bedroom, which was very spacious, and spent most of his day reading the Qur'an or putting the final touches to his will. This was not a will in the usual sense of the word since, under Islamic law, he could only bequeath one third of his fortune. This document he was working on was mainly sets of recommendations, unfinished business that needed to be sorted out, instructions concerning his funeral and the work that was in process in the family cemetery in 'Abbasiya.

Toward the end, he grew impatient with noise and would only admit in his room one or two of his children at a time. Chafaq Hanim was there all the time and only left when the doctor or one of the Pasha's two friends came to visit. Aslan Cattaoui and Yusuf Wahbah came every day; this friendship, which had lasted over fifty years was coming to a close and both of them were heartbroken. It is said that in the final days, when he no longer would, or perhaps could, take any nourishment, he would attempt to sip a few mouthfuls of broth if told that Yusuf Pasha or Aslan Pasha had sent it. Days went by, the decline was slow, painful, irrevocable. Finally, in the early hours of January 20, 1937, Isma'il Sadiq breathed his last surrounded by his sons and his two faithful friends. The women had been banned from the room, for propriety demanded that he be granted privacy during his final moments.

Muhammad, the eldest son, came out of the room and announced that it was over. At the same moment, almost as if he had pushed a button, an agonizing concert of wailing broke out, alerting the neighbors that the inevitable had occurred. These, however, lasted but a few minutes for Hussein gave orders that no one was to utter a sound because dignity and decorum required absolute silence. He was well aware that he was running counter to the custom, where screaming and wailing were the habitual expressions of grief. He lent support to his command by telling everyone that he was complying with his father's wish. This may or may not have been true, but at any rate it met with Chafaq Hanim's approval because she had always intensely disliked histrionics and unseemly outward expressions of emotion. Her daughters shared her views absolutely and were kept busy controlling the Minya contingent, who were still very much entrenched in the old ways. If they were shocked and angry at this unfeeling lack of vocal expression of sorrow, they kept their counsel. None would have dared to oppose Chafaq Hanim or disregard Hussein Pasha's orders.

There was no doubt, however, that the family was in deep mourning. Within two hours of the announcement, every sofa, armchair, and table in the house was covered by black slipcovers. How these made such an immediate appearance would have remained a mystery, had not Madame Duprée seen Umm Muhammad work in the dead of night to prepare for the fatal eventuality. The maids exchanged their colorful *gallabiya*s for black ones, and the house filled up with black-clad mourners, all of them wearing the traditional *bashnu'a*. In the *salamlik,* a continuous flow of men from all walks of life poured in to pay their respects; in the *haramlik* ground floor reception rooms, Chafaq Hanim, her daughters and daughters-in-law were in attendance all day long to receive condolences. Trays of black sugarless Turkish coffee were passed round at regular intervals—sweet beverages would have been an unthinkable breach of etiquette. Madame Duprée felt it her duty to go to Munira and offer her condolences. She had never been to a *mahzana,* hence had no idea what to expect. When she walked into the *haramlik,* she found herself engulfed in blackness and, as she later told a friend "as if projected suddenly in a dark cave where black shadows sat around crying, sobbing, or gently moaning, usually in unison but with an occasional discordant note which, for a moment, would rise above the rest in a shrill though quickly muffled wail." As far as she was concerned, the experience was harrowing because, over and above the surrounding gloom, she could not understand the verses of the Qur'an that an old woman was reciting in a deep and melodious voice.

Organizing the household for such an occasion was a major undertaking. Rooms had to be prepared, beds made up, bathrooms supplied with an adequate supply of towels, meals planned for an unforeseen number of guests, as courtesy required that mourners close to the family—the assessment of this closeness was never clearly defined—remain for the mid-day meal. It would have been unseemly for anyone in that loose category to leave without having eaten—departure would have been interpreted as a churlish expression of indifference. In the Sadiq household, the ceremonial of the *mahzana* was conducted like a choreographed ballet. Hanafi, the Pasha's head *sufraji* on the one hand, Su'ad, her sisters, and Sakan on the other, planned and successfully controlled the situation. For forty days, three times a day, tables were set for meals, one in the *salamlik* and one in the *haramlik*. Menus were based on what was traditionally expected for such an occasion. Sugar, banned from coffee cups, appeared in full force at meal times and the most exquisite desserts were prepared by the chef such as *kunafa*, *zalabya*, baklava, rice pudding, pumpkin pie or crème caramel. However, Groppi's magnificent concoctions were not ordered because they belonged to a different ritual, that of festive celebrations or joyful occasions.

Chafaq Hanim and her daughters ate sparingly. They would have preferred not to appear at meals at all but etiquette demanded that they be present, act as hostesses, and indicate by their presence their appreciation of their guests' concern. Besides, meal times were an interval, a moment of respite in the collective sharing of grief, though Chafaq Hanim was well aware that not all tears were shed out of sorrow, as some of the ladies hardly knew the Pasha at all. Nevertheless, she appreciated the fact that they all behaved as was expected of them. They came to condole, their duty was to express grief, which they did, and they were definitely sincere in their desire to conform to the norms of their world.

One very striking omission from this very traditional scene was jewelry. Cairo ladies knew better than to wear diamond broaches or earrings at a funeral reception, but the Upper Egyptian ones usually awaited such occasions to show off their dowry and riches. Socializing on a grand scale in Upper Egypt at the time was mostly restricted to weddings and funerals, which occurred with more or less the same frequency. Consequently the ladies had made it an accepted practice to wear whatever they owned, no matter what the occasion or time of day. They had to be discreetly warned that this was not done in Cairo, and might even be considered offensive by Chafaq Hanim and her daughters who would be clad in unrelieved black. Everyone complied and disappointment was offset by the excitement of the trip to Cairo and the prospect of enjoying the amenities of Munira for a few days.

One of the busiest people in the household during that period was Sakan, Chafaq Hanim's faithful maid. To her befell the duty of organizing the Thursday visits to the cemetery. In one of the choicest spots in 'Abbasiya's City of the Dead stood the Sadiq cemetery. In the courtyard and on each side of the entrance gate were two sets of rooms: the ones on the left were the *salamlik* rooms and the ones on the right, the *haramlik*. The *haramlik* was much larger for it comprised, over and above the reception room and toilet, a dining room and a kitchen. These amenities were frequent in cemeteries in Egypt. Both sets of rooms had small balconies and faced the mausoleum, an exquisite little stone building with a dome above the burial chamber. Five steps led up to it and there, two marble tombs stood next to one another, one for the Pasha with a marble inscription already in place and the other one for Chafaq Hanim. The stone floor was covered by an Egyptian rug and in front of the tombs, on a lectern, was placed an open Qur'an. Access to the actual burial site was from one side of the mausoleum, and there two alcoves had been prepared, one for the Pasha and the other for his wife as they had decided that they and they alone would be buried there together. Across the yard a very large stone terrace marked the burial site prepared for the Pasha's children, their spouses, and offspring.

The reason for which the *haramlik* was substantially larger than the *salamlik* was probably due to the fact that use of the places differed. Whereas men came to the cemetery to recite the *Fatiha*, listen for a while to a reading of the Qur'an, drink a cup of unsweetened black coffee, and then go back to the world of the living, ladies made it a whole morning's expedition, hence the need of a dining room, actually very small, and other amenities.

Chafaq Hanim, who had always been traditional in her ways and upheld with determination the accepted social conventions of her time, declared that the Thursday visit to the cemetery would be governed by the rules set by her forebears. It mattered little that January was the coldest month of the year and that she, as well as the rest of the family, was totally exhausted by the ordeal of the *mahzana*. She drew strength from her intransigent attitude and believed firmly that she owed it to her late and much beloved husband to uphold tradition and offer him, to the last, all the observances that she held most sacred.

Sakan never doubted that Chafaq Hanim would insist on the observance of all aspects of the traditional pattern. She had worked frantically with two maids to prepare baskets full of *fitir rahma* and *shulayk*, which would be distributed to the poor at the cemetery and to those who would line up at the gate of Munira. These delicate slightly sweetened loaves were delicious, therefore an ample provision had to be baked for the household as well. At 7:00 Thursday morning, Chafaq Hanim accompanied by her daughters, daughters-in-law, adult granddaughters, female relatives, and houseguests were conducted to the cemetery. There, the ladies went to the mausoleum to recite the *Fatiha* before the men arrived, while the maids headed immediately for the kitchen and the dining room to prepare breakfast. Everything had to be carried in baskets similar to the ones that contained the *fitir rahma* and Sakan had supervised herself the preparation to ensure that nothing was forgotten: the salt and pepper for the eggs, oil and lemon for the *ful midammis*, rose water for Chafaq Hanim's coffee tray, cardamom and gum Arabic to be sprinkled on live coals so as to dispel the smell of food after breakfast. The meal was served in several stages as not everyone arrived at the same time. Over and above the Sadiq household, friends and relatives flocked in a continuous stream, as the convention of the time made this visit part of the *mahzana* procedure. Did the ladies eat under such circumstances? Some did more than others, but they all shared in the ceremonial aspect of the procedure, be it only with a token cup of bitter coffee. After breakfast, as the ladies sat and listened to the reading of the Qur'an or perhaps reflected on the transience of life, Sakan, with the help of Hajj Mansur, the driver, was busy distributing the contents of her baskets to the poor of the neighborhood. Small riots usually broke out until the last loaf was given away. When the commotion died down and the shaykh had intoned the final verses of his reading, Chafaq Hanim got up, and followed by the ladies, returned to Munira.

This was an exhausting expedition both physically and emotionally, and yet, despite her extreme fatigue and immense sadness, Chafaq Hanim knew better than to shirk her duties or omit any aspect of the ritual dictated by tradition. Neither she nor her daughters ever complained and they were fully aware that self-discipline was mandatory in these moments of stress. All of them drew the strength to carry on from their training and upbringing. And so, for three consecutive Thursdays, the same procedure was re-enacted. On the fourth, however, the visit to the cemetery was, by tradition, cancelled as it precedes the fifth Thursday, the one that marks the fortieth day after burial as well as the end of the initial stage of mourning, and for that reason considered the most important of all.

The old Pasha's death had little impact on Madame Duprée and the two younger children of the Sallam family who were by then four and six years old. During the absence of its mistress at her father's house, the Zamalek household was run by Umm Muhammad to whom Fatma Hanim had delegated her authority, while 'Abd al-Rahman Pasha made it a point to be home more often to ensure that matters would run smoothly. 'Ayn al-Hayah, now a beautiful seventeen-year-old, was often taken with her sisters to Munira during the first forty days of mourning to have lunch with their grandmother. Remembering her visit, Madame Duprée was somewhat shocked that little girls—'Aliya was twelve and 'Abir ten—should be exposed to such a deeply distressing experience. She was told, however, that this was *usul*, that the girls were not too young to share in the family grief and that they were old enough to come to grips with the realities of life of which death was an unavoidable component.

The girls were marked by the experience in different ways, of course, considering their respective ages. 'Ayn al-Hayah was sad because she loved her grandmother and hated to see her suffer. She worried about the living, her grandmother, her mother, her aunts, more than she grieved for the loss of her grandfather, who had always been a somewhat remote figure in her life. She wished she could turn the clock back to happier days when lunches at Munira were joyful occasions and exciting family reunions. Yet she was also secretly proud to have been included in the group of the grown-up grandchildren. She was wearing deep mourning for the first time in her life, her dress was black, so were her silk stockings and over her hair was a black scarf pinned at the back. 'Aliya and 'Abir wore white dresses adorned with little black ribbons because they were considered too young for regular mourning. When they were taken to Munira, they were never allowed to remain very long in the drawing room with the adults. Once they had presented their respects to their grandmother, kissed her hand and then her cheek, they were led to the sitting room on the second floor to spend the day with their young cousins.

They understood very well that the occasion was a tragic one, consequently were awed and frightened. As they walked through the long drawing room toward their grandmother, passing the rows of chairs lined up back to back, they hardly dared to breathe or look around for fear of arousing nefarious powers such as ghosts or spirits. Their grandfather was dead and Madame Duprée had told them that his soul had gone to heaven, where he was happy and content looking down upon the world and all the people he loved. Was he watching them now, they wondered? In which corner of the room would he be standing? Would he be floating above them? Was he a ghost? Was he truly happy? They discussed all these issues at night after Madame Duprée had turned the lights off and told them to go to sleep.

At Munira, with their cousins in the second floor sitting room, they speculated again in whispers, assuming that such topics should not be discussed out loud. The occasion was a solemn one, they knew, and they tried to behave accordingly. Sakan, who had realized that these younger members of the family were probably under severe strain, dispatched Fathiya, a maid who had just recently arrived from her native village, to amuse the little mistresses. Fathiya resorted to the only form of entertainment she knew, and at which she proved to be very good, which was storytelling. So, for many hours, the little mourners were captivated by the adventures of epic folk heroes, such as 'Antar and Shatir Hasan, and many other tales that Fathiya had heard as a child in the village. These had become an integral part of her being. In later years, the Pasha's granddaughters would often think back on those days of mourning with a certain measure of nostalgia. In contrast to the grimness of the funeral proceedings in the formal drawing rooms of Munira, their experience was enveloped by an aura of remembered pleasure, the sweet recollection of their fascination with the epic heroes of their childhood.

In Zamalek, oblivious of the goings on in Munira, Chafaq Nour, or Cha as she had been nicknamed by her sisters, and Muhammad carried on their usual routine under the vigilant eyes of Madame Duprée. She was vastly relieved that the two little ones had not been 'dragged' to Munira as well. The very thought made her blood curdle and she was determined, had it been the case, to tender her resignation. Fatma Hanim, however, set her mind at ease and assured her that she had no such intention. The reason she had taken 'Alia and 'Abir, she told the governess, was that they were old enough to understand their obligations, and that part of growing up is to be groomed in the traditions of the family.

20

The month of Ramadan, that year, was very toned down both in Munira and in Zamalek. In Munira no one dared laugh or even raise a voice for fear of offending Chafaq Hanim, and in Zamalek, out of respect for his wife's sorrow, 'Abd al-Rahman Pasha restricted the *iftar* meal to the immediate family. For the *'Id al-Fitr*, the little girls were not given new dresses and Muhammad had a fit in the morning when he realized he would have to wear yesterday's shoes. Chafaq Hanim cancelled—no one dared to ask for how long—the Friday family reunion. Her children came to see her every day, and whoever was there shared her lunch informally in an atmosphere of subdued restraint. Chafaq Hanim had suddenly become uncommunicative. She spent her day in her sitting room gazing at the wall in front of her and occasionally gave instructions to Sakan. She clicked her worry beads automatically and whoever was in the room with her dared not speak so as not to disrupt the thoughts into which she had retreated and from which she seemed to derive some comfort. This was her way of grieving. She steeled herself into inaction, wrapped herself as it were in a cocoon of silence and introspection. Outside events no longer interested her. She seemed unaware of the sporadic unrest in the country and no longer cared that a treaty with Great Britain had been signed or that elections were to take place again. She had spent a lifetime with a man who had shared his interests with her, and now that he was gone these political issues no longer seemed to matter.

"She does not want to live any more," Fatma Hanim told her husband one evening after she had spent an afternoon with her mother, in the course of which scarcely more than a few odd remarks had been exchanged.

"Don't despair. She is still in a state of shock. You must remember that she has lived nearly fifty years with a man of your father's stature. She is naturally distraught and disoriented. Give it time. Your mother is a strong woman. She will sooner or later get a grip on herself."

"I hope you are right. Anyway, Anisah and her husband have moved in with her until the end of summer and Khadiga has promised to send Su'ad after that to run the house for her and keep an eye on things. She will never be alone. I would have sent Hayah as well but she is still too young to assume such a responsibility."

"Yes, of course. Anyway, don't worry. Things will work out eventually. They always do."

Indeed, with every passing day, the event that had so profoundly shaken the family gradually receded to the background. The requirements of daily life took over, and although Fatma Hanim still drove to Munira every day to be with her mother, at Zamalek the cloud of gloom was slowly lifting. 'Alia and 'Abir went back to school, met their friends and brought back echoes of life outside their home. The two younger ones also became aware that the atmosphere in the house was less strained. In early spring, 'Abd al-Rahman announced that the whole family would travel to Europe in the summer as he had important business to attend to in Paris. Moreover, there were still a few items he wished to acquire in order to complete Hayah's trousseau.

Hayah, now nearly eighteen, had grown into a beauty. She had had many suitors but none that either she or her father had so far deemed acceptable. It was not that she ever considered the possibility of falling in love with someone on her own, for such was not the custom and respectable young girls of the early 1930s, with rare exceptions, were not given such an option. Though segregation was mostly a thing of the past where marriage was concerned, old norms still prevailed. Hayah's upbringing and sense of decorum precluded clandestine meetings or furtive love affairs. She fully concurred with the notion that when the time came, her father would present the appropriate candidate—with the understanding that acceptance or refusal would ultimately be her decision. Hayah was her father's pride and joy, and his choice would be a difficult one because he wanted the best. He had often discussed with his daughter her expectations in marriage. Aware that she had been brought up in a refined and quasi-Europeanized environment, he knew she would not accept someone whose education or mentality differed drastically from her own.

One day, as he traveled back from the farm with Hayah, 'Abd al-Rahman met an old friend on the train, a friend he had not seen in many years. Muhammad Bey Yahya was a man of impeccable credentials, not only as a successful doctor but also as the epitome of integrity and self-respect. He too was delighted to meet his friend 'Abd al-Rahman and was particularly impressed by the beauty and demeanor of his daughter. He concluded that fate had put him on the train that day to meet a perfect bride for his son. The young man was a graduate from the Jesuit College with a degree in economics from Cairo University, fluent in French and well versed in the ways of the world. Like his father, he was both upright and imbued with a profound sense of decorum and dignity, which at times he pushed to a fault. He was young, just a few years older than Hayah, an accomplished sportsman who excelled in fencing, a sport much admired and practiced at the time. He had a caustic sense of humor, which he exercised frequently with his family and friends, but above all he never lost sight of the responsibility that lay on his shoulders as the eldest son of the head of the Juhayna tribe, the oldest Bedouin tribe in the land. Hayah was swept off her feet even before she met the young man, who was exactly the kind of person she had hoped for. There was no engagement party to speak of, as the family was still in deep mourning, and a big wedding was not even considered unless it could be postponed until after the formal period of mourning, another six months. This prospect did not suit the engaged couple, so 'Abd al-Rahman suggested that the wedding take place discreetly in Alexandria in June, a few days before the family left for Europe. It would be a very small affair restricted to the immediate families on both sides.

Madame Duprée often looked back on 1937 as the year of many events: the old Pasha died in January, Hayah married in June, and the family went to Europe once again, albeit under vastly different conditions. Chafaq Hanim was not with them to enliven the day with her amusing comments and funny requests, and Farhah had gone back to her family, her services no longer required. This time, Madame Duprée was mainly responsible for the two little ones, as Hayah was honeymooning in Italy and 'Alia and 'Abir were always with their mother. She derived much pleasure from her stay at the hotel St. Raphael where 'Abd al-Rahman had settled the family. Unlike his father-in-law, he never considered the possibility of renting a house in Passy or elsewhere for his family while he stayed at a hotel in Paris to enjoy a holiday on his own. He was very much a family man and derived his enjoyment from being with them, taking the children to museums and the older girls to restaurants.

Times change and people evolve. When in 1927 Chafaq Hanim had traveled to Europe, she had carried along with her a complete set of traditional concepts. Putting her up in a hotel would have been unthinkable as her personal habits and daily requirements would have been severely hampered. It would have been tantamount to putting her in a prison. With Fatma Hanim, her daughter, the situation was totally different because she had often traveled with her husband, had stayed at hotels, was a good companion for all outings, and he was secure in the knowledge that, whenever a business appointment prevented him from being with them, she would be perfectly capable of taking care of herself and the children. Yes, times had changed and these ten years had wrought a profound difference in the outlook of an Egyptian lady traveling abroad.

The family crossed the Mediterranean on board the Ausonia, an Italian ship. There they met many Egyptian friends who, following the trend of the time, were bound on their yearly summer exodus to Europe. Most of them were heading for one of the celebrated spas such as Vichy or Chatel Guyon to be followed by a few weeks in the mountains, usually at St. Moritz, then a few days in Paris for a final shopping spree before heading back to Cairo in late September. These were the golden days for a social group that had discovered en masse the enjoyment of European travel but were always happy to return to the luxurious comfort of their Cairene existence. Ripples of the 1929–30 international financial crisis had been felt in Egypt but these subsided into a complacent feeling of financial security, an almost quasi-assurance that all was for the best in the best of possible worlds of which Egypt was the center and Cairo the epitome. Granted that the political scene was having its regular ups and downs, its perennial upheavals, its occasional unpleasant occurrences were determinedly ignored by a majority eager to sustain the image of serene well-being and to consolidate a way of life that was enviable and meant to endure. The malaise that was already felt in Europe had not yet crossed the Mediterranean, and the possibility of war was rarely alluded to in most social circles.

The Sallams did not follow the pattern of their compatriots. They first went to Venice for a few days, as 'Abd al-Rahman had business to attend to there. During that time Madame Duprée never ceased to complain. It was, she observed, despite its many beautiful palaces, a most unhealthy city. The stagnant waters of the canals exuded an unpleasant odor from which, no doubt, dangerous fumes surely permeated the atmosphere! The Bridge of Sighs did not impress her in the least. She found it small, ill proportioned and the gondolas a most uncomfortable mode of transportation. The only redeeming aspect of their stay in Venice, as far as she was concerned, was the Hotel Danieli, the luxury and opulence of which she could not dispute. She was eager to get to Paris, her hometown, where she planned to give the children a grand tour. However, she first had to put up with the tedium of a few days at Chatel Guyon where Fatma Hanim, following her doctor's advice, had to take the waters.

Finally, on August 15, 1937, they arrived in Paris and took up residence at the St. Raphael. Madame Duprée, reflecting on the date, considered it an omen, for as she told the children, it was Napoleon's birthday. Next morning she took them to visit the emperor's tomb and, as a reward for their good behavior, bought each one of them a stick of cotton candy. In subsequent days, she took them up the Eiffel Tower from which they had a panoramic view of Paris, and while Cha was wildly excited at the big adventure of riding an elevator all the way up to the third platform, Muhammad clung to Madame Duprée and much preferred the pony ride they had taken earlier that afternoon. A few days later, they accompanied the rest of the family to the Exposition des Arts et Métiers, which was the highlight of any visit to Paris that year. Both Cha and Muhammad would remember this trip to Europe as a marvelous experience where every day brought a new and exciting outing or an enjoyable activity: a stroll down the Champs Elysées or in the Tuileries Gardens, an afternoon at the Champ de Mars to watch a puppet show, an occasional meal in a restaurant with the grownups.

Like children the world over, they were enchanted by the novelty of life abroad. The world then had not yet shrunk as it has today, distances were immense, given the prevailing modes of transportation, and Europe was an exotic wonderland. They were too young to realize how privileged they were, yet old enough to understand that they were living a marvelous experience. Best of all was the fact that during the trip they had been far more often in the company of their parents and older sisters than in Cairo, and they loved the change. As a result, the trip to Europe remained in their memory as a moment in time filled with joy and exhilaration. Even Madame Duprée had been less exacting in her demands, as if a magic wand had suddenly mollified her disciplinarian nature. The other members of the family also enjoyed this vacation. 'Alia and 'Abir felt quite grown up. They had been to so many restaurants with their parents. They, too, had been given the grand tour, sometimes with Madame Duprée and the little ones, but more often with their parents. They visited the Louvre and Notre Dame, and when they entered the Church of the Madeleine, Fatma Hanim remembered with a pang how she had teased her mother about that earlier visit. During the trip, Chafaq Hanim had never been absent from her thoughts, particularly in Paris where they had spent such a wonderful time ten years before. She longed to be back home now. Letters from Anisah had not been reassuring. Her mother was still encased in her sorrow, unwilling to reintegrate life, and resume her role as mistress of Munira. Her interest only revived when a letter from Europe arrived with news of Fatma and her family. She usually had Anisah read it several times and occasionally asked questions about their itinerary. Thereafter, she would retreat once more into herself.

"She is waiting for Fatma," Anisah told her sister Khadiga. "That is what is keeping her alive."

"Let us hope they come back soon. They have been away far too long."

"Not Fatma's choice, *abla*. 'Abd al-Rahman Pasha had a lot of business to attend to, as you well know."

"Yes, yes, it is just that I have a feeling Nayna will only start to get better when Fatma is back in Cairo."

On September 5, 'Abd al-Rahman having concluded his business, the family boarded the Esperia, the Ausonia's sister ship, for their journey back to Egypt. The trip had been an immense success and Fatma Hanim, though still mourning her father, had overcome the initial grief of the first days. Besides, they had a wonderful event to look forward to as Hayah had just cabled that she was expecting her first child.

21

Chafaq Hanim sipped her coffee very slowly. Actually, she drank it out of habit but no longer because she enjoyed it. In fact, she enjoyed nothing much any more but carried on her daily life with the calm composure that was expected of her. Her *'ulla* was on a small table beside her covered by a thin gauze to protect it from the summer flies. She still much preferred drinking from this *'ulla* than from a glass, as its water was naturally cool and did not have the metallic taste of the iced water that had flowed through a serpentine. This was her very own *'ulla* and no one ever drank out of it. Another was always placed on the northern windowsill to catch every bit of summer breeze during the day and the cool air at night. After the dawn prayer, Sakan would refill Chafaq Hanim's *'ulla* from it and replace it on the windowsill.

For the first time since her husband's death, Chafaq Hanim did not feel utterly disconsolate. Fatma and her family were coming for lunch at Munira. They had arrived in Cairo two days earlier, after an absence of eight weeks. Whenever she thought of her favorite daughter she had a little surge of pleasant anticipation. She was very fond of her son-in law and adored the children (with a marked preference for 'Alia), but most of all she felt the need for Fatma's presence. How odd that out of all her children Fatma was the only one who had been endowed with all the best qualities: intelligence, wit, and a tremendous capacity for love. "We should have named her Hanan (love, tenderness) for this is her main characteristic," thought Chafaq Hanim. But Fatma was also a good name, one she had chosen herself for she greatly admired the Prophet's daughter whose courage, piety, resolve, and strength were common knowledge in Muslim families. Chafaq Hanim's preference was sometimes hinted at by members of the family, occasionally with resentment but most often with the amused acceptance of a *fait accompli*. Hazim, the family wit, had put it very succinctly one day as they were all gathered at Zamalek for lunch. Karimah, with her usual perspicacity, had remarked that Chafaq Hanim visited Zamalek more often than any of her other children's homes. "But dear sister-in-law," he quipped, "remember the proverb, 'Feet lead wherever the heart loves.'" There the matter ended, the preference acknowledged and accepted.

The day was warm and the breeze that wafted through the north window brought with it a smell of dust carried from the Muqattam Hills. The *khamasin* season was over, but occasionally there were little bouts of easterly winds as a constant reminder that the valley was dominated by the hills, was at their mercy. Chafaq Hanim had the maids wipe all surfaces twice a day with a soft cloth because she intensely disliked the thin layer of grayish dust that settled on the furniture. Madame Duprée had suggested years ago that *grand-maman*, as she called Chafaq Hanim when speaking of her, should give orders that shutters be tightly closed in the early morning and opened up after sunset so as to keep the rooms cool and protect the furniture from the onslaught of dust. Upon hearing the suggestion, Chafaq Hanim had retorted: "If Madame Duprée enjoys gloom and wants a foretaste of the darkness of a tomb, she can please herself in her own room. Here in Munira, there will always be light during the daytime, God's light and whatever comes with it." The maids would have gladly adopted Madame Duprée's suggestion but none of them dared express an opinion.

Chafaq Hanim liked the smell of the city, the little noises that came up from the street, the clatter of the *'irq sus* vendor whose castanets could be heard when he was still many houses away and the arguments that often erupted between 'Amm Hamza, the *bawwab*, and street vendors who tried to settle down near the gate. 'Amm Hamza was a dragon protecting his territory. The Pasha had never liked the sight of these vendors who squatted with their wares, shouting out the prices to attract prospective buyers, and disrupting the peace of this residential neighborhood. Chafaq Hanim, however, had often resorted to them when in a mood to buy fresh fruit particularly mangoes, grapes, and figs in summer, tangerines and oranges in winter. She would prick her ear to catch the call of the vendor, and whenever the one she wanted was getting close, and before 'Amm Hamza had sent him away threatening him with his club, she would hurry Sakan down to fetch the man and bring him up by the back stairs to the door of her sitting room. There he would squat and the process of buying and selling would begin. First a sample of the fruit would be sent into the room for inspection, a price would be quoted to be immediately slashed down by Sakan, who was the go-between during the transaction. Scales would then be put into action, closely watched by Sakan, who never failed to accompany the proceedings by a litany of injunctions after which the sale would be concluded to everyone's satisfaction, despite the vendor's lamentations that he had 'given away' his merchandise.

In the past Chafaq Hanim had very much enjoyed these transactions because they broke the monotony of the day. With advancing age and the children away in houses of their own, she had little distraction. While the Pasha was well, he had led an extremely active existence whereas she, unable to read, had resorted to crochet to while away the hours. In time, with failing eyesight, she had to abandon this hobby, after which her only entertainment had been the regular family gatherings and her frequent transactions with street vendors. After the Pasha's death, she lost interest in this activity and lived through the day with nothing to punctuate the hours but the clicking of her worry beads.

Today however was different. She was feeling ever so slightly better because Fatma and her family were coming for lunch. And yet, there was no surge of excitement, no anticipated joy, only a very soothing feeling of reassurance. She was no longer completely alone. She loved all her children dearly and her grandchildren as well, but with them there always seemed to be a need to explain, arbitrate, ignore, or, on the contrary, express and give an opinion. There were demands made on her, expectations to fulfill, tensions to soothe, and help to offer. She had always been the giver, rarely the recipient. She blamed no one. How could she? She was the one who had created the situation. But Fatma was different. This daughter was her alter ego who never needed to be told, who understood her mother's needs without questions. With Fatma there would be quiet repose, a momentary relief to help her carry on through whatever time was left her. She was an illiterate woman who had always lived by her instinct, an instinct supported by a brilliant intellect that allowed her to feel and understand all at the same time.

Now she felt that the end was very near. Every life, as she saw it, needs a meaning if it is to survive. In her case the meaning was gone. Therefore life surely must end. She needed Fatma because she alone would understand and would help her live through the final stage with a certain measure of contentment. As a devout Muslim, she never set a date to that end, never thought next week, next month, or on the first days of spring, because to do that would be a sacrilege. Only God knows when every life will begin and end, and this knowledge as well the soul's ultimate destination are His and His alone. She did not *know* she simply felt, or perhaps wished, and turned these feelings into an instinctive certitude that bore no relation to actual knowledge.

A fly settled on the white gauze of the *'ulla*. It attracted her attention and she realized suddenly that she was quite thirsty. She waved the insect away with an impatient flip of the hand and removing the muslin took a long draught of cool water. She put the *'ulla* back on the table and carefully replaced the flimsy cloth. She settled back against the cushions of her *karawita* and smiled inwardly. "How annoyed Nadra always is at my 'bad' habits," she thought. She knew that her daughter-in-law, though she never dared express it, intensely disliked this very *baladi* habit. "Why can't Nayna use a glass like everyone else?" she had asked her husband. "Why don't you ask her?" he had answered with a mischievous smile. "Of course not! I was just wondering." The question was never asked but, though Chafaq Hanim was well aware of Nadra's disapproval, she was not angered by it because she was wise enough to accept the difference in mentality that existed between them. She belonged to the world of Zawiyat al-Baqli. She had grown up in the traditions of Sitt Halimah, and despite a long life spent with her husband in Munira and her trip to Europe, she was a woman of the nineteenth century who had fared well enough through the first part of the twentieth, her roots firmly planted, her beliefs intact, her identity unscathed. But Nadra was a modern woman brought up at the Dames de Sion Convent with a Europeanized Turkish mother and a ferocious desire to move ahead, to forge an identity that would reflect the world of polished refinement she admired and with which she wanted to identify. Could she blame her? Of course not. To each her own. An old world is dying. A new one is in the making. A better one? God only knows.

She rather liked Nadra, was amused by her constant desire to impress and genuinely admired her impeccable taste and refined way of life. "All this is good for Hussein," she thought. "The Pasha was right. He needs this kind of wife. She will help him get ahead." Yet, at times, she wondered whether Nadra would be able to stay the course and not eventually drown in too much modernity. "Probably not," she thought, "because these are her waters of which she knows every shoal and every current. She will manage to stay abreast." But how about the others? How much of the old ways will they be taught to hold onto? "He who forgets his past is lost," was one of the proverbs that often came to her mind these days. There was much truth in it and she often quoted it to the family. Her *'ulla*-drinking generation was steeped in tradition but times were changing fast and she feared the future. Chafaq Hanim sighed deeply.

She suddenly felt tired, so very tired. Her diabetes was worse again despite the fact that she ate very little. Her limbs were racked by rheumatic pains. "Old age is ugly," she thought, "and the business of dying even uglier." But today she must set aside morbid thoughts and somber reflections and reaffirm as best she can her hold on life for the sake of Fatma and the rest of the family. She must put up a front once again, set an example, and behave according to the image she has forged for herself, that of a strong woman, the giver, the dispenser of love strength and equanimity. To bear up in the face of adversity is, as she had often told her daughters, an indication of breeding, and today, she would have to draw on all her reserves of patience and understanding to cope with this first family reunion after the Pasha's death. "Thank God for Sakan," she repeated for the umpteenth time because her faithful maid had organized the whole affair without bothering her with details. Actually, all the servants knew what was expected of them, and for the most part, their loyalty and competence were beyond question.

A little while later, Sakan came in to remind her mistress that the hour of the noon prayer was almost due. Chafaq Hanim got up slowly and painfully, and leaning on Sakan's shoulder walked to the bathroom to perform her ablutions, then to her room to pray and dress for lunch. She was in deep mourning, hence she wore a *bashnu'a*. Her dresses were all floor length, long sleeved, and loose fitting. The only difference between her everyday wear and the dress she put on now was that the former was made of cotton and the latter of fine silk. Despite the heat, she wore black stockings and black shoes instead of bedroom slippers because her sons-in-law were coming and she must be properly attired. Once ready, she was helped by Sakan to settle back on the couch where she sat very still hoping for a few more minutes of respite before the impending invasion.

Eventually they all came. Kindly Khadiga dressed like her mother in every respect, with her husband, somber-looking Murad Bey, and their children. Muhammad came alone as usual. Hussein and Nadra, beautifully attired in a Lanvin creation, and Hazim and Dalia arrived with their children. Fatma, the guest of honor, was accompanied by her husband and their three older daughters, the little ones being considered too young for the occasion. Dr. 'Ali was there with his family as well as Anisah and Muhsin with theirs. They all came, and all behaved, as was expected of them, with the decorum and restraint dictated by the occasion. Hazim never raised his voice, Karimah refrained from making her usual witty remarks, Murad Bey ate in silence and avoided unpleasant observations, and Muhsin made an effort to take part in the rather stilted conversation around the table. This was not the joyful Munira reunion of the past. It was a subdued family gathering of people who had suffered a great loss and were trying as best they could to recuperate and carry on. This was *sunnat al-haya*, the law of life, to live and to die, two ineluctable components of the human condition.

Did any one of them sitting around that table on this warm September day realize how close they were to the end of an era? Possibly no one, not even intuitive Fatma because some truths are oftentimes too painful to contemplate. She had sat all the while next to her mother in an effort to make up for her long absence and tried to brighten the atmosphere by giving an account of her trip. At the end of the afternoon when they had all left, Chafaq Hanim felt drained. Sakan helped her undress and slip on a loose black night-gown. Then, as was her habit in summer evenings, she lay on her *karawita*, preferring it to her own bed as it gave her the illusion that it could hold night and its sleeplessness at bay. Sakan sat on the floor by her mistress, waiting for the moment when she would help her to bed but also taking a well-deserved rest after the events of the day.

"Everything was fine, Sakan and Usta Mabruk surpassed himself."

"Did you enjoy the kebab, *sitti?*"

"No, I did not have any."

"But you like kebab with tehina salad. He made the *imamba yalde* especially for you, did you taste some of it?"

"Yes, it was good. But you know, Sakan, I no longer have the appetite of my youth."

Chafaq Hanim closed her eyes to indicate that conversation was no longer welcome. The meal had indeed been superb: the turkey on its bed of *khalta*, the kebab and *kofta* charcoal grilled, the *imamba yalde*, the dolmas, and the cheese pâtés. The menu had been well balanced, not too starchy, not too meaty, with the right amount of salads interspersed here and there between the dishes. Yes, Sakan had organized things very well. She smiled remembering the self control exercised by Hazim who, for once, did not pile up his plate and devour what was on it with lightning speed, and Dalia, though unable to resist eating more than was good for her, had shown a measure of restraint by limiting herself to two mangoes at the end of the meal instead of her usual four. Chafaq Hanim had scarcely touched the food on her plate having been far too busy observing her sons and daughters with their families. She had been a life-long people watcher, and had derived much pleasure from her observations of human nature; now more than ever the exercise seemed important. She tried to imagine what lay in store for them, what directions they would choose once Munira and what it stood for were no longer there as a beacon to light the way, as a pole to which they were all attached by bonds of varied lengths and strengths. Did she fear for her daughters? Perhaps not, because they were molded in their mother's traditions, had drunk from the source, nurtured by her ideas, habits, and beliefs, and thus had become and would remain women of the *'ulla*-drinking lineage.

For Khadiga, her eldest, the question was moot because she was ensconced in a nineteenth century mold from which she would never break away. This had been her only affirmative action, her one gesture of self-assertion. Since her husband, whom she loved and respected, had forcefully established his male dominance and rejected women's emancipation as evil, so be it. She would go one step further in the opposite direction, turn her back on the twentieth century and retreat into the nineteenth. With the wisdom of the ancients, she had learned to limit her desires to her possibilities and come to terms with her situation by embracing it wholeheartedly. "Khadiga will be all right," thought her mother. "She is secure." Khadiga and Nadra were poised at both ends of the same pole, one finding serenity in the values of a past to which she belonged by necessity, the other looking ahead to the modern world and adopting its values with a tremendous zest for life. Both women were very secure in their own choices because they had followed their nature. Chafaq Hanim saw the difference between them and accepted it. Gone were the days when she had felt the need to control Nadra, to keep her in line, to force her into a mold that was not made for her. To be fair, she had not tried very hard because she had not wished to repeat the Malika 'Ilwi disaster.

Chafaq Hanim had never quite overcome her disappointment in her first daughter-in-law, Malika the poet, who had preferred the solitude of her little house to a happy life with her son, Muhammad. As time went by, she had learned to respect and even like Nadra, this very modern woman who always sat with her legs crossed, and had recently taken up smoking like a man. Yes, Nadra was all right because she had, despite her failings, three redeeming qualities: she was kind-hearted, intelligent, and entertaining—always ahead of Munira's time, a harbinger of novel and often curious ideas. By contrast, poor Khadiga was so predictable and so plain. For these two, she had no fear. How about Fatma? Where did she fit in the current scheme? To all appearances, she had moved quite a distance from the old ways, perhaps in order to please her husband who evidently took pride in his wife's progress—if modernity is such—perhaps under the influence of Nadra, or simply because her own nature demanded expansion toward new horizons. She had long ago given up the *habara* and the *petsha*, wore short dresses to mid-calf, used lipstick and powder, spoke French fluently—but she never sat with her legs crossed in front of her mother. Chafaq Hanim had been surprised when told that her daughter would occasionally sit in the presence of gentlemen with her face uncovered. If the notion disturbed her, she had said nothing. Fatma's social behavior was her husband's

responsibility and if, unlike Murad Bey, 'Abd al-Rahman allowed his
wife to expose herself in that way, there was nothing she could, or
indeed would, do about it.

Fatma was moving away from the old ways. The transformation
had been slow at first but had gained momentum with every passing
year. There was a time when Chafaq Hanim had worried that Fatma
might be going too far, too fast, and that she might lose her bearings.
However, she had come to realize her worries were unfounded
because Fatma's responses to events and people always reaffirmed the
'ulla-drinking lineage. Chafaq Hanim now understood that Fatma
would always steer a middle course, manage to reconcile both
worlds, be able to follow Dalia's pedestrian language and Upper
Egyptian mentality, and also be at ease with Nadra and hold her own
with·the Alexandria crowd. "Where do her preferences lie?" wondered Chafaq Hanim. "Which persona is she better attuned to? Is she
tugged one way and another, depending on the requirements of the
day?" Chafaq Hanim sighed again deeply. She did not like to speculate about such things because she feared the answer, so she silently
prayed that God would protect her daughter and her family.

She had missed the two younger ones today, little Chafaq, her
namesake, and the boy, Muhammad Hussein, whose entry into the
world had been nothing short of a miracle. It hurt her to realize that
despite her closeness to Fatma and to her daughters, the last two
were virtually little strangers. Suddenly, the answer to her oft repeated question, "What about the younger generation?" hit her like a
thunderbolt with the full force of a revelation because the question
suddenly became an answer and that answer disturbed her deeply.
Her namesake and the longed-for boy belonged to another world,
to a future lost in a horizon way beyond her vision. They did not
speak the same language! The bond had been severed, for without a
common language the generation gap becomes unbridgeable. "My
God, how did we ever allow this to happen?" agonized the old lady.
"These children cannot speak Arabic. We shall never be able to communicate, I will always be a stranger to them, an old woman whose
presence or absence is of no consequence. I could be dead already,
but what is worse, they have lost their links to their own past. They
will grow up rootless, weak. Perhaps Ahmad Bey was right after all,
maybe they should never have been handed over to a foreign gov-

erness." Despite her anguish, she recognized the value of Madame
Duprée's presence in her daughter's household. It flattered her to see
how well groomed and well behaved the children were and how
well they spoke that language she could not understand. "May God
help us all," she thought. "There is only so much one can do. Let
Him in His mercy take care of the rest."

Sakan, stretched out at the foot of the *karawita*, snored gently.
Chafaq Hanim looked at her faithful maid, her heart full of compassion. "What will become of you, my poor Sakan, after I am gone? I
should have insisted that you marry again after you husband died but
you would not leave me and I was selfish." Chafaq Hanim shifted her
body slowly and painfully. Her limbs were heavy. She could hardly
move. She craned her neck to look at the east window hoping to see
the very first hint of color, precursor of dawn, to witness that magic
moment when black turns to blue and very slowly to pale yellow
and then, with the stronger rays of early morning sun, to bright
orange. How often had she watched with awe the start of a new day,
the ever renewed miracle of the sun rising up in the sky and gradually chasing away night's blackness. But sunset had also been for her
a special time, particularly in Alexandria, when she watched the solar
disc dip into the sea and very slowly dissolve in the gradually dark-
ening water. She loved to read the description of this melting away
of the day in *Surat* Yasin:

"And a sign for them is the night,
from which we have skinned the day,
and behold they are plunged in darkness"[69]

Nothing remains as it is, and night will follow day and day replace
night forever and ever until the end of time. But now, dawn is near
and night is moving away. Chafaq Hanim hoped she would hear the
muezzin's call to prayer. She sometimes did when the wind blew in
the right direction and the city was still asleep. She loved this melodious chant, strong and powerful, which exalted God, the Creator of
all things, and called people to prayer. She had always made it a point
to perform the ritual of the dawn prayer if she heard the call and
now wished with all her heart to be able to do so again. Should she
wake Sakan to help her get up? She tried to move her legs but the
heaviness that lay over them had increased. She groped under the
cushion for her prayer beads but seemed unable to move her hand

in the right direction and suddenly she was gripped by fear. Was this
the end then? She must formulate her act of faith, she must utter the
Shihada for her soul to depart in peace, but she could emit no sound.
Her eyes moved slowly around the room as she tried to capture for
the last time the sights that had been her world for so many years,
and there, framed in the northern window, stood her *'ulla* ready for
another day. Slowly she closed her eyes overwhelmed by an intense
emotion. She knew she was dying. There was no fear but a wrenching caused by the pain of leaving all those she loved. She opened her
eyes again. There, by the couch, stood Sitt Halimah smiling gently,
and right behind her was Isma'il Sadiq, who slowly raised his hand
as if beckoning. They had come for her, and she was ready to go. The
living would carry on without her. She no longer felt desolate
because other loved ones had come to help her through the final
stage. Reassured, at peace with herself, she slowly closed her eyes
again and smiled contentedly for she heard the call to prayer and
with her last breath uttered the *Shihada*.

22

Cha stomped her little foot and kicked the ball as hard as she could across the alley. Why could she not go play with her cousins in Aunt Anisah's garden or better still, have them over for a real game of hide and seek? Why did she have to fend for herself in utter boredom because Muhammad was in a bad mood and Madame Duprée so glum and forbidding in her black dress? Life was dreary these days in Zamalek with everyone milling about the place like black ghosts and speaking in whispers.

"Your grandmother has gone to heaven." Madame Duprée had told them three days ago. "You must be very quiet because your mother is extremely unhappy. You must respect her feelings and you will behave properly as you are no longer babies, and play quietly for the next few days."

Cha and Muhammad were duly impressed and plied her with questions.

"Does this mean that Sitti Chafaq is now with Grandpa?"

"Yes, in heaven, where we shall all go if we are good on this earth."

"Is heaven a nice place?" asked the little boy.

"Oh, absolutely. It is a wonderful place."

"Why then is everybody sad?" asked Cha.

"It is not because she has gone to heaven that we are all sad. It is because we shall miss her very much."

"Still, I do not understand why we are not allowed to go play with our cousins or invite them over," insisted Cha. "It is not our fault that *sitti* has died."

"Don't be so argumentative, Cha. You must understand, child, that laughter and gaiety are not acceptable these days. You must learn to respect other people's feelings, particularly your mother's."

Madame Duprée indicated by her tone that the subject was not to be discussed any longer. Cha kicked the ball once again. Suddenly her anger subsided because a pleasant thought crossed her mind, a thought that had seemingly sprung from nowhere. A baby was coming in May, or perhaps sooner, Hayah had told her.

"Will you buy it?" she had asked her sister.

"No, God will send it to us."

Cha had wondered at the statement. If Hayah could ask God for a baby, maybe she could do so as well. However, Madame Duprée had put an end to this line of thought by declaring that God only sent babies to married people.

"But where do they come from?" persisted Cha.

"Well, during the cauliflower season, an angel places the baby in one of them and when it cries people hear it and immediately pick it up and give it to a married couple. But it must be given to people who have truly and sincerely prayed for one. In other places where storks live, a stork brings it down from heaven and places it on the roof by the chimney. How it gets down from there is a mystery, but it does and the married couple who live in the house wake up in the morning and find a baby sleeping in the cradle."

Little Cha was fascinated. She loved the story and her curiosity was satisfied. In fact, she was delighted because when Hayah's baby came she would become an aunt. That would be fun and it would make her more important than 'Adliya, her uncle Hussein's daughter, who was always trying to put her down simply because she was two years older.

"Will Hayah's baby call me 'aunt'?"

"First it must be born, then learn to speak before it can call you anything," answered Madame Duprée with a smile.

"I shall settle the question with Hayah the moment I see her. What is the use of having a niece or a nephew if I am not going to be called aunt?"

"Don't fret. Be patient child. We still have a long wait ahead of us."

The thought of the baby was a pleasant one and helped restore Cha's mood. But Muhammad was not pleased. He pedaled his little red car around the alleys, hitting from time to time the stone borders of the lawn to fake an accident, but his heart was not in it. Cha was irritating these days, always grumpy and quarrelsome. Actually, Cha was not in a bad mood. She was worried. Her mother had announced that after the summer she would go to school with her sisters, and summer was nearly over. She disliked the idea of going to school because she feared the unknown. Why could she not go on studying with Madame Duprée in the familiar surrounding of the third floor schoolroom? She had visited the school with her sisters once to attend the annual St. Catherine's Day. What she remembered, over and above the noise, the games, and the fun, was the feeling of awe that engulfed her as she walked up the main entrance stairs at the top of which stood a magnificent statue of the Virgin Mary. She had been overwhelmed by its size and gripped by a sudden fear that the benevolent smile of the statue did not dispel. She had clutched 'Alia's hand tightly because 'Alia was her protector whereas 'Abir usually pushed her around, taking advantage of the four years that separated them. The door that led to *Le Tour*, which as she was told later was the name of the convent's entrance, was open, and she had crossed it with a beating heart jostled by other girls who were in a hurry to get in.

"*Bonjour Ma Mère*," she heard 'Alia say.

"*Bonjour mon enfant, c'est donc là la petite soeur?*—Good morning, my child. So this is the little sister?"

Cha got her first glimpse of a nun. The figure in black, though smaller than the marble statue, stood very high above the diminutive five-year-old. She wore a large cross that hung on a chain over her chest, her head was covered by a black veil, and her face was framed in white cloth. The creature looked so strange and forbidding.

"What is your name, child?" asked Mère St. Thomas d'Aquin.

Cha's heart beat so hard that she could almost feel it against her ribs and in her ears. She was terrified for it seemed to her that this creature was another statue but one that could move and talk. She was not like the other adults, Cha knew. She seemed to belong to a different species, a frightening one with powers that could harm her. She had wanted to answer so as not to anger the moving statue but could utter no sound.

"Her name is Chafaq Nour," answered 'Alia, embarrassed by her sister's silence.

"Well, I hope she finds her tongue before she starts school here. Otherwise we shall have to assume that she is a nitwit."

This first encounter left an indelible mark on the child's mind and was an ominous introduction to school. She had never wanted to attend St. Catherine's Day again, or the prize-giving ceremony at the end of the school year to watch 'Alia collect almost every available one. For many years, as she walked up the steps leading to *Le Tour*, her heart would skip a beat though she was no longer consciously afraid.

But now in 1937, she was almost seven years old. According to her mother, the time had come for her to enter the forbidding world of the black and white living statues, and she was deeply worried.

As the afternoon drew to a close, Madame Duprée folded her knitting and called the children.

"Come along you two. It is almost 7:00, time for your bath and dinner."

Cha gave her ball a final kick and Muhammad ran off to reach the back stairs before his sister. The three of them walked up silently because the house was, once again, full of mourners.

In the big drawing room, Fatma Hanim sat immersed in her sorrow. The unthinkable had happened. The indestructible Nayna had died. Gone with her was a world of wisdom and formidable strength. Yet she must go on, for Nayna always said, and she could almost hear her voice now: "Nonsense, no pain is too great, for it is said in the Holy Qur'an that God in His mercy never inflicts more than one can bear." Besides, despite her immense desolation, life's demands were already pulling her in many directions. Hayah's baby was due in May and Nayna would have expected Fatma to stand by her daughter and help her through the most harrowing, yet most beautiful, experience of a woman's life. There were also the younger ones who needed so much attention, and above all, there was 'Abd al-Rahman Pasha. Fatma Hanim was very anxious about her husband because the kidney problem he was suffering from was not getting any better and doctors seemed reluctant to make a diagnosis. Fatma feared it might be serious but she was hoping it would turn out to be a minor ailment. Her mind veered all the time from intense sorrow to deep concern over her daily problems, and the tug-of-war between life and death was exhausting her. Cha was another source of concern for Fatma Hanim because, unlike her sisters who had started school with alacrity, she seemed quite averse to the idea.

"I cannot understand her," she complained to Madame Duprée. "She should be happy and excited. Instead she looks as if we are about to send her to jail."

"Pay no attention, Madame. She is a little spoiled. To be perfectly frank, I believe she is afraid to face this big adventure."

Cha was indeed quite unhappy. She hardly looked at her summer school uniform, worn from October until the second week in November. It was a shapeless off-white dress with short sleeves and a blue and white belt, the colors of the Virgin Mary as the kindly sister said while fitting her. Cha did not care whose colors they were. She hated the uniform and felt ridiculous in it, particularly as it was much longer than her own summer dresses.

"It is too long," she whispered to Madame Duprée.

"Oh no, it isn't," said Soeur Sainte Valérie who overheard her. "Kneel down and we shall see."

Cha did as she was told.

"Perfect! It is exactly as it should be, the hem turns up three centimeters above the floor." She disliked the winter uniform, worn from November to April, even more. It too was shapeless, a navy-blue dress of light wool with a high velvet collar and a matching narrow velvet band that ran the length of the bodice. The dress was all in one piece with large pleats held at the waist by a belt of the same material. Without the belt it looked like a sack of flour. Cha hated it. The material was rough against her skin and the style appallingly ugly. To make matters worse, a little cap of dark navy velvet was to be worn on the way to and back from school. This was one of the many rules of the school against which Cha was to rebel. She felt utterly ridiculous with this piece of soft velvet worn like a split sausage over the head. She hated the black knee-length stockings and the black shoes that completed the uniform. Madame Duprée suspected that this negative attitude was the expression of a deeper anxiety, the child's way of rejecting this adventure into which she was being thrust much against her will.

School began on the first Saturday in October. Cha would always remember her first day at school as one of unmitigated misery. She clung to 'Alia, would not let go of her hand, and to her sister's embarrassment, followed her into class. She spent the day sitting close to her, not uttering a sound, wishing to blend with the wall or the furniture so that no one would notice her, least of all the nuns. Though she now understood that they were not walking statues, her fear of them had not diminished. On the contrary, it had increased, as they now had official jurisdiction over her. After a while, forced inactivity became boring so she fidgeted on the bench and poor 'Alia had to restrain her as best she could. At long last, a bell rang.

"Come along. We leave early because it is the first day of school," said a relieved 'Alia. They walked over to *Le Tour* and there stood Madame Duprée into whose arms Cha threw herself seeking the security of the familiar embrace. Her cap had fallen off. 'Abir picked it up and pulled it hard over Cha's head until it almost reached her ears.

"Don't you dare remove it until we are back home," she hissed.

This was the first of many days of acute misery. Fear was like a brick wall behind which she crouched, unable to understand what was going on around her. She moved from one classroom to the other like a robot and during the recreation period she would sit on a wooden bench under a huge banyan tree that grew incongruously right in the middle of the courtyard. She spoke to no one and the other girls thought her aloof and haughty. In the afternoon, when the school bus dropped her and her sisters in front of the gate and the familiar face of 'Amm Saleh, the *bawwab*, was there to greet them, her mood would change immediately and she would run off to Madame Duprée to recount what she had seen and heard during the day. Most of all she was famished. The traditional *gouter* of brioches and jam hardly satisfied her. Consequently, Madame Duprée decided that the two younger children would be served dinner at 5:00 PM to compensate for a lunch which was served at noon and most probably was rather frugal. At the end of the first month, Cha's school results were so bad that Madame Duprée was dispatched to discuss the issue with Mother Superior.

"The child cannot read," said the venerable lady, who like her colleagues Mère St. Thomas d'Aquin and Mère St. Ignace was French and belonged to the *petite noblesse*. "She cannot do sums, has never heard of the multiplication tables, and the Arabic teacher tells me that she cannot understand Arabic, let alone speak it. She refuses to hold a pen, so we have no idea whether she can form letters. I am very much afraid we shall have to put her in the kindergarten."

"But this is impossible," retorted Madame Duprée, outraged. "She has studied with me just like her sisters. She definitely can write, do sums, multiply, and subtract, and what is more can recite three fables of La Fontaine. I can't vouch for the Arabic, of course, but as for the rest I cannot understand the problem." Mère St. Thomas d'Aquin, who was present, suggested that Cha be called to the *parloir* and gently questioned in the presence of Madame Duprée. The *parloir*, so named one assumes after its purpose—a place where one meets to talk—was a long rectangular room of majestic proportions with a crucifix on one wall and a picture of Christ on the opposite one. Jesus was portrayed with his chest split open to exhibit a heart presumably full of love for humanity, but which had the opposite effect of repelling Cha whenever she looked at it. The other pictures that hung there were of long deceased Mothers Superior who had at one time or another headed the convent. Cha was not afraid now because of the reassuring presence of Madame Duprée, who belonged to her normal everyday life.

Ever since she had started school, Cha's life had fallen into two separate worlds. The first was the world of home with her family, Madame Duprée, the servants, and everyone who behaved, acted, and lived in a way she could understand. They all ate, took baths, cried, shouted, or laughed, wore short-sleeved dresses and sandals in summer, ate candies, in other words were 'normal.' Then there was that other life, the world of the 'Mothers,' beings who wore strange clothes, walked at a measured pace, spoke in subdued voices, and were usually imperturbable. She had not yet seen one of them suck a candy or eat a chocolate bar. Did they eat at all, she wondered. Did they sleep like normal people? And if they did, would they go to bed wearing that forbidding uniform? She could not figure them out and it was perhaps from this lack of understanding that her fear had sprung.

"Come Cha," said Madame Duprée in her most gentle voice, the one she used when either she or Muhammad were ill, the voice of tender compassion and sincere affection. "Come, look at me, and recite the fable of *Le corbeau et le renard.*"

Cha remained silent because she was awfully embarrassed and did not wish to recite in front of the others.

"Come on, child. You know the fable. You have learned it with me."

The silence was growing ominous. Madame Duprée was confounded and Mother Superior looked with compassion at the poor child. Finally Mère St. Thomas d'Aquin broke the silence and in a deep, almost masculine voice declared, "This child can't speak, can't read, cannot count, or do sums. She has never heard of multiplication tables. It is obvious that she is far behind children of her age. How unfortunate that the youngest Sallam should be a moron!" This pronouncement fell like a thunderbolt, galvanizing everyone into action. Mother Superior gasped, Madame Duprée clutched Cha to her bosom, and as for Cha, she looked up at Mère St Thomas d'Aquin and in a fit of indignant anger cried out. "I am not a moron, it is. . . ." She could not go on because Madame Duprée had clamped a hand over the child's mouth to prevent the catastrophic statement that had almost burst forth. Cha was notorious in the family for her fits of rage and now was not the moment for her to indulge in one of them.

She shook off Madame Duprée's hand and in a clear, self-assured voice declaimed La Fontaine's fable in flawless French with a perfect accent. She hardly took a breath and at the last line of the poem she immediately launched into a recitation of the multiplication tables. However after three times table, Mother Superior gently took her hand and said, "*Bravo mon petit, voilà une bonne élève*—Well done, my little one. There's a good student." Cha's anger fell as fast as it had come. Mère St. Thomas d'Aquin plunged her hand into one of the vast pockets of her gown and produced a candy, which she gave Cha. The child was happy, not because she had recited her poem well but because she was no longer afraid. As of that moment, life at school ceased to be an ordeal. She fell into the pattern of what she still considered a bizarre and alien world with ease, if not total acceptance.

The ceremonial that governed the relationship between the nuns and the girls was strictly observed. Even though she wondered at the necessity of it, Cha dutifully curtsied whenever she met a nun in the corridors and uttered the mandatory "*Ma Mère je vous offre mon respect*—Mother, I offer you my respect." The sense of respect due to elders was thus drilled into them. If she chafed at remaining silent in the *réfectoire*, she gladly joined in the communal action *de grâce*, which was recited before the meal. The food she found terrible but she dared not refuse to eat it because she was told that the punishment for such unseemly behavior would be to spend the whole afternoon in front of a plate of congealing vegetables. What Cha truly enjoyed were the occasional visits to the chapel when her class would join other classes to sing hymns of praise to the Virgin. Muslims were never forced to attend, yet many of them did with alacrity. In fact, all of them were taught to recite the Pater Noster and Hail Mary in unison during the afternoon hour of free study.

During the class of manual work, called *ouvrage*, in the course of which they were taught the fine art of embroidery, the nun in charge would read to them pages of *Suzette et le bon ton*, a marvelous collection of rules of etiquette that well-brought up young ladies should live by. Christian girls studied the catechism, but not the Muslims or the Jews. All of them however, had to read *L'Histoire Sainte*, or the Old Testament. Cha loved *L'Histoire Sainte* best of all. She loved the story of Adam and Eve and shuddered at the thought of the snake. She would never have listened to the slimy creature no matter what he promised. There was a snake once in the garden at Zamalek coiled between bricks stacked up by the garage door, and a snake charmer had been called to lure it out. They had all watched from a safe distance and were horrified when three slithered out from their hiding place. Hateful creatures! Madame Duprée said they were condemned to sweep the floor with their belly whenever they moved as a punishment for their original crime.

"But, if eating an apple was so bad for Adam and Eve," Cha once asked, "why is it not bad for us?"

"Well," had answered Madame Duprée, "surely it was not the same apple."

Cha found these stories very exciting. She loved the story of Noah and often tried to imagine a boat full of animals, but there again she was confused on how lions, tigers, and crocodiles could be in the same boat as people and not devour them? And did spiders, salamanders, and cockroaches travel as well? To all these questions Madame Duprée answered as best she could but was quite put out by the crucial question that puzzled Cha more than the others.

"If God created Adam and Eve and if they had two sons Cain and Abel, where did all the people of the world come from?"

"They must have had daughters as well."

"In that case did Cain and Abel marry their sisters?"

At that point, poor Madame Duprée was at a loss, and to put an end to Cha's impossible questions answered, "You must remember that all of this·took place a very long time ago so we do not really know what actually happened, therefore no definite answer is ever going to be possible. What we know is what is written in the Old Testament and that is what we need to believe in. We know that God created Adam and Eve and we also know that the awful snake convinced them to disobey and eat of the forbidden fruit. As a result they were expelled from paradise and now we must suffer for their mistake. The lesson you must learn Cha, is that you should not ask too many questions about these things that happened so long ago. You must also try to be a good girl and in that way God will eventually allow you into paradise."

Cha was not satisfied by that answer. She could not understand why she should have to suffer for a mistake made by Adam and Eve long before she was born. Anyway, it might not have been an apple after all because Madame Duprée said 'forbidden fruit' and apples aren't forbidden. Nonetheless, she enjoyed tremendously the hour the nun spent reading these stories to an entranced audience. Rachel Behar, the girl sitting next to her in class, did not always enjoy the lesson. She had become Cha's friend because she was quiet, unassuming, and often gave her half her *pain au chocolat*. At first, Cha could not understand why she always seemed a little shy and distant from the other girls. One day, Mère St. Thomas d'Aquin was reading a passage about the pharaoh who wanted to kill the Jews of Egypt. Led by Moses, they ran away and the Red Sea opened up allowing them to walk safely to the other side. When Pharaoh and his army followed them, the walls of water closed in on them and they all drowned. Rachel looked downcast but Cha was satisfied because the bad people had been defeated and the poor Jews were saved. She looked at Rachel and could not understand her sudden shift in mood.

"You will hate me now, won't you? Because I am a Jew and Pharaoh and the Egyptian soldiers died because of us." Cha was stupefied. The idea had never occurred to her. "Of course not," she said. "Those were different Jews, and I think we are different Egyptians."

The question however had bothered her so she asked Madame Duprée to explain. The governess was hard put to find an acceptable answer, so she told Cha they would discuss it on Sunday because today Cha had too much homework. Actually she wanted to have a chance to discuss the issue with Fatma Hanim or even the Pasha, as neither 'Alia nor 'Abir had been troubled by these stories or had ever related them to the present day. Her answer had to convince, but more importantly not conflict with her parents' views.

When asked, the Pasha settled the question immediately.

"The reason I have sent my daughters to a Christian school," he told Madame Duprée, "is for them to learn about another religion and in so doing become more tolerant. Cha must understand that all of this is symbolic. Pharaoh is a bad king not because he is Egyptian but because he represents a force of evil. Therefore, she need not feel shame for being Egyptian. Besides, there were many other pharaohs who were good kings and served Egypt well. The Jews led by Moses are not better than the Egyptians they left behind, just luckier. They represent the strength of faith and are good not because they are Jews but because they believed in their leader. If Cha understands that there are good Egyptians and bad ones, good Jews and bad ones, good Christians and bad ones, she will have made a tremendous step forward in her education. I am happy she has befriended this little Jewish girl."

This answer must have satisfied Cha because she never worried about the subject again. Once rid of her initial fear of school, she became a little leader in her class. Over and above her two best friends, the Foda sisters, whom she had known since babyhood because her governess and theirs were compatriots, there were many other girls she befriended while ignoring their religious affiliation.

The question of religion, however, came to the forefront once again in the most unexpected way. Cha came home from school one afternoon in a state of great excitement. She had seen the girls who were to take their first communion. Wearing long white dresses, they had white veils that floated over their shoulders, held on by a coronet of white flowers. In one hand they held a missal and in the other a rosary. They looked lovely, eyes downcast, with an air of pious composure that befitted the occasion. They had all been through a long period of preparation, both religious and mental, in order to accomplish successfully this rite of passage into the congregation of Christians. Cha had occasionally questioned them about the meaning of first communion and been given the standard answer: now they had reached the age of reason, they should know the difference between right and wrong. When they confessed their various misdeeds to the priest they would receive absolution. This answer made sense to Cha—so much so that she ardently wished to join the ranks of the dutiful believers whose sins were erased whenever they confessed. But the nun had not asked her to join the group. This surprised, and after a while, angered her. Madame Duprée had a hard time explaining that Muslim children did not have to go through this ceremony.

"But I want to," answered Cha. "I want to wear a white long dress and a veil and a gold cross like them. I know all the prayers. I can cross myself like any of them and say, 'In the name of the Father, and of the Son, and of the Holy Ghost,' I can. . . ."

"Hush, hush, Cha. You are not to cross yourself. Your parents would not like that at all. Only Christians cross themselves. Muslims when they pray bow their head until it reaches the floor as a sign of humility before God, the Creator. We each have our own way and when you are older you will understand all this much better."

"But still, I want to be a *première communiante*, even if I do not cross myself."

"My dear, you cannot always get what you want. You must accept the difference and not envy others. Whatever your religion always remember that there is only one God and you do not have to wear a white dress, a veil, and a cross to prove to Him that you are good. He will know."

Actually the spiritual meaning of the ceremony had never been Cha's concern. All she had wanted was to share in the glamour and be made to feel special. Madame Duprée dutifully reported the incident to her employer. The Pasha was amused, but though he understood Cha's motives he realized the time had come for her to join her sisters in Shaykh Hamza's weekly sessions of Islamic instruction. Poor Shaykh Hamza had a very difficult time with his new pupil because he could not speak French and she hardly spoke Arabic. He almost gave up in despair, but not wishing to offend his cousin the Pasha, decided to apply the *kuttab* method, which consisted in having her repeat after him the same lines of a *sura* until she had memorized it. It was a painstaking and boring exercise, which Cha would gladly have escaped, had not Madame Duprée attended the lesson to control the situation. Eventually, Cha learned a few basic *sura*s but not their meaning. For that she had to wait many years until one day she decided that surely there must be much more to Islam than what Shaykh Hamza had been able to convey.

Cha's first year at school ended on a happy note because she received many prizes and was admitted to the next form. Another happy note marked the beginning of the summer of 1938 as Hayah's baby made his much expected arrival in the early days of May. Madame Duprée woke Cha and Muhammad at 7:00 AM and with a broad smile announced the good news. The children were elated and jumped up and down.

"I am an aunt! I am an aunt!" chanted Cha, to which Muhammad answered, "I am an uncle! I am an uncle!"

The whole day was a glorious one for Cha and Muhammad, and they absolutely reveled in their newly acquired status.

23

While Cha was getting her bearings in her new life as a school-girl, a momentous decision was reached concerning Muhammad's education. At the age of five, he was extremely preco-cious and like his sisters spoke French fluently, while his knowledge of Arabic was poor at best. It was thought for a while that he should be enrolled in the Jesuit College of Faggalah, which was, perhaps still is, the best foreign language school in Egypt. 'Abd al-Rahman Pasha admired the intellectual discipline they taught their students, their high academic standards, and the superior quality of their Arabic instruction. Fatma Hanim approved of the choice because the Jesuits catered to the elite, and being a French school, it would guarantee a cultural harmony between her four daughters and her only son.

The question seemed to be settled to everyone's satisfaction until an impromptu visit by Ahmad Bey one early morning in the spring of 1938. This was quite surprising, as the old gentleman never came unannounced but usually as a response to an official invitation. The Pasha was still having his early morning cup of tea in the summer sitting room, as breakfast was a meal he never took in the dining room. Not yet dressed, he nevertheless rushed down to the small drawing room where his elder brother had been introduced and apologized profusely for not being properly attired. Coffee was ordered and out of courtesy no questions were asked, for it had to be assumed that Ahmad Bey could appear whenever he wished at his younger brother's house. After the usual pleasantries were exchanged and questions related to the various members of the family asked and answered, there was a pause, which seemed to the Pasha a precursor of unpleasant moments to follow. Finally, having sipped the last of his coffee, Ahmad Bey spoke up.

"I have come, my brother, to discuss Muhammad's education."

'Abd al-Rahman was relieved for he had feared a serious problem in the family. At the same time he realized that he was in for an unpleasant half hour, as he had no doubt that the Jesuits would not meet with the approval of this staunch Muslim who, to this day, officially refused to acknowledge the presence of a Christian *khawagaya* in his brother's household. He in fact had never met Madame Duprée. Anyway, there was precious little he could do at this point except present his case and hope for the best.

"We would like to send him to the Jesuit College. . . ."

"Never!" interrupted Ahmad Bey. "Your only son shall not go to a Christian school among French-speaking people and lose his Egyptian identity. For the girls, the situation is different because manners, refinement, and a foreign language are good things for them to learn. After all, the best one can wish for them is to be refined and accomplished young ladies. What is good for them will be bad for the boy. He is an only son, surrounded all day long by women. He cannot speak Arabic properly, if at all. Do you want him to be a sissy or a little *khawaga*?"

"But what should we do? I am just trying to give him the best and everyone knows that the Jesuit College has an international reputation."

"I don't know anything about international. I only care about the national. Muhammad is an Egyptian boy, a Muslim. He must receive the education provided by his country, in the language of his country and a religious instruction befitting a Muslim."

"Where do you propose I should send him then?" asked 'Abd al-Rahman taken aback by his brother's barely contained indignation.

"To the Nasiriya School of course. It is an excellent primary institution run by the government. Instruction is given in Arabic. The curriculum is the same as that of the best foreign schools. The teachers have impeccable credentials, and since you so admire what is foreign, you will be pleased to know that a *khawagaya* is in charge of housekeeping. I would have sent my sons there had I lived in Zamalek instead of in Heliopolis." 'Abd al-Rahman knew he was defeated. Actually he realized that his brother's arguments were correct and that his initial choice would have been a grave mistake.

"It will be as you wish, my brother, and I thank you for having taken the trouble to enlighten me as regards Muhammad's best interests."

"Muhammad is my son just as much as he is yours and he carries the family name. I will not lose him to foreigners."

Reassured about his nephew's academic future and probably gratified by the Pasha's recognition of his older brother's right to interfere in important family decisions, Ahmad Bey took his leave. 'Abd al-Rahman sat alone for a while smoking one of the many Gianaclis cigarettes of the day and reflected on the wisdom of his brother's advice. Eventually, he walked upstairs very slowly, organizing his thoughts so as to present the case to his wife in an acceptable way. Although Fatma Hanim seldom questioned a decision her husband made concerning family matters, nonetheless he usually expected her approval. Would he have it this time, he wondered? Muhammad's importance in her life was paramount as well as her belief that the Jesuit College was the best in Cairo.

"Do we have a problem on our hands, Basha?" she asked.

"A problem, Fatma Hanim? Why should we have one?"

"Well, Ahmad Bey's visit so early in the morning is quite unusual. Has anything happened in the family?"

"No, he came this morning in order to prevent us from doing something we might live to regret."

"You talk in riddles, Basha. What do you mean?"

"The situation as both he and I see it is that Muhammad ought not to be sent to the Jesuits."

"Not sent to the Jesuits?" repeated Fatma Hanim stupefied. "It is the best school in town."

"Perhaps it is, but not for our son."

The Pasha then very succinctly presented the case to his wife as it had been presented to him, and to make the decision more acceptable, pointed out that most of their relatives and friends had sent their sons to the Nasiriya School. "Don't you think that Kamel Pasha Nabih, Abdel Wahab Mooro Pasha, 'Ali Labib Gabr, Muhammad Zulfikar, to name but a few of our friends, want the best for their children? They all reasoned, I assume, that since the boys are already fluent in French, it would be in their best interest to learn Arabic properly and live in an Egyptian atmosphere which is, after all, the one to which they belong."

The argument was a strong one and if Fatma Hanim was somewhat peeved at Ahmad Bey's interference in her son's life, she had the intelligence not to show it. The Pasha had decided, and though she would have preferred the Jesuits, she had to admit that the Nasiriya was a good school and catered to the best. And so the die was cast and Muhammad was enrolled in that prestigious government institution.

The Nasiriya School was housed in a palace originally built for Sa'id Halim Pasha and his wife Princess Emina Inji Toussoun; both were Muhammad 'Ali Pasha's grandchildren. The architect selected by Halim Pasha was Antonio Lasciac. This gentleman was very much in favor with the Egyptian court and was also entrusted with the building of a palace for Princess Nimetallah Tewfik, wife of Prince Kamal al-Din Hussein, one for Prince Yusuf Kamal in al-Marg, one for 'Adly Yeghen Pasha in Garden City, also known as the Sherif Pasha Sabri Palace, and the Tahra Palace in Qubba. At the outbreak of World War I, while Sa'id Halim Pasha was in Istambul occupying the magnificent post of *Sadr al-'Azam*, or Grand Vizir of the Ottoman Empire, the British swiftly sequestered his assets in Egypt. As far as they were concerned, he was an enemy alien working for an enemy state, since Britain had declared war on Turkey.

Once the palace was appropriated it was turned into a school for the Egyptian elite. The palace was located in Ma'ruf, a neighborhood that had seen better days, but was by the early 1930s definitely run down. Over the years, the palace had lost its park and gardens, and now stood right in the middle of ugly buildings and narrow streets like a jewel incongruously pinned on the chest of an old madam's faded and vulgar dress. Despite the loss of its grounds, the school itself had retained in the 1930s and 40s some of its original beauty with its magnificent marble columns, wrought iron decorations, stuccowork, and lovely parquet floors. It was run by an extremely able headmaster, carefully selected on the basis of impeccable credentials, and by an impressively qualified faculty.[70] Men such as Lutfi al- Sayed and Sa'd Zaghloul had left a very strong impact on the educational system of the country. They had clearly understood that if Egypt were ever to obtain its independence it needed an educated elite whose outlook would be focused on Egypt rather than Europe. In that respect, as in many others, time had moved on and Muhammad 'Ali's dream was taking on a new dimension: to Europeanize oneself educationally was no longer the ultimate goal but to receive an Egyptian education in Egypt seemed to be the new social order. The winds of change fanned by the nationalists, whatever party they belonged to, encouraged Egyptian families to seek an educational rapprochement with the 'national' rather the 'European.' In 1924, Sa'd Zaghloul, then minister of education, substantially increased the budget for education and if foreign schools benefited from this surge of renewed interest, certainly the government ones did so as well and even on a larger scale.

Discipline at the Nasiriya was enforced by a system of rewards and sanctions, which never included corporal punishment, except perhaps for an occasional rap with the ruler on the open palm of a recalcitrant dunce. The boys were expected to work hard, behave themselves, and learn to be true Egyptians proud of their country. The foreign matron, for indeed there was one, insisted on a mid-morning glass of milk to accompany their homemade snack.

When informed of the Pasha's decision, Madame Duprée was outraged. Her indignation was aggravated by the fact that she could not express it openly.

"I will never understand the convoluted workings of an Egyptian mind," she complained to her friend Madame Ponsot. They were sitting on one of the wooden benches that bordered the alleys of the Grotto Garden, watching the children at play. "Can you imagine this delicate, beautiful little boy in the midst of those Arabic-speaking ruffians? Do you realize the kind of language he will inevitably pick up, the bad manners, and probably skin diseases as well? Can't the Pasha see he is making a grave mistake? He is literally throwing him to the wolves."

"Come on, Madame Duprée. Things won't be so bad I am sure. Boys in my family have gone to Egyptian schools and they are fine."

"I still believe it is a mistake."

Poor Madame Duprée was beside herself with worry but stoically accepted the inevitable. On Muhammad's first day at school the whole family rose a little earlier than usual. There was great excitement in the air. Donning his new uniform of short, gray trousers, a white shirt, a blue blazer, knee-length gray stockings, black shoes, and a red tarboosh, he looked quite grown up. He drove off with his father in the family car carrying his little school bag in which Madame Duprée had put a sandwich wrapped in a linen napkin, and a white handkerchief. His first day at school was a great adventure. He never felt the fear his sister had experienced but simply took things in stride. Cha was slightly miffed because her little brother always seemed to manage with a carefree, self-assured attitude she often lacked. When Muhammad came back from school on that first day, she assailed him with questions "What happened? Did you cry? How are the teachers dressed?" To this last question she received the most surprising answer "They dress just like papa and all of them wear a tarboosh in class."

As days went by, the difference between the schools revealed itself in the daily accounts the children gave of their activities. Muhammad rapidly learned Arabic and became fluent in the language, whereas Cha distanced herself more and more from her Egyptian cultural background. Muhammad's involvement with a curriculum based on Arabic and national foundations caused his personality to change gradually as his awareness of his Egyptian identity affirmed itself. The two children, though extremely close at home, were living in totally different worlds and were subjected to vastly different sets of experiences. As a result, Cha was turning into a Frenchified little girl with a very vague underlying Egyptian consciousness, while Muhammad steadily moved away from Madame Duprée's Europeanized ministering and forged ahead to become a full-fledged Egyptian boy, reveling in the use of a language his sister hardly knew. In fact, as years went by, he and many other boys of his school became ardent nationalists concerned with political issues, and to Cha's amazement, bristled at the British presence in Egypt, a fact that had never bothered her in the least.

Many years later when both were adults, their reaction to the 1956 war was again quite different. While Muhammad and his friends of the Nasiriya School volunteered to fight the tripartite forces in the Canal Zone and ostentatiously turned their back to the Gezira Sporting Club and what it stood for, Cha, who was by then married to a committed nationalist, felt betrayed and confused. How could France and Britain, those two mighty and civilized countries she admired so much, treat Egypt in this way? It did not seem fair or right. This conflict of allegiance, this dichotomy between her official self, the Egyptian, and her other self, the Franco-British one, was never more acutely felt than in those days. And she clearly perceived then, as did Edward Said later for other reasons, that she was 'out of place,' never truly part of a definite world, never quite at ease with her reality. But in the blissful years of the 1930s Cha and Muhammad were not bothered by lofty aspirations but simply enjoyed living in the wonderful world of Zamalek at the height of its exquisite refinement.

The picture however was not as idyllic as the children perceived it. Here again was a typical characteristic of life at the time. Offspring of these privileged Egyptian families were totally protected from the realities of life. They were for the most part unaware that any hardships existed at all, and assumed that life was, as it appeared to them, secure and on the whole extremely enjoyable. They knew that they belonged to a privileged class, and from this knowledge they derived a complacent self-assurance reinforced by their quasi-total ignorance of the problems or concerns their parents faced. It was innocence in the fullest sense of the word. It is interesting to note that as these children reached adulthood, their prolonged state of innocence affected some of them profoundly. There was on their part a reluctance to emerge from the cocoon in which they had been encased and nurtured so long; rather, they used their innocence as a shield that protected them from the cruelties of life. They clung to it with quiet determination and strove to make reality conform to their conception of what it should be. Hence, a parent dying of a terminal cancer did not, as far as they were concerned, have that illness at all but was momentarily unwell. When death occurred it was viewed as a normal process devoid of the horror that illness usually connotes. The end result was the same, of course, but a cloak of make-believe was thrown over reality to make it bearable.

This was the case of the pure at heart who had fully accepted that wonderful world of childish innocence, where good was always on one side and bad on the other. Those less pure, or perhaps more rebellious, entered adulthood fully prepared—or so they assumed—to meet the world head on. Ill-equipped to face the challenge they often broke down and rarely developed their full potential. This was by no means a uniform picture. Much of the ultimate outcome depended on the degree of restriction imposed on the children: the more lax the governess, the more emancipated the atmosphere, the better adjusted were the adults. Whatever the case, there was frequently a certain aloofness among the children who belonged to the upper echelons of Cairo society vis-à-vis the rest of society they came into contact with as adults. There was a sense of separateness, an acute awareness that they belonged to a privileged, or at least different class, with the immediate corollary, which was their frequent inability to identify with the larger Egyptians community or even deal with it with ease. This was, to a very large extent, true for the Sallam family and their immediate circle. Among the girls, this attitude was carried on into adulthood, but not so much with the boys, particularly those who were sent to government schools.

Muhammad's first year at school passed uneventfully, and Cha was reconciled to the thought that his school was perhaps more fun than hers and that her little brother was by all accounts far cleverer. In June 1939, at the end of the school year, the family moved to Alexandria for the summer where both children were finally able to play their new role of aunt and uncle with their nephew, who was by then one year old. Life seemed to be smiling again on the Sallam family, and yet a crisis was in the making. 'Abd al-Rahman Pasha was definitely quite ill and doctors in Egypt strongly advised that he travel to Europe for treatment. Fatma Hanim, still in mourning for her mother, found herself in an extremely difficult situation. Hayah was expecting her second child, whose arrival was due in the third week of August, and she was reluctant to leave her daughter at such a critical time. The other children needed her as well, and above all her heart was not in it because she missed her mother. But the doctors were adamant: the Pasha had to leave. Faced with the situation, her practical common sense took over and within days the family's life was organized. Hayah and her husband offered to stay with the children and Madame Duprée in Alexandria, suitcases were packed, and in the last days of July 'Abd al-Rahman and Fatma Hanim boarded the Ausonia sailing for Marseilles.

In Paris they were received by an eminent nephrologist who confirmed the diagnosis made in Egypt and recommended surgery as the most appropriate way to deal with the problem.

"You see, Pasha, these polyps may be malignant and should be removed. We do not as yet have a remedy for such cases other than surgery."

The verdict upset 'Abd al-Rahman Pasha and his wife deeply. They went back to the hotel to think matters over. They examined the problem from every angle and since an operation was inevitable both agreed that it would be more sensible to have it done in Paris rather than wait until they returned to Cairo. However, fate decided otherwise. The next day they went back to the doctor's clinic to inform him of their decision. The eminent surgeon listened to them attentively but surprised them by his answer.

"I would advise you, Pasha, to go back to Egypt as soon as possible. Surely you realize that war is imminent and travel will become extremely difficult if not impossible once the conflagration has started. I myself do not know how long I shall be able to keep my practice going. Were I younger I would have enlisted. However, at times of war doctors are in great demand so I will put myself at the service of my country. Unless you leave immediately you run the grave risk of being stranded in France for the duration, and God only knows how long that might be."

The Pasha and his wife were stunned. They had for the past weeks been so totally preoccupied by their own problems that the international situation had been pushed to the back of their minds. Of course, they were fully aware of Hitler's demands, but like so many people they wanted to believe in the possibility of peace. Suddenly they were jolted roughly into grim reality and the prospect of impending war. Back at the hotel, they hurriedly made all the necessary arrangements and within the week they boarded the Esperia on her last crossing of the Mediterranean before the war.

24

Crossing the Mediterranean was still quite safe and the voyage back uneventful. The ship docked at Alexandria on August 26, just three days after the birth of Hayah's daughter and a few days before England declared war on Germany. The whole family went to the harbor to receive them including Cha, Muhammad, and Madame Duprée. The children were delighted because they were rarely included in the grownups' activities. They could hardly keep still and it seemed to them hours before they spotted their parents walking down the gangplank. Back at home at last, Fatma Hanim, sensing the children's impatience, opened her suitcase and extracted from it the most beautiful doll Cha had ever seen. Unlike her sister 'Abir, Cha had never cared much for dolls, preferring Muhammad's company and boys' games with her cousins. But this doll was definitely special—it could walk!

"Here, Cha," said her mother. "You just hold her hand and lean right and then left and she will bring one foot forward and then the other one."

Actually, children and grownups alike were fascinated. None of them had seen such an amazing sight: a walking doll that had no spring and needed no rewinding. Cha was delighted not just because this was a beautiful doll, but because it was different and superior to any of her sister's. This special gift made her feel special too. That night, when both children had been tucked into bed, Cha tossed and turned, unable to sleep, still in the grips of the day's events. The doll was seated at the foot of the bed, its pink organza dress spread around her, the expressionless blue eyes fixed on a point above Cha's head. Looking at it, the little girl once again perceived that she did not really like dolls at all because they were inanimate. Cha suddenly sat up in bed. "Yes," she thought. "This doll is dead, it can't talk to me and I don't know what it thinks. It's not a real person. It can't feel. It's dead." It occurred to her that grandpa and Sitti Chafaq were also dead, but in a different way. When they were alive they talked but now she could no longer see them or talk to them. They had died worse than the doll, which had never been alive. Despite the miracle of its walking, Cha disliked her doll for it brought forth sad and unpleasant thoughts. She lay down again, closed her eyes, and let her mind wander over the events of the day. Her parents were back and tomorrow there would be a big luncheon party in their honor. Muhammad's electric train would be mounted on the floor of his room. They would play with it, and perhaps the cousins would come over. Soon she drifted off to sleep.

A few days later, the family traveled back to Cairo where 'Abd al-Rahman was operated upon by his friend Dr. 'Ali Pasha Ibrahim at the Hopital Israelite of Ghamra. War in Europe had started but its impact was not yet felt in the Middle East. Madame Duprée was distraught. As a young girl, she had witnessed the horrors of World War I and was devastated by the thought of all the suffering the world would endure. Neville Chamberlain had failed. Poland was invaded and Hitler's aggressive stance was reinforced by his military successes. Everyone said that war would not last very long and that soon a solution would be found and a suitable ending would be brought to this disastrous state of affairs. But no solution seemed to be forthcoming and in the early days of June 1940 Madame Duprée's worst nightmare was realized when Hitler paraded down the Champs Elysées, desecrating her homeland with heavy Teutonic boots. "*Sales boches*," she would frequently mutter in order to relieve her inner tension.

Cha and Muhammad did not quite understand the problem. They knew of course that France was Madame Duprée's homeland and that bad people had invaded it, but these events were so far away that they had no real impact on their daily life. Madame Duprée was shrewd enough not to involve herself in the battles between governesses that ultimately led to the dismissal of Madame Gollmer from the Soliman family, and wise enough to understand that a foreigner living with an Egyptian family should avoid discussing politics particularly in front of the children. And yet, she was very amused one day when Muhammad came back from school holding the picture of a pig.

"Look at Hitler," he said

"That looks like a pig to me."

"All right, now look. I will fold the paper along those dotted lines and see what happens. Gala, gala, the pig disappears and Hitler appears."

Madame Duprée was delighted by the ingenuity of the trick.

Politics in Egypt, as in most countries of the world, moves according to the dictates of the moment, hence, while Hitler's brutality was condemned by many Egyptians who are essentially a gentle people, nevertheless the particular circumstances of the country forced others to overlook their inherent dislike of the man and his ways and, applying the motto, 'the enemy of my enemy is my friend,' they hoped for a German victory over the hated British. King Farouk, who had succeeded his father in 1936 and been repeatedly humiliated by Sir Miles Lampson, the British ambassador, hated the British, as did many outstanding Egyptians such as 'Aziz al-Masri and 'Ali Maher. In their case, to be pro-German was an indication of their profound patriotism. This was not an across-the-board attitude though. Many others, equally patriotic, knew that a German victory would not necessarily be in Egypt's best interest. 'Abd al-Rahman Sallam for one totally disapproved of Nazism and hoped for an allied victory convinced that it would mean the salvation of the civilized world.

Meanwhile Cha and Muhammad were developing a very strong sense of right and wrong because, despite all efforts to shield them from the current brutality of world affairs, they were perceptive enough to understand in the long run what they were not explicitly told. They gradually formed their own opinion about the war, an opinion that was inevitably the reflection of the bits and pieces they overheard. They came to the conclusion that the Germans were bad because they had invaded Paris, killed innocent people, and forced Jews to wear a yellow star sewn over their clothes. The British and the French, on the other hand, were heroes because they were trying to save the world from this monster. Of the Americans they knew nothing at all, until 1942 when the Seif al-Nasr villa next door to theirs was leased to the American High Command. Cha and

Muhammad, who had received bicycles for their birthday, cycled all afternoon in the garden but occasionally ventured outside, where they enjoyed the freedom of pedaling along the almost empty streets of Zamalek.

The military police at the door of the Seif al-Nasr villa would wave to them in a friendly manner. Cha did not wave back because she was quite out of her depth. This person was a stranger and she had no clue as to the proper behavior to observe. Muhammad, who was by nature much bolder, soon became friendly with these strangers and, as a reward, received chocolate bars and Chiclets chewing gum, the latter being a novelty for Egyptian children. Neither of them told Madame Duprée about their new neighbors, fearing that she might ban their outings and confine them to the garden.

Days went by uneventfully with Muhammad getting closer to the young Americans while Cha, still unable to break through the bounds of propriety, became more aloof and distant. And yet, she was positively dying to emulate her younger brother and talk to these nice young men who looked so incredibly handsome in their crisp uniforms. Little by little, as she cycled by, she would attempt a half a smile hoping that the first step would be made by one of them. Finally, the miracle happened. One of the military police, probably amused by the little girl's shyness, waved at her and gestured for her to cross the street and talk to them. As instructed by Madame Duprée, Cha looked right and left before crossing. It was 4:00 in the afternoon and the sun beat mercilessly on the asphalt, which had become soft in some places as if on the point of melting. There was no breeze, no sound of leaves ruffled by the wind, only the buzzing of bumblebees or over-grown summer flies.

Cha's hands were moist as she gripped firmly the handles of her bicycle. Just as she was about to cross the quiet street, a car drove by slowly and the figure seated at the back waved at her. It was Miss Mary Kahil,[71] Fatma Hanim's friend and neighbor. Cha waved back. She liked the kindly woman who always smiled and was so sweet and gentle. Miss Mary—as everyone called her—was a devout Catholic who attended mass every Sunday and, like Fatma Hanim and most ladies of her social milieu, worked for many charitable organizations. Cha was confident that Miss Mary would not report any untoward behavior but nevertheless decided to play it safe. She followed the car with her eyes, not daring to cross the street until Miss Mary was safely inside her house. She then walked over with diffidence, fearing that 'Amm Saleh, the *bawwab*, or one of the servants might see and report her to Madame Duprée.

She felt awfully guilty and terribly shy, but curiosity and a yearning for adventure goaded her on. Pushing her bicycle, eyes downcast, she walked toward the young man. When she looked up he was smiling broadly and producing a pack of chewing gum from his pocket, he handed it to her and said, "Come on, take it. They are very good." Cha shook her head. She felt it would not be proper to accept a gift from a stranger, let alone a man. She just wanted to say hello and prove to herself that she could be as bold as Muhammad.

"Why not? Come on, take it," he insisted. "Or are you afraid of your old man?"

Cha's face turned crimson. How dare he speak of her father in such insolent terms? No one mentioned the Pasha but with extreme respect and deference. "Old man!" This was an insult. She was so outraged that though she could speak English a little, she was tongue-tied. At the same time she knew that well brought up young girls did not quarrel in the street, whatever the offense. But her face said it all, and turning her back haughtily on the astonished young man, she pedaled vigorously to the safety of the garden.

This first attempt at emerging from the cocoon of familial protection was for Cha a bitter experience. For one thing, she had failed in her determination to emulate her brother. For another, it struck her that beyond the confines of her world, people existed who did not understand the order of things, overstepped limits, and apparently went unpunished. She decided then and there that Americans were rude, uncouth, not to be frequented. She mulled over the incident for a few days but eventually let it sink into her subconscious.

When many years later, as a young married woman, she visited the United States for the first time, she received daily jolts that shook her profoundly. There, she met many Americans who were far more educated than she was, Americans whose breeding would most certainly have impressed Madame Duprée, and on the whole, people who seemed to tower over her through their experience of life. More surprising still, she met Egyptians who, though they definitely belonged to a lower social class in Egypt, and had never experienced the refinement of her Zamalek home, yet were in many ways her superiors because their knowledge, whether empirical or academic, was far greater than her own. Her ego, as she wrote to her sister Hayah, was bruised because she realized for the first time that the way of life she had known was not the only one and not necessarily the best. Indeed, the world at large offered a great deal more than she had ever imagined.

The Pasha's operation was pronounced successful. After two weeks in hospital he was back home and resumed his normal life. Whether the removed polyps were malignant or not no one knew for sure except the patient, Fatma Hanim, and the doctor, and none of them revealed anything. The fact remains that the Pasha thereafter was a changed man. Though barely fifty-seven at the time, he looked much older. He never regained his vigor, and gradually curtailed his activities. However, his mind remained as sharp as ever before. He was re-elected to the Senate, stayed on the boards of all the companies he had been involved with, and was sought for his opinions and advice. He determinedly pursued his active life despite his weakened physical condition.

The year 1940, which in many ways was a disastrous one for Europe, brought Egypt its share of problems. In November, Hasan Sabri Pasha, the prime minister, died suddenly in Parliament while delivering the speech to the throne. The blow was hard as he was generally liked, and his ministry included some of the best men in the country such as 'Abd al-Hamid Soliman Pasha, Hussein Sirri Pasha, and Hussein Heikal Pasha. As does the sudden death of any public figure, this one shocked the nation and the question of a successor was immediately considered. It seemed for a while that the most senior member in the pecking order of the group, 'Abd al-Hamid Soliman Pasha, would be selected. However, like his friend 'Abd al-Rahman Sallam, he was in poor health and could not assume the responsibility. The choice fell on Hussein Sirri Pasha. According to many sources of the time, even if Soliman Pasha had been in good health, and regardless of his unquestioned ability, Sirri Pasha would have been selected all the same because he was the right man for the job, given the political conditions of the country at the time.

The political scene in Egypt in the late 1930s and the '40s was dominated by tensions that opposed the British ambassador and the king, the British ambassador and the Wafd, and the king and the Wafd. In this cauldron of dissention, other elements and political parties, such as the Ahrar Dusturiyin, the Sa'diyin, or the independents, added their own charged animosities and determined views. Farouk was a very young monarch, intelligent and immensely popular. Sir Miles Lampson, like Kitchener and Cromer before him, wanted to rule Egypt in his own way and impose his views on the king. Moreover he had to ensure that these internal tensions did not get out of hand, since England during the war years needed to have a stable and controlled situation in Egypt. A shrewd politician, he decided that al-Nahhas Pasha and the Wafd should ultimately become his allies because they alone could effectively control the country through the immense popularity they enjoyed. However, he needed time to pave the way for the development of an amicable relationship with the Wafd, so a preparatory interlude headed by an appropriate candidate became essential. Hussein Sirri fit the bill as no one else at the time.

As Queen Farida's uncle by marriage, he enjoyed a favored position in the Palace. At the same time, he had always maintained excellent relations with the British ambassador and his wife (unlike Soliman Pasha who, despite his knighthood, had always remained aloof from the British Embassy). Also, he had an excellent rapport with the financiers of Egypt particularly Ahmad Abboud Pasha. Finally, Sirri Pasha was politically bland. Though deeply involved in the affairs of the country, he had never belonged to any party. Consequently, he was the ideal candidate when a transitional or intermediate period was needed. To all these reasons, one might add that he was an extremely capable and intelligent man.

In 1940, war was raging in Europe and gradually its impact was felt in the Middle East. On June 10, Italy joined Germany and declared war on the United Kingdom, and on the June 11, Italian troops attacked British Somaliland. On September 13, the Italian army occupied Sollum and five days later the Egyptian border town of Sidi Barrani fell. This brought the conflagration very close to home. These Egyptian towns became for a while the focus of the struggle in the Middle East because soon enough, a British counter-offensive recaptured Sidi Barrani as well as Sollum. In fact, the British were holding their own very effectively against the Italians, which forced general Berganzoli to surrender the town of Bardi on January 5, 1941. Australian divisions entered Tobruk and British forces recaptured Somaliland. In February 1941, the German Afrika Corps appeared on the scene. The German army in the Middle East, headed by Field Marshall Rommel, was a formidable opponent.

On November 24, Rommel flung a column against the Egyptian frontier. In the ensuing days, severe fighting took place between the German and British forces, and Egypt's situation became precarious. Defeat and victory jumped in rapid succession from one camp to the other. Ultimately, on December 24, 1941, Benghazi fell to the Eighth Army. In Cairo, the situation was tense because now the war that had seemed at first so remote, fought in foreign lands by foreign armies, was suddenly very close and its danger very real. Tension was heightened because while a substantial percentage of the establishment and intellectuals hoped for a German victory, others stood firmly on the side of Great Britain, and fear of what might happen next was shared by all.

In the 'Abd al-Rahman Sallam household preparations were quietly made for a possible move to the farm at Mahalla. There was, at the time, a mini-exodus of families who thought it wiser to leave the capital before the situation got out of hand. 'Abd al-Rahman Salam was reluctant to follow the trend as he disliked panic and was convinced that Rommel would be defeated before he had a chance to invade Alexandria and march triumphantly on Cairo. He spent most of his afternoons and evenings listening to the radio and followed with great interest the daily developments on the front, whether in Africa or Europe.

The Battle of Britain was in full swing when on December 7, 1941, the Japanese attacked Pearl Harbor. With the entry of the United States into the war, the situation changed dramatically because Great Britain was no longer alone. The pro-Allies element of Egyptian society rejoiced while the others doggedly adhered to their belief in the might of the German war machine.

25

It would seem that with the enemy so close, life in Cairo would be drastically affected. This was not the case at all. In fact, despite occasional air raids and ever-present concern over the next turn of events, life in Egypt pursued its gentle course. Egyptians are, under normal circumstances, a resilient people, but in any case the war, which was causing such havoc in Europe and elsewhere, did not seem to have a tremendous impact on their daily existence. For the children of Zamalek, war was much talked about, perhaps because their families were part of the establishment and, in some cases, directly connected to the decision-making element of the government. Also, by 1942, the barrier separating children from adults was to a very large extent dropped, and everyone talked freely, particularly the governesses who never ceased to discuss the war and express opinions with the full force of a conviction based on insecurity and fear.

When, in 1942, Soliman Pasha dismissed Madame Gollmer for her pro-Nazi convictions, Madame Duprée was indignant. Although she abominated Hitler, this Teutonic vandal who was desecrating the soil of her beloved France, part of her rebelled at what was done to the doyenne of this eminent group of expatriates. Another reason might have been her intense dislike of Miss Griffith, governess to the Hussein Sirri family (and, as she later found out, the cause of Madame Gollmer's dismissal), whose Britishness rubbed her the wrong way. In any event, she vowed that nothing of the sort would happen to her. More discreet than Madame Gollmer, her political opinions were also in harmony with those of her employer.

For the children, the war had its positive as well as negative impacts. On the negative side was the fact that the long summer months were spent in Cairo. They all missed Alexandria terribly: the exclusive Sidi Bishr number two beach, the Casino San Stefano with its open air cinema, the occasional ride on the Ramleh tramway, and the carefree life of holidays by the sea. Children in the various Zamalek homes were often listless and bored. As is usually the case, boredom is conducive to mischief and the ingenuity of the Zamalekite children, some of them at least knew no bounds particularly during the summers of 1941, '42, and '43. Despite mornings spent at the Gezira Sporting Club, the afternoons proved long, tedious, and repetitive. Setting aside the sacrosanct 3:00 PM trip to the cinema on Thursdays, the children by the end of four weeks of summer vacation (and eight more to go) were always devising new entertainments, some of them dangerous. The governesses were by that time totally wrapped up in the war and the occasional feuds that erupted among themselves, so the children often indulged in pranks that could have had serious consequences. Oddly enough, these usually involved the Sallam children, their cousins Anisah Hanim's sons, the Nabih brothers, and their cousin, Nevine Sirri. Were other children in Zamalek better disciplined or perhaps less imaginative? In any event, this little nucleus of Zamalekites devised games which were not only bizarre but indicated, as a friend of the families remarked, the impact of American movies on the children's imagination.

One of these games consisted in digging a tunnel in the Nabih's garden. This was probably an attempt to re-enact the escape episode of allied prisoners of war in a German concentration camp as portrayed in a film they might have seen at the time. Since the Sirri garden was small and the Sallam's had cement-bordered alleys, the very large lawn of the Nabih's seemed ideal. The digging started at the far end of the garden and the children had no particular plan in mind other than to dig and have fun. So, like little ferrets they disappeared inside the hole, scooped up little pails of earth and emerged covered from top to toe in dried earth and mud. The exercise was exhausting, particularly when the tunnel grew in length; none of them stayed down under very long as they could hardly breathe and the crouching position was difficult to maintain. But they took turns and doggedly carried on the task. When teatime drew near, and fearing the sudden appearance of a governess in the garden, they would sneak up to the bathroom and clean themselves up as best they could. The Sallams had no problem because Madame Duprée was down with flu and Miss Griffith, being an albino, could hardly see anyway, though she marveled at Nevine's sudden fit of extreme cleanliness, as the girl seemed intent on washing her hair every day. The Nabih boys, whose garden was being savaged, had at that time no governess. They bore the brunt of the parents' collective anger after the gardener informed their father that the children were playing an odd game.

"They are digging a hole," he told the bemused parents.

"What do you mean a hole? Are they trying to plant a tree?"

"No, not a hole, a tunnel."

"A tunnel?" exclaimed Kamel Pasha and his wife in unison.

"Come see for yourselves. The lawn is ruined," lamented the old gardener.

When Kamel Pasha viewed the extent of the damage he was aghast. His first thought was for the danger incurred by the children because anyone walking over the tunnel would inevitably have crushed a child digging down there. Besides, sooner or later the tunnel was bound to cave in since it was not held up from the interior by a supporting structure.

The story made the round of Zamalek society, and even went beyond its borders, the naughtiness of these children being greatly talked about. After a period of restriction, during which the children were confined to their respective houses and the Thursday trip to the cinema cancelled for a while, the incident was eventually dismissed as a childish prank and soon forgotten. Life resumed its normal course with its mixture of repetitive occupations, occasional fun but mostly boredom. The Sallams spent their afternoons in the Nabih's garden where the tunnel had been filled in, but where there were trees to climb and games of hide and seek to be played until sunset.

One afternoon, as they were sitting under the shade of the garden's only mango tree, they thought up another 'project' to satisfy their current yearning for adventure. It was never clear thereafter which one of them came up with the idea; it was daring, and definitely adventurous. They named it 'the moon secret' for it was to be executed at dead of night when the moon was full and consequently the streets not in total darkness despite the mandatory blackout in force at the time. What fired their imagination and spurred them on was the element of danger involved because their plan was to get out of bed around midnight, sneak out of the house in their night clothes, and meet mid-way between the Sallam's house, the Nabih's, and the Sirri's. At first, they opted for the Greek Embassy as a meeting point, but it was considered unfair for the Sallams whose house was too far round the corner. After much discussion, they settled for the Seif al-Nasr villa, oblivious of the fact that military police stood at its door. That night Cha and Muhammad went to bed at their usual summer time, which was around 9:00 PM. By 10:00, they could hardly keep their eyes open. By 11:00, Muhammad was fast asleep but Cha was determined to carry on the project. She got out of bed, walked up and down her room and finally at the appointed hour woke Muhammad, having practically to drag him out of bed. Groggy, he followed his sister like a sleepwalker.

Both children crept down the back stairs, walked confidently to the front gate, which oddly enough was not locked, and with beating hearts found themselves in the street. Despite the moon they were engulfed in total darkness, or so it seemed to them. The acacia tree in the neighbor's garden rose majestically, its branches spread out like giant arms. Cha drew closer to her brother. They started walking on tiptoes afraid to make the slightest noise. A cat whisked by and hid in a hedge. Cha repressed a cry of fear and clung to Muhammad. Keeping close to their garden's railing, they crept very slowly toward the meeting point. Suddenly they heard a booming voice shout, "Stop! Who goes there?" They froze for a second, petrified, but the imminent danger that threatened them and the catastrophic consequences of their behavior galvanized them into action. They turned on their heels, ran back to the house up the three flights of stairs, and jumped into bed in a state of total panic. In the morning they overslept and in the afternoon they went back to the Nabih's looking sheepish for they had failed the test of courage. As it happened, they found that the others had behaved in exactly the same way. Apparently, the guard at the Greek Embassy gate had perceived unusual movements around the Sirri and Nabih villas and fearing burglars had cried out in alarm. The children spent many days thereafter discussing their missed adventure and derived much pleasure at recounting in minute detail every moment of their experience.

What may appear today as a very innocent prank was actually a very serious one, which could have had dire consequences. At a time when 'proper' young girls were not allowed out of the house unaccompanied, for any of them to be caught on the street at dead of night in their pyjamas in the company of three boys would have provoked a scandal of momentous proportions. They would have been branded 'bad girls.' Their reputation would have been tarnished despite their parents' position in society, or perhaps because of it.

Frustration brought on by summers in Cairo was one aspect of the situation. The war, however, had a positive effect on the Zamalek children as well, because it was during that time that they discovered the Gezira Sporting Club and its amenities. With the discovery of the club as a source of entertainment, this young generation of Egyptians, along with children of select families from other residential neighborhoods of Cairo, developed an interest in sports. Most of them took up tennis, some of them squash, and all of them delighted in the use of the pool. 'Abd al-Rahman Sallam, however, did not wholly approve of his daughter going to a swimming pool. His Upper Egyptian conservative mentality rebelled at such emancipation. He disliked the idea that his daughter should follow in that respect the ways of the foreign community of Cairo. To be daily in the company of boys wearing a swimming suit could be conducive to undesirable consequences, not the least of which were expectations of independence, which he was unwilling to accept. At the same time, being eminently wise, he realized that it could be just as bad to frustrate the child by depriving her of the fun, or imposing upon her a discipline different from the one followed by the rest of the group. A compromise was attempted: Cha was told she could swim three days a week but the other days she would sit by the pool or play tennis while the others swam. This was not enforced for very long because Fatma Hanim, aware of her daughter's rebellious nature, realized that it would, in the long run, have negative consequences. Besides, she did not actually disapprove of the practice, and if she did not allow herself to openly contradict her husband, she made it her business to convince him that the issue had best be left alone and Cha allowed to swim as often as the others.

So, the war brought to these young people an opening into a totally different world from the one known to the previous generation. At the club they met children of varied backgrounds, offspring of embassy personnel, army officers, or the foreign community of

Cairo. They befriended, among others, Sir Walter Smart's son, Mickey, whose brutal and untimely death in 1943 devastated them all.[72] The Zamalekite children of the 1940s very quickly blended into this expanded group of new friends, absorbed the ideas that were offered to them and thoroughly enjoyed this new dimension brought to their life. If the younger generation perceived the war, more or less as an event that deprived them of summers by the sea but opened up new vistas through the Gezira Sporting Club, their elders found themselves involved in much more complex sets of events and situations.

Someone once observed that never in its history had the city of Cairo witnessed a more brilliant 'social season' than the one that encompassed the war years. It was dazzling, varied in its activities, and seemed unending. The social scene was dominated by the king and his court on one side, and the British ambassador and his court on the other. The king of the land was young, handsome, and though he never wielded the autocratic power of a Louis XIV, yet like the Sun King, he radiated an aura of charm and glamour that attracted like a powerful magnet the socially active upper class. The mass of the people worshiped from afar, but the establishment, irresistibly attracted by the light he radiated, tried to get closer and bask in the warmth of these august and glorious rays. With a smiling face and charming manners, Queen Farida, his consort, was a lovely young woman, barely twenty years old when the war broke out. Soon after their marriage, the couple became a role model for the Egyptian society over which they reigned, and as a result, it became the fashion in the '40s for girls to marry when still in their early teens. These formed one of the social poles.

At the other pole stood Sir Miles Lampson, the British ambassador, whose six feet and rubicund face exuded all the arrogance of a representative of His Britannic Majesty's government in a satellite of the Empire. Lady Lampson, Jacquetta, tried as best she could to neutralize some of her husband's more abrasive attitudes but she had limited powers and consequently little impact. Tension between the two poles was clear from the very beginning. Many other forces deepened the chasm that was developing into a drama that almost ended in disaster on February 4, 1942. Farouk, like his cousin, 'Abbas Helmy II, was a patriot at heart and like him had the kind

of pride that precluded the acceptance of Miles Lampson's authoritarian and arrogant attitude. When war broke out, 'Ali Maher, a
Germanophile, was prime minister and the king's advisor. He had
built a strong case in favor of the Axis to which the king lent a
favorable ear. Whether Farouk really admired Hitler and National
Socialism is debatable. More likely he adopted an attitude that
expressed his rejection of the British occupation of Egypt and, more
specifically, of Sir Miles Lampson. It seemed to be a personal
vendetta and his immediate entourage never let him forget 'Abbas
II's forced abdication in 1914. Members of the establishment were
never officially summoned to take sides but inclinations or preferences were often clearly expressed, though there were politicians
such as Mustafa al-Nahhas who clamored his patriotic convictions
while at the same time becoming the Embassy's man, the one chosen to run the country. Because of the Anglo-Egyptian Treaty of
1936, Egypt was kept out of the war and in May 1940. Cairo was
declared an open city.[73]

During the war years Cairo did, in fact, become an 'open city,' as it
included such an amazing variety of nationalities. When war broke
out, there were over 1,000 Germans in the country actively engaged
in proselytizing for the party. They were immediately rounded up and
interned in concentration camps. There was also the Italian colony
that had lived in Egypt for many generations and suddenly found
itself on the wrong side. There was the Greek contingent whose
members straddled the social ladder such as the Zervudachis, the
Perakos, the Benachis, the Salvagos, down to the grocers such as
Vazelakis, whose shop in Zamalek was for generations a landmark of
quality goods, and seamstresses, embroiderers, and artisans. This
colony took on the mantle of Homeric grandeur being representative of a small nation that was valiantly defending its homeland against
the German–Italian aggressors. Feuds and enmities were often
expressed in the form of anecdotes that ran the salons of Cairo. One
in particular was a favorite during the early days of Italian victories:
two women—one Italian, the other Greek—in a cinema are involved
in a heated argument. The Italian boasted that Italy had successfully
invaded Greece, to which the Greek woman replied, waving her red-
lacquered finger nails in the face of the other one, "Ah, but not for
long! Soon all our fingers will run red with Italian blood."

There were also the royals who sought sanctuary in Egypt from the devastation of their countries. Among them were King Zog of Albania with his wife, Geraldine, and their young son, Leka; King George of Greece with his German-born wife, Frederika, and their three children, who spent some time in Alexandria on their way to South Africa; and King Victor-Emmanuel of Italy with his family. But above all there was the British contingent made up of officers on leave from the front, and embassy personnel who formed the nucleus of the Europeanized entertaining that went on at the time. The Egyptian Syro-Lebanese and the Coptic families of the upper crust were among the first to intermingle freely with the British officers and embassy personnel.

Women such as Dora Plant,[74] Swiss born Gertie Ghali,[75] GertieWissa,[76] Marie Wissa[77] and many others gave brilliant soirees attended at first mainly by the foreign contingent but gradually by Egyptians as well. Marie Wissa's parties were as sought after as Momo Marriott's, wife of Brigadier Sir John Marriott and one of the outstanding hostesses of war-time Cairo. Marie transformed the basement of her house into an attractive private nightclub, where she received her guests on a lavish and grand scale and very quickly became a fixture of the Cairo social scene of the time. Chez Marie, her private nightclub, became as famous among the glittering elite as the tulle *voilette* that always veiled her eyes and her very long aquiline patrician nose. Competing with Marie's parties were the ones given by Samira and Samiha—pronounced by them Smiraa and Smihaa— the two lovely daughters of Sadiq Pasha Wahbah, the son of Yusuf Pasha Wahbah. Born and bred in Cairo, they never went to school in England or even lived there for any length of time, yet they both spoke English perfectly with the clipped Oxonian accent, which they assumed, no doubt, to be the quintessential language of British nobility. Whether this was a pose or whether it came naturally is unimportant because they did it very well and consistently. They spoke French fluently with a definite British accent to underscore their linguistic preference and ability. Oddly enough, neither of them, particularly Samira, had any doubts where their allegiance lay: they were Egyptians, proud descendants of a glorious pharaonic past. But they would also, in all probability, have disagreed with their cousin, Dr. Magdi Wahbah,[78] who once declared, "to be French-speaking was to think of Cairo as home, but to believe that Paris was the navel of the world."[79] As far as the Sadiq Wahbah girls were concerned, this navel was most probably situated somewhere around Buckingham Palace. Their guest list often included British officers whom they wished to impress with the refinement of their Egyptian way of life because none of these Coptic ladies ever forgot they were Egyptian first and foremost and any identification with the occupier was a matter of social convenience.

Over and above the common fray was the Egyptian royal family. By tradition the royals never mixed freely with society and with very few exceptions their social intercourse was limited to formal occasions. King Fuad had by all accounts been an autocratic and domineering person. He enforced with vigor the protocol of the Ottoman court, which was based on the strict segregation of sexes. The Queen could not be seen in public with her face uncovered. On set occasions she would receive formally at Abdin Palace female members of the royal family, ladies of the diplomatic corps, wives of Egyptian cabinet ministers, and the like. Seated on her throne, surrounded by ladies of the royal household in decreasing order of precedence, she would greet with a smile the lady presented to her by her lady-in-waiting. It is said that when King Farouk acceded to the throne, he went one step further than his father, as at first he would not frequent the royal family at all. According to some sources of the time, he was following his father's advice to keep a distance from his relatives. This may or may not be true, but in the first years of his marriage he was definitely very aloof with his family.

Queen Farida could not understand why she was not encouraged, or even allowed, to mix freely with her in-laws. Actually, no one in her family could understand the reason for such reserve until one day Farouk confessed that he distrusted them. Queen Farida was not satisfied with the answer and being very persistent by nature nagged her husband continually on that issue. The situation, changed quite suddenly in the most natural manner. When Empress Fawziya of Iran came back to Egypt for a visit after the birth of her daughter, she was received with all the splendor that a grandson of Khedive Isma'il could lay out for his favorite sister. By force majeure the royal family had to attend the official festivities. Not wanting to be outdone, all the senior members of the Egyptian royal family follow suit and gave parties in her honor, which, according to a witness of the time, were magnificent. All the princesses wore their tiaras, diamond necklaces, and matching pendant earrings. All of them glittered by the beautiful display of family heirlooms despite the fact that some of them were in somewhat straightened circumstances. But noblesse oblige and the round of parties seemed endless.

One of the most outstanding parties was given by Princess Chivekiar in the course of which the king had a marvelous time being entertained by his father's ex-wife. King Farouk realized that there was no longer any point in maintaining his reserve toward his family, especially since he now owed them return invitations. Socializing on a grand scale that started off among the royal family soon penetrated the next rung of the social ladder, that of the high middle class and again through the efforts of Princess Chivekiar. To entertain the king was definitely one of her objectives, but she decided to be not only the most lavish hostess in town, but its foremost philanthropist as well. Killing two birds with one stone, she gave sumptuous parties in her palace, which were also charity benefits. These parties were attended by the royal family and Egyptian high society. Eventually, party giving and party going became the name of the game and the excitement grew as apparently the royal family and Egyptian society discovered a new and extremely pleasant way of life.

Events all seemed to conspire to propel society further into this social whirl. A war was on and efforts had to be made to keep the spirit up. At the same time, Egypt suffered several epidemics that inflicted tremendous hardships on the poorer classes. Charity balls, the proceeds of which were given to the stricken victims of the most recent calamity, became a solution that offered itself quite naturally as ladies rallied around Princess Chivekiar's call to arms. She indeed set a pattern with her fabulous extravaganzas, orchestrated and organized with the help of her son, Prince Wahid al-Din, an esthete, who adored parties and was his mother's darling. The ease with which Egyptian society of the 1940s took to this somewhat modern form of philanthropy was quite amazing.

The success of these parties was largely due to Princess Chivekiar whose lack of beauty was compensated by her intelligence and very strong personality. She soon realized that good food and a congenial atmosphere were not enough to turn her parties into unique events. She therefore, decided to enliven her soirees with charming *tableaux vivants*. Where the idea originated is not clear, though someone at the time advanced the opinion that she was perhaps trying to emulate, albeit on a smaller scale, the fabulous parties of Versailles. Whether in her palace of Munira or the Muhammad 'Ali Palace in Shubra, the imagination with which the various scenes were construed seemed unlimited. The actors were selected from the upper class youth and good looks were mandatory. No effort was spared to give each tableau its perfect finish. To achieve this end, she secured the help of professionals from the Egyptian Opera House.

One of them was a certain Mr. Nashaty, of Syro-Lebanese origin, who, with the help of a French choreographer, worked relentlessly to train the young actors in the various roles they were assigned. The 'scenes' were varied and always original. Guests milling slowly around the vast gardens would move from the representation of a Spanish nightclub with dancers tapping heels and clicking their castanets to the sound of the most exotic flamenco, to a Viennese café where couples dressed in nineteenth century crinolines and tailcoats waltzed the whole night long. On one occasion, the master choreographer with the help of Mr. Nashaty presented a scene of Neptune rising from the sea, holding his trident, surrounded by Naiads. Pulling his chariot were sturdy young men wearing a horse's head mask, followed by little dolphins, eight-year-old girls dressed in gold lamé swimsuits embroidered with sequins to imitate fish scales and holding their tail by a hook slipped on their little finger. Many years later, one of these little girls, Laila Hegazy (Mrs. Adel Gueneina) still recalled the fun she had with her friends on these grand occasions. This particular tableau was spectacular because it included the oceans of the world, controlled by Neptune, God of Water. Nothing was left to chance and every detail was scrupulously examined to ensure verisimilitude. Daily rehearsals took place for several weeks before the party under the exacting eye of Mr. Nashaty and his colleagues, and seamstresses worked at the Chivekiar palace to create costumes, draperies, décor, or whatever else was needed.

These parties were so successful that despite advancing age and poor health, Princess Chivekiar carried on almost until her death in 1947. One of the last she gave was noteworthy not only because it was perfect in almost every way, but because it provoked a mini-scandal in Egyptian society. On that occasion Mr. Nashaty had sug-gested that a glimpse into the past of the Turkish court would be appropriate. Princess Chivekiar readily agreed as she immediately foresaw the sumptuous effect that could be achieved through a recreation of a Sultan's court. The main role was held by Isma'il Naguib, a handsome young attorney, who stipulated before accept-ing the role that no pictures of him be taken at close range as he had no wish to appear in the daily press dressed up, even as a monarch. Though Egyptian society had made giant steps toward modernism, certain social conventions were still upheld. Flattered as he must have been, Isma'il Naguib nevertheless felt the need to protect his real life role and the prestige it carried.

In any event, once the Sultan was chosen, attention was given to the girls who were to play the role of slaves in his harem. There again, selection did not proceed as smoothly as was expected. If most upper class Egyptians loved the idea of such parties and adopted with alacrity the concept of 'philanthropic entertain-ment,' which was relatively new in a society where two decades earlier women were still veiled, dogged conservatism and adher-ence to traditional values occasionally had the upper hand. This was precisely what happened when one of the girls was told by her fiancé, a young diplomat in the Ministry of Foreign Affairs, that he would under no circumstances allow her to play the role of a slave in a harem, even for one evening, however worthy the cause. Everyone tried to make him change his mind but as he pointed out, he was the descendant of one of the oldest families in the land and tradition forbade his future wife to behave in a way he considered unseemly.

His decision was not negotiable. She would have to choose: it would be either him or the Sultan. Egyptian society buzzed with the news of the impending disaster that was about to strike this young girl as a broken engagement was bound to reflect negatively on her reputation. Most people sympathized with her but assumed that in the end she would forgo the glory of one night and opt for the secu-rity of a very brilliant marriage. As it turned out they were wrong. Probably foreseeing a life of Upper Egyptian restrictions, she opted for the Sultan and the engagement was broken off. Mr. Nashaty was delighted, the selection proceeded apace and the party was an immense success.

The story of the young woman ended a few years later on a happy note. After a short, unsuccessful marriage, she met her ex-fiance again. His views on life may have altered significantly because they picked up where they had left off, married, and lived for many years in perfect harmony.

26

While Princess Chivekiar was thus actively engaged in her socio-philanthropic activities, other Egyptian ladies did not remain idle but carried on the movement initiated by Hoda Sha'rawi. They sallied forth with tremendous energy and enthusiasm into the field of social welfare. With the help of the royal princesses, they launched many philanthropic societies such as Mabarrat Muhammad 'Ali (The Muhammad 'Ali Philanthropic Organization) and al-Mar'a al-Gadida (The New Woman) to help the impoverished classes of the country. In an effort to emulate the splendid role played by the International Red Cross, they gave a new impetus to the women's Egyptian Red Crescent (headed at first by Nahed Sirri, followed by Djenan al-Shawarby). Ladies, who a decade earlier had still been totally engrossed in family affairs, were now very actively engaged outside their home. Surprising as it may seem today, they took to their new life as active working women like fish to water. However, one must remember that from the harem life of their ancestors, they had learned the arts of organization and planning.

Harems were not, as has usually been described, a boring place or a prison. Quite the contrary, in an affluent one life was gregarious and bustling with activity. It was usually a complicated household where hierarchy and strict protocol were observed. To give orders judiciously became second nature to these ladies and, as 'Afaf al-Sayyid-Marsot observes, "That quality was to stand them in good stead when later on they sat down in a committee to plan how to set up and run a hospital. . . . Above all, they knew how to manipulate people and how to delegate authority."[80] Among them and noted for their driving power and initiative were Fatma Sirri,[81] Hedeyah Barakat,[82] Sophie Ghali, Mary Kahil, Amina Sidki,[82] Ateya Abu Usbu', and Aisha Sirri to name but a few. Whether for the Mabarrat Muhammad 'Ali, the Mar'a al-Gadida, or the Red Crescent, there was always a charity affair being organized for a worthy cause.

Cairo during the war years was a wonderful place to be, particularly for the privileged classes, as life was cheap and all commodities were available on the local market, not only the essential ones but the superfluous and often the extravagant as well. This situation lasted until the end of 1943. When war first broke out, it had been perceived by social Cairo as an unfortunate event that was taking place elsewhere. As it drew nearer home, society seemed to function on several levels at the same time. Political Cairo was polarized, anti-British or anti-Axis, and social Cairo seemingly unperturbed, carried on the rounds of festivities while poor Cairo hoped that 'Muhammad Ider,' alias Hitler, would eventually win the war, oust the British, and reestablish the economy of the country, which, at their level, was perceived as unsatisfactory. It was not uncommon in those days for lower-middle class Egyptians to name their newborn sons Hitler. Stirred by world events, a hodgepodge of humanity was actively engaged in pursuits of one kind or another, and while the country was not officially at war, yet the war was a backdrop against which actions were measured and decisions taken.

It seems incongruous that the blitz years of London should be paralleled by the glitz years of Cairo. The point is that the horror of Hitler's bombing of the British capital was not overly publicized in Egypt so as not to demoralize Allied troops fighting on the various fronts. More important still was the fact that Great Britain had to appear strong, otherwise Egypt might be reluctant to provide the facilities upon which the British war machine depended heavily. And so, the round of parties and festivities went on and the *mashrabiya* screens that had segregated Egyptian women for so long gradually became relics of the past. Contact between British officers and Egyptian families became more frequent. The former returning from the front welcomed the hospitality that was lavished upon them in the course of sumptuous dinner parties, while the Egyptian hosts enjoyed exercising this novel and exciting way of life.

The year 1941 witnessed a great social event: the wedding of Doddy, daughter of prime minister Hussein Sirri Pasha, and Mahmud Younes, the scion of one of Egypt's most prominent families.

A problem presented itself from the start. Queen Farida, who was Doddy's cousin, wanted to attend the wedding. However, the rules of protocol instituted by King Fuad, Farouk's father, prevented her from doing so if foreigners were invited. This dilemma was shared by King Farouk who wanted to please his wife, and the Sirris who had to invite more people than just the immediate family. To get out of this impasse and solve the problem, King Farouk announced that he would offer a party—the first one—which would be restricted to the royal family and the young couple's families. Consequently, Doddy Sirri and Mahmud Younes were given two weddings, a royal one on May 22, 1941, and the other one four days later. These events were extremely lavish and it is to the credit of Nahed Sirri, the bride's mother, that she was able to obtain a perfect blend of European finesse and oriental opulence. Both weddings were held at the Sirri home, now the residence of the Tunisian ambassador in Zamalek.

To allow more space, Mrs. Sirri requisitioned her neighbors' gardens, the Zulficar's and the Kirdani's, so hedges were swiftly cut down with the owners' blessings. The bridal cortege was composed of six young girls in white tulle dresses encrusted with silver bows, and six young boys in formal evening wear. Tahia Carioca, the famous belly dancer, whose figure at the time was surprisingly svelte considering what it became later, led the procession as it moved very slowly down the steps, toward the *kusha* erected in the garden to face the royal table. Following Tahia was her chorus singing the traditional wedding song punctuated with the tingling of their metallic castanets. This was as far as Mrs. Sirri Pasha would go toward giving her guests a taste of Orientalism. There were no other Egyptian forms of entertainment. On the other hand, hidden from view in the Kirdani garden was a balalaika ensemble that gave background music once the *zaffa* was over and the bride and were groom finally seated in their *kusha* surrounded by their bridesmaids and pages.

Doddy was a lovely girl of sixteen with large black eyes and a charming smile that revealed pearl-like teeth; Mahmud was one of the most handsome young men of his generation. They made an extremely romantic couple whose youth and beauty greatly enhanced the magic of this enchanted evening. Of course, the royal presence lent its glamour, as did strains of violin that wafted seemingly from nowhere, enveloping the garden with the delicate softness of their music.

The buffet was sumptuous and entirely managed by Hajj 'Abd al-Hakim, the Sirri's chef, and his brother Hajj Muhammad, 'Abd al-Hamid Soliman Pasha's chef. A somewhat incongruous note, however, should be mentioned: the family maids, some of whom had been with the family for many years, followed the *zaffa* holding candles that were the same as the bridesmaids' and wearing fineries made for the occasion. Though they must have looked odd in their brightly colored *gallabiya*s, no one criticized their presence, in fact, some of the guests remarked that having them there was rather touching. Despite Mrs. Sirri's strict instructions, one of them dared a ululation the moment she set eyes on the king. His Majesty was greatly amused and indicated that he would like to hear more, a request the maids readily complied with, sending forth shrill tremolos that drowned, for a few moments, the songs and the music. This evening was a gift from King Farouk to his queen. He gave her the pleasure of appearing before her family in full regalia as the Queen of Egypt, but at the same time he adhered to the protocol established by his father. The second evening on May 26 was a repeat performance of the first one without the royal family but including members of the diplomatic corps, Egyptian officials, and all the friends who had not been invited the first time. It was the outstanding event of the year.

It was also a momentous event in Cha's life. Nevine, her friend and the bride's sister, had told her all about the preparations and supplied endless details. Never in her wildest dreams did she assume that she would attend such a regal affair. And yet the miracle occurred. One morning as she was about to leave for school, her mother came into her room and with a smile of anticipated pleasure asked, "Would you like to be one of Doddy's bridesmaids?" Speechless, Cha nodded vehemently.

"Well then, this afternoon after school you shall come with me to Madame Paradisi to be fitted for the dress you are to wear."

From that moment onward, Cha lived in a state of chronic exhilaration. She thought of little else and her joy at having been chosen was only equaled by the pride she felt. She loved the dress, which seemed to her the most beautiful she had ever seen and was delighted to hear that her long braids would be let lose for the occasion, held back by a garland of tiny flowers. She talked of nothing else all day long and poor Madame Duprée had to endure a multitude of questions about the ceremony to which she actually had few answers. When the great day arrived her excitement knew no bounds. Finally at 8:00 PM she was ushered with the other brides-maids into Mrs. Sirri's dressing room where they were to remain in utter seclusion until the bride was ready. Finally the procession was organized, and when the sirens were heard in the street announcing the arrival of the royal party, Cha found herself moving slowly as in a dream, clutching her lit candle with both hands as if to draw support from it. Her heart beat so hard she could feel the pulse in her ears. Her mouth was dry and as she walked down the stairs she feared for a moment that her legs might betray her. The very thought petrified her so she steeled herself to walk ramrod straight as Madame Duprée had instructed, hardly daring to move her head.

"Smile," someone hissed in her ear. She turned slightly and saw Hayah who pointing at her own lips smiled broadly. Cha realized that she had been frowning but to smile was, for the moment, beyond her power. Suddenly they were in the garden and she saw King Farouk for the first time. She had never imagined that anyone could be more beautiful than this incredibly handsome man seated at a long table with a lady on each side. She knew, of course, that one of them was his mother Queen Nazli and the other one his wife Queen Farida. Queen Farida looked enchanting. In her hair was an aigrette of very soft white feathers that moved with every tilt of her head. She wore beautiful diamond earrings that sparkled and reflected the various sources of light in the garden. The other lady, however, impressed her more. Queen Nazli that evening looked particularly regal, almost forbidding. Her huge heavily kohled black eyes looked on the surrounding scene with indifference. The majesty of her person was enhanced by the incredible pendant earrings she wore and her unsmiling dark red lips were pressed together, perhaps in an effort to hide her prominent teeth. To the ten-year old she looked formidable.

As the procession moved slowly toward its final destination, the ladies of the family showered the bride and groom with *badra*, or gold coins, which fell around, on tables, ladies' hair, onto the lawn and with a tingling sound in sherbet glasses, some empty, others still half full. Coins that fell on the floor were later picked up by the servants, the guests helping themselves to the ones that fell within their reach. The bridesmaids and pages had been instructed to ignore this golden shower and not try to retrieve any of it. As far as Cha was concerned, the evening was pure enchantment from beginning to end. At one point, as she was standing with some of the bridesmaids, she saw the youngest of the royal princesses come over to speak to Nevine. This was Princess Fathiya who, apparently bored by prolonged seating at the royal table had been allowed to join her cousin, Nazli Sabri, and the other girls. Cha looked at her with curiosity. She had often wondered what a princess would look like. The girl was rather plain and wore a dress, which Cha noted with some pride, was not as beautiful as her own. On her wrist was a little gold watch but none of the diamonds and beautiful jewels worn by her older sisters.

"She is like me," thought Cha, "treated like a baby, always made to feel that the older sisters have more privileges." She suddenly felt sorry for this girl so, in order to attract her attention, asked, "What time is it, please?" Princess Fathiya looked up surprised, probably taken aback by this breach of protocol. Nevertheless, she answered politely but in a subdued audible voice, "Five minutes past midnight," and blushing she immediately turned away. Cha for her part had sensed the princess's shyness and discomfort. Shortly after, Queen Nazli got up, walked over to the group of young girls "Come along, darling," she told her daughter. "It is past midnight. Time to go home." The child immediately got up and followed her mother to join the rest of the royal family. Cha was immensely surprised. "Home?" she thought, "Do princesses live in a home? Why did the queen not say palace for surely that is where kings and queens live? A palace is not a house. A home is a house but a palace is much bigger so how can it be called home?" She was bemused because up to that point she had believed that royalty belonged to a superior or, at any rate, different category of beings. Cha, for her part, had no wish to go home. She wanted the evening to last as long as possible. She had scarcely eaten when dinner had been served and now felt ravenously hungry. Although the grownups had already eaten, buffet tables were still laden with an impressive amount of dishes. Foregoing the ones she knew, she helped herself to the ones she had never seen. She was told by her friend Nevine that on her plate was a piece of *chaud-froid* (cold chicken wrapped in cream with truffle) and a slice of *canard à l'orange*. She liked neither.

With the passage of time, this wedding took on for Cha an aura
of unmitigated happiness on a grand scale. However, after it was over,
she experienced the inevitable feeling of letdown as well as the slight
depression, which are often the aftermath of intense joyful emotion.
There was a more serious reason for Cha's unease, which was the
atmosphere of strained anxiety in the house brought on by the
Pasha's failing health. She knew that her father had undergone a serious operation, the nature of which she was never told, and was aware
that the war situation could have an impact on his health. 'Abd al-
Rahman Sallam spent most afternoons and evenings listening avidly
to every bit of news he could garner. As the war progressed, his disapproval of Hitler increased steadily and his pro-British sentiments
grew in proportion. In the summer of 1942, the situation was so bad
that he feared a German victory which would inevitably mark the
end of the world as he knew it and possibly the destruction of the
moral order in which he had always believed.

It mattered little now that Sir Miles Lampson was obnoxious, or
that the British were taking advantage of his country. On their
side lay norms he could understand, and Egypt's struggle against
them was fought according to acceptable rules and for legitimate
reasons. He could not accept the pro-German attitude of some of
his compatriots. As far as he was concerned, Hitler and National
Socialism were definitely beyond the pale, and as he told Fatma
Hanim one evening in November 1941, "An evil we know is
preferable to an evil we don't know and cannot understand." He
had not involved himself in the whirl of social activity that
engulfed Cairo society, as it suited neither his health nor his natural inclination, but he encouraged his wife to take part in whatever she deemed acceptable.

The summer of 1941 had been a relatively quiet one in the
Western Desert as Hitler was occupied with the eastern front. On
June 22, 1941, the German army invaded Russia, and on July 12, in
Syria, Vichy forces agreed to an armistice. Meanwhile the economic situation in Egypt had not improved at all. Between August 1939
and September 1941 the cost of living index had risen by 45 percent. Hussein Sirri, who had become premier in November 1940,
was not popular with the masses because he projected, through the
media, an image of aloofness. Furthermore, he was thought to be

too pro-British in a context of generally pro-German popular public opinion. He was also resented for having, at the instigation of the
British Embassy, taken certain decisions that were extremely unpopular. One of these concerned the price of cotton, which Sirri presented to the Egyptian Parliament as a fait accompli. Britain had
tried to buy Egypt's cotton crop at a reduced price, but the ensuing
uproar forced Great Britain to raise the price for the benefit of large
cotton plantation owners; the difference was paid by the Egyptian
government through increased taxes.

The war in the desert was carried on with relentless energy and
determination. On November 18, 1941, a British offensive,
'Operation Crusader,' started and Sidi Rezek was captured by the
Eighth Army. Field Marshall Rommel retaliated with his Twenty-
first Panzer division, which neutralized the British army and defeated its piecemeal attacks, and on November 24 he crossed over the
Egyptian frontier. Fighting went on savagely with tremendous loss of
life on both sides. Finally, on December 24, 1941, Benghazi fell to
the Eighth Army.

As the war raged on the Western frontier, social Cairo was still
engaged in its pleasant pursuits though somewhat less actively, and
political Cairo became more and more entrenched in its polarized
attitudes. Hussein Sirri's unpopularity increased with every turn of
events. First he was criticized for having agreed to the arrest of
Hasan al-Banna, head of the Muslim Brotherhood, then for the
unpopular legislation which reduced cotton acreage, finally for having, through his economic policy, triggered a hoarding syndrome
among merchants and clients alike. What provoked his downfall, and
one of the worst crises of Farouk's reign, was his decision to break
off relations with the Vichy government. This was a move that had
repeatedly been requested by Miles Lampson, but the government
had dragged its feet because of the pro-Axis public opinion as well
as the fact that there were still about 300 Egyptian students in
France who could not be brought home in time, including some
who had no wish to return. Hussein Sirri prevaricated as long as he
could, keeping in mind that Egypt was not at war and that his countrymen were, for the most part, opposed to such an action.
However, in early January 1942, he could no longer refuse the
British ambassador's pressured demands.

The king at that time was in Aswan with his wife and mother, greatly irritated by the two ladies' open discord. Queen Nazli, his mother, had never accepted her son's marriage to Safinaz Zulficar, a daughter of one of her ladies-in waiting. When she became queen her name was changed to Farida.[84] The young queen never forgave her mother-in-law and, with the impetuosity of youth, antagonized her as often as she could. At Aswan, the situation soon became unbearable, and the king found himself caught up in a most unpleasant domestic situation. That might account for the violence of his reaction upon hearing that his government had severed its ties with the government of Vichy. He flew into a rage over what he considered an encroachment on his royal prerogatives. He voiced his anger in a telephone conversation with his prime minister and reproached him in abrasive terms for having taken this decision without consulting him and demanded the immediate resignation of the minister of foreign affairs. His anger was fanned by 'Aziz al-Masri, one of the most pro-German politicians in the country, who seized this opportunity to discredit Hussein Sirri. It is to the credit of the latter that he immediately rose to the situation and the inborn pride and self-respect of an Upper Egyptian gentleman took over spontaneously. He answered that he could not comply with this request but would offer his own resignation instead. Furthermore, he stated quite clearly that he took exception to the way in which the king had treated him, as neither his age nor his position as uncle by marriage to the queen made it acceptable. The king, somewhat calmed, pacified his prime minister, who thought it wiser to let the matter drop for the moment though he did not request the minister of foreign affairs' resignation.

The situation in Cairo became volatile, with demonstrations in mid-January to protest against Great Britain's involvement in Egyptian affairs. The Muslim Brothers entered the fray and, having whipped up the general feeling of discontent, were soon joined by the students of al-Azhar University. At the same time, news from the front had taken a turn for the worse as on January 28, 1942 Axis radio reported the capture of Benghazi. On February 2, Hussein Sirri resigned while students demonstrated shouting the ever-recurrent slogan of 'Down with the British.'

In the Sallam household the atmosphere was somber. The Pasha spent the greater part of the day shut in his ground floor office to listen undisturbed to the radio. Fatma Hanim was distressed. She realized the gravity of the situation and was particularly upset at the reversal of fortune of their friends, the Sirris. Both she and her husband concurred with Hussein Pasha's political moves and wholeheartedly admired the way he had handled the situation. Unlike Miles Lampson, who having obtained what he wanted allowed himself to criticize Hussein Sirri, they did not consider that the latter had made a 'mistake' in cutting off relations with the government of Vichy for such was his duty as well as his right as prime minister.

The matter of Sirri's replacement became crucial. The British ambassador judged that the interim, or preparatory, period had lasted long enough and that al-Nahhas Pasha and the Wafd were now ready to take over. The king, however, would not hear of it. He disliked and distrusted al-Nahhas, the choice of his archenemy. On the morning of February 4, 1942, the Embassy's position was made clear and King Farouk was served with the infamous ultimatum: either call in al-Nahhas to form the new government or abdicate. Abdin Square was cut off and facing the palace were British tanks and armored cars. The king, in a surprising show of political acumen, agreed to bring in a Wafdist government and in so doing saved the monarchy, much to the annoyance of Sir Miles Lampson, who had thus been outmaneuvered. During this crisis, Hussein Sirri's attitude toward the king was impeccable. Setting aside his resentment at the way the monarch had treated him, he rushed to the palace to offer his unconditional support. Peace was made between the two men and this in turn led to a rather unexpected episode in the strange and often convoluted developments of life in Cairo during the war: the marriage of Nini Sirri, Hussein Sirri's eldest daughter.

Field Marshall Rommel was still at the gates of Alexandria threatening the city with impending invasion, while accounts of his exploits inflamed the imagination of young Egyptians. On June 25, 1942, Field Marshall Auchinleck was named Commander-in-Chief of the Eighth Army. Three days later Rommel's forces took Marsa Matrouh and on July 1 the Panzer army reached al-Alamein. The Germans seemed driven by an invincible power as they rushed across the desert, oblivious of sand, flies, and the scorching heat, obliterating all resistance that tried to obstruct their mad drive toward Alexandria. Rommel's problem, however, lay not in what was before him but in what was behind him, namely his supply line. Ultimately, lack of adequate supplies forced him to stop his advance, and under British attack, to withdraw. The battle of al-Alamein ended with a victory for the Allied forces and marked a turning point in the development of the Second World War.

Meanwhile, the situation in Cairo had become very tense. Families were moving to their farms to avoid the expected air raids and the first encounter with the conquering army. The Sallams stayed on in town as the Pasha decided to postpone the family's exodus until the last possible moment. Cha and Muhammad, as well as their cousins and friends, were aware of the situation, as governesses and adults no longer took precautions when speaking before them. Madame Duprée was distraught: the 'boches' would soon be in town and much as she feared for her employers she feared even more for herself as her pro-Gaullist sentiments were well known. "I have no doubt," she told Fatma Hanim, "that I shall be sent to a concentration camp. I shall most assuredly die there and be buried in a mass grave. I shall never see France again!" Fatma Hanim had no patience for these lamentations, as she was herself consumed with anxiety. In the midst of the rising tension, she received a strange telephone call from her friend Nahed Sirri who asked her to come over immediately as she had a very serious matter to discuss. Fatma Hanim walked as fast as she could the small distance that separated their houses. She was ushered into the upstairs sitting room where she had been preceded by Nahed Hanim's sister, sisters-in-law, and two friends.

"Come in, Fatma. Help us with this new problem."

"What on earth is happening? Are the Germans in Alexandria?"

"Not yet. But His Majesty has informed Hussein that he wants us to organize a wedding for Nini."

Nini had, for some time, been engaged to Muhammad Hashem, a young lawyer. No wedding plans had, so far, been made because of the political situation. Nini was also Queen Farida's cousin and best friend, and was often invited to spend the day at Abdin Palace. A strong friendship between her and the royal couple ensued. King Farouk enjoyed Nini's company and appreciated in particular her forthrightness, a quality he seldom encountered among his entourage. He apparently decided at one point to bring Nini's prolonged engagement to its proper conclusion. This, at any rate, was the reason he advanced to explain a decision that must have seemed incongruous at the time because the Germans were just a few miles from Alexandria and the invasion of the country seemed imminent. Fatma Hanim, for her part, was stupefied upon hearing the news.

"A wedding?" she exclaimed "But the Germans will be in town any moment now. Surely His Majesty realizes that it would not be proper if you have a party for whatever reason while we are in danger of being invaded by the enemy."

"Well, my dear," retorted 'Akila Hanim, Nahed Hanim's friend and Queen Farida's Lady-in-waiting, "it is all a matter of perspective. Who is the enemy? Farouk is now enchanted because the British are being beaten within an inch of their life."

"Besides," added Nahed Hanim, "Farouk, as you well know, is very fond of Nini and he really feels it would be unfair to deny her a wedding party. Bad enough that she is getting married after her younger sister, at her own insistence if I may add, without aggravating her any further."

"But a wedding, Nahed, my dear?" persisted Fatma Hanim.

"Well, nothing like we had for Doddy last year of course. It will be a simple affair. The king will come with very few guests, and we are to invite the immediate family only and few close friends. He will have to approve the list, of course. Now, can your cook come over to help ours?"

"Certainly."

"I will be needing a few other items as well. I have prepared a list for each one of you so please take a look at it and let me know if you can supply what I need."

An hour later Fatma Hanim walked back to her house still not believing what she had just heard. 'Abd al-Rahman Pasha was waiting for her in the summer sitting room.

"What did Nahed Hanim want that was so urgent?"

"You are not going to believe this. The Sirris are planning a wedding for Nini."

The Pasha stared at his wife for a moment rendered speechless by what he had just heard. Then he burst out laughing uproariously!

"Good for them. Nahed Hanim must be in seventh heaven. She likes nothing better than a good party. Besides, no one that I know can organize one as well as she can."

"But the Germans will be in town any day! How embarrassing if they arrive just as we are having the *zaffa*."

"Well, in that case they will join the party no doubt and have a taste of our hospitality."

"Come on, don't joke about such matters. The situation is very serious. I wish they would postpone this affair at least until matters clear up a little."

"You are right. The situation is too grave for us to be flippant about it. However, I have a feeling that the Germans will never reach Alexandria, let alone Cairo. But how did all this come about?"

"The king has requested it."

"Well, after what Lampson did on February 4th, I am sure His Majesty is enjoying himself tremendously and wants to celebrate. I also think that he is trying to make up for his rudeness to Hussein a few months ago. When is this wedding to take place?"

"Next week, on July 2nd."

On that day, Jim Bowker, first secretary at the British Embassy, had been busy burning confidential papers and documents that should not fall into enemy hands. The atmosphere at the embassy was of febrile and despondent activity. At 8:30 PM, exhausted after hours spent sorting out documents, Bowker decided to drive home for a shower and a change of clothes. His house on Ibn Zanki Street in Zamalek was across the street from the Sirri residence. As he turned his little green Morris from Hasan Sabri Street into Ibn Zanki, he was surprised to see from a distance all lights ablaze at the Sirri's. He had almost reached it when the traffic was momentarily stopped by the royal motorcade and to his immense surprise, Bowker saw Their Majesties step out and walk into the house from which emerged the sound of ululation. Bowker could not understand any of it. Had Sirri Pasha taken leave of his senses? Did he not know that the country was facing enemy invasion? What on earth was going on inside that house? He drove into his garage, locked his car, and walked over to the policeman standing guard at the corner. Without speaking, he made the standard questioning gesture with his hands.

"*Farah*," answered the policeman "The Pasha has a wedding celebration." Bowker could not believe it. He went back to his house and called Hussein Pasha.

"Congratulations, Pasha. I have just heard that a wedding is underway in your house."

"Yes, indeed," answered Sirri Pasha briefly.

"Surely, Pasha, this is not prudent for the Battle of al-Alamein is also underway."

"Not now as I have just received information that Rommel has been forced to retreat."

Bowker was rendered speechless. After a few seconds he asked, "Are you sure, Pasha?"

"Would I have said so otherwise?" retorted Hussein Sirri, who then replaced the receiver and walked slowly back toward the study that led onto the pergola. He stood for a moment there and suddenly was struck by the irony of the situation. At the far end of the pergola sat the king with his family and close friends, the pro-German contingent of the evening. In the study, clubbed together in restrained mood were the pro-British guests, friends, and family. The demarcation line between the two groups was fluid, with servants going back and forth, while occasionally someone from the study group would walk over to the pergola at the king's behest. It truly looked like a separation of forces. Of course it was not, but merely a question of protocol. No one could approach the royal presence unless invited to do so by the king who, on that evening, seemed quite content to limit his socializing to members of his entourage. As Hussein Sirri viewed the scene, Midhat Bey, a relative known for his wit and occasional malice, approached his host and with a wicked smile whispered, "His Majesty is in high spirits tonight. He must be anticipating a German victory."

"Is he now?" answered Sirri Pasha.

"Why else would he be here tonight? For surely he is celebrating more than Nini's wedding."

Sirri Pasha did not bother to answer, and walking over to the king gave him the latest news of the front, after which all the guests were informed. Those present that evening gave different accounts of the soiree, but all agreed that Farouk's reaction to the news of Rommel's withdrawal surprised them all. They had expected annoyance masking anger and disappointment. Instead they realized that Farouk was genuinely pleased, reassured as to the immediate fate of his country. According to a well-informed source of the time, Farouk's pro-German attitude was a nose-thumbing pose to irritate Miles

Lampson, but the king was, in fact, too intelligent to contemplate with any measure of satisfaction the occupation of Egypt by racists and fascists, whether German or Italian.

After Nini's wedding, the general atmosphere in Cairo lightened somewhat. This first defeat of Rommel cast doubt on the ultimate victory of the Axis forces. All through that summer of 1942, Egypt's Western Desert was the theater of fierce battles with victory jumping like a tennis ball from one camp to the other. On August 18, Field Marshall Montgomery took up his new post as commander-in-chief of the Eighth Army. This brilliant strategist with piercing eyes, a beak nose, and an often-abrupt manner, was determined to out-fox the fox and soon became a legend in his own right. On September 7, faced with the possibility of a crushing defeat, he stopped the battle to recoup, making diversionary movements and limited offensive thrusts. On October 23, his big offensive started, and all through autumn until November the battle raged and the two military geniuses were pitted mercilessly against one another in a mortal combat from which only one could possibly emerge victorious. Rommel finally lost, defeated not by his enemy alone but by his own Führer who had been unable to sustain his supply line. On November 4, 1942, the Panzer division began its final withdrawal from the dessert.

27

During that summer of 1942, while the war raged on the Western front of Egypt, Cha, Muhammad, their cousins, and their neighbors, the young Zamalekites, spent their holiday in relative calm. Though they were all aware of the danger of the German offensive, they were too young to be overly worried by it. In fact, at least as far as Cha was concerned, the world of adults was so dominated by news from the front that suddenly more freedom was granted than ever before. Parents could not be bothered with details of the children's daily routine, and the governesses who could hardly cope with their own deep anxiety, often became more permissive. It suited these worried ladies perfectly to sit in one of the families' gardens, sip tea, and converse with their compatriots while the children were out enjoying their newly found freedom. Cycling around Zamalek became an acquired right, though in Cha's case there was the proviso that she never be out alone, in other words that Muhammad should be with her all the time. One afternoon, however, the weather was hot, Cha particularly trying, and Muhammad in bed with a cold. The frustrated twelve-year-old nagged her governess relentlessly.

"If Muhammad can go out alone, why can't I? I am two years older!"

Madame Duprée could not quite understand the reason herself therefore, in order to get some peace, she finally gave permission. "Very well, you may go but for no more than ten minutes. I will keep an eye on my watch."

This proved to be an unfortunate decision because just as Cha was turning the corner at full speed, her father's chauffeur-driven car met her head on. Collision was averted by the driver's fast reflex while Cha, totally oblivious of the accident she had just escaped, waved proudly to her father. 'Abd al-Rahman Sallam could not believe his eyes. What on earth was his daughter doing alone in the streets of Zamalek? Had Madame Duprée taken leave of her senses? And where was Muhammad? Had the world gone mad? Usually extremely self-controlled and not given to bouts of ill-temper, the Pasha opened the car door before it had fully stopped and started getting out as fast as his slowed down movements would allow. He called Idris, the head *sufraji* and demanded to see Madame Duprée immediately. Fatma Hanim upon hearing her husband's angry voice looked down from the banister on the first floor and started down the stairs. Madame Duprée rushed in from the garden where she was entertaining Mademoiselle Carère, the Attal family governess. The Pasha glared at her and the poor woman, never having experienced her employer's anger in all her years with the family, was very alarmed.

"Where is Cha, Madame Duprée?"

"Cycling, Pasha."

"Where is she cycling?"

"Around the block."

"Alone? You allowed my daughter out of the house unaccompanied?"

"But Pasha, this was only for ten minutes. She will be in any moment now and Zamalek streets are quite safe."

"They are not Madame Duprée. I almost ran her over. Furthermore, it is not just a question of security but of propriety, of manners, of what can be done by a young girl like Cha and what should never be allowed if she is to preserve her reputation."

Madame Duprée's cheeks were scarlet, 'Abd al-Rahman looked at his watch and Fatma Hanim, who had rushed down, stood there silently praying for Cha's immediate return. The three of them let out sigh of relief when they heard her call out, "Madame Duprée, I am back."

Later on that day, 'Abd al-Rahman Pasha called Madame Duprée to his study. He realized that his anger, though justified, had been excessive, perhaps because of the near fatal accident his daughter had narrowly escaped. At the same time, he was deeply disturbed. What he had witnessed that morning was the sign of change, a change that, like his mother-in-law before him, he feared because it carried too many intangibles over which he had little power.

"Come in, Madame Duprée. The reason I have asked to talk to you is not only to reassure you that you do have our absolute trust, but also to remind you of certain guidelines that need to be clarified. While I strongly believe in the norms of our conservative society, I also realize that Cha's world is very different from her sisters.' That is understandable since she is quite a bit younger and the war has had a tremendous impact on our way of life. We will have to go along with the change but not lose sight of the fact that uncontrolled freedom can have catastrophic consequences."

"I quite agree," answered Madame Duprée, mollified by the Pasha's conciliatory tone.

"Good! I will give Cha permission to cycle around the block alone occasionally, but no longer than five minutes at a time when alone. Though I would still much prefer it if her brother were to ride with her as it would be more respectable."

"Very well, Pasha. I shall see to it that she follows these instructions."

The issue could have been settled then and there had it not been for Cha's rebellious and angry reaction. As her father was discussing with Madame Duprée, Fatma Hanim talked to her daughter and gave her the same message. The girl flew into a rage.

"Why am I always treated differently? I cannot do what my sisters do because I am too young and now you are telling me that I cannot cycle around Zamalek as I please unless Muhammad is with me. Why should he be allowed to leave the garden unaccompanied, but I may not unless I tag along with him? I am older, two years older, but you are treating me as if I were younger."

"It is not a question of age," answered her mother patiently. "It is because he is a boy and you are a girl. In our society, girls do not go out alone but boys do. It is a question of respectability and decorum."

This explanation did not appease Cha at all. It all seemed so unfair and she perceived the fact that being born a girl was a calamity. This despondent mood lasted for days. She was unhappy, listless, and unwilling to take advantage of the little freedom she was granted, so the bicycle remained in the shed.

This summer of 1942 was a difficult one for Fatma Hanim despite the Allied victories in the early days in July. Her husband's health was not getting any better and Cha was proving more difficult with every passing day. Nearly twelve years old, she felt disoriented, inadequate, and at odds with her surroundings. Despite her grandmother's valiant attempt to safeguard her from the onus of being a fourth daughter, she deeply felt her undesirable position and, as is often the case with children that age, she plunged headlong into attitudes that oscillated from rebelliousness to lachrymose self-pity.

"It will pass, Madame," said Madame Duprée at the end of a particularly difficult day. "*L'âge ingrat* is painful, but it will pass."

"I really hope so," sighed Fatma Hanim. "We just need some good news to cheer us all up and take her mind off her resentments."

Some good news was actually in the offing as Fatma Hanim's husband had that very morning informed her that 'Abir had received a proposal of marriage. Though she felt her daughter, at the age of fifteen, was still far too young to marry, yet it pleased her to know that she had been noticed by an excellent family. She voiced her reservations however to which her husband answered, "I am fully aware that 'Abir is still very young and perhaps not yet ready to settle down and be responsible for a family. Sooner or later she will have to adjust to the idea and this young man is eminently acceptable. This is the kind of calculated risk we should take."

"I see your point and yet I fear it is too soon, much too soon."

Abd al-Rahman drew on his cigarette and made no reply. He knew his wife was right and yet he had made up his mind. In fact, he had been waiting for quite sometime for such a proposal. He wanted to settle this question fast, have one more issue taken care of, one less problem for Fatma Hanim to grapple with after his death. By August 1942, he no longer had any hope of a full recovery and had convinced himself that he would not live much longer. Though he faced death with courage, he was reluctant to discuss it openly with his wife. A certain inhibition prevented him from exposing his most intimate thoughts on the subject. He knew that his reasons for accepting this marriage proposal were valid but at the same time wished to spare her the pain of sharing the burden of his knowledge.

He preferred to carry on the pretense of good health and a bright outlook. And yet he had to convince her that 'Abir was not too young and that marriage at that point in her life was right for her; the main thing was for her to be entrusted to someone of value who would protect her and give her time to grow up at her own pace. The prospective young man was certainly someone he felt he could trust. Anyway, the girl was fifteen and a half years old and quite mature for her age since she shared her older sisters' lives and was thrown in with the adults all the time. She was very bright, had received a very good education at the Mère de Dieu. She was a voracious reader, full of energy, both physical and mental, and quite accomplished in many ways. Other than her age, there did not seem to be a good reason to refuse a good proposal now and risk waiting for another one, which might not be as good. Besides, 'Abir had already indicated her willingness to become a wife, like her sisters and her friends, Nini and Doddy Sirri.

Fatma Hanim respected her husband's reticence. She understood his dilemma but had no wish to embarrass him by admitting her knowledge. She knew the reason for his eagerness to settle 'Abir in a life of her own, but she was still convinced that the girl was too young. With this thought she sighed deeply.

"What is wrong Fatma Hanim? We are not discussing a funeral but a wedding. What nicer thought is there? You should be more like Nahed Hanim and start making up lists, these innumerable lists that precede all her social activities."

"So, Basha, you have decided to accept Rashwan Bey's offer?"

"Yes, I have and will let him know soon."

"And when is the wedding to take place?"

"My dear, you know very well that this decision is not mine to make. Rashwan Bey or his son must set the date. All I can do is warn them that I cannot have a wedding in my house as long as Rommel is camped at al-Alamein. Don't look so downcast, your daughter will be fine, besides she is not much younger than Queen Farida was when she married and the king had not reached twenty years of age."

A few days later 'Abir became officially engaged.

At the end of summer, when the danger of a German invasion of the country was less acute, Fatma Hanim broached the subject of the wedding having no doubt that it would be a small affair because of the war and her husband's health. She did not like protracted engagements and believed that a promise of marriage, once given, is binding. Furthermore, she was quite tired of having two governesses in the house and wished to be rid of the chaperone as soon as possible.

"When are we having the wedding?" she asked her husband one morning at breakfast. "Zaynab Hanim led me to understand that they are ready and would like to celebrate as soon as possible."

"Not yet. Not as long as Rommel is around."

Finally, in November after Rommel's withdrawal and the capture of General von Thom, the commander of the Afrika Corps who replaced him, the danger of a German invasion of Egypt seemed to be definitely set aside. On November 8, Allied troops landed in North Africa and the war took a new turn as the action transported itself elsewhere.

28

During that summer of 1942, Cha viewed the world of adults with expectation, curiosity, and occasionally with a little twinge of fear. She had realized that there was a great deal about that world that she could not understand. Although it was governed by grownups with so much power over her young life, there were things over which they seemed to have no control. Her father was not getting any better. How was it that all these doctors could not rid him of this problem that made his hands shaky and his walk so slow? And there was this General Rommel who would be entering Cairo at any moment now. No one was able to stop him, not the king, not all the generals, not anybody in fact. For the first time ever she suddenly felt the urge to turn back, to retreat into the security of her childhood years, and keep the world and its dangers at bay. On October 10, 1942, she celebrated her twelfth birthday quietly with her cousins and a few friends, with a little tea party in the huge Zamalek dining room. 'Abir came in with her fiancé for a few minutes, glowing in her new status of an engaged woman. Acting very much as a grown up, she accentuated her condescension toward the younger crowd. Under normal circumstances, Cha would have been irritated by her sister's patronizing attitude, but she was not. Suddenly, looking at the young couple she thought, "Thank God it is not me. I still have a choice. My life has not been settled for me yet!"

When school started that year, she went back happily, looking forward to meeting her school friends again. Cha's life was split very neatly into two separate wholes: there was school and there was home, and each had its own set of activities, its own very defined atmosphere. With the exception of very few girls who met her parents' approval, she was not encouraged to socialize with other girls.

Cha did not mind this division but rather liked to keep her two worlds apart. It was almost as if she were making daily trips from one country to another. Sometimes, when a quarrel erupted between her and one of her 'home' friends, or some unpleasantness arose, she would comfort herself with the thought that tomorrow she would be back in her other world, the world of quiet discipline, that other place which was so very different from her home. The converse was also true, because when she bristled at the staid and often boring convent routine, she would mentally transport herself out of it and find solace in the more congenial atmosphere of her home life. This was an escape mechanism that served her well during her difficult pre-adolescent years.

One day, in early December, 'Abd al-Rahman surprised the family with the announcement that he intended to throw a huge party in celebration of 'Abir's wedding. Fatma Hanim was taken by surprise as she had assumed all along that a big wedding was definitely out of question.

"Are you sure, Basha? Would it not be better if we have a simple ceremony, just the family and a few friends? Then we could offer the young couple a nice honeymoon."

"I intend, in any case, to offer them a honeymoon, however, with the war on, the possibilities are limited. Palestine could be an acceptable choice, as I doubt if either of them would want a trip to Upper Egypt. Nevertheless, I also want to have a big wedding with all the family, in-laws, relatives, and friends. I shall extend an invitation to His Majesty as well as to my colleagues and ex-colleagues in the ministry."

Fatma Hanim was speechless. After a while, she regained her composure and calmly said, "It seems to me that we shall be dealing with a gathering of over 500 people."

"I would say that is more or less what I had in mind. How about December 31st? That would be a pleasant start to the new year. I've no doubt the evening will go on until the early hours of January 1st."

"Yes, of course that would be nice. I assure you, however that neither 'Abir nor her fiancé expect so much. 'Abir is quite reconciled to the idea of a small wedding."

"There, you have just said it—'reconciled.' Why do you want to deprive the child of the joys of a big wedding? I certainly don't.

Besides, we should celebrate in our own way the end of the German presence on our borders. I would not have done it had Rommel still been around. Hussein and Nahed had no choice, as it was a command performance ordered by the king. This is not our case. Now the time has come for us to celebrate."

From that moment on, feverish activity became the order of the day in the Sallam household. Lists were made, bridesmaids selected, and caterers called in. 'Abd al-Rahman had, from the start, declared that his daughter's wedding would be a very oriental affair, quite different from the one the Sirris had for their daughter Doddy. There would be no pages to walk with the bridesmaids. The girls, twelve of them, would be wearing salmon pink moiré dresses to offset the bride's white one. Tahia Cariocca, the famous belly dancer, was invited to view the grand staircase and establish her repertoire accordingly. She was asked to limit her songs to the most traditional ones and to walk down the stairs very slowly as a beautiful *zaffa* should never be hurried. Fatma Hanim organized a chorus of ululation performers whose shrill crescendos would accompany Tahia's singers to create the perfect blend of sounds traditionally associated with an oriental wedding. There would be no balalaika ensemble hidden behind trees, for the garden would be entirely covered by a huge tent and transformed into a dining hall with tables set all around and upon which the buffet would be served. 'Azzuz al-'Ashshi, the most famous caterer at the time for oriental food, was asked to produce the best and most elaborate menu his kitchen could supply. The dining room was prepared for the royal family should they make an appearance.

The high point of the evening, however, was the promised attendance of Umm Kulthum, dubbed 'star of the East' by her admirers, who had become over the years one of Fatma Hanim's friends. To have her perform at the wedding was a shared honor: the Sallams had the social standing and Umm Kulthum had the crowning of success. And sing she did, all through the night accompanied by her famous *takht* (oriental orchestra). She sang of love, mostly unrequited, which might seem odd under the circumstance. She sang of yearning, of desire, of joy, and of sadness. The lyrics of the outstanding composer Riyad al-Sunbati with the poems of Ahmad Shawqi, known as the 'prince of poets and the poet of princes, were carried by her golden voice to unparalleled degrees of excellence. At 5:00 in the morning, having performed with enthusiasm, the great singer's last song finally came to a close and an early morning breakfast was served to the valiant guests who had remained to the end.

Cha had been allowed to stay up as late as she wished but was not enjoying herself. To begin with, she did not like her dress at all and much preferred the one she had worn at Doddy's wedding. This one made her look fat and awkward; the flat-chested little girl of ten was now a plumpish twelve-year-old who stooped to hide her developing bust. She hated having a bust because it made her different from her brother and cousins, and the moiré dress buttoned down the front seemed stretched to capacity, almost ready to burst. Moreover, her feelings were hurt because she had overheard a conversation between two ladies who had criticized the evening. They were *nabilas*, or lesser princesses, who were complaining of boredom and felt quite out of place in this very oriental evening despite the beauty of the house and the lavishness of the reception. Cha hated them for daring to make such ugly remarks about the wedding. It pained her that her parents' tremendous efforts should be dismissed as 'boring' though, if truth be said, she was bored herself. Most of her friends had left after the buffet and only their parents and other adults had remained to enjoy Umm Kulthum's entertainment. She did not like Umm Kulthum at all and could not understand the fuss over this woman who was not pretty and whose music was so discordant to her ears. There were, of course, moments of excitement just like at Doddy's wedding. Walking down the grand staircase, she had felt immensely proud that this should be her home.

She was delighted to see the Queen quite close as she walked to the first floor sitting room where she was to spend the evening with her ladies-in-waiting while the king and other gentlemen were taken to the ground floor drawing room. His Majesty had not requested two wedding ceremonies this time because he knew the house was large enough to accommodate everyone without breach of protocol. Also, under his wife's influence, King Farouk had become more flexible in the application of court etiquette. Cha was still very much impressed by the glamour of royalty and, as she was getting ready for bed, she thought of nothing else but the beauty of the Queen and the awe-inspiring presence of the king.

As she drifted off to sleep, a thought of infinite pleasure crossed her mind: "Now, I am Mademoiselle Sallam. I am next in line and I have finally become important."

January 1, 1943 was a day of recuperation for the Sallam household. Fatma Hanim slept until noon and the Pasha, though an early riser, allowed himself to linger in bed until 9:00 AM. The servants went quietly about their business putting the house back in order. The gardener surveyed the damage to his garden not knowing where to begin while workmen were methodically dismantling the giant tent and folding up the tables. Madame Duprée, in her third-floor bedroom, was still in a daze. She was exhausted, not having slept a single minute in her exhilaration at having been part of this fabulous evening. She recalled all the stages of the preparations: the baskets of flowers that poured seemingly in an endless flow, had to be sorted out by color and placed according to a plan, the white and pink ones near the *kusha*, the other colors scattered around the house and in the tent. The upstairs winter sitting room had to be provided with little dishes of sugared almonds, chocolates, and marrons glacés, as well as heaters to keep up a decent level of warmth. Powder rooms on the ground floor and bathrooms of the first floor, scrubbed to their shining pristine newness, had to be supplied with embroidered hand towels and tiny crystal vases with one rose in each. These chores had been her responsibility and she had handled them with her usual efficiency.

She had watched everything with fascination not wanting to miss a single detail of the proceedings, and she had been profoundly impressed by the spectacle of such oriental splendor. She had cried when watching 'Abir in her beautiful white brocade dress, her veil held by a tiara, her lovely face framed by the silver threads of her tally, walking slowly toward her destiny. At that moment, she had wondered at the wisdom of launching this girl into life so unprepared to meet its many daunting challenges. "She will have to learn very quickly if she is to survive. God knows how fast she will be able to do so!" She then looked for Cha and spotted her among the bridesmaids, so serious, straight backed, holding her candle and gazing at the crowd below, seemingly unperturbed. "May God preserve my Cha," she prayed silently, "and may she not throw herself into the world before she is ready." This morning Madame Duprée felt drained of energy and was suffering from a splitting headache. Duty called, but for the moment she could not bring herself to leave her room and start her working day. "A few more minutes of peace and quiet," she thought, and leaning her head against the back of her *bergère*, closed her eyes, and fell asleep.

In the afternoon the telephone rang constantly. Everyone wished to thank the Sallams for the lovely wedding and the perfection of its organization. Inevitably, comparisons were made in society between the two outstanding Zamalek weddings: Doddy Sirri's in May 1941 and 'Abir Sallam's on December 31, 1942. Each one of them represented an aspect of current Egyptian society, the westernized one and the oriental one, and each in its own way had been a resounding success. For those who had, like Nahed Sirri, opted for avant-garde attitudes and mores, Doddy's wedding was much more to their taste, but for the others who still held unto the past and its traditions, 'Abir's was absolute perfection.

Actually, these two weddings of the early-1940s were a fairly good example of the social evolution that was taking place in the country. Here was a society trying to forge a new identity for itself. It was attempting to overlay its years of Orientalism, now considered outmoded by the pioneers of the modern movement, with attitudes, stances, and social practices that belonged to a different world. Ironically, this was the world of the current invader, or the potential invader, but invader nevertheless and basically different. Whether it was the British or the German models that were observed by Egyptian society, they were European and certainly not Oriental. Fatma Hanim represented moderate conservatism. She navigated in mid-stream and, as her mother had predicted, stayed the course and remained in large measure within the bounds of the world in which she was born. Nahed Hanim, on the other hand, steamed ahead full blast and while respecting the moral integrity of her Egyptian background, she superimposed upon it the newfound values and social mores of the European world she so admired. While Fatma Hanim never in her life uncovered her shoulders in public, Nahed Hanim was photographed at a ball in the early 1940s looking radiantly beautiful in a gorgeous full-length dress that left her shoulders bare. No one at the time criticized her since everyone tacitly agreed that the world had changed. The war had introduced new ways and people were free to choose what suited them best.

A few days after the wedding, Mrs. Donovan, the British chaperone, tendered her resignation to her relieved employer. "Thank God this episode is over," Fatma Hanim told a friend over the telephone. "Our two governesses were soon going to be at each other's throats!"

After the Christmas holiday, Cha went back to school filled with her newly acquired sense of self-importance. She was now the only daughter left in the house, the one who would be courted by prospective suitors. Not that she desired marriage. In fact unlike her sisters, she had no intention whatsoever of settling into conventional matrimony. The fun lay in being the center of attention, of being sought while standing aloof. She reveled in this new status, and though her brother was still the only son, the mental world she evolved in now was one in which a boy had no place. Cha always adored her brother despite the many privileges he enjoyed, and her resentment had never been focused on him, but on the social conventions of her family, the adults who were bent on curbing whatever freedom she felt was her right. For the time being, however, she set aside her preoccupation with independence because her mind was busy on an altogether different level. Never in her young life had her ego soared to such heights of complacency and self-indulgence.

Madame Duprée was not pleased with this new phase of Cha's development but, with the wisdom born of long years of experience, she decided to let the child enjoy her little moment of glory. However, she had not anticipated what would happen at school. The nun in charge of Cha's class overheard a few smug remarks she uttered in front of her classmates and to teach her a lesson in humility, she chose the weapon of ridicule. For a whole day, she addressed the girl in class as 'Mademoiselle Sallam Pasha' stressing the title and accentuating with a repressed smile the ludicrous appellation. Cha was profoundly mortified and brutally brought down from her self-erected pedestal. The lesson was cruel but it bore fruit for never again did she dare mention her father's elevated position, least of all his title. Had the nun known what sadness and hardship lay in store for Cha, she might have shown more kindness.

In any event, as days went by, elation over the wedding's success wore off and life in the Sallam household resumed its usual pattern. 'Abd al-Rahman Pasha was totally engrossed in news from the front and listened to all available bulletins, which he supplemented with information garnered from his colleagues. He followed the movement of Allied forces in Russia, North Africa, or wherever the battle raged. By the end of 1943, he no longer doubted the defeat of Germany was just a matter of time. Fatma Hanim, for her part, was totally involved in her social work and, consistently encouraged by her husband, she spent most afternoons with ladies who, like herself, worked for charitable organizations. As for Cha, her initial elation over being the center of attention soon wore off as she very quickly experienced the other side of the coin.

She found herself thrown into the limelight, which was not at all to her liking because with it came additional curtailment of her independence. She was told that running around on a bicycle would have to be abandoned as well as her constant companionship with boys. A period of dejection followed. She felt completely at odds with her family and knew that she would have to put up a strong fight to secure a certain amount of freedom. Though she still went to the 3:00 PM Thursday movie with her brother and cousins, followed by high tea at one of the Zamalek houses, oddly enough, she enjoyed these outings far less than before. She felt a little awkward, almost as if these were childish activities and one ought to move on to more adult pursuits. Actually, what disturbed her deeply was her awareness that the boys themselves seemed to have lost interest in these outings as well, to have outgrown them and were possibly involved in other activities in which she had no part. She felt left behind at a time when she needed the reassurance of their undivided allegiance.

The summer of 1943 was hard on Cha. She was approaching adolescence, at odds with her surroundings, insecure in her relationships, hating her appearance, and generally dissatisfied with her life. With Rommel safely out of the way, families were again able to spend a few summer weeks in Alexandria. The beach of Sidi Bishr number two experienced an influx of Cairene tourists and the Casino San Stefano had its daily quota of guests. There again Cha felt left out because at the beach the boys were allowed to wander off on their own while she was expected, after her swim, to sit in the cabin with the grown ups. More often than not, she found herself nursing a grievance of one kind or another, particularly when she became aware that some of her girl friends were enjoying more freedom than she was ever allowed. The irony of her situation galled her. Here she was, almost thirteen years old, treated as an adult whose reputation depended on the limitations that were imposed upon her, while on the other hand, these limitations made her look like a child in front of the other girls. She was far too young and inexperienced to understand that the society to which she belonged was going through a very rapid transformation toward modernism and that her family, her mother in particular, were reluctant to be front runners but held to the middle course as it seemed safer and more reasonable. By the end of summer, she looked forward to going back to school again, that haven of security where all girls submitted to the same rules.

Cha's problems with her life took on a different dimension one day in early November. She woke up, as was her habit, a few minutes before Madame Duprée came in to open up the shutters and fill her room with light and early morning bustle. This morning, however, Cha stretched, yawned, stretched again, assuming that Madame Duprée would be in any moment. She watched a single ray of light that crossed her room through the partially opened shutters, and the little specks of dust that floated in it, moving incessantly as if pursuing an activity controlled by a master plan. After a few minutes of daydreaming, she sat up in bed wondering at her governess's delay. Alarmed, she jumped out of bed, threw her dressing gown over her shoulders and, not bothering with slippers, ran to Madame Duprée's room. She knocked twice and receiving no answer slowly opened the door. What she saw made her gasp. Madame Duprée was sprawled on the floor in a dead faint and a rivulet of blood trickled down her forehead where she had hit the brass railing of her bed.

"Madame, Madame," cried the child frantically. Unable to move the older woman, she ran down to her mother's room screaming for help. A while later, an ambulance carried Madame Duprée to hospital while Cha sat in her room crying. There was no question of going to school, actually no one pressed her to get dressed and meet the school bus as the household was in a state of confusion and no one was paying much attention to the children. While their parents went to the hospital, the children stayed home to fend for themselves as best they could. Both of them were devastated, Muhammad perhaps a little less so than his sister as he had come to consider Madame Duprée as belonging more to Cha; he was a man and governesses were for girls. Later in the day, 'Abd al-Rahman and Fatma Hanim came back looking grim. They gave no details but warned the children that Madame Duprée would not be back for a few days. She never did come back. She had suffered a massive stroke and died peacefully the following night.

When she heard the news, Cha was heartbroken. She did not cry and showed no open reaction. She simply went to her room and sat there looking at the floral pattern on the wallpaper. She followed the movement of the foliage that stretched up to the ceiling, paralyzed by a primeval fear. "It is not fair," she kept thinking. "It is not fair." Madame Duprée had been so strong, so powerful, so much in control of herself and her surroundings. Suddenly this pillar of strength was gone and Cha perceived her own mortality with acute awareness. More important, she saw with clarity the frailness of human life and understood with bitterness that the only certainty one has is that death will inevitably come. Her attitude toward death had, so far, been casual as she always thought of it as happening elsewhere, to other people. Both death and the people who were struck by it were abstractions over which she never worried much, particularly as it was not a topic usually discussed in front of children. Even the thousands dying on the battlefields or in bombed cities were also abstractions and as far removed from her life as the planet Mars. Nothing of the sort happened in Zamalek. Her grandparents had died, but they were old and it was therefore natural that they should die. What else could they do? She knew that people could not go on forever. That was still fair, acceptable. But with Madame Duprée it seemed all wrong, as if the rules of the game had not been respected, as if the pattern had suddenly gone berserk.

On that day, Cha quite suddenly became an adult. Whatever innocence of childhood she retained was only at surface level. The reality of the human condition had hit her with full force. She understood the meaning of transience and consequently developed a fear of time, implacable partner of death that plods along at an unchanging pace while everything else forever changes.

29

For many days Cha followed her routine like a robot. She had to take a daily bath and make sure her uniform was neat and her shoes scrubbed. She had to go to school and study. She had to carry on with her life. She wanted Madame Duprée to be proud of her and, from wherever she was, know that Cha had learned her lesson well. This was her way of grieving.

A few days after Madame Duprée's death, Fatma Hanim started looking for a replacement. She was just as disconsolate as her daughter because Madame Duprée had been a constant and amiable companion for many years. Much as she disliked the idea of having a stranger in the house, it was inevitable since Cha was not allowed to go out on her own. In those days, finding an adequate replacement posed no problem as foreign emigrants and expatriates swarmed in this haven of relative calm. The war was raging elsewhere now and Egypt, as always, was the land of plenty, the place of gentle inaction, where immobility masks change like the Nile, whose waters glide smoothly, inexorably toward the sea, hiding under their tiny ripples treacherous whirlpools and dangerous currents. The solution to the Sallams' quest presented itself almost immediately.

Anisah Hanim phoned her sister a few days after Madame Duprée's funeral and offered their own governess as a replacement. "We have decided that our boys are too old for a governess and we plan to dismiss Madame Ganteau. Would you like to hire her in place of poor Madame Duprée?" The idea seemed very good. Madame Ganteau had apparently been satisfactory and although the maids had reported occasional acts of brutality against the boys, she had the necessary qualifications. She claimed to be related to the Ganteau family, who had been established in Egypt for many years and was part of the Cairo social scene. For a reason never clearly explained, she was said to belong to a poor branch of the family. It was whispered by other governess that the branch was nonexistent and the link a figment of her imagination. However, since the Ganteaus never denied the allegation the story took hold and her pedigree was thus established.

She had told Anisah Hanim when she hired her that she was British of Maltese origin, though she later also said that she was a raya, which according to her meant that she had no defined nationality. This may or may not have been true, but whatever the case it certainly solved the problem of political allegiance since she could not pretend to have any. She spoke English—which she said was her mother tongue—very well, but French with a terrible accent. She had impeccable manners, pushed her love of decorum and etiquette to exhausting extremes and seemed to be the ideal duenna for a recalcitrant thirteen year old. Cha was not consulted nor expected to be. In fact, she did not mind Madame Ganteau who was always such fun and full of amusing stories. And yet, she resented the fact that anyone at all would replace her beloved Madame Duprée.

Her feelings were ambivalent. If she accepted readily the presence of this new governess, would it not indicate an ungrateful lack of feeling for a person to whom she owed so much? She therefore held back, retreated into the safety of her room and tried to sort out for herself the proper attitude to observe. The governess felt the girl's reticence and being herself insecure and unkind, misunderstood her motives. She took an instant fearful dislike to Cha, knowing very well that her presence in the house depended largely on being accepted by her new charge. Muhammad presented no danger because, like his cousins, he was beyond her jurisdiction. Oddly enough, since the children were still very often together, sharing their activities and outings, it seemed that Madame Ganteau was everybody's governess.

In order to secure her position and safeguard her status as the eminent educator, she simply adopted the British motto, 'Divide to rule.' She immediately devised little schemes to ingratiate herself with Muhammad and her erstwhile charges, Anisah Hanim's sons, and created a united front of admirers and confidants from which Cha was deliberately excluded. The child could not understand at first what was happening. Why was Muhammad suddenly hostile? Why were the boys laughing at her behind her back? Why were they always in Madame Ganteau's room having fun and the moment she came in silence fell like a lid over a tin box? She felt excluded and definitely unwanted. Since she could not understand the reason for such animosity and was too proud to ask, she retreated within herself in agonies of self-doubt. It never occurred too her to complain to her mother for this was simply not done! Besides, what could she tell? Madame Gateau never raised her voice or dared lift a hand to her as Fatma Hanim had made it clear from the start that this was unacceptable. The boys, like Cha, did not understand the game that was being played either or the fact that they were used like pawns on a chessboard. As far as they were concerned, Cha had become a spoilsport, always glum and unhappy.

Meanwhile, the situation in Cairo was delightfully pleasant. Albert Soussa had inaugurated the 'Auberge des Pyramides,' which very quickly became one of the favorite haunts of King Farouk and his clique immediately followed by the 'in' people of the social establishment. Egyptian hostesses like Dora Khayat, Marie Wissa, Nahed Sirri and many others competed with one another to give the best parties, the most lavish or the most refined. More often than not the king would make an appearance and his hearty laughter could be heard over the after dinner conversation. According to a witness of the time, the great days of wartime Cairo came after the battle of al-Alamein despite the fact that an epidemic of cholera was causing havoc among the poorer classes. The political atmosphere of the country was at its usual steady tension like a casserole gently stewing over a low fire.

Al-Nahhas Pasha, after the humiliating performance of Miles Lampson, the British ambassador, was running the country while, according to well-informed sources, being himself run by his young and greedy wife Zaynab al-Wakil. His popularity with the masses had somewhat decreased as he seemed unable to control the economy and word had spread that he was the man of the British. The king was gaining ground over his enemies, Sir Miles Lampson, now Lord Killearn, having been elevated to the peerage, and al-Nahhas. In an attempt to strengthen his popularity, he drew closer to the Coptic contingent by occasional gestures such as the donation of 400

Egyptian pounds for the restoration of St. Catherine's Monastery. At the same time Hassanein Pasha, his mentor and advisor, orchestrated a campaign to discredit al-Nahhas and his wife. With the help of Makram Ebeid, a dissident Wafdist and founder of the Kotla Party, he inspired the writing of a book, later dubbed the Black Book, which exposed with clarity Nahhas' abuse of power and his nepotism.

Galal al-Hamamsy, a bright young journalist, scion of one of Damietta's best families, wrote most of the book, methodically researched all its allegations against the premier and his wife, checked his sources carefully, examined all documents to ensure their authenticity and ultimately produced an embarrassing condemnation of the country's ruling party. He subsequently paid for his audacity and courage with eighteen months in a house of detention. But the deed was done and al-Nahhas' reputation severely tarnished. In the Sallam household, the general feeling as regards the Black Book and its authors was of unmitigated support. Fatma Hanim visited Galal's mother, a woman of great courage and forbearance who held her head high and, despite her deep anxiety over her son's welfare and future, never complained but carried on her daily life with composure and serene self-respect.

'Abd al-Rahman, though concerned over the political developments of the country, was totally engrossed in the war. He now lived the life of a semi-invalid, rarely ventured out and spent most of his day reading or listening to news bulletins. He knew that once the maelstrom was over, the world would never be the same again. Would this war in effect put an end to all wars? He doubted that, but worried more about the change that was bound to happen and whose magnitude he could not visualize. He knew that his life expectation was short and that the new world that was in the making and would appear after this universal slaughter was over would be one in which he would have no part. It saddened him because he would have welcomed the challenge while aware that the new values, new ideas, and different concepts were fraught with danger, particularly for the older generation.

And so, while 'Abd al-Rahman Pasha watched with keen interest developments on the various fronts, Cha was engaged in a battle of her own. She knew that Madame Ganteau was the enemy who had declared war with no apparent reason and was pursuing it with relentless cruelty and ingenuity. The war of nerves, the attacks on the emotions, feelings, and sensitivity of a vulnerable thirteen-year-old were a source of unending pleasure to the governess. This at least was how it started because Cha had then no clue as to the older woman's vicious behavior. Cha was disconcerted, almost disoriented, and wrongly assumed that if she tried to please her governess, she might be accepted and the taunts, humiliations, and barbs would cease. Soon enough it became apparent that there was no way she could placate Madame Ganteau. The woman hated her and was determined to make her miserable. Having reached this conclusion, Cha decided that the only solution would be to retreat even more within herself and find refuge in her books. She became a voracious reader, and to all the nasty remarks of the governess opposed an inscrutable silence and haughty disdain.

Disregarding totally the governess whose permission she supposedly had to seek before going anywhere in the big house, she would, every afternoon, sneak down to her parents' floor and spend an hour or two with her father. Suddenly her life took on a new turn for she discovered a parent whom she had always adored from far but had not really known. By the same token, 'Abd al-Rahman delighted in her company and realized that she was not an ordinary thirteen-year-old. She did not seem interested in the childish occupations of her age, rather she seemed to derive an inordinate pleasure in conversation of a more serious nature. The war was, of course, the main topic or perhaps the starting point from which radiated other topics such as the evil of dictatorship, the difference between nationalism and chauvinism, and the importance of patriotism, which led to a discussion of identity and self-knowledge. 'Abd al-Rahman discussed these lofty subjects in a simple way to reach the child's mind. He marveled at the fact that she never seemed bored but listened avidly with unwavering attention.

For Cha these were golden hours. For the first time in her life she understood the meaning of privilege. This was what she had been seeking all along, not the limelight or the glamour of being a pasha's daughter living in a handsome house full of servants, but to have the undivided attention of an adult who treated her as an equal, who addressed her mind in order to enrich it, and who did it out of love. Looking at her one afternoon after a particularly rewarding session of questions and answers, 'Abd al-Rahman Pasha was pleased: his little 'catastrophe' was developing rather nicely. The pattern was thus set. Every afternoon, while Madame Ganteau was taking her nap, Cha would sneak down to her father's sitting room where he would be waiting with daily, renewed interest.

Ultimately Madame Ganteau found out what was going on and tried to put a stop to it by claiming that Cha should be punished for not taking permission before going down, as the Pasha should never be disturbed. Cha for a moment panicked but immediately took hold of herself and in a calm, detached manner told her governess, "My father expects me in his study. If I do not appear within the next five minutes he will send for me and I shall have to tell Idris that you did not allow me to go down." She then sat at her desk, opened a book and pretended to read. Ganteau was livid, she could not fault the girl therefore knew she had lost the argument.

"Very well then. Go down if you must. Anyway your father is a very sick man so you might as well enjoy his company while it lasts."

The poisoned arrow hit the mark with accuracy. Cha steeled herself not to show the depth of her feelings, the anger, frustration, and hatred she felt for her tormentor. She knew her father was ill but that did not necessarily mean he was going to die, or did it? But of course he was going to die. It was inevitable. Her moments of happiness would soon be over. And yet, if he were truly dying, why then did her mother go out and leave him alone in the study? Surely that was not possible, people were not just left there alone to die, certainly not a pasha.

"She must be wrong," thought Cha. "She wants to frighten me, she wants to make me miserable and unhappy because she hates me. I will not let her see how much she has upset me."

"Thank you for your kind permission. I shall go down now and perhaps stay a little longer than usual because I have very important things to discuss with my father," said Cha. Not giving the governess a chance to answer, she dashed out of the room, scrambled down the stairs and ran to her father's study. But she stopped at the door gripped by a terrible sense of foreboding. "He may be dead," she thought. "He may have died all alone while listening to the news, he will be sitting there not breathing anymore, not hearing, not seeing. . . ." These thoughts jostled with one another in her mind and she was paralyzed with fear. The eerie silence of the vast hallway seemed filled with supernatural presences, angels or demons, or perhaps souls of her grandparents and Madame Duprée who had come to fetch her father. She had no fear of death. In fact, there were days when she looked forward to it, not in a spirit of despair but more through curiosity about what lay beyond the veil. Today, however, she abhorred it because she knew that if it came, it would be for her father and she would be left behind, alone once again. Her feet seemed glued to the floor when suddenly she heard her father cough and the sound like a whiplash broke the spell.

"Come in Cha. What are you doing standing there like a statue? And why are you late this afternoon?"

"I had too much homework," answered Cha at the mercy of conflicting emotions. Her father was still alive so there was profound happiness, but there was also fear as he might not be there tomorrow or the day after. "Life is so insecure," thought the child.

"What is wrong Cha? Why are you pensive today?"

"Nothing is wrong. I was just thinking that life is very frightening."

"Frightening? How so?"

"Well, one never knows when one is going to die, or become ill, or anything."

"You are not making much sense. Are you afraid of death?"

"Not really. . . ."

"Well, are you or are you not? You must decide which it is before we proceed any further."

"Well, I am not because I am still too young to have committed very many sins and so, if I do not go to heaven straightaway I shall spend very little time in purgatory. One thing worries me though. We have been told at school that little children who die before they are baptized never go to heaven but stay for ever in a place called Limbo. I should hate to go there, and I might have to after purgatory because I have not been baptized."

"Well Cha, Limbo might be a nice place, might it not? If I follow your line of reasoning all unbaptized people will find themselves there sooner or later which means all the people you have known and loved in this life."

"Oh no, only children go there. In fact, just babies in most cases. And anyway, how about the others? I mean us. I would like to go to heaven in the end because there I would meet everybody, my grand-parents and your parents, whom I have never seen, and people like Louis XIV, Queen Marie Antoinette, Napoleon, who must surely be in heaven by now."

"So, my curious little girl, you want to meet people, enlarge you circle of acquaintances. What a socialite you are?"

"No, no, that is not what I meant. . . ."

"I know, I know I was just teasing you. Look Cha, you must not think of heaven as a place of temporary enjoyment like going to the cinema or to a party. Heaven is the reward for a life well-lived."

"What does that mean?"

"It means first of all that all people, whatever their creed, are eli-gible candidates. In other words, if you are not baptized you have just as much chance of going there as your Catholic friends at school. God is fair, and it would be false to assume that a little baby who has done no wrong would be condemned to wander for all eternity among other babies in Limbo simply because he has never been baptized. Look Cha, what happens in the hereafter is God's business. What happens down here is what we should be concerned with. But now to go back to the point of you being frightened. Can you pinpoint to the source of the fear since you said you did not fear death?"

Cha remained silent trying to sort out her ideas.

"You do not have to answer Cha because I know well what is worrying you. It is not your death you fear for as you said you view it as an exciting adventure, it is the death of those you love." Cha nodded imperceptibly and a tear ran down her cheek. Her father ignored it but in a calm manner continued. "This is wrong, for no one knows when the hour has come. It may be now it may be ten years from now. Do you propose to spend a lifetime of worry? Do you believe that this is a 'good' way of life? To my mind this would be wanton waste and a good person should never waste anything, not time or energy or misplaced emotion."

A while later, Cha went back to her room and pondered on this conversation with mixed feelings. The worry about her father was still there like a persistent headache but, at the same time, she per-ceived the corollary of a fact she had understood long ago. If time is the enemy pushing relentlessly ahead, unstoppable, unconquerable, moving humans like a herd of cattle toward the inevitable threshold, time was also the friend, the companion of the hours of sorrow that would erase distance and ultimately reunite those who in this life had known and loved one another.

By the early days of 1944, the ultimate outcome of the war in Europe was viewed with definite optimism. It was not over yet, however the light at the end of the tunnel was no longer perceived as wishful thinking but as a tiny glimmer that grew with every passing day. In Egypt, the social-philanthropic movement spread to Alexandria and to the main cities of Upper Egypt particularly Asyut and Minya. But it was in Cairo that the ladies were most active. Fatma Hanim, encouraged by her husband, participated with enthusiasm in all projects and took her role of treasurer of one of the societies very seriously. Actually, all the ladies who had until quite recently been ladies of leisure demonstrated an impeccable professionalism in their approach to social work. 'Abd al-Rahman Sallam was proud of his wife's achievement and did not mind her frequent absence, as he needed time alone to sort out his affairs. He felt sure he would not survive another year as his strength was declining steadily. His main worry was the tremendous responsibility his wife would have to face after his death. Though his eldest daughters were safely married and settled in lives of their own, there were still the two younger children, particularly Muhammad, his only son, whose education had hardly begun. There was also the big house in Zamalek, his pride, which he realized would be an unnecessary burden for Fatma Hanim. "It must be sold," he thought. That evening, when his wife came back from yet another meeting, he broached the subject of the sale of the house.

"I have been thinking that we should move into a smaller place now that the girls are married. . . ."

"Move to another place?" interrupted Fatma Hanim "Whatever for?"

"This house is far too big. A smaller one would be more convenient"

"More convenient for whom? I have no problem running this house. What is the matter, Basha? Why this sudden decision?"

"It is not a decision, just an idea that I should like to examine with you."

"Well, as far as I am concerned, I do not believe for one moment that we shall be happier living somewhere else. At any rate, what brought this on?"

The Pasha had no wish at this time to discuss his real motive. Talking about the future, a future in which he would have no part was very hard for him, and yet he had to give a reason and a convincing one as well.

"The house, as I have just said, is too big. I am getting on. My movements have slowed down ostensibly. I can no longer negotiate the stairs with ease."

"We could install an elevator."

"Yes, we could but this would not make the house shrink. Anyway, it was just a thought. Let us not talk about it anymore."

"Now I have planted the seed, let it germinate," thought 'Abd al-Rahman. He knew it was a wise decision no matter how painful. There was no urgency. What mattered was his wife's acceptance of the idea for without that, implementation would be exceedingly difficult. He knew that she would discuss the issue with Hayah and expected the latter would react negatively because she loved the house and shared her parents' pride in it. He was much surprised, however, when Fatma Hanim reported that Hayah agreed with her father. Ever the practical member of the family, Hayah had understood his reasons and despite her emotional attachment to the family home, realized that the sale would be in her mother's best interest. She understood perfectly that her father did not consider an immediate sale but rather an option to be given serious thought should the need arise, and decided to be perfectly frank with her mother.

"I believe the house should be sold eventually because running such a big place will be too great a burden for you alone. I believe Papa wants the house to be sold after his death, not before."

A shocked silence had followed Hayah's declaration. Her father's eventual demise had never been discussed openly before. This sudden allusion of 'after' on the part of Hayah distressed her mother, who knew the time had come to drop the pretense at least with her eldest daughter.

"You are right," she sighed. "But may this not happen for a very long time."

The matter was dropped and for the next few days, life at Zamalek went on as usual: 'Abd al-Rahman was still engrossed in the developments of the war, Fatma Hanim attended her daily meetings, and the children pursued their routine supervised by Madame Ganteau.

Cha's relationship with her governess had gone from bad to worse. There seemed to be no limits now to the goading of the governess who was immensely frustrated at the child's apparent insensitivity. She never seemed to be able to hurt her deeply enough because to the renewed aggravations the girl opposed an impassive front, a mask of cool detachment. Matters were bound to come to a head. They eventually did and brought about the immediate and unexpected dismissal of the governess. One late afternoon, after a particularly enjoyable session with her father, Cha found Madame Ganteau waiting for her at the top of the stairs.

"Ah, here you are at last. What do you think you are doing bothering your father all afternoon? Don't you know he is a very sick man? At any rate, as I told you before, enjoy it while it lasts. You won't have him for much longer."

Cha gave no answer hoping to put an end to the conversation, but Madame Ganteau had apparently decided to give the screw another turn.

"You know, of course, that after your father's death you will be sent away."

"Sent away? Why?" cried Cha, forgetting her self-imposed discipline of silence.

"Because, my dear, this is the custom in your country. You will be sent to uncle Ahmad Bey in Heliopolis."

"But why uncle Ahmad Bey? Why can't I go to Aunt Anisah? I know her, I hardly know him."

"Again, because such is the custom in Egypt, it is the paternal uncle who has precedence over the maternal relatives."

"But why can't I stay here with my mother and Muhammad?"

Madame Ganteau smiled her crooked smile and pretended reluctance to give an answer.

"Why, Madame? Why?" cried Cha hysterically.

"Well, if you must know, there are two reasons. The first one is that Muhammad is a boy and, according to the law, should remain with his mother wherever she goes. You see the boy is his mother's protector. You are just a girl. The other reason is that this house will probably be sold and Muhammad with your mother will have to find some other place to live, probably a little flat somewhere."

"Why must the house be sold? Why can't we just stay here as we are?"

"Because, after your father dies, you will be ruined."

Cha stood stock still for a few moments unable to react, watched with glee by Madame Ganteau who knew that she had dealt a cruel blow and torn to shreds the girl's mask of detachment. However, she did not anticipate the violence of the child's reaction or the unprecedented response it provoked. Cha ran out of the room, grabbed the telephone that was nailed to the wall in the vestibule and dialed her sister Hayah's number. Madame Ganteau, who had returned to her room assuming that Cha had run off to hers, heard her sob while trying to speak to someone. In a panic, she rushed out and watched in stunned silence as Cha struggled to control her voice and become coherent.

"Why do I have to be sent away, Hayah?" she sobbed. "Why can't I go to the flat with Muhammad?"

"Who ever said anything about sending you away or about a flat? What flat? What are you talking about?"

"We shall be ruined after Papa dies, and I am to be sent away to live in Heliopolis with Uncle Ahmad Bey as I am just a girl and Muhammad and Mama are going to live in a little flat somewhere. I want to go with them. I can't. . . ."

"Wait a minute," interrupted Hayah. "Whoever told you this story is lying. Was it one of the maids? One of the boys?"

"No, it is Madame Ganteau, and she knows."

"She knows nothing, and don't believe everything you hear. You will never be sent away whatever happens and I am coming over right now to get to the bottom of this affair."

Cha still crying, replaced the receiver and turning round faced her governess. The latter, hiding her panic behind an amiable mask, asked Cha in a sweet and gentle voice, "Cha, my dear, why did you do that? You should not have telephoned your sister. Now she will come over and tell your mother something I told you in confidence. You know how much I care for you. As a matter of fact, I am sure your mother will do everything in her power to keep you with her."

But it was too late for Madame Ganteau. She had gone too far this time and there was no turning back. Cha despised her now for she perceived the woman's panic and was totally repulsed by her. She went back to her room, closed the door firmly, and tried to calm herself down. She wondered at the outcome of her outburst. Would her mother scold Madame Ganteau for having upset her? Would she be angry with Cha for having called Hayah? Would Madame Ganteau take revenge on her for having accused her? Never in her young life had Cha been so close to a death wish as she was at that moment. "If only I could lie down, fall asleep, and never wake up again," she prayed silently.

An hour later, Muhammad rushed into her room looking very excited. "Have you heard the news? Madame Ganteau is leaving."

"Who told you? What happened?"

He was about to answer when Fatma Hanim and Hayah came into Cha's room, both of them looking rather strange.

"Cha," said her mother. "I want you to tell me exactly what happened between you and Madame Ganteau."

Cha's long tale of woe burst forth and with it all her pent up anger and frustration. Both Fatma Hanim and Hayah were profoundly shocked and the shock turned to anger.

"But why did you never say anything?"

"I was afraid you would not believe me. Besides, the boys were on her side. They like her."

"I don't," said Muhammad. "I did at first but then I saw how nasty she really is. Do you remember how she would make me leave the table while we were having dinner to go feed the cats that live on the roof of the garage? I was afraid of the dark. She made me do it and said I was a coward and that she was teaching me to be courageous. I hate her too."

Fatma Hanim was deeply disturbed. Both her children had been victimized by a sadist while she had been totally unaware of what was going on. Hayah remained silent. She had just witnessed her mother's interview with Madame Ganteau in the course of which the latter had tried to defend herself, claiming that she had merely tried to prepare Cha to the eventuality of her father's death.

"What about the sale of the house," asked Hayah. "Who told you about that?"

"No one at all, I can assure you. I was just teasing Cha. She is so smug about the house I was simply trying to give her a lesson in humility."

"Humility!" interjected Fatma Hanim. "You must be out of your mind. And all this nonsense you told her about Egyptian law and about sending her away! How dare you tell a child of thirteen such lies? Anyway, it is obvious that the children dislike you. I will, therefore, no longer require your services."

Cha and Muhammad remained in Cha's room as long as Madame Ganteau was packing as neither of them wanted to see her or say good-bye. Cha was exhausted by the emotional trauma she had just undergone. She was confused, disoriented, like a person who, having spent many months in a dark cell, is suddenly released. Was it possible that she was at long last rid of the monster? She dared not believe it yet because the woman was so cunning, she might still find a way of reinstating herself with her employers. A while later, a triumphant Umm Muhammad knocked at the door and, in a conspiratorial tone of voice, announced that Madame Ganteau had left. After Madame Ganteau's dismissal, Hayah and her mother discussed at length the ugly episode. They thought it might perhaps be a good time now to broach the subject of the sale of Zamalek with the children.

"They must be given time to adjust to the idea. Now that Madame Ganteau has made such a mess of things, we might as well turn some of it to our advantage. She has mentioned the sale of the house among other things so I imagine that sooner or later one of them will bring up the subject."

"Yes, I suppose they will. Anyway, better wait until they do before we rush into premature explanations especially as we have agreed to postpone the issue until later."

'Abd al-Rahman had been informed of the latest developments in the affairs of his household. He too was extremely angry and upset. The very thought of the governess's outrageous behavior disturbed him deeply. "Maybe Ahmad Bey was right after all," he thought. "Maybe we ought never to have employed foreign women to take care of our children. We try to do the best we can and suddenly *we* find ourselves defeated by one vicious woman. Anyway, the deed is done. Let us hope the children have not been too deeply hurt by the experience." Fatma Hanim for her part was full of remorse because she felt that she had been remiss. She had been too trusting and assumed that Ganteau, like Madame Duprée, would care for the children and be good to them.

"What shall we do now?" she asked her husband. "Should we look for a replacement for Madame Ganteau or do we abandon the idea of a foreign governess? Muhammad does not need one, but what shall we do about Cha?" 'Abd al-Rahman did not answer immediately. Oddly enough, the whole issue seemed to revert to the sale of the house. If they were living in a smaller place, it would be much easier to supervise the governess, and yet he knew that the concept of the sale was not yet ripe and its implementation not fully worked out. Actually, he wanted to go on living in his home for whatever time he still had. He could not bear the thought of the upheaval, both emotional and physical, that such a move would impose. He was satisfied to know that his wife and eldest daughter accepted the idea and most probably would put it into effect after his death. For the time being, however, they would all remain here. Hence the problem of the governess presented itself once again and with some urgency since Cha was not allowed out on her own. The new person would have to be very well recommended and closely supervised.

"Whoever comes will be hired on a temporary basis and her position made permanent only if Cha likes her," he told his wife. "You see, Fatma Hanim, how it will be easier for you to supervise a governess in a smaller place?"

And so the quest for a new governess started all over again. Cha was so relieved to be rid of Madame Ganteau that she was perfectly content to sit in her room and read. She still had her afternoons with her father though they were not as frequent as before. Her mother seemed to be going out less often and her sisters were constantly coming over with their husbands. She often sat with the family now but she did not enjoy these evenings as much as she had enjoyed the privacy of her conversations with her father. Theirs had developed into a very special relationship and Cha realized with sadness that the moment was over. "It is always this way," she thought. "Good things never last. Well, bad ones don't either, like Madame Ganteau. My father is right: life gives and life takes away, or is it time?"

Finally, a few days later in the spring of 1944, Madame Capsalis, the Greek ambassador's wife phoned Nahed Hanim Sirri and told

her that she was looking for a good home for her daughter's governess. The girl, Helen Capsalis, would be sent to school in Athens
after the war and her parents felt that a Greek governess—if one
could be found in Cairo—would be better for her now. However,
the English lady they had was so nice, they hated the thought of dis-
missing her without finding her an adequate position. Nahed Hanim
phoned her friend Fatma Hanim and within a week Cha found herself in the company of Miss Prudence F. McKay. Miss McKay, as she
was always called, was Ganteau's antithesis. There was no guile or
viciousness in that woman, no twists and turns of the mind that led
to intrigues, wickedness, and cruel behavior. She was a very kind,
quiet, and unassuming woman whose modest demeanor hid a vast
body of knowledge gleaned from a lifetime of travel. She was the
epitome of British gentility, almost Victorian in her punctilious
adherence to the 'proper' conduct of a lady. She always dressed for
dinner, a meal that both Cha and her brother now shared with their
mother and frequent guests. At precisely 5:00 PM , her tea would be
served in her third floor sitting room and every day, undeterred by
Cha's negative response, she offered her charge a cup of tea. She
never gave up until, one day, Cha told her, "But Miss McKay, you
know I never drink tea in the afternoon."

"I know my dear, but it is proper that I should ask and, at the same
time, whether you have a cup of tea or not is immaterial. The proper behavior is that you should keep me company while I have mine."
Henceforth, every afternoon Cha sat with Miss McKay who very
slowly sipped her tea and ate a slice of raisin cake. "Be careful when
you serve tea, Cha," said Miss McKay. "Always pour milk first and
then the tea. Never fill the cup to the brim, and never stir the sugar
or put the spoon in the cup." Cha was surprised. Madame Duprée had
always poured milk after tea. "*Un nuage, rien qu'un nuage*—A cloud,
just a cloud," she would occasionally say, because as she explained,
pouring it into the tea allowed her to assess the right color of the beverage. At teatime, Miss McKay conversed with Cha and enlarged her
horizon. She talked about England during the reigns of Edward VII
and George V and of how young girls in her day lived and behaved.
She described the city of London and its main landmarks, chatted
about the royal family, and even allowed herself a spot of gossip about
the 'terrible' Mrs. Simpson who had made the handsome Prince of

Wales abandon his throne in order to marry her. "His mother never forgave him, my dear, because he forgot his duty as king."

What Cha liked best of all were the tales of China where Miss McKay had resided for a number of years as 'lady companion' to the teenage daughters of a British Embassy employee. China, as far as Cha was concerned, was the other end of the world, and she was fascinated by her governess's tales of people who bandaged their daughters' feet to make them smaller, who were always bowing and wore their hair in a pigtail down the back. Miss McKay told her about an empress who had spent her life in a secluded palace and people said she had been covered from top to toe with beautiful jewels. Cha was encouraged to express her opinion and gradually she began to enjoy her 5:00 PM teatime sessions with Miss McKay.

While Cha was thus infused with her daily quota of culture and general knowledge, the war in Europe pursued its course with relentless vigor. June 6, 1944, was a great day in the Sallam household. 'Abd al-Rahman never stopped listening to news bulletins over the radio and followed with trepidation the Allied invasion of Normandy. His excitement was such that he could not sit in his armchair but walked slowly the length of his study smoking his Gianaclis cigarettes, stopping now and then to concentrate on a news item that seemed to be of particular importance.

"This is the beginning of the end," he told his wife.

"Do you think the Germans are going to throw the invading army back into the sea?"

"Of course not. Eisenhower and Churchill have prepared their plan of action. No, I believe they will progress inland and Hitler will be defeated." Fatma Hanim wondered whether her husband was being overly optimistic; the Germans were putting up a very strong defense and casualties on both sides were horrendous.

Miss McKay acquired a map of France and every afternoon after tea would show Cha the reported progress of the Allied forces on the Normandy coast. Muhammad soon joined his sister for he became interested as well in the development of an event which, as far as he was concerned, seemed to have been there ever since he was born. Actually, he was seven when war started and yet it had been such a dominant element in his life that he sometimes wondered what it would be like without it. Sainte Mère l'Eglise became familiar to the children as the first village of France to have welcomed the Allied invasion. Miss McKay told them endless tales about the French resistance and the courage with which they fought the enemy on their soil. They were all heroes as far as she was concerned and her admiration for de Gaulle was unlimited.

"He is a fine man," she told the children, "a man of courage and integrity." When de Gaulle came to Egypt, she would have loved to pay her respects with the French delegation of Cairo, but being British she felt it might not be appropriate. She was a little envious of Madame Ponsot, the Foda girls' French governess, who had been included among the privileged group. On the appointed day, Madame Ponsot wore a dress she had prepared for the occasion, made up of the three colors of the French flag. On her left shoulder she had pinned her Croix de Loraine. Poor Madame Ponsot occasionally felt as if she were riding a roller coaster in seventh heaven when the Allied forces won a battle and down again when they suffered a defeat. After Madame Duprée's death, she had felt bereft and lonely, unable to share her deep anxieties, as she trusted no one, least of all Miss King, who lived with the Foda family having once been Madame Foda's governess. Miss King annoyed her for she was a stiff-necked Englishwoman devoid of compassion, whereas Madame Ponsot was a kindly soul who, despite her hatred of the Germans, readily accepted the presence of the young German pilot who had literally dropped from the sky onto the cotton field of the Foda farm.

The poor boy had parachuted out of his flaming plane and still dazed, had been picked up by the peasants who eyed him as a curiosity, but nevertheless fed him and sheltered him in the barn. Hussein Bey, who was always informed of whatever happened on his property, turned a blind eye to this intrusion and 'officially' ignored the presence of an enemy alien in his domain, while unofficially, he gave orders that the young pilot should be well treated. Consequently, after having spent one night in the barn, he was moved to a room in the guesthouse where he remained until the end of the war. It might seem strange that an anti-German Egyptian gentleman should have shown such compassion to an enemy alien, and yet it fits with the Egyptian frame of mind, which is basically generous and hospitable. As far as Hussein Bey was concerned, 'Fritz' was a young boy, barely out of his teens and, like so many of his compatriots, the victim of

Hitler's machiavellian ambition. However, notwithstanding his generosity, he still remained a conservative Egyptian at heart and therefore gave orders that the 'prisoner' should never come anywhere near his daughters.

The allied advance which started on the beaches of Normandy in the west and the Russian advance that crept up toward Berlin from the east gradually squeezed the German war machine and crushed it like a shell caught within the pincers of a giant crab. When the Sallam family went to Alexandria that summer of 1944, the talk was no longer of 'if' but of 'when,' and by September an Allied victory seemed almost certain. The conquest of Italy brought with it tales of terrible battles and frightful casualties. The patriots joined ranks with the invading army and the fascists found themselves faced by a cruel choice: abandon the Duce or be caught in the crossfire. When in April 1945 the Germans themselves gave up on Benito Mussolini and abandoned him to his fate, the world was given an illustration of Sicilian type revenge. Pictures of the Duce and his mistress Clara Petacci strung up by the feet were splashed all over the front pages of the international press. The Sallam children heard the story, of course, and poor Miss McKay found herself in a very embarrassing situation. She could explain well enough the execution of the dictator, but what about the woman? Her Victorian sense of propriety precluded the discussion of the particular role played by Clara Petacci in the Duce's life.

"One does not discuss mistresses with children," she told Fatma Hanim who, of course, agreed. Cha and Muhammad, who knew perfectly well what a mistress was, mischievously teased her by asking seemingly innocent questions.

"Why did the lady have to die as well?"

"She was not a lady, Muhammad. She was a bad person."

"Why was she a bad person? What did she do? And why did they string her up upside down?" persisted the boy.

Before Miss McKay could answer, Cha promptly replied, "For the whole world to know what kind of underwear she wore."

"Ha! Ha! Maybe she wasn't wearing any at all," replied her brother with mirth.

"This will be enough, children," scolded Miss McKay whose complexion had taken the dark hue of a beetroot. "This discussion has lasted long enough. There will be no more talk of this ugly episode. But for your information, she was wearing trousers."

Actually, and despite her hatred of Mussolini, her sense of fair play was outraged. She expressed her disapproval quite openly as she wanted to draw a lesson of moral rectitude that would benefit her charges. "One should always treat prisoners decently," she said. Besides, she did not like communists and had heard that this was the act of leftist hooligans. However, she made no mention of communists in her argument as, in fact, she knew very little about them other than that they had caused a revolution in Russia and massacred its royal family. Her integrity was such that she refused to broach a subject about which she was not adequately informed. Still, she had her opinion and it mattered greatly that the children should know the right moral behavior whatever the circumstances. The children for their part had, in the course of the long war years, developed very definite opinions as regards public events. They knew without doubt that Hitler was the villain of the story and Mussolini his stooge. Their interest in the latter's execution, however, had very little political overtones but stemmed essentially from the morbid curiosity common to adolescents of their age, a kind of childish voyeurism, and they intended to make the most of it particularly as they enjoyed the fun of teasing Miss McKay.

Whatever mirth they could derive from the Mussolini episode was welcome as it helped alleviate the sadness of their life. 'Abd al-Rahman, after a long struggle with illness, died quite suddenly on February 13, 1945, a few months before the end of the war. Fatma Hanim and her eldest daughters steeled themselves to meet the challenges of the *mahzana*. 'Abd al-Rahman was a public figure and his funeral, as that of his father-in-law before him, was a grand affair. His coffin was carried out of the house by pallbearers drawn from family members, preceded by his life-long secretary who carried a cushion upon which were pinned the many decorations he had received in the course of his successful career. There followed the male members of the family, officials, friends, and acquaintances who had come to pay their last respects and accompany him to his final destination. His only son was not among the mourners because Fatma Hanim decreed that he was too young to be involved in that aspect of the adult world.

Muhammad was deeply shaken by his father's death though he had never drawn as close to him as his sister. He had loved a father who had always been kind, generous, affectionate, and never scolded. He was proud to be his son. For Cha, the sense of loss was acute and the sadness profound, and yet, oddly enough, she experienced a strange relief. For the past three years at least, she had lived with the fear of her father's death, had thought about it almost daily, had wondered how and when it would happen. She had imagined scenarios all of them possible and all of them painful. Now, the worst had happened, the threat was no longer there and she was relieved. She remembered vividly the discussion they once had about life, death, and the hereafter and the role of time in the framework of human existence. "Time is on my side now," she thought. "Every passing day will bring me closer to him." She was not actually thinking of her own death, but jumping a stage, was looking ahead to a place in time where they would be together once again. It was, on her part, a defense mechanism, her way of coming to terms with her present reality.

Cha had, so far, never been a religious person. In fact, whatever religion she knew was the Catholic one taught by the nuns at school. Her parents, though religious themselves, had, strangely enough, never tried to enforce the teaching of Islam on their children. Their son's religious education was undertaken by the government school he attended, and the girls would pick up whatever was necessary from their mother and Shaykh Hamza. The system worked very well for the three older girls but for Cha the situation differed totally. The first twelve years of her life had been taken over by Madame Duprée who was a devout Catholic. Her Muslim friends at school were, for the most part, in situations akin to hers, all of them sharing a profound admiration for the ritual of the Catholic mass. Their own religion seemed so dry by comparison. Poor Shaykh Hamza had a very hard time with Cha who never learned her *suras*, was unable to recite them correctly, or even to pronounce some of the words. Since the Qur'an is full of marvelous stories, she always managed to turn the lesson into a storytelling session totally devoid of spiritual substance. After her father's death though, she felt the need to draw closer to her own religion, the one her father had always practiced, so as to ensure their promised final reunion.

"It is safer that way," she thought. " I must follow the same path or else I may get lost." She translated this primeval fear of the unknown as a need to conform, or perhaps to accept without question her allotted place. "If God had wanted me to be a Catholic girl he would not have sent me to a Muslim family."

She had abandoned her worries over Limbo, considering the whole issue a rather childish one. She was not an infant, not even a child any more and must act accordingly. It occurred to her that she should make her position clear—short of announcing her sudden conversion, which might have drawn ironic comments from the boys and the rest of the family. Suddenly, she became a very assiduous student of Shaykh Hamza. The poor man could not understand this amazing transformation but was nevertheless elated. Cha promised herself that she would no longer recite the Pater but limit her nightly prayer to the *Fatiha*, and she would not attend Mass anymore because Shaykh Hamza told her that to kneel in front of statues was a form of idolatry. She listened in awed silence and absolute concentration to the kindly man who wanted to instill into his erstwhile recalcitrant student the basics of Islam. She drew the line, however, when he broached the subject of the five daily prayers preceded by the required ablutions. "This I will not do," she declared to the bemused teacher. "I shall pray to God in my own way." He wisely did not press the point. Cha was not ready for that ritual; she was still too close to her chapel-going days. She was quite simply deliberately willing a spiritual transformation but was unable to completely surrender to her new faith.

After the *mahzana*, life resumed its normal course in Zamalek. Hayah, 'Aliya, and 'Abir who had stayed with their mother the first few days went back to their respective homes, mourners were still coming in every day but proceedings were far less dramatic than the ones at Munira when Isma'il Sadiq and Chafaq Hanim had died. Furniture was not shrouded in black, the children were not deprived of their radios, and the general atmosphere of the house was one of controlled sadness without spectacular expressions of grief. But Cha, who was just fourteen years old, was dressed in black. Her opinion on that issue had not been sought as it was assumed she would wish to follow the custom. She was no longer a child and it was her duty to acknowledge before the world the loss she had suffered. Cha actually complied willingly because in that particular instance she had no wish to be different from her sisters. She wanted to conform. Miss McKay would have much preferred that the child be left alone and allowed to resume her normal activities but, of course, she could not express her opinion as it would have been presumptuous to criticize the manners and customs of her employer. This worked well enough as long as Cha was at home—she was kept from school for a whole week—among her family, sharing a common grief. However, when she went back to school wearing her black dress of mourning, she suddenly felt embarrassed. The feeling of being singled out in that way, of being considered different, was extremely distasteful.

It seemed to her that she was asked to play a role, that of the mourner who was not entitled to laugh, or smile, or run and be herself, but had instead to observe at all times the composure of controlled grief. She knew grief, she missed her father, she was unhappy, and yet this public display of sorrow upset her deeply and her desire to conform gradually disappeared. She also noticed that girls at times avoided her, perhaps because they were discussing topics of fun, movies they had seen, or parties they were planning to which she was not invited and at any rate could not have attended. It seemed to her at times that she was branded as a culprit, penalized for having suffered a loss and she resented the added grievance. And yet she knew that she had to conform to society's demands and the traditions of the family. It was a harrowing experience, a time of profound turmoil. And all the while she was observing the family and trying to figure out what impact her father's death would have on their lives. She knew she was never going to be sent away because she implicitly trusted her mother, who had assured her that it would never happen. But were they ruined as Madame Ganteau had told her? It seemed not. The servants were all there. The house was full of people. Meals were as abundant as before, and there was even talk of summer in Alexandria. Yet a persistent nasty feeling was at the back of her mind all the time, gnawing at her sense of security. One afternoon as she was standing before her open cupboard trying to decide which of her two outfits was less dismal, the black skirt with the black blouse and jumper or the black dress with the high black collar, when Muhammad burst into her room, his face flushed, in a state of great agitation.

"Have you heard the latest?"

"What is it? What has happened?"

"They are going to sell the house."

In a flash, Cha caught onto the cause of her persistent discomfort. Of course, the house! Madame Ganteau had said as much that day. She had almost forgotten about it, so wrapped up as she had been in other worries and concerns. She stood stock-still in order to control what she felt to be the imminent collapse of her world. All the fears, tensions, and anxieties of the past few months rose up to the surface and engulfed her like a giant wave.

"Have you heard, Cha. They are selling the house?"

"I heard, I heard. But are you sure? Who told you?"

"Idris and the people are in the drawing room right now. They want to visit every room. I won't let them see mine. Never!"

"Don't be a baby, Muhammad. If they have decided to sell the house there is nothing we can do about it except perhaps find out the reason. Do you think we are ruined?"

At that point Umm Muhammad knocked at the door and told the children that their mother wanted to see them in the drawing room. They looked at one another and while Muhammad stood helpless by the door, Cha slipped on her black dress with the high black collar and followed her brother to face the news of the impending disaster.

When the prospective buyers had left—an elderly couple who looked sweet and kind but whom both children hated on sight—Fatma Hanim had a long conversation with them. She explained the situation in simple straightforward terms: selling the house had been their father's wish; the place was too big for just the three of them; they were to move into a beautiful duplex in Zamalek; they would be just as comfortable but much cozier than in the big house; they would not move out before the end of the school year, so they had ample time to organize themselves.

"Are we ruined then?" asked Cha.

"Ruined? Of course not. I told you once before, forget what Madame Ganteau told you. We are not selling the house because we are ruined but because it is the practical thing to do under the circumstances. Anyway, I do not wish to live here any more now that your father is no longer with us." The decree was final. "Life gives, and life takes away," thought Cha, except that it seemed to her at that moment that it usually took far more than it gave.

Both children were crushed. This was their home, their very own place. How could strangers take it away from them? These people were going to use their rooms, sleep in their beds, entertain in the drawing room, and boast about the grand staircase, show it off to their friends, and pretend it was theirs. It would never be theirs. They were not born there. They belonged to some other place. The children's indignation was profound and the hurt very deep. Each expressed revolt in a different way. Cha as usual, retreated within herself, reluctant to show her feelings, seeking solace in the solitude of her own thoughts. Muhammad on the contrary, raved and ranted, splashed ink over the blue wallpaper of his room and locked himself up for a whole day. It seemed unfair. First his father and now this new catastrophe! He spent the time devising plots to make the deal fall through but got nowhere and finally gave up knowing that resistance was impossible. He was just twelve years old and life was unfair. In the late afternoon, Miss McKay decided he had been given enough time to vent his anger.

She knocked at his door and in an enticing voice said, "Come out of your room, Muhammad. I have something to show you." The boy opened his door and saw Miss McKay standing there all dressed up and with her hat on. "Come, we are going for a little walk, not far, I have something to show you. Please tell Cha to come along as well."

Both children followed their governess and wondered what she was up to. They walked round the corner, crossed the main artery that separates both sides of the island, and after about fifteen minutes she stopped before a handsome building at the edge of a very large garden overlooking the Nile.

"Isn't this building beautiful?" she asked.

"Yes it is," answered Cha politely "Who lives here?"

"We shall very soon, my dear. The flat we are moving into is lovely, you shall have a room next to your mother's on the first floor and your bathroom, which you will share with no one, is in green marble. Muhammad and I are on the upper floor and our rooms open onto a huge terrace where you shall entertain all your friends, as many as thirty or more at a time if you wish."

The children gaped in silence. The novelty of the situation pleased them. Their spirits lifted immediately and they showered Miss McKay with questions. How big was the flat? How many rooms does it have? Would they have new furniture for their bedrooms? How soon could they bring their cousins over to see it? They seemed reconciled to the idea of moving out of the villa and into a totally different environment. Quite suddenly, despair was replaced by satisfaction. They were still young enough to be able to shift gear at a moment's notice and find new reasons to be happy. The three walked back to the house, the children's mood temporarily restored and Miss McKay satisfied by her achievement. She knew, of course, that elation would not be permanent and that frequent bouts of depression lay ahead. For the time being, however, the situation was under control.

What happened next belongs to a period Cha later recalled as her Limbo state. She was neither here nor there, no longer part of the big house, not yet installed in the new. Her life was changing, of that she had no doubt, and its direction headed toward the unknown, which seemed, during her better moments, full of promise. As a four-teen-year-old, she looked forward to the change oblivious of the heartbreaks that would inevitably be part of the process. It was decided that the family would move out at the end of June and the buyers had agreed on that important stipulation. Thereafter, feverish activity took over in the Sallam household. Cha's suppression mech-anism had been so strong that, in later years, she could never recall what exactly took place during that time. How was the furniture moved out? Was there a period when the house was bare, stripped of it belongings like an empty shell? Who decided what was to be taken and what left behind?

She could not remember the hustle and bustle that are usually part of such moves, periods of disorder, of chaotic preparation, or, perhaps on the other hand, the orderly marching out of the family's belong-ings. It was as if she had been transported elsewhere, as if she had not been in the house at all during that period. As an adult, she under-stood that this amnesia had been her way of handling the difficult part, the slow and very painful wrenching from her home. Strangely enough, the only day she remembered with clarity was the final one. It remained etched in her memory, perhaps because she had made the conscious effort of recording the last moments. Meanwhile, war had come to an end, and while everyone rejoiced, May 8, 1945 was a sad day for Cha. She wished her father had been alive to witness the victory of the Allies and the end of Hitler, and bitterly regretted that he had not lived long enough.

June 24 was the day Fatma Hanim had selected to move out, as it was the last day of school for Cha, so it seemed to be a convenient date. Cha woke up at her usual hour, donned her summer uniform, which was cream colored and considered appropriate as a *demi-deuil* color. Unlike her married sisters, she was not expected to wear black for a whole year. Nonetheless, propriety and decorum required that the move toward normalcy be slow and proceed in stages. In early April, Fatma Hanim had gone through the standard formal question, "Would you like your summer wardrobe to be black, or would you prefer to wear light colors: white, beige, pale gray?"

Cha was embarrassed because she feared that an eager response might give the wrong impression or indicate on her part a lack of sensitivity to the family's circumstances, or perhaps a lack of faithfulness to her father's memory. And yet, with the resilience of youth, she felt quite ready to move on and drop mourning black that had encased her like a shroud for so long. Her mother sensed her embarrassment so she decided for her.

"You have worn black long enough. Your summer wardrobe will be in *demi-deuil* colors, and in the fall you shall wear colors again."

Cha's relief was evident. She was ready now to turn the page and move on to the next stage of her life. She had never, in fact, associated what she wore with the loss of her father but, on the contrary, quickly rebelled against a social convention that did not do justice to the immensity of her loss. In any event, the pale colors of her wardrobe were a great improvement over the depressing ugliness of black. Wearing her summer uniform, she felt dressed up as if she were going to a party. She looked at herself in the mirror, swirled right and then left and joyfully picked up the white gloves that were mandatory for the prize-giving ceremony, and put on her velvet beret. She was ready now and at long last reinstated among her peers, no longer wearing the mesh of sorrow.

Prize-giving day at school was always a grand occasion, very solemn and formal. She expected to win many prizes, having worked hard all year and looked forward to the event. She heard the loud horn of the school bus. Time to leave. She ran down the back stairs and when she reached the oak staircase was tempted for a moment to slide down the banister one last time. She thought better of it though, and walked down very slowly wanting to savor these last moments. No one was in the hall at this early hour, so she stood there for a moment, looked round one last time so as to store in her memory as much of it as she could. She then peeked into her father's study which looked so empty, so still now, bereft of his presence, and saw on the desk his bronze lion, cast by the artist in a crouching position forever ready to spring and attack. She walked down the six marble steps of the vestibule flanked by the other lions, the tame ones she had often ridden as a child. She stroked the mane of the right-hand one, the one she always claimed was hers, leaving the left-hand one to Muhammad. So many memories!

She felt sadness creep up threatening to destroy her firm resolve, but pushed it back fiercely. Life had taken so much away, surely it would now give something back in return because such was the order of things. The horn sounded again. She turned to the door, and steeling herself for the final break, pulled the bronze handle firmly and rushed out into the sunlit morning. It closed behind her with a click, which, like a sonorous full stop, put an end to that period of her life. She boarded the bus, sat at her usual place, and as it drove off, she did not look back but fixed her gaze on the moving scenery of Zamalek and let her mind wander over the exciting day that lay ahead.

Notes

1. The origin of the name Zamalek is not clear. It has variously been ascribed to: a) a derivation of the Arabic term *dhu al-mulk*, (i.e., the one who has ownership) in reference to property owners on the island; b) squatter's huts that were scattered all over the island, particularly the northern side; the term derives from the Turkish word for hut.

2. In his very informative article, "Guezira Sporting Club Milestone," Samir Ra'fat writes: "A moving spirit behind the club's creation was a Captain Humphreys of the mounted infantry. Not only did he participate in the selection of the Club's grounds, but was also instrumental in the design of its first racecourse which had a 'distance' of a little over one mile. . . ." (*Egyptian Mail*, February 10–17, 1996).

3. Edward Said, *Out of Place: A Memoir* (London, Granta Books, 1999), 45.

4. Princess Chivekiar, King Fuad's first wife. After her divorce from King Fuad, she married Seif Allah Yusry Pasha, divorced again and later remarried Ihamy Pasha.

5. Hoda Sha'rawi, *Harem Years: Memoirs of an Egyptian Feminist (1879–1924)*, trans. Margot Badran (Cairo: American University Press, 1998).

6. In the late 1980s and early 1990s, two more bridges, or fly-overs were added to service the increasing flow of traffic: the Sixth of October Bridge and the Fifteenth of May Bridge.

7. The first Qasr al-Nil Bridge was a toll bridge. The breakdown of prices is rather interesting: 2 Egyptian piasters (2 Pt.E.) for a loaded pack of camels, 1 Pt.E. for an unloaded one, 1.15 Pt.E. for a loaded donkey, 0.15 Pt.E. for unloaded ones, 1.15 Pt.E. for large loaded buffaloes *(gamus)*, 0.15 Pt.E. for smaller ones, etc. For more on the subject see: Muhammad Kamal al-Sayid Muhammad, *Asma' wa musamiyat min tarikh Misr al-Qahira* (Cairo: al-Hay'a al-Misriyah al-'Amma lil-Kitab, 1986).

8. Samir Raafat, "If Lions Could Speak: The Story of Kasr El Nil Bridge," *Medina*, November 2000.

9. Although harems and slavery have disappeared from Egyptian life, polygyny remains as an integral part of society. The difference between today's practice and the nineteenth century one is that whereas the latter was unconditionally accepted, even admired, the former is usually frowned upon. Multiple

households are less common than before. Though probably related to the harem system, the practice persisted longer among the rural community. The reason for the continuation of family households there was the cost of cultivation. In Egypt, irrigation depends on waterwheels and wells, both systems being way beyond the means of the average landowner. By the 1930s, the practice became far less common among the upper class. It is not clear whether multiple households are on the wane or, on the contrary, reappearing in full force in the urban middle class. Rising cost of living and shortage of available housing often make it imperative for young couples to go on living with their parents after marriage.

10. The term as used in this context has a different connotation than the standard one. There is no degradation implied here; ladies living in the harem had been sent there since childhood, had grown up with the family and identified themselves with it. Not to be confused with slaves sold on the market by slave traders.

11. *Nabil* is a royal title given to offspring of a royal person and a commoner.

12. Hassan Hassan, *In the House of Muhammad 'Ali* (Cairo: American University in Cairo Press, 2000), 60.

13. Hayworth-Dunn, the British historian, claims that although women were taught to read the Qur'an, *Surat* Yusuf was a chapter usually omitted, the assumption being that the behavior of some of the women mentioned in it was immoral. This seems doubtful because the text was available for all to read. For more see: J. Hayworth-Dunne, *An Introduction to the History of Education in Modern Egypt* (London: Frank Cass, 1968).

14. Such was the case of Princess Chivekiar's mother. She was a Georgian slave of great beauty who married one of Muhammad 'Ali's grandsons.

15. The term is used loosely as there is no formal adoption within the framework of Islamic law.

16. Muhammad Sultan Pasha was one of the outstanding Egyptian personalities at the time of Khedives Isma'il and Tewfiq. He was the first president of the newly elected Chamber of Deputies and had a tremendous influence on the *A'yans,* particularly in Upper Egypt. At the start of the 'Urabi Revolt he gave his support to 'Urabi, as did most *A'yans.* At one point however, he withdrew that support tipping the balance in favor of the Khedive's forces. 'Urabi's defeat at Tel al-Kebir and the occupation of Egypt by Great Britain followed soon after. Sultan Pasha's 'defection' was immediately interpreted by 'Urabi's followers as an act of treason. Whether this was the case remains to be proven. A more likely interpretation, one that corresponds to what was written about him by contemporaries, could be advanced: like 'Urabi he resented the treatment of Egyptians by Turks; however, he soon perceived the limitations and overweening ambition of 'Urabi. He understood that nothing short of the leadership of the country would have satisfied that officer, who had neither the training nor the intelligence required for the position. A victory for 'Urabi would have ushered in Egypt a military dictatorship headed by a lesser man, which would have been, as far as the proud Upper Egyptian gentleman was

concerned, more detrimental to Egypt's welfare than the continued presence of the hated British. This interpretation though conjectural is plausible.

17. The sister had one daughter who later became the wife of Mahmud Fahmi al-Nokrashi Pasha, one of the pillars of the Wafd Party. In December 1948, while prime minister of Egypt, he was assassinated by a religious fanatic.

18. 'Ali Mubarak Basha, 1823/24–1893. At one time minister of education and author of a multi-volume topography of Egypt: *al-Khitat al-tawfiqiya al-jadida li-Misr al-Qahira*, published in 1888.

19. Lambert Bey (1804–1864), engineer employed in the construction of dams on the Nile and at one time director of the School of Engineering in Cairo. He studied the work of J.M. Le Père, an eighteenth-century French engineer, on the possibility of piercing a canal through the Isthmus of Suez.

20. J.C.B. Richmond, *Egypt 1798–1952: Her Advance towards a Modern Identity* (New York: Columbia University Press, 1977), 12.

21. Ibid., 2.

22. For more on the history of educational missions abroad see: Ahmad 'Izzat 'Abd al-Karim, *Tarikh al-ta'lim fi Misr* (Cairo: Matba'at al-Nasr, 1945).

23. The order of primogeniture succession was such that Muhammad 'Ali was succeeded by his grandson, 'Abbas I, who was the oldest surviving male member of the family. Upon his death, he was succeeded by his uncle Sa'id Pasha who was a few years younger.

24. Khaled Fahmy, *All the Pasha's Men* (Cairo: American University in Cairo Press, 1997), 282.

25. Antoine Clot (Clot Bey) 1793–1868. French doctor who became Muhammad 'Ali Pasha's personal physician in 1825. While in Egypt, he reorganized the country's health programs and sanitary services.

26. Verdi's *Aida* had been commissioned for the occasion but was not ready on time so *Rigoletto* was given instead.

27. Hanna Wissa, *Assiout: The Saga of an Egyptian Family* (Sussex: The Book Guild, 1994), 67.

28. Pierre Crabites, *Americans in the Egyptian Army* (London: Routledge, 1938), 2.

29. Ibid., 5.

30. Fahmy 1997, 89.

31. Crabites 1938, 8.

32. Ibid., 191.

33. Isma'il Siddiq (al-Mufattish) was Khedive Isma'il's half-brother and trusted confident. He engaged in dishonest dealings, consequently fell out of favor and was exiled to the Sudan. According to some sources, he was assassinated.

34. William Loring. *A Confederate Soldier in Egypt.* (Dodd, Mead, 1884), 423–430.

35. Wissa 1994, 103.

36. "The most famous deputy irrigation inspector of the later 1880s and early 1890s was Ismail Bey Sirry, deputy irrigation inspector of the fourth sector (Central Upper Egypt). From time to time, Sirry would submit a report about the circumstances of irrigation in his district that *al-Ahram* would reprint in full. In fact, one of these reports had so impressed Colonel Ross that he sent it

to Zaki Pasha, the minister of public works who ordered two copies to be produced, one to be submitted to the minister of interior and one to His Royal Highness the Khedive. Given this success, it is no wonder that Sirry continued to be promoted until he became the minister of public works in 1908, and one of the most famous ministers to occupy this post." Quoted from: Labib Younan Rizk, *Al-Ahram Weekly*, December 8–14, 1994.

37. It is interesting to note that the *kitab*, or formal signing of a marriage contract as we know it today, is of recent origin. In 1921 a law was promulgated whereby a written agreement between the parties became mandatory. Up to that date, there had been quasi-total reliance on *'urf*, or tradition, and *usul*, or application of that tradition.

38. For more on the subject see: Afaf Lutfi al-Sayyid-Marsot, *Women and Men in Late Eighteenth Century Egypt* (Austin: University of Texas Press, 1995).

39. *Sura* 112 of the Qur'an that proclaims the oneness of God.

40. Darrel Bates, *The Fashoda Incident of 1898: Encounter on the Nile* (Oxford: Oxford University Press, 1984), 126.

41. *Irrigation in the Valley of the River Po, Northern Italy*, an account of the mission undertaken for the Egyptian government in the summer of 1899.

42. It is interesting to note that after the 1952 Revolution the position was reversed. During the Nasserite period and for a number of years, *ahl al-thiqa* once again replaced *ahl al-khibra* with the predictable disastrous consequences.

43. Hunter, F. Robert. "Egypt's high officials in transition from a Turkish to a modern administrative elite, 1849–1879," in *Middle East Studies*, vol. 19, no. 3, July 1983: 283.

44. Afaf Lutfi al-Sayyid-Marsot, *Egypt's Liberal Experiment: 1922–1936* (Berkeley: University of California Press, 1977), 218.

45. al-Sayyid-Marsot 1977, 222. However, when the promise did not seem forthcoming and in the light of Britain's callous behavior, Lutfi al-Sayed firmly adopted an anti-British stance.

46. Alfred Milner, *England in Egypt* (London: Arnold, 1892), 205.

47. For more on the formation of the Egyptian army at the time of Muhammad 'Ali see Fahmy, *All the Pasha's Men*.

48. Samir Raafat, "Groppi of Cairo," *Cairo Times*, June 15, 1996.

49. Amira Sonbol, trans. and ed., *The Last Khedive of Egypt: Memoirs of Abbas Hilmi II* (Reading, UK: Ithaca Press, 1998), 73.

50. Ibid., 83–84.

51. Ibid., 87.

52. Usually refers to Upper Egyptians. Here, however, the term has a derogatory connotation, i.e., uncouth, vulgar.

53. Wissa 1994, 277.

54. Richmond 1977, 178.

55. Ibid., 180.

56. Ibid., 181.

57. George Young, *Egypt* (London: Benn, 1927), 248.

58. This is the official version, the one usually cited by most historians. It appears, however, that members of the Milner Delegation (if not Milner himself) held

preliminary meetings with a high-ranking Egyptian official. For more on the subject see: *Conversations between Sir John Maxwell and H.E. Sirry Pasha* (December 11, 1919 and December 12, 1919), 85–87 at the Bodleian Library, Department of Western Manuscripts, Oxford University (from 132, no.7, shelf mark Ms Milner Dep. 448).

59. Upper crust of society. As Hunter defines in his book *Egypt under the Khedives, 1805–1879: From Household Government to Modern Bureaucracy*: "Egypt's high officials were known as '*al-dhawat*' an Arabic plural which means upper class or aristocracy," 80. Isma'il Sadiq's concern was based on the generally accepted social norm that marriages should only be contracted between equals socially and economically. Shari'ah law in fact supports this view. The principle implied in that law is that the husband must be able to offer his wife the same standard of living as she had enjoyed in her fathers home.

60. Relatives on the father's side represent the strong line or '*asab,* relatives on the mother's side the weak line. However, when a matrimonial alliance is being sought, maternal uncles play a very important role because through them the mother's lineage is checked and its importance, or lack of, established.

61. "Dr. 'Ali Ibrahim was born in Alexandria in 1880. An eminent surgeon, he became the Minister of Public Health and later the president of Cairo University until his death in 1947. He started collecting art objects in 1910 and by the twenties he started focusing on Islamic art particularly on carpets and ceramics. Within the course of 27 years he collected over 800 pieces forming a first-class collection. Only two months after his death, the Museum of Islamic Art bought the whole collection of ceramics, 378 pieces, 42 panels of tiles, 26 pieces of Iznik and Kutahiya ceramics, 36 pieces of metalwork and 127 carpets." Quoted from: Ahmed Muhammad Dabb', *Gordes Carpets in Egyptian Collections*, M.A. thesis, American University in Cairo, 2000, 9.

62. The *karawita,* also called in colloquial Arabic *kanab stambulli,* is a long rather wide settee with cushions at the back and small cushions across (usually two, one on top of the other) used as armrests. *Karawita*s came to Egypt, probably imported from Turkey, in the mid-sixteenth century and were standard pieces of furniture in homes well until the early twentieth century. People sat on them either cross-legged in the scribe position but more often over one leg bent at the knee and the foot of the other leg resting on the edge of the seat. In order to accommodate this very oriental posture, the divan had to be deep and the transversal cushions high enough to make the arrangement comfortable. With the impact of European culture and education that were gradually taking hold of the upper middle class, seating habits changed dramatically. It was no longer considered acceptable for ladies and gentlemen to fold limbs over seating furniture or indulge in a slouching position. To 'sit up' became the norm. Besides, most homes of the upper echelons of society were now furnished with European style furniture and *karawita*s gradually disappeared from the scene. They were often relegated to the servants' quarters or the reception rooms in cemeteries. Perhaps the most famous example of a *karawita is* the one upon which is seated Muhammad 'Ali Pasha of Egypt in a portrait which has often been reproduced in art and history books.

63. 'Visit baskets' were for the rural- and low-middle class social groups of the time the equivalent of a box of chocolates or a bouquet of flowers for the upper crusts of society. It usually contained farm produce and home cooked food such as *fitir mishaltit* or stuffed pigeons. The variety and the quantity of the offerings varied according to the person's financial ability but were usually considered mandatory. The practice is now slowly dying out.

64. "He can fear but cannot be shamed" is a common Arabic saying used to describe a person who is cowardly and insensitive regardless of religious affiliation.

65. No sugar, very little sugar, some sugar, sweet.

66. Qasim Amin, *The Liberation of Women: A Document in the History of Egyptian Feminism,* trans. Samiha Sidhom Peterson (Cairo: American University in Cairo Press, 1992), 5.

67. Agati was the most important silversmith in Egypt in the nineteenth century and well until the mid-twentieth.

68. The Older Pasha, which in that case also means the grandfather.

69. *Surat* Yasin, verse 37. Author's translation.

70. For more on the Nasiriya School see: Samir Raafat, "The Grand Vizier's Palace," *Cairo Times,* June 7, 2001.

71. The Kahil family is of Syro-Lebanese origin, mentioned in 'Abd al-Rahman al-Jabarti's monumental history of Egypt: *'Aja'ib al-athar fi-l-tarajim wa-l-akhbar.* Miss Mary was a very wealthy woman who devoted most of her time and money to philanthropic pursuits and was noted for her kindness and amiable disposition.

72. Sir Walter Smart (Smartie), married in 1931 Amy Nimr, whose father Nimr Pasha founded *al-Moqattam* newspaper. They had one son, Mickey. On January 17, 1943, the Smart family took a picnic in the desert. Eleven-year-old Mickey picked up a bomb stick that exploded in his hands. He died a few hours later.

73. "On 30th May, Ali Maher drew up a proclamation declaring Cairo an Open City. The measure, designed by international law to protect the urban population of a neutral state from enemy bombardment, would not technically come into force while British troops were in the Citadel and the Kasr el Nil Barracks, but inside the city limits. The Ambassador and Service Chiefs, furious at having been taken by surprise, had no intention of moving their troops. Cairo's status remained ambiguous." From Artemis Cooper, *Cairo in the War, 1939–1945* (London: Hamish Hamilton, 1989), 47.

74. Dora Plant, née Khayat, who comes from an outstanding Egyptian Coptic family.

75. Swiss born Gertie Ghali, wife of Merrit Ghali who, after the 1952 Revolution, held for a brief period a ministerial post.

76. Gertie Wissa, daughter of Zaki Bey Wissa and Shafigah Khayat.

77. Marie Wissa, daughter of Akhnoukh Fanous and Balsam Wissa and wife of George Wissa.

78. Dr. Magdi Wahbah, son of Mourad Pasha Wahbah and grandson of Yusuf Pasha Wahbah. He was professor of English literature at Cairo University and, during Nasser's regime, undersecretary at the Ministry of Culture.

79. Magdi Wahbah, "Cairo memories," *Encounter* Magazine, 1984, 74–79; quoted in Artemis Cooper, *Cairo in the War, 1939–1945*, 27.
80. Afaf Lutfi al-Sayyid-Marsot, "The revolutionary gentlewoman in Egypt" in *Women in the Muslim World* (Boston: Harvard University Press, 1978).
81. Fatma Sirri, daughter of Sir Isma'il Sirri Pasha and wife of 'Abd al-Hamid Soliman Pasha.
82. Hedayah Barakat, wife of Bahyeddin Barakat Pasha, regent of Egypt after the 1952 Revolution.
83. Amina Hanim Sidki, wife of 'Aziz Pasha Abaza and daughter of Isma'il Sidki Pasha.
84. "King Fuad, out of veneration for his mother, whose name, Ferial, began with an 'F' had wanted all his children's names to start with the same letter." Quoted from: Hassan Hassan, *In the House of Muhammad 'Ali*, 46. King Faruk following the tradition established by his father changed his fiancee's name from Safinaz to Farida and named his three daughters: Ferial, Fawzia, and Fadia. He broke the pattern however when he married Narriman Sadik whose name he did not change. The only son he had with her is called Ahmad Fuad.

Glossary

'abaya	Cloak.
abla	Respectful form of address to an older woman.
abriq	Water pitcher with spout.
'alim	Learned man, particularly in religious matters; scholar.
'ammiti	Father's sister.
Anna	Mother in Turkish.
'asaliya	Honey sweets.
babaghannug	Eggplant and *tihina* salad.
baladi	Usually what is native or essentially Egyptian. It can also be given a derogatory connotation, i.e., that which is vulgar or not refined.
baqala	Scamp.
bashnu'a	Black veil that covers the head, ears, and throat. Worn at funerals or when one is in mourning.
bawwab	Gatekeeper.
bulagh	Peasant's slippers.
dhawat	Upper echelons of society.
duktur	Colloquial Arabic version of *doctor*.
Effendi	Used as a title of respect for men, equivalent to *gentleman* or *sir*.
farah	Wedding ceremony; more generally, any joyful occasion.
Fatiha	Opening *sura* of the Qur'an. The reading marks the official announcement of a couple's engagement. Most other transactions are also preceded by a recitation of the *Fatiha*.
feddan	1.038 acres; approximately 4,000 square meters.
fellah	farmer; peasant (plural: *fellahin*).
fitir mishaltit	Pastry cooked with a good amount of ghee and formed into large rounds, usually served with cream and molasses (or honey) for dessert, or with salty white cheese.
fitir rahma	Literally, 'bread of mercy'; sweetened loaves of bread given to the poor at the cemetery.

ful midammis Boiled fava beans, a staple of the Egyptian diet.

habara Headdress of black opaque cloth that covers head and shoulders.

halawa tahiniya Candy sweet made from sesame oil and sugar.

hilba Fenugreek.

hummusiya Crunchy chickpea snack.

'Id al-fitr Feast that marks the end of the month of Ramadan.

imamba yalde Eggplant with raisins and herbs.

insha'Allah God willing.

'irq sus Drink made from licorice root.

'izwa Power derived from clan solidarity.

gallabiya A long, loose garment with full sleeves, worn especially in Muslim countries; jellaba.

karawita A long and wide oriental settee.

khalta A mixture of rice, nuts, raisins, and chicken liver.

khawaga Foreigner, usually European, non-Arab (feminine: *khawagaya*).

kirdan Necklace.

kitab Marriage contract.

kofta Meatballs.

kunafa Fine angel hair pastry blended with nuts and rosewater syrup.

kusha The bride and groom's seating arrangement at their wedding.

kuttab Qur'anic school; lowest elementary school.

mahzana Funeral proceedings.

mashrabiya Latticed screen of turned or carved wood used to designate windows or grills, a hallmark of Islamic domestic architecture, offers privacy to women from passers-by.

Ma'udhatayn The last two *sura*s in the Qur'an, usually recited to invoke God's protection from the evil eye, or more generally, from harm.

mihallabiya Dessert made from milk, flour, and sugar.

milabbis Candy; sugared almonds.

mufattish ray Irrigation inspector.

mughat Hot, thick, syrupy beverage made of ground tree bark, sprinkled with chopped grilled almonds and nuts.

mulukhiya Jew's mallow soup.

Nayna Title given to a mother or grandmother.

petsha White gauze veil that covers face from the nose down.

sadd al-hanaq Dessert made of sugar, honey, flour and occasionally cinnamon.

Sa'idi Upper Egyptian.

Sammadiya *Sura* that proclaims the oneness of God.

saqa Water carrier serving villages with no running water.

shabka Gift from the groom to his bride to seal the marriage agreement; literally, 'that which binds.'

Shihada An Islamic act of faith: I declare that there is no God but Allah and that Muhammad is His Prophet.

shulayk Sweetened bread distributed to the poor at the cemetery.

Si Sir; short for *Sidi*.

sinibar Pine nuts.

Sitt Madame.

Sitt al-kibira The older lady. Term of address usually given to the grandmother.

stambulina Black overcoat buttoned down the front.

sufraji Waiter.

sunna Islamic tradition based on the *hadith*, or Prophetic sayings.

sura Chapter of the Qur'an.

talli Silver threads worn by a bride.

tamanni Official salutation to the monarch, large sweeping gesture of the right hand from the heart (that loves) to the lips (that praise) to the forehead (that reveres).

ta'miya Ground, seasoned, and fried fava bean or chickpea patties; falafel.

tamr hindi Beverage made of tamarind.

Tayza Respectful form of address to an older lady.

tihina Thick sauce made of sesame paste.

'ulla Clay water pitcher without spout or handle.

'umda Village chief (mayor).

umm 'ali Dessert made of crushed wafers, milk, cream, and nuts.

Usta Title for a driver or master of a craft.

usul Correct behavior according to tradition.

uzi Baby lamb.

wali Governor.

ya Abu Father of.

Yafandim Respectful form of address to a socially superior person.

Yakhti A form of address meaning sister.

zaffa Wedding procession.

Bibliography

Abbas Hilmi II. *The Last Khedive of Egypt: Memoirs of Abbas Hilmi II*, trans. and ed. Amira Sonbol. Reading, UK: Ithaca Press, 1998.

'Abd al-Karim, Ahmad 'Izzat. *Tarikh al-ta'lim fi Misr.* Cairo: Matba'at al-Nasr, 1945.

Amin, Qasim. *The Liberation of Women: A Document in the History of Egyptian Feminism*, trans. Samiha Sidhom Peterson. Cairo: American University in Cairo Press, 1992.

Bates, Darrel. *The Fashoda Incident of 1898: Encounter on the Nile.* Oxford: Oxford University Press, 1984.

Cachia, Anna. *Landlocked Islands: Two Alien Lives in Egypt.* Cairo: American University in Cairo Press, 1999.

Cooper, Artemis. *Cairo in the War, 1939–1945.* London: H. Hamilton, 1989.

Crabites, Pierre. *Americans in the Egyptian Army.* London: Routledge, 1938.

Description de l'Egypte, ou, Recueil des observations et des recherches qui ont été faites en Egypte pendant l'expédition de l'armée française. Paris: Imprimerie Imperiale, 1809–1828.

Fahmy, Khaled. *All the Pasha's Men.* Cairo: American University in Cairo Press, 1997.

Hassan, Hassan. *In the House of Muhammad 'Ali.* Cairo: American University in Cairo Press, 2000.

Hayworth-Dunne, J. *An Introduction to the History of Education in Modern Egypt.* London: Frank Cass, 1968.

Hunter, Robert F. "Egypt's high officials in transition from a Turkish to a modern administrative elite, 1849–1879," in *Middle East Studies*, vol. 19, no. 3, July 1983, pp. 277–291.

———. *Egypt under the Khedives, 1805–1879: From Household*

Government to Modern Bureaucracy. Cairo: American University in Cairo Press, 1984.

Milner, Alfred. *England in Egypt*. London: Arnold, 1892.

Muhammad, Muhammad Kamal al–Sayid. *Asma' wa musamiyat min tarikh Misr al-Qahira*. Cairo: al-Hay'a al-Misriyah al-'Amma lil-Kitab, 1986.

Richmond, J.C.B. *Egypt 1798–1952: Her Advance towards a Modern Identity*. New York: Columbia University Press, 1977.

Said, Edward W. *Out of Place: A Memoir*. London: Granta Books, 1999.

al-Sayyid-Marsot, Afaf Lutfi. *Egypt's Liberal Experiment: 1922–1936*. Berkeley: University of California Press, 1977.

———. "The revolutionary gentlewoman in Egypt" in *Women in the Muslim World*. Boston: Harvard University Press, 1978.

———. *Women and Men in Late Eighteenth Century Egypt*. Austin: University of Texas Press, 1995.

Sha'rawi, Hoda. *Harem Years: Memoirs of an Egyptian Feminist (1879–1924)*, trans. Margot Badran. Cairo: American University Press, 1998.

Wissa, Hanna. *Assiout: The Saga of an Egyptian Family*. Sussex, UK: The Book Guild, 1994.

Index